WHEN THEY WERE BOYS

Also by Larry Kane:
Ticket to Ride:
Inside the Beatles' 1964 and 1965 Tours
that Changed the World
(Running Press, 2003)

Lennon Revealed
(Running Press, 2005)

Larry Kane's Philadelphia
(Temple University Press, 2000)

Death by Deadline,
an e-book novel
(Dynamic Images, 2011)

WHEN
THEY
WERE
BOYS

The True Story of the Beatles' Rise to the Top

Larry Kane

RUNNING PRESS
PHILADELPHIA · LONDON

Books published by Running Press are available at special discounts for bulk purchases in the United States by corporations, institutions, and other organizations. For more information, please contact the Special Markets Department at the Perseus Books Group, 2300 Chestnut Street, Suite 200, Philadelphia, PA 19103, or call (800) 810-4145, ext. 5000, or e-mail special.markets@perseusbooks.com.

ISBN 978-0-7624-4014-6
Library of Congress Control Number: 2013938630

E-Book ISBN 978-0-7624-5095-4

9   8   7   6   5   4   3   2   1
Digit on the right indicates the number of this printing

Cover and interior design by Bill Jones
Edited by Greg Jones
Typography: Adobe Garamond and Neutra Text

Running Press Book Publishers
2300 Chestnut Street
Philadelphia, PA 19103-4371

Visit us on the web!
www.runningpress.com

To Donna, Michael, Alexandra, Doug, Jen, Aiden,
Benjamin, and Peyton

CONTENTS

ACKNOWLEDGMENTS

There are so many people to thank, but let me start with Bill Harry, Tony Barrow, Sam Leach, Allan Williams, Yoko Ono, the staff at Studio One, Ron Ellis, Ellen Ellis, Freda Kelly, Denny Somach, Louise Harrison, Jerry Blavat, Julia Baird, and Tony Bramwell. Also thanks to Chris Carter of KLOS and XM–Sirius Satellite Radio, Alan White, Rod Davis, Colin Hanton, Colin Hall, Len Garry, Hunter Davies, Colin Fallows, Kathy McCabe, Mac Walter, Dave Forshaw, Sir Ron Watson, Joe Flannery, Jude Southerland Kessler, Mark Lapidos, Bruce Spizer, David Bedford, Ed Jackson, Roag Best, the White House Social Office, June Furlong, Horst Fascher, Pauline Sutcliffe, Billy Kinsley, Billy J. Kramer, John Rose, Tony Guma, Jodi Blau Ritzen, Dr. Mike Brocken, Joe Ankrah, Jonathan Davies, BBC TV, Buz Teacher, Spencer Leigh, Kevin Roach, John Gannon, Theo Somach, Jim Turner, Kevin Donahue, Marc Hudson, Joe Johnson, Andre Gardner, and Tim Riley.

Special gratitude to my family, to whom this book is dedicated; literary agent Faith Childs; the book's editor, Greg Jones (this makes three books with him); and Running Press Editorial Director Jennifer Kasius, Publisher Chris Navratil, Photo Consultant Sue Oyama, Designer Bill Jones, Project Editor Annie Lenth, Tina Camma, Allison Devlin, and Gigi Lamm.

Thanks to all.

FIRST WORDS:
PRESENT DAY/VIOLENT PAST

From Alpine Valley to the East Wing of the White House

When the former Richard Starkey began his rendition of "Yellow Submarine," we all started to scramble, looking for some shelter from the storm on this sweltering summer night at Alpine Village in East Troy, Wisconsin. As he would sing later, "It Don't Come Easy."

It was 1989, the summer that Ringo Starr & His All-Starr Band was created, and the 37,000-seat venue nestled between Chicago and Milwaukee was under attack from the gods of water and lightning. There was no place to hide as our TV team scattered backstage under canopies, under anything we could find, seeking shelter.

Three hours before, the sun was shining during the afternoon sound check when the drummer and I sat on stools on the stage, sharing, during a video-taped interview, some memories of the Beatles' historic North American tours of 1964 and 1965. In the first of those unforgettable summers, I was a twenty-one-year-old newsman with a ticket to ride to cover young Ringo and his three extraordinary bandmates. It was an unlikely assignment for a man who can't hold a tune or even dance to one, but it began an odyssey, a true life adventure, that would bring me onboard not just for two summers of touring plus parts of the 1966 tour, but for a lifetime of adventure and memories.

My life experience would include fifty-six years of covering news, often having to cover my behind in some really bad and violence-filled places. My love of politics would lead me to presidents, senators, governors, mayors, and politicians of all stripes. I also went to jail, as a visitor, chronicling the life-after-political-death of many a corrupt politician. I anchored the TV news for a long time, and reported on all sorts of stories. But I would always be tethered to the one story I originally didn't want to cover. For—and this is the truth—I never wanted to travel with "the boys," as insiders called them early on. After all, in early 1964 I had predicted to my puzzled bosses that the "mop tops," as the Beatles were unceremoniously described by the grown-ups of the time, had no real future. My talent for forecasting the future was bogus.

Tell me in 1964 that I would wind up writing three books on the "Fabs," as Starkey would later call them, and I would suggest that you were smoking dope, which many of you may have done at one time or another.

The interview with Ringo went well, but the skies were clouding up. By showtime it was a driving rain, like a tropical storm, and the promoters invited us to the green room, the warm and fuzzy green room, which I will forever remember as the magic room. It was there that I found out what Ringo Starr was *really* doing.

My wife, Donna, who rarely accompanied me to news events, was checking out the green room. Donna, who loves photography, had taken pictures of my reunion with Ringo earlier. The green room was subdued. There was an unkempt skinny guy sitting in the corner, looking lonely, sipping a Coke, and sporting a thousand-mile stare into nothingness. I introduced myself. With a sheepish handshake, he said, "I'm Joe Walsh." Joe Walsh of the Eagles? Yes, it was. On the other side of the room, E Street Band saxophonist Clarence Clemons had that always-cheerful look.

Not far away, munching on some food, was Dr. John, the king of the piano, the pride of New Orleans. And the hits just kept on coming in the magic room: Nils Lofgren; musician supreme, the one and only Billy Preston; drummer Levon Helm; bassist Rick Danko; and drummer Jim Keltner. "Amazing," I thought. Ringo had made magic, assembling an all-star lineup of musical greats to supplement his limited repertoire. Could Ringo alone sustain a McCartney-like concert for two hours or more? Probably not. But in the process of putting together this extraordinary collection of artists, he had created a knockout concert; it was more than just a casting call to help rejuvenate stifled careers of fellow artists. For the ex–Beatles drummer, this was, in fact, the beginning of redemption. And it was an experience he was delighted to share.

I walked outside, under a large canopy. It was still raining. I sat down at a picnic table and started reflecting on this strange and sensational reunion between the two of us.

"It don't come easy." It didn't for Starkey, aka Ringo, whom I watched slowly walk down a narrow, metal staircase, dressed in a bathrobe with a towel draped around his neck. He waved, tenderly, and smiled as he prepped for act one of the show. After all, the drummer had been given up for lost before he finally found a way to surface from oblivion. And that's why the magic room was so magic, and the evening so special. It was especially so for the men assembled in that room, the flesh and bones of stars whose spotlights had faded, legends scattered to the winds by a changing business. Some of them, like Ringo, were felled by substance abuse; others by fate. No surprise was it at all that some of the band members in this most-unusual green room were in the process of resurrection. Lazarus would have been proud.

With a little help from his friends—and they, with a lot of his own help— Ringo was unselfishly prepared to chart the course for the rest of his career. It was an act of grace, a display of kindness; it was part of the fiber of the boys who, back in the Liverpool days and nights, made the joy and dreamed of the music they could make and the stories they could tell. In an era of celebrity misfits and coarse role models, the four dreamers from so long ago still stand out, for their character as much as their intrigue. And there is plenty of that, as you will soon learn.

The road to glowing stardom and success is paved with more than gold. It is hard and scathing, and sometimes treacherous. We all know what happened at the end, which to this day has been an endless ending to an unlikely story. But the story of how Richie and his three mates came to that point really starts at the beginning, and I'm talking here about the exit from the womb, and the arrival in a dark, dank, and battered city, where all hell was breaking loose in a daily struggle for survival. It was there, amid the crushing bombs and abject poverty, that the story of the Beatles really began.

On the 1989 stage in Wisconsin, Ringo feigned a loss of memory as I quizzed him about the touring days. After a few minutes, his mind seemed to stir. His eyes lit up. We recalled together the crazy nights and the crazier crowds and the tumult.

At the end, he just smiled.

"Remember, Larry."

"Yes?"

"We were just boys then, just boys."

"Just boys," he added for emphasis.

The "boys" became men and the men endured in a way that few world icons endure and evolve, making an imprint larger, in some cases, than the tenure of some world leaders.

***

The spotlight moves 1,200 miles east to 1600 Pennsylvania Avenue, the White House. The date is May 30, 2010.

The sun shines brightly on the East Wing of the president's house. An anteroom is set up for cocktails and finger food, the invitation-only crowd beaming with the excitement generally reserved for a superstar. But this was not Barack Obama's night. The superstar is somewhere inside the intense security wall of the White House. On event days, his own security bubble resembles the president's, its layers so deep. But on this day, his private security detail waits outside. After all, the star is inside the president's bubble.

The East Wing is known as the first lady's wing, including her offices and the headquarters of the White House Social Office, which has carefully planned this special evening.

I arrived, along with other invited guests, holding what was described to me as the hottest ticket to any White House event in decades—the annual concert (taped for later broadcast) and presentation of the Library of Congress Gershwin Prize for Popular Song. The recipient was Paul McCartney, who was, at the early hour of my arrival, not to be seen. As I walked down the corridor of the ground floor of the East Wing, I saw other entertainers gathering, along with members of the McCartney family led by Paul's affable brother, Mike McCartney. But with the excitement building, I had little understanding of the grandeur and scope of the extravagant event I was about to witness, until I scanned the embossed program booklet and the profiles inside, listing a collection of creative genius:

> British singing sensation Corrine Bailey Rae
> Rock legend Elvis Costello
> Dave Grohl of Nirvana and Foo Fighters
> Piano jazz legend Herbie Hancock

Grammy winners Emmylou Harris and Faith Hill
The Jonas Brothers
Chinese pianist Lang Lang
Jack White, rocker and actor
Jerry Seinfeld, strictly for laughs
Stevie Wonder; would he sing "Ebony and Ivory" in duet?

It was a breathtaking lineup. And at 7:25 p.m., a voice somewhere in the East Room announced, "Ladies and gentlemen, the president of the United States, the first lady of the United States, and Sir Paul McCartney."

Paul, dressed in a black show suit, with a collarless shirt, took to the stage and immediately started into "Got to Get You into My Life." I watched him carefully. I thought, "It's like, well, it's just like 1964 or 1965 all over again." Frankly, since I was the only one in that room who had been there in person, stage-side, during those heady times in the sixties, it was a clock stopper—but there was also a shocker. The years had put some age lines on the famous boyish face! But the body moved quickly to the rhythm of the music, and the classic composer and cowriter of the most delicious anthology of music in the modern era wasn't missing a beat. Was I the only one who could appreciate all the years that passed, and the continuity of vibrancy that remained in the never-ending story of Paul and the "lads," as the older American reporters liked to call them in those blood-flushing, enrapturing early days? I think so. I know that I was probably alone in my thoughts, but I was beaming quite naturally at the irony of fate, time, and the coincidence of my presence.

The next ninety minutes were bathed in greatness, the kind you rarely see on one platform on any given night. As the other artists sang, Paul sat in the front row, mouthing the words and enjoying each unique version of some of his greatest hits. "How amazing," I thought. "All the way from Merseyside to these heights. All that way in a journey of fame and glory, but never conceding excellence." And yes, Paul and Stevie sang "Ebony and Ivory." And yes, it was unbelievable.

When the music ended, the forty-fourth president of the United States, Barack Obama, took the stage. His brief but thoughtful comments illuminated the meaning of the honoree.

BY ITS VERY DEFINITION, POPULAR MUSIC IS FLEETING. RARELY IS IT COM-
POSED WITH AN EYE TOWARDS STANDING THE TEST OF TIME. RARER STILL
DOES IT ACTUALLY ACHIEVE THAT DISTINCTION. AND THAT'S WHAT MAKES
PAUL'S CAREER SO LEGENDARY. IT'S HARD TO BELIEVE THAT IT'S BEEN
NEARLY HALF A CENTURY SINCE FOUR LADS FROM LIVERPOOL FIRST
LANDED ON OUR SHORES AND CHANGED EVERYTHING OVERNIGHT. . . .

OVER THE FOUR DECADES SINCE, PAUL MCCARTNEY HAS NOT LET
UP, TOURING THE WORLD WITH THE BAND WINGS OR ON HIS OWN;
ROCKING EVERYTHING FROM SMALL HALLS TO SUPER BOWLS. HE'S COM-
POSED HUNDREDS OF SONGS OVER THE YEARS, WITH JOHN LENNON,
WITH OTHERS, OR ON HIS OWN. NEARLY TWO HUNDRED OF THOSE SONGS
MADE THE CHARTS—THINK ABOUT THAT—AND STAYED ON THE CHARTS
FOR A CUMULATIVE TOTAL OF THIRTY-TWO YEARS. [LAUGHTER AND
APPLAUSE.] AND HIS GIFTS HAVE TOUCHED BILLIONS OF LIVES.

I enjoyed the remarks, although I believe the president did not adequately
cover the enormous and creative influence of John Lennon on Sir Paul's life
and times, which were and remain our times as well. But even that miscue
couldn't diminish a very special moment in time.

Soon the show was over. The people, about two hundred of them, were
exiting to a brief postevent reception. I walked across the room and said,
"Paul, it's Larry."

He looked back. And then he shouted, "Oh my God, it's Larry! It's Larry
Kane! Look at *you*."

"Look at you," I answered.

He grabbed me in a big bear hug. He whispered, "It's so great to see you."

We chatted the private chat of people who have shared the same experience, and both thoroughly enjoyed our brief reunion.

The truth is that I have never been a "fan" of anything. I've always enjoyed
great performances, but that special night, in of all places, the White House,
I felt like, acted like, and was totally enveloped in fandom. And as I left the
East Wing a little later and hailed a cab, I started thinking back over the years

and realized just how truly lucky I was to have been part of the beginning. But of course, my beginning with the Beatles was not the real beginning, which occurred long before 1964 and has always been a subject of fascination and mystery.

After all, Paul was just a boy when it all began—a little younger but just as wise as his writing companion and fellow genius John Lennon and the leader of the All-Starr Band, and a bit older than George and his guitar-mastering magic fingers.

I first met the Beatles in February 1964 during their brief visit to the States, and first joined the Beatles on tour on August 18, 1964. But two decades before that, their journey began. This is *that* story.

Was the Beatles' success story improbable? Yes, more so than you know. But it is a story where all things *were* possible. In many ways, the prequel to the Beatles' arrival in America was more exciting than the main event.

Filled with characters dimmed or forgotten by the lapses of history, marked at times by despair and defeat, punctuated by moments of drama and fate, this story was mostly created by the energy and talent that overcame the most overwhelming odds.

My search for the characters was daunting. There are no doubt lies reported in this book, because there are so many contradictory reports. But everyone gets their moment of truth.

This is also a story about a city and its people. Alfred Lennon and his wife, Julia Stanley, would burn their own bridges of love and companionship in the parks and bedrooms of Liverpool, but flickers of art and banjos and guitars would burn inside a son. Harold Harrison, a friendly bus driver and stalwart union leader, taught his wiry son to respect the music, and to listen to its wonderment. James McCartney of the north side brought a middle-class work ethic and a charismatic personality to his son. And the less financially endowed Starkeys of the South Side of Liverpool saw their shy and sickly son, obsessed by the music, emerge into a man, and a talented one at that. The Sutcliffes encouraged their only son, Stuart, to paint *and* to play guitar. The legendary Mona Best played den mother to her drummer son, Pete, and to the early makeshift band. A tense, consistent, and frequent writer, Bill

Harry, wielded a pen as mighty as a guitar, and he had plenty of company—the likes of Beatles pressmen Tony Barrow and Derek Taylor, and others. The promoters, some of them still promoting, are vibrant in life and in recollection. The catalyst, Beatles manager Brian Epstein, is the most fascinating of entrepreneurs, provocative and endearing.

There are many heroes and heroines, risk takers, doubters, and hundreds of others who claim a piece of the history. To the people of Liverpool, their names stand beside the rich and the famous as architects of a revolution in culture. Sit beside early Beatles promoter Sam Leach, or longtime Beatles insider Tony Bramwell, or the original Quarrymen, and you feel what it was like to be there when the beginning began. You sense the uncertainty, the determination, the doubts, and the perilous flights of fancy and dreaming that live in young people. Ironic, isn't it? Youth is fleeting, but in the case of the Beatles, the music freezes them in time.

Time is the greatest enemy of history. Real events and people are distorted, exaggerated, and often forgotten. We are dependent on individual and collective memories. And there are so many people who try to shape their stories to suit their own biographies. That is expected. After all, what is memory but a hazy, subjective reconstruction of the vivid reality from so long ago?

Such is the history of the Beatles—conflicting stories, betrayal, love (lots of that), intrigue, and real or imagined adventure, some of which I shared while touring with them.

But about one fact there is absolute certainty. Before the world noticed, before the glare overwhelmed them, it all came together in the period from 1957 through 1963, when they were boys.

And it was all preceded by a bloody nightmare that would define the city and the boys.

Madness Above the Mersey

Jim McCartney would stand on the rooftop and watch. The glare of fires burning on the waterfront of the river Mersey would make his eyes squint and his stomach turn. He would glance out over the neighborhoods of his city and wonder how close the bombs would come. He was a volunteer—his job was to observe and report fires, and then, after the strange whistle of bombs hit the air on their way down and then exploded on the ground, Jim would fight the fires, and silently hope beyond hope that the killers in the sky would miss him. Jim, considered too old at thirty-eight to join the fighting forces, and hampered with a childhood injury, was determined to do his part.

A mile away, his wife, Mary, was delivering babies by darkness, another player in the drama that was Liverpool. For Mary and Jim, their only solace was that their first son, Paul, was born after the blitz had stopped. During the bombardment, German bombs strangled their city, but the heroism in the middle of the hell was a tribute to the stalwart fabric of the British and their undying hope to always see another daybreak. But daybreak also brought with it the shocking sights and smells of the tragedy.

That odious gas escaping from its destroyed pipelines, the smell of lathe and burned metal, and the stink of sewage streaming through the streets— it was unforgettable. As the horrified citizens emerged from the shelters, they discovered piles of soot several inches deep, and ultimately, the feared sight—lifeless beings extricated from the rubble.

As in all historic bombing campaigns, a few minutes late or early could decide the fate of an individual. On July 7, 1940, Elsie Starkey was late, but also early. As her son Richard entered the dark world of poverty she lived in at 9 Madryn Street, the first air-raid warnings were sounded. Fortunately, the height of the blitz started a few months later. Richard Starkey was born one month later than he was due, but early enough to survive the bombs.

Some people—wounded, dazed, and disoriented—wandered the remains searching for relatives and friends. Animals, left behind in the hurry to find safety, were clueless victims. Anticontamination units moved through the narrow streets to contain the filth and protect the living. The citizens of the city knew, quite privately because the enemy didn't know the extent of the damage, that thousands were dead and dying.

Bus conductor Harold (Harry) Harrison managed to maneuver his vehicle in and around shattered streets. He was a thin man, with intense dark eyes and a great love for his wife, Louise, and three children, including the youngest, Peter, born during the horrific blitz. A fourth child, George, the spitting image of his father, would arrive in 1943.

Harry, like his fellow wartime mates, experienced the suffering firsthand. Day by day, the toll was mounting.

In the end, the count was 4,000 dead in Liverpool—second only to London's loss of 30,000 in the extended aerial carnage. More than 6,000 Liverpool homes were gone, and nearly 200,000 damaged. The city was a shooting gallery. The blitz by the German Luftwaffe continued from Christmas 1940 until early in 1942.

But fate would have its moment, defying the destruction. On the evening of October 9, 1940, a woman could be seen running in the dark, fearless in the face of fear, heading for the Oxford Street Maternity Home, as it was called then. It is said she missed the explosion of a land mine by a few minutes. One thing is certain: a few hours earlier the Germans had launched another attack on populated areas. This attack did not stop Mary Stanley, known as Mimi, sister of Julia Stanley Lennon, from getting to the maternity home. Julia, a beautiful and caring young woman, married to merchant seaman Alfred Lennon, had just given birth to their first child, John Winston. Mimi, a strong-willed woman—some would say extremely stubborn almost to the point of defiantly immovable—was quoted as saying, "This was the one I was waiting for," as if it were her own child. The sisters were close, but Mimi viewed herself as a guardian to Julia. Inevitably, years after the bombs and war ended, Mimi's "wait" would take a historical turn, and the controversy over her role would live into the next century.

The blitz ended when the twentieth century's most prolific mass murderer, Adolf Hitler, turned his attention east toward the Russian threat against his expanding domain of death and fear. But the damage had been done.

The city of Liverpool and its environs had been a likely target. The port on the river Mersey, a waterway that would be romanticized by the young bands of musicians that roamed the streets fifteen years later, was the entry port for over 90 percent of raw war materials that arrived from other countries. Liverpool, whose great wealth was secured as a port of call several hundred years prior, was *the* port of call for the lifelines of World War II, and the gateway to the West. The Germans, diabolical in their bombing campaign, tried to stop the flow and kill the morale. But the mounting deaths, and the additional pain and suffering, only emboldened the populace to resist and fight daily for survival. Rationing of all resources was standard, but there was one critical commodity that the people of northwestern England had in abundance, and that was, quite simply, hope.

There was, and remains today, a sense of pride in the northwest of England. Is its sense of superiority unbound? No. But the mothers and fathers and children who grew up amid the ruins, many of them limited by economic duress caused by war, learned that, while London was the capital, the people of Liverpool would never afford themselves anything but first-class status in British society. Much of that moxie emerged from survival in the war, and it was on display when the greatest band in the world emerged from the port city, at first denied by the London music scene, and later embraced by Her Majesty's empire, and the rest of the human universe.

Liverpool is also a city of remembrance, whether it is the simple grave of the young retailer-cum-band manager, Brian Epstein—a member of Liverpool's small Jewish community who catapulted Britain's greatest entertainment exports to fame and glory—or the small, crumbling stone marking the resting place of the mother who produced a musical genius, both of whom died much too early. There are the houses of the famous and the hospitals where they emerged. But superseding the famous and those who were left behind is the spirit of the city's working-class people, nurtured over decades of seeking a better life for their successors and etched in the courage burned into their souls by the great aerial bombardment.

Perhaps the most famous nod to the past is the church that remains standing, remarkably, in the heart of the city. On May 5, 1941, a German bomber dropped a firebomb on St. Luke's Church. Today, when you walk aside the church, you dwell on the beauty of the structure, until you look closer and notice, chillingly, that its insides are gone, destroyed in the attack. While "Merseyside," as the people call Liverpool, has been reconstructed with contemporary multilevel shopping malls and a large waterfront development, the shell of St. Luke's remains erect to this day, a memorial to the thousands who died in the second great war, and to the hundreds of thousands who survived.

The aerial attacks brought the city to self-imposed darkness amid the lights-out warnings that were strictly observed, lest the Germans spotted a flicker and attacked it with added intensity—for history shows us that the Luftwaffe rarely made the humane distinction between strategic targets and those with no strategic value at all. And so darkness itself became a terrifying ordeal.

June Furlong tried to live with the darkness of war. She would later make history posing for a young art student who would achieve undying fame long after his heart stopped beating. She was ten years old when the bombs started dropping.

"We would sit around the table during the blackouts. The only illumination [was from] the paint on the railings of the narrow staircase. I practiced piano in the dark, studied in the dark, sat in the dark, and heard the news that my cousin, a pilot, was shot down and killed. It was truly terrifying."

Furlong still shudders to think what else could have happened. Recalling the fright, she talks of one fateful night. "An incendiary device came crashing through the roof," she tells me.

She remembers the moment, her eyebrows arching, her face still showing the pain of the memory, sixty years later. "We sat under the table in the dining room. As the house shook, so did my body. It was so bloody frightening."

When the bombers stopped, even before the war ended, Furlong and her generation remembered the way it hardened the souls, and brought people together.

Furlong, who would play a role in the education of John Winston Lennon, is a woman of great enthusiasm, and has an undying love for her city. Her lips widen, her eyes glow, her voice becomes high-pitched and cheerful as she talks about the suddenly unchained people of her city and their ultimately positive reaction to the war.

"It [brought out] the best in people. People who didn't talk for years started talking. Friendship and dependency in war was second to none. We had street parties, jellies [candies], and parades. They were filled with music."

She beams with the wise counsel of a woman who has been there.

"Let's face it. It was the music that kept us going."

The music kept Liverpool going, but so did the differences, the dividing lines that infuse the energy of a great city. And those differences are fascinating, starting with the country's most popular sport.

In 1892 the Liverpool Football Club was born. By the year 2000, Liverpool F.C. was declared the most successful English soccer team of the twentieth century. Yet, the team was not the first one established in the city. Over a decade earlier, in 1878, Everton F.C. was founded. And today the two teams' respective stadiums sit right across the way from each other. The Liverpool team is known as the "Reds," and Everton is the "Blues." For many years the teams were divided by religions—the "Reds" were viewed as the Protestant team, the "Blues" as the Catholics. Indeed, Liverpool is one of the few cities in the world with two massive cathedrals, Protestant and Catholic, tall and becoming, facing off each other in a neighborhood not far from where the Beatles went to school.

Many years after soccer arrived, another major arrival would change the fate of a city and the world. This was, of course, the arrival of the guitar boys, who in 1957 replaced the banjo and washboard stars they had worshipped. A teenage band, in raw form, arrived on the scene through a circuitous journey, on streets hardly paved with gold, but rather lined with the trapdoors and quicksand of decision, fate, and competition. The surviving four boys of the band never wavered in their meteoric rise to immortality. It is an irony that in today's Liverpool, many of the younger generation embrace these boys with less intensity than the rest of the world, but ask any one of them which four men made the greatest statement of independence to the elites of the English south, and they know exactly where their modern-day heritage was born.

Yes, it is a city of contrasts and great pride, and like all cities, was founded on illustrious contradictions.

The city's eponymous soccer club earned its success in no small part by the spirit of its fans. Generations of Liverpool fans and players have moved through the sacred grass of Anfield, their home from the beginning. And in the modern era, the team and players have marched to the beat of their theme song, "You'll Never Walk Alone," borrowed from the musical *Carousel.*

The song was recorded by Gerry Marsden, the leader of Gerry and the Pacemakers. Although Marsden lived in the shadow of the Beatles, he had a successful career in his own right, and is beloved by Liverpool soccer fans for the song, which is, in itself, a major contradiction. Marsden may be the voice of the "Reds," but it is said that he was actually a fan of the "Blues" until he was thirteen. Fans will rarely walk into each other's stadiums, but when it comes to Marsden's soccer preferences, no one really cares.

But to all others: beware. These are sacred grounds, and one should never enter the wrong turf. The Reds and the Blues play in separate stadiums, facing each other, just like the towering cathedrals. Each stadium holds over 40,000 fans. The economies of modern communities suggest a single stadium could better serve both fan bases. But to date, loyalty and sacred heritage are more important than money.

It is true that a soccer fan never walks alone in Liverpool, just as the besieged residents of the war's blitz knew that their backs, if not their houses, were covered. The friendliness of the people even today is catching. I have never met a cabdriver in Liverpool who didn't ask where I was from, nor did any man or woman ever balk when I walked up to ask directions. I have never seen such a city where happiness is not bounded by social or economic standing. People may call you "luv" and, believe me, they really mean it. The accent is thick with a slightly Irish brogue, and sometimes it is hard for the visitor to understand. So, on occasion, you have to ask, "Can you please repeat that?" And they do, willingly.

In Liverpool, no one ever really walks alone.

The people who endured the bombings, the postwar mothers and fathers who looked forward, not back, and the parents of the boys in the band who kept saving money for their sons, worried that the bubble would burst.

And the boys themselves? They were not always saints, but like their fellow citizens, they always had people covering their back. These people were so important, and in many ways, so ignored by history. Surrounded by a cast of characters no writer of fiction could ever invent, blessed with inordinate talents and a determination to succeed, ordained with tons of luck, and destined to narrowly escape the dangers of their path, they wrote their history, and gifted their joy to a surprised world.

And it all began in the coastal city in northern England, where life, some of it soaked in rain, can, in itself, be a daily surprise.

WHEN THEY WERE BOYS

Part One:
Stirrings

The milkman makes his rounds, smoking and dreaming. Little Paulie pines for his mother, tinkles with the piano. George has his own bus, sort of. Pete studies hard; Richie not so much, instead listens to Donegan, while Johnny Boy scrapes up the money to buy the contraband 45s, hoping for a peek at the Everlys. Paulie loves the bicycle and the comb and strumming the strings of his future, while the milkman terrorizes teachers with a vengeance. The teachers have no clue. The hearts are beating fast, the stomachs churning, the dreams lighting up the dark of the night, along with the booze, the cigs, and the sounds on the radio from the small country that dares to play the censored music. There are stirrings, and seeds planted; will they grow?

Treachery, honesty, desire, respect or lack of it, wealth, native talent and talent acquired, lucky breaks, winning by design, love found and lost, leaving your mentors in a fog of mediocrity, respecting your contemporaries, frailty, power, revising your history, living in the truth, peace, violence—all of our lives' histories are padded with pieces of all of the above, including the four boys who would become the best-known music stars of all time.

These factors of life combine to make our histories, but as time moves on, and people vanish to a different world, legends remain that often are not true.

One of the legends is the "rags to riches" story that emerged from Liverpool after the success of the Beatles, who in this book will often be referred to as the "boys," as they were in their day. When they were boys, and with only one exception, they really didn't all rise from the depths of poverty.

Scholar Mike Brocken of Liverpool Hope University has studied the reality for decades:

THE BEATLES, INCLUDING PETE BEST, WERE FROM SOUTH LIVERPOOL, A LEAFY SUBURBAN AREA AND COMPLETELY DIFFERENT THAN WHAT WAS PORTRAYED—WORKING-CLASS, LOWER-MIDDLE-CLASS, IMPOVERISHED BACKGROUNDS. OF COURSE, THIS DID NOT INCLUDE RINGO, WHO CAME FROM A MORE UNDERPRIVILEGED AREA OF LIVERPOOL. THE REALITY OF THE CLASS BACKGROUND IS COMPLETELY DIFFERENT THAN WHAT HAS BEEN PORTRAYED HISTORICALLY, QUITE DIVERGENT FROM DEPICTED

NARRATIVE, REALLY. THE BEST FAMILY WAS A PROMINENT FAMILY WITH A GRANDFATHER WHO WAS THE LIVERPOOL BOXING STADIUM PROMOTER. HIS MOM WAS A POWERFUL AND FORCEFUL WOMAN IN HER OWN RIGHT. THEY RAN AN UPSCALE CLUB. THOSE AREAS AND IDEAS OF RACE, WEALTH AND INFLUENCE, DEMOGRAPHICS REALLY NEED TO BE TAKEN INTO ACCOUNT IN THOSE EARLY YEARS IN PARTICULAR. THEN YOU CAN START TO UNDERSTAND THE NARRATIVE THAT DOESN'T REPEAT THE SAME OLD MATERIAL OVER AND OVER AGAIN.

THESE LADS, WITH THE EXCEPTION OF RINGO, CAME FROM A RELATIVELY COMFORTABLE AND A RELATIVELY AFFLUENT PART OF LIVERPOOL, ALTHOUGH IN THEIR EARLY DAYS, THE FAMILIES OF GEORGE AND PAUL WERE FINANCIALLY STRESSED. THE PERCEPTIONS ABOUT THE DISTRICTS OF LIVERPOOL NEED TO BE ADDED INTO THE EQUATION. EVENTUALLY, THEIR FAMILIES COULD AFFORD TO PROVIDE THEM WITH GUITARS, AMPLIFIERS, AND SOMEONE TO RIDE THEM AROUND IN A VAN.

So, to begin, it was more like threads.

Threads. There are enough of them in the story to stretch a quilt from Liverpool to London. The boys were, like all boys, discovering new threads to their future at every moment. Theirs was a world, like that of all children of exploration, with some odd places. As little more than toddlers, little Paul McCartney and skinny George Harrison would play with friends in the Speke neighborhood, sometimes dangerously toying with German bombs that were, depending on whom you talk to, unexploded or harmless, probably the latter. Speke was a neighborhood of 25,000 people, many World War II veterans and their spouses, bringing up children in the British version of the postwar baby boom. It was busy with pedestrians and bicycles, this area near the airport. That airport doesn't exist today, but the new one, John Lennon International Airport, is sparkling and not far away.

In 1943, William Howard Ashton was born in the Bootle section of Liverpool. He says,

IT WAS A REALLY TOUGH NEIGHBORHOOD, VERY BLUE COLLAR. YOU GREW UP EARLY WITH A PLAN . . . MINE WAS TO TRAIN FOR THE RAILROAD AS ENGINEER.

I DID THAT, BUT IN THE END, MUSIC WON OUT. LIKE ALL THE FAMILIES IN BOOTLE, MY PARENTS INSISTED THAT I HAVE A PLAN. WHO KNEW WHAT WOULD HAPPEN? YOU DID YOUR BEST, PRAYED A BIT, AND HOPED SOMETHING WOULD HAPPEN. THE HARDER YOU WORKED, YOU HOPED THE BETTER CHANCE YOU WOULD HAVE, BUT LUCK AND CIRCUMSTANCES WOULD PLAY A PART. I WASN'T A BEATLE, BUT I HAPPILY RODE THE WAVE.

Inspired by the boys playing at Speke and that "Lennon guy," William became Billy J. Kramer, the strikingly handsome leader of the group Billy J. Kramer and the Dakotas. He would get close to the famous ones and receive a great gift someday: the words and music of their songs to record himself.

"Liverpool may have been seen as a tough place," Kramer says, "but my growing up was filled with memories of playing in the streets of Bootle, finding fun in the streets and love at home."

For John Winston Lennon, the middle name in honor of the great prime minister, life at home was a bit more complicated, as, it turned out, his own life would become. He had a birth mother and father, and he had a surrogate mother and father, and while he was well cared for in his younger days, he was strained by confusion, and with it, an angry side developed that would make him both popular and controversial, even in boyhood. His birth mother purchased an acoustic guitar, and while her sister Mimi, John's surrogate mother, generally disdained popular music, mother Julia was happy to dance and sing with him. These were moments in time he would never forget in the years after his mother passed on.

The drummers had contrasting childhood lives. Pete Best was born in India, and by the time he came to Liverpool, his mother, Mona, was separated from her husband. Mona, it turned out, was energized and ambitious, and would protect her sons at any cost.

Richie Starkey grew up in a poverty-stricken neighborhood, raised mostly alone by his divorced mother, Elsie, who was loving, and always worried. When he turned six, she had reason to worry herself sick. Her little boy slipped into a coma. When he emerged after two months, his recovery from a serious illness was arduous, but eased by his first musical experiences banging on a tin drum.

James McCartney, to become known to the world as Paul, was smart enough to get into the prestigious Liverpool Institute High School for Boys at age eleven. Paul often shared bus rides with George Harrison. The two, sharing interests of music and guitars, would get together and play, and talk, and play some more. George, a year younger and a grade apart from Paul at the Institute, told me that "I think Paul thought he was a bit better than me. You know what eighteen months' difference is when you're young." Paul would admit later in many conversations that he acted superior to George. The bus driver's son, too, blamed it on youth, although he admitted that after an undistinguished education at Dovedale Primary School, he was fortunate, by way of passing his eleventh plus exam, to gain entrance to the Institute.

While Paul benefited from his father's early work in jazz, a career cut short by the financial reality of the times, George was mentored and encouraged by his mother, Louise. He became, courtesy of his thoughtful parents, the proud owner of a very used acoustic guitar. Paul did a trade-in, sacking his father's old trumpet for a similar guitar, which with some difficulty and a change in the strings he learned to play his natural way, left-handed. He loved the guitar and especially appreciated the tips he got from George. He seemed to intensify his interest in music and learning after his life was turned upside down by tragedy on October 31, 1956. Like his future bandmate John, Paul lost one half of his loving support team.

John had left his first school, the same Dovedale Primary School where George attended, a few years behind him, to join Quarry Bank School, where he made friends and decided to form his first band. John never met George at the school, nor would he until Paul McCartney introduced the guitar man to him in 1958.

Richie, like George, disdained school, but George managed to do well. Richie did not do well, though he aspired to a better life with his interest in music. But from the ages of six to thirteen, he became a truant, and once again faced serious illness. Despite the illness and serious drug and alcohol issues, Richie managed to hold on. Music kept him going, even though, unlike the others, he had little musical inspiration from family.

Pete was a superior student, and even as a young boy, he was being touted as a future teacher until his mother decided to open a nightclub. It was there, at the Casbah, that his pulsating love for the drums began. Pete benefited from a stable family, as did Stuart Sutcliffe.

Thin. Handsome. Eclectic. Stuart had all the family love that John wanted as a child. Stu and John were really a case of man-to-man friendship, an intimacy that few achieve in a lifetime. Theirs was a story that only death could stop.

For John, James, Richie, George, Stu, and Pete, the musical legacy of Liverpool was being passed on. The city was rich in its history of music, and music, the love of it, was what tied their interests together. The stirrings of the early fifties brought them together in unusual ways. It all began with the original leader—his self-taught talents of wit and words, the questioning of his own beginnings, and a tremendous level of guts and raw courage.

But as you'll learn along the roadway of dreams, there were accidents and near-misses from the early fifties until 1963. Fate is not often in our hands. Nor is fortune. Talent and ability are not always rewarded. Circumstances sometimes override even the most ambitious efforts of mere mortals.

In truth, when they were boys, the sometimes-dangerous sequence of events could have produced a different ending, one the world might never have noticed.

CHAPTER ONE

THE MILKMAN

"When he acted like that, sometimes I wanted to give him a smack."
—Colin Hanton, Quarrymen drummer

*"He was just a little boy . . . who was saddened that his mom
was not around and his dad was not around."*
—Yoko Ono

*"He tried to hide his pain, but he had a lot of it,
especially after what happened to our mother."*
—Julia Baird, John Lennon's sister

THE MILKMAN WAS A DREAMER. Without his dreams, the band might have never been.

The sun's rays, on a lucky day, are making their way through the rooftops of Liverpool. The solitary figure moves quietly over the sidewalks, dropping off the fresh milk at his appointed rounds. He is hungry and, as always in the morning hours, filled with anxiety, a smidge of anger, and a touch of daydreaming—the kind of fantastic dreams that fill us with hope as teenagers. Chances are that he is thinking about music and creating a reasonable amount of mayhem during the day ahead. In young John Lennon's mind, the milk delivery is a necessary means to an end, a few extra pounds, a purchase here or there of American records, a chance to chart his future, undaunted and barely affected by the doubts of the adults in his life. Above and beyond everything he was—friend, lover, son, nephew, brother, student, milkman—he was an incessant dreamer and devilish manipulator. His small, piercing eyes—whether as an infant in diapers, a late teen in a black leather jacket, a young star on tour from 1964 through 1966, or a worldwide icon—always told you the story. Even on the bandstands with his washboard and banjo friends—the Quarrymen—the eyeballs, and the muscles surrounding them, spoke volumes. When he giggled, which few witnessed, or when he was making a point with humor, he stared at you directly, his eyelids rarely blinking, and at times, not at all. During the moments when he was intense or quite serious, the eyes turned into a frightening stare. No wonder some of his teachers thought he was a menace. The eyes could look cold. As they say, "If looks could kill."

During his shows, when he played to the crowd, his eyes stared straight out, as if he were rocking the joint for an audience of millions. One on one, in intimate moments of emotion and eloquent conversation, he would give a wistful look, as if to show sincerity. I was always stunned at his eye contact with the audiences. His flashes of humor, that ability to jump ahead of the thought, respond in a second or two to a statement or a question, were amazing, if not superhuman. The boy, making his deliveries, and the man, later offering his words to the world, never stopped thinking his special thoughts, or about what he would say next. His personality and his imagination were something special, a package of excitement, sometimes so special and rudely honest that it became excess baggage on the travels of his life, but always, in the end of the remarks, refreshing the world with courage and conviction.

The milkman takes a deep drag on a cigarette as he circles back to the small home. As he comes through the door, the cigarette is gone. It wouldn't be accepted in this house. He knows he has just a few minutes to gather up some tea, maybe toast with jam, a short conversation, if any at all, and it will be time to head off to school. It will be a long day, but music from the radio the night before is still filling his mind—Buddy Holly, Gene Vincent, the Everly Brothers, good old Lonnie Donegan. Lately he has been obsessed with George Formby Jr., the man who grew up in Lancashire, the tart comedian who also sang. The milkman has searched in great wonder for information on George, a banjo-ukulele man who eased out of Merseyside to reach the world of comedy and movies. After all, John thinks, how many infants could lose their sight and regain it after a violent sneeze? How many children at the age of seven could have a short career as a jockey? How could

Formby, whose voice alone could make you laugh so hard, create separate stage and recording careers that brought so much joy to people during the Depression and war? And could John become, like Formby, a man who created comedy and song with rich double meanings, like Formby's risqué tune "With My Little Stick of Blackpool Rock"?

It was not lost on John that "My Little Stick," a trademark song for Formby, king of comedy from 1934 to 1945, was banned by the BBC. John would take it as a badge of honor that years later, his relatively harmless song "Imagine" was banned on hundreds of American radio stations because it simply stated that there could be a better world without wars and the divisions of religion. John was amazed by Formby. Along with Donegan, Vincent, and the Yanks (an expression he learned from his mother, referring to American musicians), there was enough inspiration to incite the most curious of teenagers. Sadly, by the time he was seventeen, the mother was gone, and now he relied on his music boys, quiet Uncle George, an unsung hero in his life, and his formidable aunt, Mimi, who raced to the hospital during the bombing blitz to see little newborn John Winston, "the one" she had been waiting for.

He was at times both angry and hopeful, and always resented the establishment around him—the teachers, the pompous, and anybody with a hint of bullshit. In his world, there was no room for that. He was also glowing or prickly, and there was very little in between. This mood swing, nonchalant to sensitive, would continue for all of his life.

Most of all, the milkman was an incessant dreamer. Dreaming was his first real profession. He did it all the time. During an argument we had on the 1966 North American tour, we debated the Vietnam War. He told me, "I dream of rescuing Americans before they go off and get killed." Then, realizing that I was going into military service that summer, he offered me a job in the Beatles organization. "You could become an expatriate," he said. I replied, "You've got to be kidding." He said, "Not at all."

Did he dream of becoming famous? Yoko Ono's favorite time with her husband was late at night, before bed, when the pillow talk about both of their younger lives came to the forefront.

"John told me that at Mendips [John's childhood home] he wasn't dreaming of becoming a big thing like the Beatles. He was thinking of music, but he, his early years, he was a little boy who was saddened that his mom was not around and his dad was not around. He always wanted to find out about his dad, but through it all he dreamed of excellence."

Transferring those dreams from daydreams to reality has always been the supreme challenge for human beings, especially young people. But in this case, the life was fiercely complicated by a family conflict that could rip into one's insides. Rising above such a situation—a part-time mother, a vanished father—and dealing with a surrogate family could be so difficult. Such obstructions were a challenge for John Lennon as a preteen, as a teen, and even as a Beatle. But John had his own weapons, his own emotional shields to blunt the sadness, the vulnerability.

There is no doubt that the left-handed guitarist, Paul McCartney, was, is, and always will be a workaholic. Friends like Bill Harry and Tony Bramwell will tell you so.

Quarrymen banjo player Rod Davis, who was closer to John and really didn't know Paul, says that John Lennon was also a hard worker, but an unremitting dream machine.

"He was, in my day, a cocky kind of guy, a young guy with a pointed nose who liked to start trouble, but yes, a dreamer. . . . He was also cynical," Davis says. "Would I ever see him as a peace activist with a beard and long hair? Never in those days, mind you. But then again, he was unpredictable. That's what made him so exciting."

Quarrymen bassist Len Garry (now vocalist for the modern-day version of the band) says John was a good listener, but it's what he didn't listen to that took him where he thought he wanted to go. John had encouragement, but an enormous amount of negative energy around him.

"That guitar; that's what it was all about," Garry remembers. "Aunt Mimi told him, 'That guitar, John, you'll never make a living out of that.' Did John listen? No. He didn't listen to anyone who disagreed with his hopes. He followed his talent. Lots of people will tell others, 'You can't do that,' and that affects people. But John wouldn't be denied. There was a drive that was both admirable and overwhelming."

Quarrymen drummer Colin Hanton recalls, "John could be impossible sometimes. He was driven to extremes. He could be almost near violent. When he acted like that, sometimes I wanted to give him a smack. But he was always determined to be something, to stand above."

Davis, a current world traveler and surfing enthusiast, will always remember John as tough and sensitive, two traits hard to reconcile as a teenager:

FIGHTING BACK, AND HARD, WAS A LENNON TRADEMARK. . . . I NEVER KNEW HE WAS A SENSITIVE HUMAN BEING, ALTHOUGH OF COURSE HE DID WRITE POETRY; HE DID WRITE THINGS FOR THE SCHOOL MAGAZINE. BUT HE WASN'T FLOWERS AND BIRDS AND CLOUDS AND STUFF. I MEAN, HE WROTE A POEM CALLED "THE TALE OF HERMAN FRED," WHICH WAS PUBLISHED IN THE SCHOOL MAGAZINE, AND WAS QUITE AMUSING. SO HE HAD THIS ABILITY TO EXERCISE TOUGHNESS, BUT HE DID NOT VIEW HIMSELF AS UNMANLY BECAUSE HE ENJOYED WRITING. HE COULD BE CHAOTIC IN THE CLASSROOM, THOUGH.

Psychologists like to tell us that we are what we think we are. Unfortunately, that doesn't work for everybody, but for John, it was always a work in progress—the challenge of channeling his childhood loneliness and constant despair into the real-life messages of hope, love, and loss that showed up in the songs he wrote both with Paul and after the Beatles. To this day, John Lennon may be the most autobiographical of songwriters, unashamed for the rest of us to share his ordeals.

One can image the loneliness he felt in the mid- to late fifties, and the reasons: a mother struck by a car and killed when he was seventeen; a father who had supposedly vanished from his life; the hostile failure of his teachers to recognize his creative endeavors; and the lack of mentors, save for the recording artists he worshipped.

So, inevitably, imagination took over. It is not without coincidence that his most iconic song is "Imagine."

The photograph of John sprawled out on his narrow bed in Mimi's home, reading and sketching and listening to records, is the most compelling. His second-floor bedroom at 251 Menlove Avenue is still locked in time today, much like the sitting room below. The furniture is circa 1955, and the walls are as they were. Like many British homes, it has a name, Mendips. The home provided John a room with a view, a bright and shiny view of the world outside. When I glance around the narrow room I can imagine the teenage world of the smoking milkman as he lay in his bed, reading, getting up to look at the avenue, quietly shaving in the bathroom, fantasizing about being on stage, rocking like the famous rockers, infuriating his teachers, and dealing with his kind Uncle George and his upright and strict Aunt Mimi, guardian of the young empire, dominatrix of the household, surrogate mother, for a time, and puritanical challenger of everything John.

Mimi was a force, although Freda Kelly, the teenage secretary to Beatles manager Brian Epstein, and one of the closest people to Mimi, has a different take. Kelly was the main liaison to the Beatles' parents. When she first met John and Mimi, months after she went berserk with the rest of the crowd at the Cavern, she was in a different position. Now she saw John as a wild and creative and unchained force. In Kelly's view, five years after the death of John's mother, Mimi was quite necessary.

"She was like my father: old school," she says. "John needed controlling. He was a rebel. She was a woman who was trying to do the right thing, doing her best to guide and bring him up right. She was a lovely person who didn't suffer fools gladly. Her imagery as a tough, unrelenting woman is not the whole story."

Brian Epstein's lifelong friend Joe Flannery sees the aunt's assertiveness from a different angle: "There is no doubt that Mimi, who was someone who loved him beginning at birth, saw and understood John's vulnerability, and believe me, he was vulnerable."

Mimi. George. Mendips. Along with the mother he loved, they were John's world.

From the age of five, when he was brought into Mimi and George's life, until twenty-three, John lived at various intervals at Mendips. At the age of seven, he wandered in the small but lush backyard, bordering on Strawberry Field, a home for orphans. He often, in moments of daring, scaled the fence to join the children. He enjoyed their company for years. During a 1975 interview, John told me, "Most of my memories in those days were with the other children. I liked being with them. But Mimi was not happy." Did he sense a commonality with them? Did he feel like an orphan, too? I never asked him those questions, but once again, as it happens so often in this story, the fence-jumping, Mimi-defying excursions made their way into song.

When Mimi scolded John for jumping the fence, John said, "C'mon, Aunt Mimi, they can't hang you for it." Later, in the words of the song "Strawberry Fields Forever," it was "nothing to get hung about."

Sitting on his narrow bed, posters of contemporary entertainers on the walls, John would read late into the night, sometimes sleeping just a few hours before heading out to his milk rounds. Mimi's husband, George, one of the motivators of John's teenage years, used the home as a refuge for learning. Mimi's strong-willed sense of discipline extended to her husband. George enjoyed his time with John. Mostly they talked about the need to read. John became a master reader. His interest in contemporary news reports was intense by his fourteenth birthday. John started reading the "Just Williams" children's series at ten, and graduated to *Alice's Adventures in Wonderland* and *The Wind in the Willows*, a 1908 novel of mysticism, camaraderie, and adventure, channeled through four animal characters with human-like features and traits: a mole, a rat, Mr. Toad, and Mr. Badger. The book is a classic, and the young fence-climber was fascinated by its fantasy. At the age of ten, he would share some of the stories with his friends on the "other side" at Strawberry Field.

John was mostly peaceful at home. School was another story. He alternately puzzled and tortured his teachers at Quarry Bank. He was, as Stuart Sutcliffe's sister Pauline describes, an "anarchist." There may have been reasons.

Boyhood buddy and bandmate Rod Davis says John, like him, ventured into a scary environment at Quarry Bank. It was somewhat formal yet surrounded by young goons trying to mess up the school day.

"So we had our nice little blazers with our Quarry Bank stags on and our little gold stag heads around the cuffs and so on. And we were a target for all the toughs. We were the bright guys, just for going to Quarry Bank School. So therefore we were the targets for all of the guys who decided they were going to take it out on us. So, John's technique was to develop a hard exterior, and that worked quite well."

John was both angry and insightful, but determined to disrupt classes with outbursts, the distribution of graphic and sexual sketches, and other odd gifts. When teachers would scold him, he looked dumbfounded, with a "not me" look, an external innocence, as if to say, "Nothing to get hung about."

Eventually, for a short period, John became one of the "toughs" himself, to prove his mettle.

And later, along with his friend Pete Shotton, John became one of the intellectually stimulated students; he would and could excel, depending on the day. As John plowed his way through the books, interested more in hearing music from the States than focusing on the sciences or math, teachers were frustrated by his pranks. One of them was heard to say, "This boy is bound to fail." Failure at times, in the school setting, was something John dealt with gracefully, sometimes with humor and sarcasm. But he also made it clear to teachers and friends that he was very interested in music and art.

Quarry Bank's headmaster, William Pobjoy, knew that despite his questionable grades at times, John was very smart. In an act that caused some of the teachers to question his own credibility, Pobjoy helped John to get into the Art Institute (now John Moores University), where his relations with intellectuals and pseudo-intellectuals would make him even more of a young revolutionary. Although he would meet future wife Cynthia there, along with great friends Bill Harry and Stu Sutcliffe, John's grades were dismal. Some years later, John answered a fan letter from a student at Quarry Bank. In reference to the headmaster who indirectly paved the way to advance John's destiny, John wrote, "After all, it was he who got me into art school, so I could fail there, too, and I can never thank him enough."

There is plenty of confirmation of John's indifference to the standard rules of education. June Furlong, our heroine who once braved German bombings in total darkness, became a successful life model and worked at the Art Institute. Sitting in the coffee shop of a modern Liverpool movie house, June smiles broadly as she tells me that John's close friend Stu Sutcliffe was engaged in the learning process, while John seemed less so.

"Stuart was the student. John was the inquisitor and activist, more involved with the other students, a little bit distracted, but I must add, the perfect gentleman at the same time."

So we know that John as a student, at both his middle and high school, was highly suspect. The only time he seemed to meld at Quarry Bank was when he talked music, and subsequently formed his very basic skiffle band, the Quarrymen, affectionately named after the school he had so warmly accepted as his own in more ways than one. And it is in that pursuit, the desire to play his heart out for anyone who listened, that John Lennon, in his early teens, found his obsession, influenced by his birth mother along with a spark from good friends.

Colin Hanton remembers the traits of character that the confused but driven teenage John brought to the band.

"He was a leader but he didn't bang the table and say, 'I am the boss.' Whatever he wanted to sing, there was no point arguing. We just went along with it. He led gently, so to speak. Where John went, we followed. He wasn't a tyrant or anything, most of the time."

Was he fun to play with?

"Oh yeah. He was a great laugh. There was no middle ground with him. If he liked you, he liked you. If not, then he wasn't going to be funny about it. I must add, too, that he was rarely afraid of trouble."

And trouble was always just around the corner.

Johnny's Great Escape: First Rush

Trouble did come in one of the Quarrymen's early concerts. It was an important event because it showed young John that he had a power, in addition to the music, that would carry over to the days of the Beatles. It was, in a word, seduction. Some men and women develop the art of seduction as life goes on. John had it at an early age, and he broadcast what he was looking for with his eyes, his hips, and his voice, sometimes high but always entrancing.

June 22, 1957, was a day to remember, or forget, depending on whom you were. If you were John Lennon, it would be an early lesson in the perils of sexual animal magnetism—aka John Lennon putting girls in heat.

Rosebery Street was putting on a bit of a street festival, part of a citywide celebration of neighborhoods. The Quarrymen were booked, and set up their instruments on the back of a lorry. In American terms, that would be a flatbed trailer behind a truck—not very glamorous, but they *were* fifteen years old.

Dealing with nerves was never part of John Lennon's preshow routine—not until he downed some mind-altering drugs, such as Preludin, to stay awake in Hamburg, or heavier drugs post-1964 on the worldwide tours. Generally, though, in the early days, John was not afraid. Early on, his onstage sexual appeal to women was clear—especially when he belted out hard-rock songs.

In an incident I'll call "Johnny's great escape," black women in the Rosebery Street crowd rushed the wagon, screaming for John, reaching out. Their hands were up in the air, their faces showing sexual energy toward the animated boy leading the band. And the black boys in the crowd became incensed; John was poaching on their turf.

Eyewitnesses described a frantic scene, as the Quarrymen realized that the girls seemed to be excited by John, heat glowing from their cheeks, while their male friends wanted to put down the musical maniac who was turning them on. Their eyes were filled with a look that said, "How dare this bloke with the guitar incite our women!"

Colin Hanton has vivid memories of the concert, performed to a racially mixed crowd:

THAT WAS ON ROSEBERY STREET. I WAS WITH THE LADS AND WE WERE ON THE BACK OF THE WAGON. I WAS WAY ON THE OTHER SIDE BUT I COULD SEE THE GROUP GETTING RESTLESS. AND I LEANED DOWN AND SAID TO ONE OF MY DRINKING BUDDIES IN THE CROWD, "WHAT IS GOING ON OUT THERE?" AND SOMEONE SAID, "THEY ARE GONNA GET JOHN LENNON!" THAT WAS IT; WE JUMPED OFF, GOT OUR GUITARS, ETC., AND WENT INTO SOMEONE'S HOUSE. JOHN RAN DOWN THE STREET . . . QUICKLY.

ON SEVERAL OCCASIONS, WHEN THIS TYPE OF THING HAPPENED, I WAS NOT HAPPY WITH HIM. JOHN WAS VERY GOOD AT TALKING HIS WAY OUT OF TROUBLE. THERE WAS NEVER REALLY ANY TROUBLE TO SPEAK OF . . . ALTHOUGH THERE WAS GREAT POTENTIAL.

Len Garry, who once fancied himself a young teen idol, remarks that despite whatever was going on in John's personal life, his childhood buddy had a certain panache, a daring charisma, and a determination that he admired.

Garry, who admits he was a bit envious of John's appeal, remembers the near riot on Rosebery Street:

REMEMBER, EVERYTHING WAS CLOSE IN. THERE WAS NO SECURITY, JUST OUR LITTLE BAND AND THE CROWD. THE GIRLS WERE GETTING CLOSER AND CLOSER, JUST STARING AT JOHN, WHO WAS WIGGLING HIS HIPS A BIT. AS THE GIRLS GOT CLOSER, THE BOYS SEEMED TO BE GETTING ANGRIER. JOHN DIDN'T CARE. HE LOOKED STRAIGHT AT THE GIRLS. NO FEAR. NOTHING. COLIN [HANTON] WAS LOOKING SCARED. SO, AS THE RIGHT TIME APPROACHED, WE ALL TOOK A RUN TO SAVE OUR LIVES.

Running for his life—first in Liverpool, and later in the fan-filled arenas of America and the world—would become old hat for John. But for forty years he tried to run, but couldn't hide, from things beyond his control: the confusion of his childhood, the love he was given, and the affection that was taken away. Love was central to John's life—real love or the lack of it. John ran from the crowd that day on Rosebery Street, but he could not hide from the dimensions of his early life and the confusion that enveloped it.

Mom and Mom, and the Sister Act

The gravestone is marked with the names of her children. It is inscribed: "Mummy, John, Victoria, Julia, Jackie." It stands isolated in a Liverpool cemetery along with the graves of thousands. An unusual work of art sits alongside the grave—the tiny stone sculpture of a kitten, a fond farewell from her more austere sister, who assumed the mantle of parental leader.

Beneath the earth, the eclectic and unpredictable mother would never hear the lonely strains of "Mother" and "Julia," songs written by her firstborn to remember her by, and to scream out for her.

There is one absolute in the life of the mad and funny genius whose scrape-filled marathon to immortality gave us the Beatles: his childhood and teenage years were filled with a confusing angst, and the spillover affected his adult life.

It all starts with the story of Mother, and there are many versions. The question is: Will the real Julia Stanley Lennon please stand up? After all, Julia, you did affect so much in a very short time.

The boy who was running the race to greatness had, within him, a storm of emotions about his mother, a British beauty with a loving touch. To say that Julia Stanley Lennon was an attraction to men is an understatement. To label her a harlot, as many writers have, is an exaggeration of a woman's needs and the consequences of bad choices.

Painted, tainted, and applied with a broad brush, the story of Julia's life and her impact on John is debated passionately and often. Inevitably, recorded history is often trumped by the priorities of family. The writers seek the testimony of the past; the family members search for their own truth, where historical accomplishments are much less meaningful than the story of what really happened around the kitchen table.

Welcome to the kitchen table of the Stanley and Lennon families, and the debate that still rages.

Julia was thin and tiny, striking and adorable. Her personality was cheerful, but there was an underlying insecurity—a neediness to be loved, and the inevitable desire for financial security in the bleak period after the Depression. But first and foremost, Julia was a woman of passion.

Although she died in the middle of the last century, the strong debate over her role in John's life is still central to his story. The *conventional* story of Julia's life is not remarkable in the history books: young beauty gives birth to the son of her husband, Alfred Lennon, often described as a seafaring deadbeat, although he was hardly that, sending money home to Julia from his various ports of call. Their marriage dissolves, but the lively and spirited Julia has a series of affairs, and three other children. John's first sister was named Victoria Elizabeth. The father was a soldier; his name was Taffy Williams. In due time, Williams left the scene. The baby girl was offered for adoption and raised by a family in Norway. Ironically, Julia Baird Lennon learned as she grew older that her sister was nearby. She met the woman, now named Ingrid, who told her that she actually grew up in Liverpool and Hampshire. Mother Julia's next love interest was John Dykins. Never official, it was a common-law marriage that remained in place until Julia's death. The couple had two girls, Julia and Jackie, born in 1947 and 1949. At first Dykins was loving, but was often elusive, and later was quite abusive. The elder Julia suffered beatings at his hand. Dykins never wanted young John in their household. He was keenly aware that Mimi had taken responsibility for John's upbringing in his early years. She relished the relationship. What's missing in the narrative of John's life is the many overnight visits to his real mother's home. For his part, Dykins was quite happy that Aunt Mimi was handling John's parenting, along with her sweet and pliant husband, George. In the early fifties Julia saw shreds of a family coming together as John and his sisters would interact. It was a splintered family, but still, she felt, family.

That's the conventional story. Then there is Julia Baird's version.

In the words of Paul McCartney, in a 1968 interview with me about his use of LSD, "The truth is sometimes painful."

Julia Baird makes you think about the truth, which for her has been a painful and life-altering experience. In the world according to John's oldest sister, much of conventional history about his childhood was rewritten by their Aunt Mimi.

Baird, who bears a great resemblance to her brother, sits in the back room of the modern version of the Cavern, on Mathew Street, in 2010. She is extremely intense, almost nervous about recalling the past, as she did in her book *Imagine This*, which gave the people of the world a different look at her mother and the family dynamics:

> WELL, ESSENTIALLY MIMI LIVED ELEVEN YEARS LONGER THAN JOHN DID. IN THAT TIME SHE WAS ABLE TO REINVENT HERSELF TOTALLY. THINGS SHE COULD NOT DECIDE ABOUT MY MOTHER WHEN JOHN WAS LIVING STARTED SUDDENLY APPEARING. . . . WHEN JOHN HIMSELF DIED SHE WAS ABLE TO WHITEWASH OVER MY MOTHER. . . . I ALWAYS USED TO JOKE THAT IF MIMI HAD LIVED ANOTHER TWENTY YEARS, IT WOULD HAVE BEEN SOME DREADED FAMILY SECRET BUT SHE WOULD HAVE BEEN THE ONE TO GIVE BIRTH TO JOHN!

Baird is determined that future generations get the real story.

This intensely serious and sensitive woman sips her water, stares around at the Cavern's walls, and declares that even her own origins had been slammed by her aunt.

MIMI HAD CONJURED UP A STORY THAT MY MOTHER HAD MOVED INTO A
HOUSE WITH MY FATHER [DYKINS] AND TWO CHILDREN, MY SISTER AND I,
ALLUDING THAT HE WAS OUR FATHER AND SHE WAS NOT OUR REAL MOTHER.

JOHN IS JOHN. JOHN IS A WORLD ICON. PEOPLE WILL BE WANTING TO
KNOW ABOUT JOHN WHEN WE'RE LONG DEAD. I DON'T WANT MY MOTHER
TO HAVE *NEVER* BEEN IN THE STORY.

The family story came apart when mother Julia, leaving Mimi's house after tea, crossed Menlove Avenue and was struck and killed by a car driven by an area constable. It was July 15, 1958. John was seventeen years old, and his music was beginning to enter the magical phase. It was a loss that brought fits of rage, nightmares, and anger to John for the rest of his life.

Julia Baird, at the time shell-shocked, devastated by the loss of her mother, remembers how John tried to hide his tears.

"He was so ripped apart. He tried to hide his pain, but he had a lot of it, and it didn't go away . . . not ever, especially when it came to her."

Nigel Walley, an original member of the Quarrymen, and later manager of the group, had left Julia Lennon at a bus stop near her home. He was the last person to see her before the fatal accident.

"John could hardly face the funeral," Walley recalled. "John didn't want anyone to see him crying. For many months after her death he wore black in her memory."

John, like Paul, who also lost his mother in his teenage years, may have never recovered. It was a big hole in his life, but he rarely talked about it.

On the Beatles' chartered Electra airplane in August 1964, John Lennon had heard that my mother had just died. He found out from Paul McCartney, who was sharing thoughts with me on losing a parent.

"How are you, Lawrence [my birth name is Larry but he liked to call me that]? How are you doing?" John asked.

"Okay," I said, the memories still lingering then after my mom's death at the age of forty.

"Well, it's hard. I know. My mum was killed in our neighborhood."

He explained the accident, the feeling of loss. It was comforting.

"What was she like?" I asked.

"Well, she loved music. Bought me my first guitar. Taught me music. We played together, laughed and sang."

There was no mention of Aunt Mimi and her role in raising John, nor was there any outward sign of bitterness, just a bittersweet sadness in his face.

I wasn't savvy enough in those days to probe further. After all, when you're twenty-one, who thinks of writing history? Who actually believes, in the time that you are living your history, that you will pursue the recording of it in the future?

The official history of Julia's life has been studied in books, films, and hearsay. Her real effect on the future star has been minimized and discredited by the ravages of time and misconception. The truth is that the part-time mother served a major purpose and, probably outside of Yoko Ono, played the most significant role in inspiring the young and confused John. Let's be honest—it's much easier to taint and paint a woman of allegedly questionable repute than it is to discredit a seriously intense woman like Mimi, who after complaining to social services co-opted Julia and took control of John's daily life.

Well, almost. Mother Julia was always present in the background, especially when it came to music. She was dedicated and cheerfully determined. And she was a charismatic woman, with striking looks.

"She was very tiny, like me," Yoko Ono says. "John used to make the connection between the two of us. John respected all five Stanley sisters, especially Mimi. But he had an enduring love for his mother, [who] in many ways was like a sister, while Mimi was more of the authority figure. He loved both, but his love for his mother was, as I said, enduring."

As an adult, John would reflect on his mother's choices. With love and affection, Yoko remembers:

"'My mom would go to bed with someone who gave her a silk stocking,' he would tell me. While he knew about his mother, he wanted to know more about his dad. But he knew his mother because of what she gave him."

And that was a lot.

Julia Baird was eleven when her mother died. She has spent years attempting to correct the impression that Julia Stanley Lennon was an afterthought and, frankly, she has the memories to back it up.

While Mimi banned tape recorders in her house, John would often go to Julia's house and they would sway together and hold hands and listen to the music of Elvis Presley. John's sister recalls:

MY GRANDFATHER JOHN CAME BACK FROM THE MERCHANT MARINE WITH A BANJO AND A MONKEY. HE PLAYED THE BANJO AND IT WOUND UP IN OUR HOUSE, ACTUALLY IN MY BEDROOM. HE TAUGHT MY MOTHER HOW TO PLAY A BANJO AND SING. MOTHER TAUGHT JOHN HOW TO PLAY THE BANJO. SHE WAS VERY, VERY MUSICAL. SHE BOUGHT JOHN HIS FIRST GUITAR. MIMI BOUGHT HIM HIS SECOND GUITAR. JOHN PLAYED THE GUITAR LIKE A BANJO AT FIRST, BUT MOTHER TRANSITIONED HIM TO GUITAR. SHE LOVED THE TIME WITH HIM. WHEN HE CAME OVER, JACKIE AND I WATCHED THE TWO BONDING MUSICALLY. SHE LOVED HIM LIKE A MOTHER WOULD LOVE A SON. AND HIS EYES WOULD LIGHT UP WHEN HE CAME OVER. SO WOULD OURS. WATCHING THEM TOGETHER WAS VERY SPECIAL.

So, why, I ask Baird, would Mimi portray her own flesh and blood, her own sister, in a negative light, and falsely broaden her own role in John's life?

Baird stares straight at me and says, "She had been rigid in many ways. . . . I think that, at the end of her life, she was struggling with how she had lived her life."

Baird feels that Mimi did give John guidance and some level of discipline, but that mother Julia gave him an emotional connection. She also pointed out that while married, Mimi had an affair. So, she says, the dignified aunt was flawed after all. The truth is that husband George had lost a small fortune to gambling. Mimi was devastated and became involved with a boarder. The affair, in Julia Baird's view, contradicts the view of Mimi as a tidy, controlled, faithful guarantor of ethical standards.

As far as her own mother, the namesake insists that the tag of a young, frivolous lover is absurd.

"Fred [John's father, Alfred] and my mother were courting on and off for ten years. How much more conventional can it get?"

More important than the subject of virtue is the effect that both women had in developing young John. Music from his mom, and something much different from her sister—together they produced a legacy of women with impact.

"When John finally took me to meet Mimi," Yoko remembers, "Uncle George was in a corner like no one could see him. John always said that in that household, in that family, men didn't mean anything. The women at times so dominated that men couldn't voice their opinion."

Was Mimi as stern and intense as she has been portrayed?

"First of all," Yoko says, "Mimi was a handsome woman. Mimi said, 'I always loved him.' It must have been tough for Mimi. She was one of five sisters. She *was* tough, but I think in a loving way. She wasn't musical like her sister Julia, but the discipline she handed out was good for John."

It was an interesting tween and teenage environment that John Lennon lived in. Yoko continues, "Mimi was not into popular music and art, so John learned the classical music from Mimi and her art. Mimi wanted John to be a tweedy type, and she thought and told John he could be anything. She loved Van Gogh and certainly influenced John's art and drawings."

There was another aspect of Aunt Mimi that Yoko delights in:

SHE WAS VERY INTELLIGENT. VERY PERCEPTIVE. IN THE HOUSE ONE TIME SHE SAW PAUL SITTING ON A STOOL REHEARSING AND JOHN WAS ON THE FLOOR. SHE KNEW HE [PAUL] WAS PRETTY AND TALENTED AND HAD A WAY WITH PEOPLE. MIMI WARNED JOHN [ABOUT PAUL'S AMBITIONS]. SHE WAS SUSPICIOUS. JOHN WAS NERVOUS ABOUT PAUL BECAUSE MIMI WAS WARNING HIM. JOHN WAS MORE OUTGOING. LATER HE LOVED HELPING RINGO AND GEORGE, ESPECIALLY HELPING GEORGE MAKE "SOMETHING" INTO A SINGLE. ALL THE WHILE, PAUL WAS SUGGESTING THAT JOHN WAS REALLY DOING NO FAVOR, BECAUSE HE FELT THE OTHER THREE COULD BECOME A GROUP "AGAINST ME."

So, the prospect of a conflict between the two giants of contemporary music was a prophecy of protective Aunt Mimi.

Of course, Yoko never met mother Julia. But she did stay in close touch with Mimi, even in the years after John's death.

About Mimi's affair, Yoko says, "That would mean she is only human, maybe not as hard and cold" as she has been portrayed.

Julia Baird, on the other hand, is emphatic about Mimi's affair—perhaps to deflect from her mother's own challenges? Maybe, but the fact is that all of the Stanley women were attractive, and sought after by men. No surprise, then, that the central figure in our story became a young man in hot pursuit of women as aggressively as he was seeking the lore of rock 'n' roll.

The domestic education was an unusual one for the skinny boy who would have to tiptoe out of the house. When that didn't work, when Mimi heard him and would whisper through the walls, "John? Is that you, John?" he would remain undaunted and would sneak out, whether to climb the fence to visit the boys at Strawberry Field, or later, to wander out for a smoke or to meet with a girl.

Mimi scared John but also disciplined him in a productive way. Mother Julia pleased him, with valuable time spent on entertaining and enlightening him. There was no heavy lifting or tension on John's visits with his mother, but then again, part-time mothering does have its benefits.

On the key point of the impact on a child's mission into life, mother Julia had great influence, even on his art:

MY MOTHER HAD INFLUENCE ON THOSE FAMOUS SKETCHES. SHE TAUGHT JOHN, ME, AND MY SISTER TO DRAW IN BLACK INDIA INK ON WHITE PAPER. IT WAS THOSE MOMENTS, WHEN MY MOTHER LOVED HER ADORED CHILD, THAT SHAPED HIM, ALTHOUGH FRANKLY, HE WAS PRETTY WELL SET WITH HIS OWN MIND.

IN ORDER TO WRITE MY BOOK, I GOT IN TOUCH WITH A SCHOOL FRIEND OF JOHN'S—DAVID EPSTEIN. SADLY, HE GOT THIS DISEASE CALLED FARMER'S LUNG. HE WAS A BEEKEEPER, NOT A SMOKER. HE MUST HAVE GOTTEN IT FROM ALL THE PESTICIDES. WE GOT TO BE FRIENDS SINCE I WROTE THE BOOK, AND HE SENDS ME LITTLE BLACK-AND-WHITE SKETCHES OF CREATURES. I SAID THEY LOOK FAMILIAR. HE SAID, "I WONDERED WHEN YOU'D ASK. YOUR MOM GAVE ME THE PENS." I RANG HIM STRAIGHTAWAY AND SAID, "PLEASE SEND THEM TO ME." HE DID, AND THEY ARRIVED ON MY MOTHER'S BIRTHDAY. AND I RECOGNIZED THEM STRAIGHTAWAY.

I always wondered whether the young John Lennon knew he had uncommon talent. He certainly carried himself with a swagger as a twenty-three-year-old, so I assumed that he believed in his abilities.

"He knew when he was eleven that he was a genius," Baird says. "He said, 'If there is such a thing as a genius, then I am one.' There are people who just know. But it still didn't come easy. They said they did eight hundred hours of rehearsal in Hamburg alone. Then they repeated it here. They were hardly an overnight sensation. They worked at it really hard. They worked it hard for seven years."

She emphasizes, "It didn't come easy."

Nothing came easy for John. Could life have been that carefree and consequential for a child searching for a father, torn between two adoring and dramatically different but equally volatile sisters? The apparent prodigy walked the line between ruination and reinvention all of his life. He soared and then he sank, and when barely out of his teens, he made a fateful mistake.

***

Sitting in 2010 in the old classroom in the Art Institute, at John's desk, I glance over to the row that Cynthia Powell sat in. It was this classroom, traditional in its seasoned wood and elevated rows, where the eyes of John and Cynthia first met. It was eye contact and blushing first love.
Sister Julia Baird says,

AS FAR AS JOHN, IT WAS TRUE LOVE FROM THE BEGINNING. I REMEMBER IN THE COURTSHIP DAYS, SHE WAS BRIGITTE BARDOT–LIKE. [JOHN HAD AN OBSESSION WITH BARDOT.] SHE [CYNTHIA] HAS THIS GREAT BONE STRUCTURE, HIGH CHEEKBONES AND ALL. SHE STILL LOOKS GREAT, BUT SHE IS A GREAT PERSON INSIDE, TOO. IN THE DEVELOPMENT OF JOHN, SHE DOESN'T REALLY GET THE PRAISE SHE DESERVES FROM THE HISTORY WRITERS, BUT DURING SUCH A CRITICAL CREATIVE TIME IN HIS LIFE, SHE GAVE HIM THE ATMOSPHERE TO MAKE IT WORK.

Four years after John and Cynthia's intense relationship began, the beautiful Ms. Powell advised him that she was pregnant. The times and his own personal philosophy meant that marriage was a mandate. The baby, Julian, was born in April 1963. Young sisters Julia and Jackie became aunts at a very young age to Julian.

Time and subsequent remarriages by Cynthia Powell Lennon have not changed Julia Baird's view of her. "She is a wonderful person. She has a great son [Julian]. During those years, she was dutiful and faithful. Jackie and I love them very much."

For John, in that era, the marriage was a stumbling block, but he never let anyone know until years later. Although John was viewed as caustic and uncaring, he loved his son, but in that relationship, he lost his way. He rarely bonded with Julian. When May Pang—John's former secretary and girl-friend for eighteen months in 1973 and 1974—arranged for Cynthia and Julian to visit the couple in California, a maternal instinct on the part of May, there were some flickers of chemistry between father and son, but apparently not enough to sustain a close relationship.

In the professional style of the early Beatles, John could be caustic, but the memories of his peers tell a lot about the young leader.

There are those who say that people never change. It is true that John's hard side was always there, but the softer, unselfish piece of his personality, always on view, has rarely been chronicled.

Billy J. Kramer has the stories to prove it. His legal name was William Howard Ashton. When young star Billy Kramer began his ascent in Great Britain, John, his contemporary, suggested that he add the middle initial "J." to his stage name, telling him it was "much stronger." And in an extraordinarily unselfish act, John graciously offered two songs to him.

"It was my twentieth birthday. We were all at Bournemouth. John surprised me, said he had a song exclusively for me. It was called 'Bad to Me,' a Lennon-McCartney early creation. He also offered me, 'Do You Want to Know a Secret,' and it became a hit in Britain even as the Beatles released it on their own."

"What was the motive?" I ask.

"He liked me, and it was really quite unselfish. I did ask him to let me cover 'I Want to Hold Your Hand.' I think it was a stretch. This was during a meeting at Abbey Road. He smiled and said, 'I think, Billy, we are going to save that for ourselves, if you know what I mean.' I laughed, too."

To put the caring, unselfish side of Lennon in perspective, consider this: Billy J. Kramer was a competitor, yet Lennon went out of his way to help Kramer's career. In one of the early *Mersey Beat* polls, Kramer finished third behind the first-place Beatles. Although they shared a manager, Brian Epstein, for a while, Kramer was a genuine, viable contender. Still, the song "Bad to Me" was written by John, *for* Billy, during a vacation in Spain. John's generosity for people he genuinely respected was unlimited. "Bad to Me" became a number-one hit for Kramer in England in 1963, and hit the top ten in America. It was the first hit penned by Lennon (although "Lennon-McCartney" is on the credits, as was their agreement) for another artist to make it in America.

Much has been said about the style and substance of John Lennon. My own work has been criticized by people who never met the man as much too soft and sometimes patronizing. From his youthful womanizing to his violent temper, the view of John is complex, but the facts and the testimony of the living and dead, speaking of John's lifelong musical philanthropy, are the truth.

Billy J. Kramer views John's musical offerings as proof of the nature of the man, even as a young and aspiring entertainer.

"This was a complete man, a person who really cared about people, but real people. I guess we hit it off. I know everybody says how he and the guys changed life and entertainment, but in this case, he really changed one life: mine."

Another Billy, Billy Kinsley, founder of the band the Merseybeats, remembers the generous nature of the boys during so many concerts at the Cavern, Tower Ballroom, and Litherland Town Hall. Kinsley has vivid memories of John:

He was the leader, even at twenty or twenty-one. He did it with his body language. He could be a bit caustic. Paul was very pleasant and courteous, as was his style. George was quiet then. And Pete, my friend to this day, was subdued but [was], and is today, a kind and sensitive person. I think John set an example for courtesy; John would do anything to make you comfortable, and he did it with humor and a smile. He almost, at times—and sometimes with his hands and his smile—cheered on the other bands, especially Billy J. and our band. I know he had his issues in the time, but he was a real man, kind and giving.

"Kind and giving." Did his teachers know that John had the potential to be a giver as well as a taker?

It is amazing in life, isn't it, that the real potential of people is often over-looked in the standards set by the people who guide us through the early years. And remember the famous quote by a teacher, "This boy is bound to fail." It's an easy one to remember, isn't it? How many fine teachers may have missed the potential of their students?

As you look at the infancy and maturation in the life of John Lennon, you may think of a question: Was the teacher talking about a grade, a course, a test, or the triumphs and travails of a life itself?

"Grading" John Lennon? Try it at your own risk, but know one certainty: whether it was the period when he was a "boy," or his budding success and fame in 1963, John was closer to that complete man that Billy J. talks about—brooding, triumphant, confused, indignant, determined, soothing, unselfish, irresponsible, sensitive, and giving.

From the boys at Strawberry Fields, to the kids chasing him at an early Quarrymen gig, to the invitation to Paul to join his band, and to his mag-nanimous gestures to fellow artists like Billy J. Kramer and Billy Kinsley, even during his own struggle to succeed, John was a complete man.

Maybe it was the childhood mystery of his parents' challenges, or the anti-establishment protest at schools, but the middle-class boy who would become a millionaire and an icon championed the real people. On tour, he constantly criticized "the authorities" for keeping the crowds so far away.

"All they want is a wave, just a wave of a hand, Larry," he would tell me on tour.

For people like Billy J. Kramer and Billy Kinsley, John would offer help and sympathy. The "working-class hero" in him surfaced whenever he met people he felt were challenged economically, many of whom lived in Merseyside.

That part of him, the anarchist turned human-rights fighter, was wonderful to watch. Just as he perceived his own wants and needs, the amazing, some-times caustic and unpredictable leader of the boys wanted a perfect world.

That, along with personal ambition, is usually the end result of imagining the future. John Lennon could be a malcontent. He was constantly frustrated and, at times in his life, often drunk. He could be violent, as you will discover, graphically, later in this story. His affections were reserved for only a few, and then, in bursts of love, they flowed faster than an overflowing river. In youth, and later, he was a man who abhorred bullshit, and didn't suffer obstructionists lightly. But watch out! If you got in his way, he would throw you under the bus, and a few blocks later, check to see if you were really dead.

Complex? The word is too minimal to explain him. He was a lot of things.

But above all else, the man who penned the immortal "Imagine," the milkman who walked his teenage beat, was a dreamer.

CHAPTER TWO

INSPIRATION, PERSPIRATION, AND ADMIRATION

*"Lonnie Donegan. All of us listened to him, you know. Inspiration, of course.
We all wanted to be Lonnie."*
—Ringo Starr

Lonnie—A Bit of a Lad

For the milkman and his current and future cohorts, there was plenty of inspiration. But one man, who sang in an unusual staccato voice and used the barest of essentials, set the early standard.

In 1959, a novelty song made its way to number five on the record charts in the United States. At the time, I was in twelfth grade and worked part-time at a Top 40 radio station. You couldn't miss the song, but who knew the singer of this wacky melody had almost single-handedly changed the music scene in Britain? The tune was catchy, its lyrics fun. It was called "Does Your Chewing Gum Lose Its Flavor (On the Bedpost Overnight)?"

The artist was the most successful solo artist in British history. And there was, in his life, a dual legacy—he scored twenty-four hit records on the British charts, and he was the greatest musical influence for the boys who became the Beatles, and for almost every other British artist or group of the time. An original member of the Quarrymen, the learned Rod Davis, remembers the sound and the man.

"Lonnie Donegan? When you look at the pictures of the Quarrymen, in the beginning, we were all emulating Lonnie. I truly believe, in fact, his songs, so successful, were borrowed from America."

Lonnie Donegan, the lad, was "the King"—that is, until the lads, ironically, ended his reign. Once a jazzman, the Scotland-born Anthony James Donegan was to the kids and adults in the 1950s what Elvis Presley was to America at the same time.

Skiffle had been around for many years before Lonnie emerged from the nightclubs of London and discovered a uniquely American style of country music—the raw and spiritually inspired folk and blues music made by the likes of Woody Guthrie and Leadbelly. In 1954, he recorded Leadbelly's "Rock Island Line," later immortalized by Johnny Cash. Donegan, washboard and guitar in hand, catapulted the song to solid gold in Great Britain that year, and it also became his first top-ten song in the United States.

What was skiffle? Skiffle was a mixture of folk, jazz, blues, and some country. Most of the artists created their own instruments, like the washboard and the tea-chest bass.

To get the real feel of Donegan's music, take a listen, as John Lennon did, to "Rock Island Line," and feel the fast-paced flavor of the artist, relying only on primitive instruments and the speed of his delivery. There are no sophisticated arrangements, just the almost eerie sound of Donegan's storytelling with a hint of a church revival, his voice breaking into different cadences of emotion. To the country-music-addicted Richard Starkey, Donegan's music, and that washboard humming in the background, sounds fresh and very different even in the modern day.

To the teenagers of the early and mid-fifties, listening to Lonnie Donegan's no-frills style, his energy, and his haunting and "new" sound was not just a treat. It was an opportunity.

"He was the first person we had heard of from Britain to get . . . to number one. . . . We studied his records avidly. We all bought guitars to be in a skiffle group," says Paul McCartney. "He was the man."

The sense of opportunity, in fact, empowered young John Lennon to form a skiffle group.

"Lonnie Donegan was like a god to us," recalls Rod Davis. "If he could do it, we could do it. John was really inspired by Donegan. It was a true case of hero worship, plain and simple."

Of the four Beatles, John, Paul, and George were so impacted by Donegan and an appearance he made in Liverpool in 1956 at the Empire Theater that they were inspired to buy guitars. Richie Starkey was crazy about Donegan, too, as well as country music. In my vast archive of audiotapes, several episodes feature all the Beatles talking about influences. There were mentions of Johnny Cash, Fats Domino, Elvis, and Little Richard, of course, but the only person uniformly mentioned by all was Lonnie Donegan. And remember, these interviews were conducted within a few years of their rise to fame, so the veracity of their thoughts was not tarnished by memories fifty years later. Ringo talked about Donegan with me in the summer of 1964.

"Who was the most influential to you, all of you?" I asked.

"Lonnie Donegan. All of us listened to him, you know. Inspiration, of course. We all wanted to be Lonnie."

Paul was so inspired by Donegan that father Jim paid fifteen British pounds to buy him his first guitar. George was likewise inspired, and borrowed three pounds from his mom to buy a secondhand guitar. But that wasn't enough for George, whose idolatry of the suave and handsome Donegan, and his music, had no boundaries. George investigated the whereabouts of the superstar in Liverpool. He knocked on the door again and again until the star emerged. The curious, stargazing George refused to leave without an autograph, which he got.

The original Quarrymen were dazzled by Donegan. Many of their informal concerts leaned heavily on his songs. Colin Hanton was infatuated with Donegan's music. "We loved 'Rock Island Line,' 'Railroad Bill,' 'Midnight Special,' and all the songs. It wasn't rock, more folk, but John rocked with it anyway, getting up there and holding his guitar close, chest high. In his mind, at that time, he *was* Lonnie Donegan, and nothing could stop him."

When the Quarrymen first played in earnest at the Cavern on August 7, 1957, John offered to play a version of "Don't Be Cruel," the Elvis favorite. But the club's management reminded him that rock 'n' roll was forbidden at the club. John improvised with his own version of the song in Lonnie's skiffle style. Eventually John, Paul, and George would rock the place into the history books. But in the beginning, they were forced to improvise, and with the addition of Paul into the band, the future Beatles did a creative imitation of Lonnie and his style.

Key to that style is something that goes beyond the music—a stage presence that would be emulated by the three Beatles front men (Ringo being in the back). Donegan held his guitar close and high, and nearly swallowed the microphone when he sang. Look at Lonnie and you see the influence on John—his guitar pulled up high against his chest, his neck held high, his mouth so close to the microphone's metal. Even in the beginning, with the Quarrymen, John Lennon was Lonnie Donegan. Lonnie's charisma when performing was loved by all genders, and he knew it. He had the reputation of being a "bit of a lad," an English expression for a ladies' man, with very serious talents in the arena of social interaction. His stage presence led the way to an intense social life, several marriages, two cases of open heart surgery, and a career that had serious ups and downs.

More than any of his personal "ups" was his impact in the fifties on the young "wannabes" in Britain.

"When the boys walked through the streets of Liverpool, or for that matter, any city, they envisioned themselves as Lonnie—his hair, his walk, his skiffle sound, the cadence," remembers Alan White, longtime drummer for the band Yes, who also joined John Lennon and the Plastic Ono Band on various recordings, including the classic song "Imagine."

"I grew up to all the British rockers. They grew up to Donegan. He may have had the most influence on the so-called British Invasion period. . . . His impact was mostly in the fifties, but it was mostly felt by some of the young stars of the sixties," White says.

Ironically, Donegan's star faded as the Beatles' star emerged, partly because of his failure to embrace the rock 'n' roll wave. So, the man who so completely inspired them became a victim of his own inspirational success, and of theirs.

Eventually the Beatles and other fervent admirers paid him back. In the late seventies, Paul suggested to Donegan that he reprise some of his skiffle music hits. An album, *Puttin' on the Style*, was released early in 1978. The list of musicians backing him up included Ringo Starr, Elton John, Leo Sayer, Brian May of Queen, and Lonnie's regular band. Ringo made appearances on the tracks "Have a Drink On Me" and "Ham 'n' Eggs."

Lonnie Donegan spent twenty-four more years writing songs, trying to revive his career and his health. He was keenly aware of his effect on the British groups, and especially the Beatles, whom he admired so much. He received a written tribute from George in 1997, in a foreword to the book

Skiffle by Charles McDevitt. George wrote, "Of course, Lonnie Donegan was the reason so many of us loved skiffle."

At the millennium, Donegan was honored by the queen. Two years later, after another heart attack, he died in the middle of a national tour. Ironically, his death came when he was en route to a memorial concert honoring George Harrison.

John Lennon once told me, "Yeah, Chuck Berry, the Everlys, Little Richard—they were all important to us. But no one, not one single person, was more important than Lonnie Donegan."

Music Addiction

"We did everything we could to get our hands on American music—
anything. For most of us [in Merseyside] it was as important
as drinking and eating."
—JOHN LENNON

America had its baby boomers, born after World War II. Britain's war started earlier, and so did its baby boom. It began in 1938—the extraordinary birth explosion known as the "bulge." The boys were all part of that people explosion. Like millions of other young people in Britain, they joined in a mass coming-of-age, little knowing that they would help lead it.

On the cusp of international fame, the boys, part of the "bulge" generation, were still hungry to listen and learn, and their role as "students" of the art of music provides an insight into the group's early power dynamics.

Throughout 1962 and 1963, the Beatles were hooked on music—totally addicted, captivated—and they couldn't get enough of the stuff. In fact, finding the right product was paramount. And there were two ways to get the music. Radio was the key, though it was scarcely available. But there were other ways to get the stuff.

And the "stuff" they wanted was mainly American music. Some records, by established stars, were available in stores. Brian Epstein sold many of those two-sided 45-rpm records in the record store his family owned. But the songs of less established stars, many who would set musical standards for the future, were hard to get. Or even hear.

There is no way to underestimate the impact that American pop music had on the 1962 and 1963 Beatles.

Joe Flannery, lifelong friend to Brian Epstein and early manager of the Star Club in Hamburg, says, "They spent most of their free time—mind you, there was not a lot of that—listening to 45s. They listened and listened, and exchanged records. John and George would listen together, Ringo by himself; he favored country. Paul listened to everything."

Bill Harry, a member of the "bulge" generation, describes a social and cultural vacuum, especially on the radio:

THE FIFTIES WERE THE YEARS OF A BULGE OF TEENAGERS IN LIVERPOOL. THERE WERE MORE TEENS AT THAT TIME THAN ANY TIME BEFORE AND AFTER. I ACTUALLY THINK THAT IS WHEN THE TERM "TEENAGER" WAS INVENTED—IN THE FIFTIES. SUDDENLY WE WANTED OUR OWN THINGS. WE HAD BEEN DOMINATED IN THE MEDIA BY THE GENERATION OF PEOPLE OLDER THAN US. BRITISH RADIO, OR THE BBC, WAS THE FAMILY FAVORITE, THE WORKER'S PLAYTIME. NOTHING TO DO WITH ROCK 'N' ROLL OR THE MUSIC TEENAGERS WANTED.

Future promotion executive and Beatles' buddy Tony Bramwell remembers the swap meet that was going on every week, and the hunger for the music:

I HAVE TWO OLDER BROTHERS, AND GEORGE WOULD BRING RECORDS AND WE WOULD SWAP RECORDS. SAME WITH PAUL; HE WOULD BRING HIS RECORDS. THEY WOULD POP INTO MY HOUSE AND BRING RECORDS THAT THEY GOT IN THE PAST FEW WEEKS LIKE THE EVERLY BROTHERS AND CARL PERKINS AND STUFF. AND I HAD BUDDY HOLLY AND CHUCK BERRY. WE WOULD SHARE OR SWAP OUR RECORDS. WE USED TO SAVE OUR POCKET MONEY AND BUY RECORDS. IF THERE WAS ONE WE REALLY LOVED, IT WOULD BE STUCK ON THE REPEAT CONTROL ON THE RECORD PLAYER.

Bramwell and the boys, who were a few years older than him, would crawl under the covers in their bedrooms and take in Radio Luxembourg. He recalls,

ENGLISH RADIO WAS PRETTY CRAPPY. THEY DIDN'T HAVE POP MUSIC PROGRAMS [ON] THE BBC. WE USED TO LISTEN TO RADIO LUXEMBOURG

FROM THE DUCHY OF LUXEMBOURG. THEY WOULD HAVE THREE-, FOUR-HOUR MUSIC PROGRAMS SPONSORED BY RECORD COMPANIES. DECCA. CAPITOL. EMI WOULD HAVE AN HOUR. MERCURY WOULD HAVE AN HOUR. MAYBE EACH A HALF AN HOUR—BUT SOMETHING LIKE THAT. WE WOULD BE LISTENING AT NIGHT IN YOUR BEDROOM TO CRACKLY PRE-TRANSISTOR RADIOS. THEY DIDN'T HAVE TRANSISTOR RADIOS YET—CAT'S-WHISKER RADIOS. IT WAS LIKE LISTENING TO AN UNDERGROUND STATION. IT WAS FUN.

From 1957 on, the kids of the so-called bulge were hungry for the "new" music that was being played in the States. But that is not all. *Mersey Beat* founder Bill Harry says it was a real cultural revolution. In many ways, he says, it was quite anti-establishment:

WE HAD NO DECENT ROCK 'N' ROLL ON THE RADIO. IT WAS CONTROLLED. THE ONLY RADIO WAS THE BBC. WE *HAD TO HAVE* RADIO LUXEMBOURG BEAMED OVER IN ORDER TO GET ANY DECENT ROCK 'N' ROLL ON THE RADIO. SUDDENLY TEENAGERS FOR THE FIRST TIME WANTED THEIR OWN CLOTHING, THEIR OWN IDENTITY. BUT WE COULDN'T HAVE IT BECAUSE THE MEDIA WAS ON A DIFFERENT SORT OF LEVEL. EVERYTHING WAS CONTROLLED BY MOGULS, THE BUSINESS PEOPLE. CLOTHING—EVERYTHING—WAS CONTROLLED. MANIPULATING TEENAGERS. AND THAT WAS AN EXAMPLE OF WHAT IT WAS LIKE. WE WANTED OUR OWN VOICE—WE HAD TO CREATE OUR OWN DESTINY, OUR OWN VOICE.

The boys were constantly searching for their voice. John, Paul, and George studied songs and discussed styles until their throats were dry from talking, or until their eyelids closed. Although they were enamored by the big names of music, they were also impressed by daring artists who were willing to break through.

One thing that all four Beatles were serious about was rolling out their reel-to-reel tape recorder and listening to any recordings they could find. I can say, from watching their in-flight, hotel, and pre-concert routines, that Ringo and George were as serious as John and Paul about learning all they could about other people's music. There were two amazing moments on the

Beatles' North American tours, aside from the Elvis Presley meeting: the brief but exciting meeting in a trailer at Tulane Stadium in New Orleans with Fats Domino, and the backstage meeting with Johnny Cash at the Cow Palace in San Francisco.

These meetings were very revealing. Although the artists they met in America were thrilled to meet *them*, the boys were more like fans than contemporaries. Whether it was Joan Baez, Elvis, or the young Bob Dylan, the Beatles seemed thrilled, and in awe. America was always a marker for music excellence to the Fabs, unaware that, in those early days, they were becoming the markers of the musical future.

Monitoring the rest of the world's music, especially the American stars and one-hit wonders, took second place to priority number one: perfecting their sound on stage. Having covered sixty-three Beatles concerts in 1964, 1965, and 1966, I can say that their relentless pursuit of perfection made them the tightest and most nearly perfect performing band in history. They mirrored their early stirrings. Listening to the music, *carefully* listening to the music, John and Paul, with a heavy assist from George and Pete, were determined as early as 1960 to find the best music there was, put their own touches to it, and never settle for a bad night. They did have plenty of bad nights, but after a certain record retailer named Brian Epstein showed up, most of the bad habits, like eating on stage, vanished.

It all started with their obsession with devouring American music. Getting the music was not easy. But they had help.

Their record supplier during the early sixties was a young guy named Ron Ellis, who was and still remains a renaissance man. For years he has offered a uniquely important insight into the later influences on the boys. In his nearly fifty years of work, Ellis has been a group manager, promoter, singer, author, publisher, broadcaster, researcher, concert deejay, and one of the "go-to" guys when you are seeking the truth on Merseyside.

For four years, night and day, he researched the Beatles and John Lennon for controversial author Albert Goldman. Goldman's book, *The Lives of John Lennon*, was despised by Yoko Ono and members of the Lennon family, almost universally. About one thing, almost every Beatles expert agrees: Ron

Ellis's recollections of his eyewitness accounts of the Beatles' early performances, and their musical influences, is second to none. The book that
he worked on for Goldman is not the first controversial book on the
Beatles. Ray Coleman's book, *Lennon: The Definitive Biography*, is beautifully
written, but the author, for some reason, glosses over John's eighteen-month
relationship with May Pang in 1973 and 1974. Even the man considered to
be the gold standard of Beatles biographers, Philip Norman, reserves just two
sentences in his Beatles biography, *Shout*, to the Lennon-Pang relationship.
Ellis will not reveal his opinion of Goldman's work, but he guarantees that
the research was impeccable. In the cutthroat world of Beatles history in
Merseyside, where second-guessing and rewriting history is an art form, no
one will challenge Ellis's work.

Back in 1963, Ellis was a shrewd and enterprising young man who had the
fix in with a pen pal from America, Ronnie Kellerman. Kellerman would
ship the albums, or records, to Ellis, who would deliver them to two successful British groups: Billy J. Kramer and the Dakotas, and the Searchers.
Eventually Ellis reached out to the Beatles, and for good reason; he knew
they were getting to the point where they could afford the albums.

As always, it was the great leader of the group, the most avid reader and
listener, who wanted the most.

Ellis had a tidy little business going. And he tells me that John was his best
customer. John's shopping list provides an insight into the great songwriting
learning curve that John was always willing to tackle. Ellis remembers:

"The records that John ordered were ones by the harder-edged R&B artists
such as Dr. Feelgood, Inez & Charlie Foxx, Bobby Blue Bland, James Ray,
and Rufus Thomas. George went for the Coasters and Ben E. King. Ringo
wanted everything in the catalog, particularly the most obscure gospel
albums. They all wanted Tamla Motown records which hadn't been released
in this country."

"What about Paul?" I ask.

"Well," he says, "that's a story that comes a bit later."

WHEN THE RECORDS ARRIVED FROM THE STATES, I RANG JOHN AND HE
SAID THEY THAT WERE PLAYING AT THE FLORAL HALL, SOUTHPORT, THE

FOLLOWING WEEK. AS I LIVED ACROSS FROM THE FLORAL HALL THEY AGREED TO COME TO MY HOUSE AFTER THE SHOW AND HAVE SOME SUPPER AND COLLECT THEIR RECORDS. TURNS OUT IT WAS THE DRAMATIC DAY WHEN THEY DISCOVERED THAT THE BEATLES WERE INVITED TO THE ROYAL VARIETY PERFORMANCE [IN NOVEMBER]. THAT, LARRY, WAS AS BIG AS IT GOT. THE ROYAL FAMILY WOULD BE THERE, AND SO WOULD EVERY PRESSMAN IN THE WORLD. IT WAS HUGE. I WENT BACKSTAGE AT THE FLORAL HALL AND WE AGREED THAT, WITH ALL THE EXCITEMENT, I WOULD DELIVER THE RECORDS LATER. JOHN, GEORGE, AND RINGO ADDED SOME NEW TITLES TO THEIR LIST, BUT PAUL SAID NOTHING.

Ellis is a keen observer. A man who understands the nuances of human behavior, he was, even as a young man, fascinated by the dressing-room behavior of artists, which in the case of the 1963 Beatles was telling. He saw them backstage twice: once in Southport, and then at the Odeon in Liverpool for the group's triumphant Christmas concert in December 1963. It was there that he finally delivered the records to John, George, and Ringo.

AND WHEN I WENT IN, THEY WERE ALL IN THE DRESSING ROOM AND PAUL MCCARTNEY WAS MINCING ABOUT, IMITATING BRIAN EPSTEIN, "OH, 'ELLO, BRIAN," AND THIS SORT OF THING, TAKING THE PISS OUT OF HIM. GEORGE WAS A QUIET PERSON; JOHN WAS VERY PLEASED TO GET HIS RECORDS; RINGO WAS, WELL, LET ME TELL YOU WHAT HAPPENED. BILLY J. KRAMER AND THE DAKOTAS WERE ON THE BILL AT THE TIME AND THEY'D HIDDEN RINGO'S POLO SWEATER. AND THEY MADE HIM CRAWL AROUND THE ROOM AND BEG BEFORE THEY'D GIVE IT BACK TO HIM.

"They . . . liked him?" I ask.

"Oh yeah, they were just joking with him, you know?

SO I LOOKED AT MCCARTNEY AND I THOUGHT, "THIS IS SOMEBODY WHO'S ON A DIFFERENT LEVEL." JOHN WAS IN IT, YOU KNOW, FOR THE LAUGHS AND THE MUSIC AND THE BIRDS [WOMEN] AND EVERYTHING. RINGO WAS ENJOYING THE RIDE . . . HE WAS LUCKY; SUDDENLY NOW HE'S A NATIONAL STAR, YOU KNOW? JOHN LOVED ALL THE MUSIC AND FUN, BUT YOU FELT MCCARTNEY'S ON A DIFFERENT LEVEL HERE—HE'S A

BUSINESSMAN, PLAYING AS A MUSICIAN. THAT'S THE IMPRESSION I GOT. HE WAS VERY SUPERCILIOUS.

I THINK HE CAN SEE THE BIG PICTURE, HE CAN SEE WHAT'S GOING TO HAPPEN TO THE BEATLES, AND HE WANTS TO BE IN THERE MAKING SURE HE CONTROLS IT.

Ellis, who was a fan and curious observer, saw many of the boys' earlier concerts, and with those, got a good sense of their dynamics.

GEORGE, I THINK, WAS AN AMIABLE SORT. AND I THINK GEORGE WAS AS TALENTED A SONGWRITER AS MCCARTNEY AND LENNON WERE, BUT HE NEVER GOT THE OPPORTUNITY. GEORGE, I THINK, WAS JUST AS TALENTED BUT HE MOVED IN A DIFFERENT DIRECTION. AND I THINK HE WAS HALTED BY THE BEATLES BECAUSE HE WOULD HAVE PROBABLY BEEN BETTER WITH OTHER MUSICIANS, WHICH HE EVENTUALLY DID, AND THEN THE WORLD SAW GEORGE'S REAL TALENT.

MCCARTNEY WAS THE BUSINESSMAN. I THINK HE WAS THINKING, LIKE, "WE'VE GOT A GOOD THING GOING HERE, I WANT TO BE IN CHARGE OF THIS."

While listening to Ellis talk, I had a flashback to Mal Evans's comments to me, both in Nassau and in Britain, in 1968, about the talents of George Harrison. You will meet Mal later in this book, and in a very personal way.

"You want to know the truth?" asks Ellis. "The truth is that John is the leader Beatle, George is the deep-thinking Beatle, Ringo is the fun Beatle, and Paul is the cute one. But Paul, when it comes to business and those things, Paul was the shrewd Beatle. But I tell you, Larry, that George . . . well, is very talented . . . very."

Mal knew the inside of the group more than anyone. And researcher Ellis has deeply delved into the idea that Paul and John were controlling George's destiny as early as 1962.

"Lennon and McCartney were controlling what was said," Ellis tells me. "'We'll give George a song; we'll give Ringo a song.' I think they put George in the category of Ringo. A song for Ringo, a song for George."

The sense of Paul's quiet ambition and manipulative powers were shared by both Beatles press officers, Derek Taylor and Tony Barrow, who play a pivotal role later in this saga. But my own dressing-room experiences, in 1964, were different. Paul never grimaced in my presence. In fact, he "cracked up" at some of my questions. He did, by his comportment, show an aversion to any sort of controversy. He treated Epstein with respect in public, but privately complained to John whenever he believed Epstein was too controlling.

Ron Ellis, in addition to his work in music, is also a deeply respected football (soccer) writer with a keenly developed intuition on team dynamics. Today he teaches adult education courses in music, with one course being dedicated to the Beatles. His stories on the boys are intriguing, along with his analysis of the early group dynamics that flowered into super success, and eventually, contributed to the group's disintegration. But one can argue that the group's breakup was not the end, but just the beginning of the road from early stirrings to enormous success, worldwide domination, and eventually, a state of idolatry and musical immortality.

The Quarrymen—More to the Story

> *"Out of this rock, you will find truth."*
> —Motto of the Quarry Bank School

> *"We were crap, really, just crap."*
> —Colin Hanton, on his assessment of the band's talent level

Before Paul, George, Stu, Pete, and Ringo joined John to form the Beatles, there were the fascinating Quarrymen.

The students and some of the early buddies at the Quarry Bank middle school who joined John Lennon to form the original lineup of the Quarrymen—Pete Shotton, Eric Griffiths, Rod Davis, Len Garry, and Colin Hanton—in their legend have more than compensated for the memories of John's malicious academic malpractice. The surviving Quarrymen today find solace and gratification in the fact that they were the pre-Beatles and helped John achieve at least the earlier part of his destiny. They knew that John was a little "off-balance," as former drummer-boy Hanton would say, but they also knew that his recklessness and vigor for danger was also an asset, especially when he had to make a fast escape.

Hanton's buddy to this day, Rod Davis—scholar, senior pro surfer, and perhaps the intellectual of the group—remembers how the school they attended shaped their future.

"What we [in England] call public school is a paying school. What you [in America] call public school, anybody can go to. We had a good time, studied hard—at least some of us did."

Quarry Bank was filled with teenagers with dreams. It was a school with strict behavioral standards. That made it a great challenge for John Lennon, who relished his role as troublemaker. But he was also a world-class teenage organizer, recruiting other musicians to join his band. With their washboards, drums, and tea-chest bass, and the nervy leader at the helm, the boys from Quarry Bank performed whenever they were asked. There was very little money, just the pride of a scraggly band of teenage musical novices.

The modern-day views of the Quarrymen are filled not with melancholy, but with a sense of wonder about the history they didn't realize they were making.

"I mean, it was great being on stage in front of all your friends," Davis recollects, "and, you know, Auntie, Grandmother, and all this kind of thing. It's of quite more significance over the years because, you know, we realized later on how important it was . . . although none of us really wake up and wish we were a Beatle."

That importance is shared by many of the Quarrymen, but Davis offers a rare admission.

"You know, I'm really not a Beatles fan. But I am proud of the early times with John and especially of all the fun we had in our reunions over the years."

Len Garry, who became an architect, is an introspective man who occasionally offers some frank dialogue about that period, and enjoys the reunions. He has a different perspective.

"At the time, I thought I had talent. Still do, my friend. I can still sing well," he says.

I can attest—Garry *can* carry a tune, and his stage presence is marvelous. He laments, "I mean, I could have made it."

He smiles broadly.

"But the truth is: I didn't. So the end result is I get to be with my friends and travel the world fifty years later."

The trio of Davis, Garry, and Hanton are the remaining touring Quarrymen. Although Garry has pride in his early work, drummer Hanton doesn't see it that way. He takes you back to the day with a startling reality check, deflating the ballooning romanticism attributed by many, including me, that the Quarrymen were an important step on the road to the Beatles.

"First of all, Larry, we were crap, just crap," Hanton admits. "We were sweating our brains out, we were so nervous. I am talking about layers of perspiration. We were not all that close, although some of us became closer in time. I think the main misconception is how the Quarrymen felt when John left to form the Beatles. Of course, he didn't leave the Quarrymen to form the Beatles. . . . Different people came and went from the Quarrymen. It just evolved after he left the Quarrymen. He had no intentions of forming another band, I don't believe."

Ironically, Hanton, the Quarryman who played longest with John, has the dimmest impression of those days, especially after Davis left the band, with little fanfare.

"No, it didn't upset me [when Davis left]. I was right there with John, Paul, and George right up to early 1959, but the experts told me late 1958. Then I left. I had had enough. I walked out after one drunken session—we blew our chance, I believe. We didn't even have our own car. We had to carry our own equipment, drums and everything, on public transport. Eventually I had had enough. We weren't going anywhere."

I ask, "In terms of the relationship that . . . you [and John] had, and that Len had with John, was it a buddy relationship, or was it just an association? Were you close friends? Did he like you?"

"If he didn't [like you], you knew it," Hanton says.

HE EITHER TALKED TO YOU OR HE DIDN'T. . . . I NEVER CONSIDERED THAT WE WERE BUDDIES, BUT THAT WE PLAYED TOGETHER. WE WERE FRIENDLY, THOUGH. HE TOOK ME TO MEET HIS MOTHER—NOT MIMI, BUT JULIA— WHICH CAME AS A SURPRISE. HE WAS LIVING WITH MIMI, BUT WE NEVER

KNEW [JULIA] AS HIS MOTHER; JULIA WAS MORE LIKE HIS BIG SISTER
THAN HIS MUM. AND YES, SHE WAS VERY GOOD-LOOKING, PLEASANT, AND
FUN-LOVING. AND SHE WAS MUSICAL, TOO. SHE WOULD GET THE BANJO
OUT WHEN JOHN ACTED UP, SKIPPED SCHOOL. MOST PEOPLE WOULD
KICK HIM OUT, TELL HIM TO GET BACK TO SCHOOL, ETC., GET MAD—BUT
NOT HER. SHE JUST GOT THE BANJO OUT AND STARTED STRUMMING.

So, although he met and mostly enjoyed John's unpredictable company, in
the world according to Hanton, the Quarrymen were just an unsuccessful
teenage adventure.

"We were just lads trying to have a great time and impress some of the girls
along the way. Nothing serious or businesslike about it, really. Not in the
early days."

Hanton is a realist. While he savors the later "reunion" career of the
Quarrymen that started in 1997, he has no regrets from the earlier days. His
comments on his career path are telling, humble, and most enjoyable.

WE DIDN'T HAVE THAT KIND OF TALENT. I WASN'T GOOD ENOUGH. I
REMEMBER I HAD TO GO SOMEWHERE AND TAKE TIME OFF FROM MY
APPRENTICESHIP AND THE BOSS SAID, "ARE YOU SURE YOU WANT [TO BE
IN] THE UPHOLSTERY BUSINESS, OR DO YOU WANT TO BE A BAND MEM-
BER?"—SOMETHING LIKE THAT. HE DID END UP GIVING ME THE DAY OFF,
BUT MADE ME REALLY THINK ABOUT IT. I COULD HAVE GONE WITH THEM,
ACTUALLY, BUT WOULD HAVE ENDED UP LIKE PETE BEST IN HAMBURG. I
WOULD HAVE ENDED UP WITHOUT A TRADE. I WAS NOT A GOOD STUDENT.
I WAS GOING TO BE LEFT WITH NOTHING. I WASN'T GOING TO GIVE MY
TRADE UP AS AN UPHOLSTERER FOR AN UNKNOWN OUTCOME. I WASN'T
THAT GOOD AND KNEW IT. WHEN I STOPPED IN LATE 1958 OR EARLY 1959,
I PUT MY DRUMSTICKS ON TOP OF THE WARDROBE. AND WHEN THEY ASKED
US TO DO THIS ONE-OFF CONCERT IN 1997 TO RAISE MONEY FOR ST. PETER'S
CHURCH HALL, I HADN'T PLAYED DRUMS FOR FORTY YEARS . . . AND SAID,
"NO! I COULDN'T PLAY BACK THEN; WHY WOULD I BE ANY BETTER NOW?"
SO THEY JUST SAID, "LET'S JUST MEET AT LEN'S HOUSE AND HAVE A LOOK."
PETE SHOTTON SAID, "WHY DON'T WE JUST GET TOGETHER AT LEN'S
HOUSE." I TOOK MY DRUMSTICKS DOWN FROM THE WARDROBE, WHICH MY

WIFE HAD BEEN THREATENING TO THROW OUT FOR YEARS. WE HAD SUCH A BLOODY WONDERFUL TIME IN LEN'S HOUSE, LIKE WE WERE NINETEEN AGAIN. FORTY YEARS DISAPPEARED, AND WE DID IT EXACTLY THE SAME— NOT BETTER, NOT WORSE—JUST THE SAME.

Hanton has sweet memories of the school and the boys, but when it comes to perhaps the most important moment in modern music history—the first meeting between John and Paul—he's a bit uncertain. It was also the day of the biggest performance in the young life of the boys from Quarry Bank. "It was summer 1957, at the Woolton church fair. I saw some guys talking to John in this wooden shed on the Woolton church property where Boy Scouts hung out and we kept all the equipment and our coats. I was playing drums and Boy Scouts were playing their trumpets. I saw Ivan [Vaughn] come in, and this other dark-haired lad, and I didn't know who they were, and they were talking to John. The dark-haired lad, I realized [later], was Paul. And that is when they met."

Paul's arrival was the beginning of the end of Rod Davis's musical career, although he still plays a mean banjo and guitar. That meeting is emblematic of a great pairing of talent, when John met Paul amid the burning sun of summer, an innocent meeting, a chance encounter. And I wonder, what if it had rained and young Paulie couldn't ride his bicycle? Would he have walked? Or would he have stayed home? It is just another "what if" in a wondrous story of trial and error—in those days, mostly error.

CHAPTER THREE

PAUL—YESTERDAY

"He wanted to be accepted, loved, and always appropriate. He viewed criticism as a dagger, and adoration as a source of support. He avoided confrontation like a plague. He was a politician. He was so good at it, that in some other life, he might have been elected prime minister."
—Tony Barrow

"[My dad] just said . . . 'Well, you're never going to make any money . . . in a group.'"
—Paul McCartney, in a 1964 interview with me

"Paul was the Beatle, from the very beginning, who wanted to sustain a good image."
—Derek Taylor, in an interview with me in the mid-eighties

Jim and Mary and Paul and Michael

Rumor has it that the oldest son of Jim and Mary McCartney was able to comb his streaking black hair with one hand as he held the handlebar of his bicycle with the other, all the while anticipating his arrival at the church in Woolton for the historic first meeting with John Lennon. James Paul McCartney had just turned fifteen. It was only eight months since the death of his mother. Life had been cruel to the music-loving cyclist with the locks of black hair, the slim teen body, and the hopes of becoming a professional musician. The roots of his life dated back, as those of so many children in Britain in the 1950s, to the nation's fight for survival. In fact, the McCartney family had its start beneath the surface.

Jim McCartney met Mary Mohin in an air-raid shelter, the earth shaking around them. The parents of Paul McCartney, humble and loving, were married on April 15, 1941. The sirens again wailed after the ceremony, and so their wedding night was spent with family and friends in a shelter. That was life in Britain in the forties.

Although the road was bumpy and surrounded by intrigue, their first son, James Paul McCartney, born June 18, 1942, would become one of the twentieth century's most famous people.

His friends, the close ones from the old Liverpool days, called him Paulie. The media has renamed him "Macca," a rather meaningless and unflattering abbreviation of his last name. His mom and dad have always called him Paul. The people of the British Empire, and most others, have called him "Sir" since Her Majesty, Queen Elizabeth, knighted him in 1997.

Paul was a charming boy. He captivated his parents and relatives, endeared himself to neighbors, and at a very young age made himself a mesmerizing and seductive sex symbol through a sly demeanor, cutesy smile, and hips that would move even when his feet stood still. When he bicycled to the church at Woolton in July 1957 for what would be a historic, life-changing meeting with John Lennon, it is said, by eyewitnesses—how could they possibly remember the detail?—that in some miraculous way, he kept his hair intact on that windy summer day, in anticipation of meeting girls. As I can tell you from witnessing it less than ten years later, Paul was artfully creating a winning combination with women—a personal presence accompanied by the most powerful force of seduction. Paul talked to girls, and later, young women, with an intense seriousness. His words and intimate conversations were powerfully accentuated by a fleeting touch, or the wink of an eye.

It's truly a pity that, in our own early years, so many of us failed to emulate Paul's real secret to the art of romance: he used words, words spoken softly and with respect. He was a natural conversationalist who was truly and sincerely in love with his prey, at least at the given moment. Eventually that special talent would land him in the arms of a woman he loved for more than thirty years. But in the early days, Paul McCartney was a professional practitioner of beguiling girls and women into his bed with a manner befitting Casanova and Romeo. His parental guidance was filled with advisories on respect, and so he always showed respect to the women on tour whom he lured for intimacy. Which is why his answer to a personal question I asked in 1964 was surprising for a man of his young age and romantic skills.

"What would you want in a wife someday?" I asked.

"Well, most of all I would want a woman who was sensitive to my needs," Paul said. "Good looks would be nice, but not the most important thing. Fashionable is okay, but not high fashion. Most of all, I would want to love someone who has a great sense of humor."

When I first met Paul McCartney, soon after he turned twenty-two, I was blown away by his charm and his boyish grin, but I knew right away that he was aiming to please. Most people want to be liked, but Paul was almost obsessed with being loved and adored. He still is. Even after achieving supreme success as one of the most talented writers, artists, and performers in rock 'n' roll history, and despite the lifetime security of being a billionaire, and in stark contrast to his now royal pedigree and universal fame, Paul is really just the same old Paulie from the beginning, trying to be loved by everyone. He still seeks that face-to-face approval that only mega-concerts bring, and still adoringly treasures the praise and applause, whether it comes in the press that he tries to control, or from his fans of all ages who are still out of control for anything Paul.

And those legions of fans are forgiving. When Paul attempted to change the songwriting credits on certain "Lennon-McCartney" masterpieces to "McCartney-Lennon," fans objected. But then they let it be. After all, it was Paul being Paul, and despite this walking paradox of personality, insecurity, daring stage majesty, and artfully creative music, Paul McCartney remains the gold standard of the world's superstars. He also maintains presidential-like security inside an organization best described as a bubble. Inside the bubble are press agents, fellow musicians, confidantes, and loved ones. The bubble is never penetrated. Even staff photographers, over the years, have been required to show their work to Paul or his censors before it leaves the confines of the bubble, especially on tour.

Yet the bubble has not always worked as it should. Paul McCartney's failure to provide routine access to reporters has ironically resulted in grossly distorted views of him, based on secondhand information, rumors, and innuendo. Clearly, Paul has never really learned that when reporters do not have information, they tend to guess, or worse, rely on distortion. And, sadly, they make mistakes. It is commonly known that Sir Paul will never do an interview without knowledge of the subject matter ahead of time, which is not uncommon in the superstar industry. But it wasn't always that way. In the early days, from 1962 to 1970, Paul was the most accessible and approachable of the Beatles. John was also available, but he always took an arm's-length approach, even to me in the beginning. And George and Ringo were available, yet perhaps not as much in demand as John and Paul.

While Paul disdains criticism of any kind, the fans understand a little more than he does that in real life, it comes with the territory. And because of that, the millions who love his music and appreciate his wondrous talent are happy to dismiss a few verbal indiscretions here or there. After all, for what Paulie-Macca-Paul has brought to this world, he gets a pass, doesn't he?

The Beginning

How did this amazing climb to the mountaintop begin? It almost didn't.

Although Jim and Mary offered love and support to their two children (Paul's brother, Michael, was born in 1944), there were true moments of caution. Why not? In the 1940s and 1950s, parents were, as they are today, anxious about their children's ability to make their way in the world, especially those parents who had endured the years of depression and war.

Life wasn't easy for the McCartneys in post-Depression Britain. Mary worked as a nurse and midwife, her career blooming even as the mild-mannered and attentive Jim sought better jobs. He worked as an inspector for an engineering company, and as a cotton salesman. They moved several times. In postwar Liverpool, they lived in a tenement for a while, then two residences in the growing Speke neighborhood. Speke was the location of the airport, and it was off the runways where young James Paul McCartney, little George Harrison, and thin and younger Tony Bramwell went scavenging for spent German bombs. The McCartneys, buoyed by an economic upturn, wound up at 20 Forthlin Road in Allerton in 1955.

For Jim, a champion of hard work and ethical behavior, and Mary, the woman who helped bring so many babies into the world, labor was required to feed and maintain a decent life for their children. That high standard left an indelible impression. There was a special urgency about taking the right steps to guide the boys in the right direction.

And there was no lack of inspiration. Unlike the divided family loyalties of young John Lennon, the McCartney brothers had a clarity and sense of purpose that were forged into their psyches.

So, when Jim warned Paul about the dangers of relying on a career as a musician, he was less an obstructionist than a concerned father. Jim, the courageous volunteer firefighter, who fought through the flames and rubble that the Luftwaffe left behind, sounded the warning to his son.

Paul, with deep respect for his dad's memory, shared with me the conversation.

HE JUST SAID . . . "WELL, YOU'RE NEVER GOING TO MAKE ANY MONEY . . . IN A GROUP, AND YOU MAY BE ENJOYING YOURSELF, BUT YOU STILL HAVE TO HAVE SOME MONEY TO HELP YOU LIVE," YOU KNOW. SO HE SAID, "GET A JOB AND [PLAY MUSIC] IN YOUR SPARE TIME." . . . [SO] I DID GET A JOB. . . . BUT BECAUSE WE WERE PLAYING LUNCHTIME SESSIONS, I COULDN'T STICK TO IT . . . HAVE TO KEEP RUNNING AWAY EVERY AFTER-NOON, YOU KNOW. SO I GAVE IT UP, AND LUCKILY, WE MADE IT. . . . AND SO NOW, LARRY . . . HE'S VERY THANKFUL I DIDN'T TAKE HIS ADVICE.

Jim and Paul and his younger brother, Mike, later a celebrated musician and photographer, forged a closeness rarely found among teenagers and parents, especially after Mary died in 1956, following surgery for breast cancer.

The boys, shattered by their mother's death, lived for a while with relatives but reunited with their grieving father a short time later. It was a unifying coincidence that both Paul and John lost their mothers in their teenage years. That was a big hole for both, though Paul had a better support team in his father and brother.

The father and his oldest son had something that John Lennon would have given just about anything for: a relationship as a child with a grown man built on love and respect.

Paul told me years ago, before the media-blackout years of his life, "Dad is a very encouraging man, even though he wasn't crazy in the beginning about my career choice. He was . . . a wonderful man."

Boyhood buddy and longtime Beatles associate Tony Bramwell, who looked up to Paul and still does, remembers, "The McCartneys were sweet people, always welcoming. Some of us felt it was a home away from ours."

Kevin Roach, who works in the Liverpool Record Office and wrote *The McCartneys: In the Town Where They Were Born*, has gotten closer than any chronicler to the essence of the McCartney family.

Roach says the McCartneys were quite typical of many families in the forties and fifties.

"They were a down-to-earth working-class family. And theirs [Paul and Michael's] is a positive story of two boys growing up in Liverpool, searching for their path."

He recalls the neighbors and friends who described them as close.

"Every family in Liverpool protects each other. Even if they didn't have fame, the families of a working-class city would guard their interests like gold in a vault."

When Roach was researching his book, he made a golden discovery. At age ten years and ten months, Paul wrote an essay at the Joseph Williams Primary School in Speke. The essay, about the coronation of Queen Elizabeth II, was written in attractive and neat cursive handwriting. One of his teachers entered the essay, unknown to Paul, in a citywide competition. Paul won and was feted, with his smiling parents present, by the Lord Mayor of Liverpool. He was said to be quite nervous on stage—odd, considering what a stage presence he would eventually create. It was his first public appearance, and his first press notice. It was only months later that he entered the Liverpool Institute High School for Boys, a prestigious school. (Today the school is called the Liverpool Institute for Performing Arts. The Institute's number-one patron is James Paul McCartney.)

The well-written essay, discovered by Roach in the city records, became the subject of a tug-of-war. Mike McCartney, who served Roach well as liaison to Paul for the book, insisted that Roach return the essay to Paul. A surprised Kevin Roach didn't know what to do.

"Paul insisted that it was his. Turns out he didn't even know it existed. But it wasn't mine. In actuality, the copyright belonged to the sponsor of the original contest: the Liverpool City Council. I went back and forth with Mike, and eventually Paul relented. He did get a copy, a digital copy, which I'm told is locked in a vault."

The minor episode is nevertheless typical of the strong feeling of owner-ship that the McCartneys have.

"They are very guarded," Roach reiterates. "Remember that they are prob-ably the most investigated and examined family in the world. They will defend. They will not respond to malicious material, nor will they offer much in the way of quotes."

One example of the McCartneys' reticence is their failure to respond to a real lie that made the rounds over the decades. In light of this preposterous accusation, Roach performed an extraordinary investigation, in his own right, that helped the McCartney family.

Flyers distributed on the perimeter of the 1964 farewell salute to the Beatles at Liverpool City Hall charged that Paul McCartney was the real father of a little boy. Was it a shakedown? No one knew for sure until recently, when the young man in question proved to Roach and John Gannon—his coauthor on *The Beatles: Living in the Eye of the Hurricane*—that there was no way Paul was, indeed, his father.

Roach's description of a family unwilling to address even its own honor is telling of its extreme caution. With the exception of the early days, and entertainment-oriented interviews, both McCartney sons can really be described as a closed book. Paul is a sensitive man, perhaps just as eager to be viewed in a positive light today as he was in those rarified early days. Michael McCartney is constantly afraid that access to him will injure his brother. I admire the brothers' all-for-one-and-one-for-all posture. It is com-mendable, but dangerous, especially when less responsible elements of the contemporary media look for dirt. "No comment" to most people means the subject of a report has something to hide. And to the public eye, perception always seems to trump reality.

That air of protectiveness is a positive tribute to the bond of family, yet it is also a bond of silence that opens the family up to distortions.

About two people in their lives, there is no mystery. Father Jim, who was also in a band as a teenager, was extremely supportive. Mother Mary was determined that Paul follow a disciplined path. She was happy that, at the time of her death, Paul was on a steady road to becoming an academic.

Kevin Roach and other McCartney watchers agree that there was an irony in the tragic loss of a mother.

"Most people believe that her death may have inadvertently freed him up, given more space to pursue his dreams. You really have to wonder," Roach says. "Paul's dad was always a fan, what Americans would call a cheerleader, a devoted dad who always beamed with pride. There were certainly generational differences, but he was more with it in understanding changes in culture than a lot of moms and dads of his own generation."

Jim was also a source of musical inspiration, playing his favorite hits from the forties on his home piano, and creatively rigging up an electrical extension connection, complete with earphones, from the radio in the living room to the boys' bedrooms. This handiwork allowed the boys to enjoy Radio Luxembourg in their beds. While other parents disdained the early moments of rock 'n' roll as vulgar and dangerous, Jim McCartney was able to shed his classical and jazz history to understand that his boys were embracing the music for *their* times.

Young Paul rarely enjoyed his music classes at school. Early on, though, he thrilled at the hands-on approach of learning on his own. One of his greatest investments was trading in the trumpet his dad gave him for an acoustic guitar that cost fifteen pounds.

For Paul, there was always a passion for music, as witnessed on November 5, 1956, when his hero, his own music man, Lonnie Donegan, played the Liverpool Empire Theater. Paul could not get a ticket, so he stood outside with other fans hoping to catch a glimpse of his idol—in retrospect, it was an ironic mirror image of the fans who would do anything to get a glimpse of the Beatles in years to come. So the boy who would become world-famous stretched out his neck and caught a glimpse of inspiration Lonnie, not knowing that his friend George Harrison had been funded by his parents to get tickets. George was inside on *all* the Donegan concerts, and would tell people later that he "was never the same."

In the coming months, Paul would take to riding the streets with a good friend and classmate, Ian James. They had guitars on their backs. They were ready to rock, but there were few takers. Paul started treating his guitar as a holy object, tuned and at the ready. All he needed was an audience.

Although George was the ultimate guitar man, throughout his life, Paul has also treated his strings as an extension of his body and his mind.

Even in private moments, like the relaxing hours in the rear of the tour plane, you could see Paul playing and listening to the sounds of his guitar. I would look back to the Beatles compartment on the Electra every now and then. John was always reading. They were all smoking. And above the haze of the cigarette smoke, I would always see Paul working on his guitar.

It should be noted that Gentleman Jim, as he was called by the Liverpool elite, scheduled Paul for music classes, but young Paul disdained formal musical lessons and relied more on his "ear." Neither he nor John ever read music then, but what ears!

Beatles researcher Ron Ellis agrees with writers Roach and Gannon about the young Paul McCartney.

"Paul was sensitive to a point, but he covered it up well with a cheerful disposition, while John used his abrasiveness as a Teflon cover."

Freda Kelly says the gene pool made a big difference for handsome, young Paul. Kelly became close to the senior McCartney. Kelly, the fan-club maven, had constant contact with the families. She could sense from Gentleman Jim that he had given Paul the basics for success at personal communications.

"We called him Uncle Jim," Kelly says. "'Don't call me Mr. McCartney,' he would say graciously.

"Uncle Jim was proud of his oldest son, and his desire to succeed, but he was also ferociously protective. Paul and his brother loved him, really respected him. I remember on Wednesdays he would come to the NEMS [North End Music Stores, Brian Epstein's Liverpool headquarters] and take me out for coffee. I have to say I really adored him. . . . I really did. He was just a marvelous man. It was easy to like him. He was a man of deep respect, and ferocious support of his boys."

"Did you adore him as much as you adored his son?" I ask.

"Well, that's another story. You'll never get that one, Larry."

We both laugh.

"I had a crush on each one of them at one time or another, but Paul just had this magical sense of hopefulness. He was a man who would always think about tomorrow, like his dad, Uncle Jim."

Throughout his life, as a little boy, in school, and as the bike-riding guitar man, Paul was an optimist.

The boys' frequent press man and assistant to Brian Epstein, Derek Taylor, remembers, "We would get into jams, something would happen, and he would always emerge somewhere or other and smooth it over. He got us out of difficulties. I always described it as 'the Mary Sunshine approach' to life."

Kelly also remembers a similar optimism.

"Paul was always confident. He never really changed. He may live in a different world now, all rarified and that, but I can imagine that underneath it all, he's the same as he was."

Kelly, one of the most admired people on the Liverpool scene, recalls a teenager brimming with panache.

"For a man his age, he exuded warmth to everybody he met. And remember, this was a great offset to John's directness."

Brian Epstein, whose savvy catapulted the Beatles, knew that John was the true leader. But Brian also enabled Paul.

"Brian Epstein's arrival on the scene," Bill Harry remembers, "affected the transition that turned John's boys into Paul's men. Brian allowed the leadership to change, but still gave John all the affection and respect that he needed. Make it clear. Brian allowed a big change—John's group became Paul's group, not necessarily in public, but certainly helping to shape the group in private."

Along with all the positives of Paul's early life, and his sterling career, there are some other behavioral traits to explore, which began early and lasted forever.

A Blow for Equality

While Ringo, from the early days until today, always seemed annoyed by the vagaries of celebrity and public life, Paul has always enjoyed contact with people. He seems to need the adoration, which is not uncommon in show business, and because he is Paul McCartney he enjoys the luxury of controlling information and situations. The real story on the firing of Pete Best has direct links to Paul, as you will soon read. The independence and power that Paul exhibited at the time of the group's breakup showed him as territorial, and obsessed with taking appropriate credit. His desire for control over media content began early. It was difficult for me to penetrate his political or spiritual views during interviews, unlike with John and Ringo. But on one subject, he was forcefully outspoken. John always seemed to be the conscience of the group, but Paul took the lead in this particular case.

It happened during the 1964 tour. I advised the Beatles in their Las Vegas hotel suite that their upcoming concert at the Gator Bowl football stadium in Jacksonville, Florida, was going to be racially segregated. Immediately it was Paul who stood up first and said, "Well, that's rubbish. Tell them we are not going to play there if Negroes [the term used by many in the sixties] are seated separately."

John echoed, "No way." And the rest followed. The Gator Bowl management balked at first, then acquiesced. The concert was not segregated—the first time that happened in the legendary stadium. Paul's lead on this issue was emblematic of his affinity for artists held back because of race—a striking irony for a British lad who grew up in an atmosphere full of racial and religious prejudice.

Before the Gator Bowl experience, it was Paul who encouraged the group's embrace of Joe Ankrah and his magical all-black vocal group, the Chants. Watch an old video of the Chants, who began in Liverpool, and you will be enchanted by their demeanor, stage presence, and wonderful harmonies in the doo-wop style. Ankrah told me, "It was bad enough that the modern moods [racism] never gave a black group a chance, but if not for Paul and his friends, we would have never stayed together. . . . In fact, I think that meeting the Beatles changed the direction of my life."

Ankrah also makes it clear that, in a sea of intolerance, Paul and the Beatles stood out, and stood up for him and his bandmates.

"They were very cool guys, and meeting them gave us a look at real opportunity."

The very week that the Beatles' "Love Me Do" had made the charts in the UK, Ankrah gambled. It was October 12, 1962. The boys had just finished a concert at the Tower Ballroom in New Brighton, backing up the legendary Little Richard. A day earlier, Ankrah had arranged for a meeting with Little Richard at Liverpool's Adelphi Hotel, once a bastion of hardened segregation. Ankrah, impressed with the American artist's defiance in actually staying at the Adelphi, was in awe as the two conversed about music and racism and life in Britain. Little Richard invited Ankrah, as his guest, to the Tower Ballroom a night later. Ankrah made his way to the dressing room, where he met Little Richard and was approached by John Lennon.

IT WAS AFTER THE SHOW, LARRY. I WAS WARMLY GREETED BY LITTLE RICHARD. THAT SEEMED TO IMPRESS LENNON, WHO ASKED ME IF I WAS AN ENTERTAINER. AND THAT'S WHEN THE OTHER [BEATLES] BAND MEMBERS CAME AROUND. I EXPLAINED TO THEM THAT I HAD A GROUP, BUT NO BAND . . . THAT MY MUSIC WAS A CAPPELLA. THEY SEEMED GENUINELY INTERESTED, ESPECIALLY JOHN AND PAUL. I WAS A BIT STUNNED WHEN PAUL INVITED ME TO THE CAVERN AT A LUNCHTIME SESSION AFTER THEY RETURNED FROM A HAMBURG GIG. LITTLE RICHARD SEEMED PLEASED. THIS WAS SERIOUS. IN FACT, PAUL EVEN WROTE A NOTE SECURING OUR ADMISSION TO THE CAVERN. HE SAID, "LET'S SEE WHAT YOU DO."

The following week the Chants, led by Ankrah, arrived at the Cavern at lunchtime. Fate would have it that they couldn't get in until the time the crowd was pouring out.

"I will never forget the smell of the place," Ankrah says.

THE CONDENSATION AND SWEAT, PERSPIRATION WAS STICKING TO THE WALLS. IT WAS OVERWHELMING, A HUMAN SMELL AND VERY CONFINING, BUT IT GOT VERY EXCITING, ESPECIALLY WHEN PAUL WAVED FOR US TO TAKE THE STAGE. WE SANG "THE DUKE OF EARL." PAUL'S EYES LIT UP. GEORGE STOOD UP, JUST STARED, AND JOHN RAN OVER TO THE PIANO AND STARTED BACKING US UP. HE MISSED A FEW BEATS, BUT HONESTLY, WHO CARED? I DIDN'T KNOW THEM WELL, BUT I KNEW, SOMEHOW, THAT A BARRIER WAS CRUMBLING.

The future of the Chants was still cloudy at that time, but history shows that Joe Ankrah and the Chants received a formal invitation to the City Hall celebration in 1964, Liverpool's formal farewell to the boys. A token invitation in a time of change? Maybe. But it was a breakthrough, an unheard-of gesture, and it happened just two months before Paul led the way along with his bandmates to integrate the Gator Bowl in Jacksonville.

It has always been fascinating that a young man surrounded by the post-war anti-Semitism and racial mores of Liverpool, a man so averse to controversy, would reach out so early in his career to strike very public blows against hatred.

In one of our earliest interviews, I broached the subject of race to Paul McCartney.

"What about the [racial] barriers being broken in the music business?" I asked.

His answer was fascinating in its simplicity and reasoning. (It should be noted again that his use of the word "Negro" was commonly accepted at the time.)

IN SOME OF THE WORST PLACES IN AMERICA, YOU GET NEGRO ENTER-
TAINERS MIXING IN WITH WHITE PEOPLE. ACTUALLY IT'S ALL STUPID
BECAUSE I REALLY DON'T SEE ANY DIFFERENCE BETWEEN A NEGRO AND A
WHITE PERSON. IT'S LIKE YOU GO TO THE SOUTH OF FRANCE AND YOU
GET A LITTLE TAN. IF YOU GO DOWN INTO TUNISIA YOU GET A LITTLE BIT
OF A DARKER TAN. IF YOU GO DOWN TO THE GOLD COAST OF AFRICA,
YOU GET A VERY DARK TAN AND SUDDENLY YOU BECOME A NEGRO. THAT'S
ALL . . . THEY HAVE A VERY DARK TAN AND NOBODY WOULD EVER THINK
OF DISCRIMINATING AGAINST A MAN FROM FRANCE OR TUNISIA, BECAUSE
THEY ARE NOT QUITE NEGROS. IT'S A FUNNY THING, BUT ONCE THEY
BECOME NEGROS . . . THEN THE DISCRIMINATION COMES IN. JUST CAN'T
SEE IT. IT'S ALL STUPID TO ME.

He made the remarks with such innocence and sincerity, and it was both a rare and reasonable explanation.

When it came to Joe Ankrah and the Chants, the young black group The Exciters, who opened for the Beatles at the Gator Bowl in 1964, and scores of other nonwhite entertainers along the way, Paul was truly color blind, and in the early to mid-sixties, that was not an ordinary characteristic in a world filled with hate and dissent.

Paul was fully confident in his various stands against hatred. In addition to opening doors for Joe Ankrah as a teenager in Liverpool, he did the same for the young people, especially the talented singer Mary Hopkin, a few years later. He introduced me to Hopkin in the Beatles' office in London in 1968, and played me the tape of her recording, "Those Were the Days." Paul was more confident than even Mary that the song would be a success. It was truly amazing to me that such a young man would already be in the business of mentoring, whether it was helping to give a break to a black man facing barriers, or a young woman yearning for a break.

Confidence was always a strong characteristic of Paul McCartney's existence, even on the day of a meeting that would change his life.

"The Meeting"

The meeting was not set in concrete, but it wasn't really accidental. Three people played a role. Ivan Vaughan was a mutual friend of John and Paul, and was hopeful the two would meet. Quarryman Pete Shotton advised John that the Woolton event was a good opportunity for the band. Both Shotton and Vaughan, along with Nigel Walley, the Quarrymen's teenage manager, pushed John hard to talk to the pastor and secure the engagement for the band. Separately, Vaughn had urged Paul to go, as well. There are differing accounts of who the real catalyst was, but all three played a role. The "matchmakers" were hopeful that something would happen, but it was really a situation of wait and see.

Young Paul pedaled hard on his cycle journey to Woolton. In his heart, did he know what the day would bring? Do any of us know? One thing was certain—when he got there, his friend Ivan would take him to meet the leader of the band. It was a hot summer day in Liverpool, so the bicycle trip to St. Peter's Church in Woolton must have been strenuous. After all, Paul was out to impress. He was wearing a white sport coat and dark pants. He had been talking to his friends, including the official introducer, Ivan Vaughn, about his dream of getting into a band. Would John Lennon consider it? Although hindsight shows this meeting as monumental, to Paul, in the moment, it was just a chance to join a real band.

Despite the myth and the glory of that first meeting, the reality is that Paul and John knew of each other before that meeting, albeit very little. The families had some contact, and John was aware, according to Tony Bramwell, of the death of Mary McCartney in late 1956. Within a year, both boys would have something tragic in common.

The beautiful afternoon was marked by floats, fanfare, and music. The annual crowning of the Rose Queen was an important event in the Woolton neighborhood. So many accounts remain of the day, but none as descriptive as that of Julia Baird, John's half-sister.

THE ENTERTAINMENT BEGAN AT TWO P.M. WITH THE OPENING PROCESSION, WHICH ENTAILED ONE OR TWO WONDERFULLY FESTOONED LORRIES CRAWLING AT A SNAIL'S PACE THROUGH THE VILLAGE ON THEIR CEREMONIOUS WAY TO THE CHURCH FIELD. THE FIRST LORRY CARRIED THE ROSE QUEEN, SEATED ON HER THRONE, SURROUNDED BY HER RETINUE, ALL DRESSED IN PINK AND WHITE SATIN, SPORTING LONG RIBBONS AND HANDMADE ROSES IN THEIR HAIR. THESE GIRLS HAD BEEN CHOSEN FROM THE SUNDAY SCHOOL GROUPS, ON THE BASIS OF AGE AND GOOD BEHAVIOR.

THE FOLLOWING LORRY CARRIED VARIOUS ENTERTAINERS, INCLUDING THE QUARRYMEN. THE BOYS WERE UP THERE ON THE BACK OF THE MOVING LORRY, TRYING TO STAY UPRIGHT AND PLAY THEIR INSTRUMENTS AT THE SAME TIME. JOHN GAVE UP BATTLING WITH BALANCE AND SAT WITH HIS LEGS HANGING OVER THE EDGE, PLAYING HIS GUITAR AND SINGING. HE CONTINUED ALL THROUGH THE SLOW, SLOW JOURNEY AS THE LORRY PUTTERED ITS WAY ALONG. JACKIE AND I LEAPED ALONGSIDE THE LORRY, WITH OUR MOTHER LAUGHING AND WAVING AT JOHN, MAKING HIM LAUGH. HE SEEMED TO BE THE ONLY ONE WHO WAS REALLY TRYING TO PLAY AND WE WERE REALLY TRYING TO PUT HIM OFF!

Baird does not mention her nemesis in life and in death, Aunt Mimi, although she, too, was present. Mimi arrived on the church grounds while

John and the Quarrymen were performing in the afternoon. John, startled by the presence of the square-jawed and intense aunt, was nervous. He tried to beat the nerves by starting to sing the words, "Oh, Mimi. Oh, Mimi is coming down the path. . . . Oh, Mimi." Mimi, some neighbors later recalled, was aghast at John's outfit, especially the shocking jeans—skintight and all that. Not far away from Mimi was Paul, who watched intently as the Quarrymen entertained the crowd.

Drummer Colin Hanton played at the legendary Rose Queen concert in the afternoon but was not there for the evening concert in the church hall when Paul was introduced to John by mutual friend Vaughn. But two weeks later, after Paul joined the Quarrymen, Hanton became very impressed with two aspects of the life of the fifteen-year-old.

"Paul was a very nice young man, very well spoken," Hanton recalls. "Paul was like a schoolboy, preppy, more refined, if you will. Yes, he was pretty much more middle class, or climbing up the ladder."

Although Paul would be forever known for his songwriting and vocal skills, Hanton remembers his work on the strings.

I REMEMBER THAT HE WAS AN EXCELLENT GUITAR PLAYER. HE WAS A GOOD TALENT. THAT IS WHY HE IMPRESSED JOHN SO MUCH. THAT IS WHY JOHN THOUGHT IT WAS A GOOD IDEA TO HAVE HIM IN THE GROUP. I DON'T REMEMBER HEARING HIS SINGING IN THOSE DAYS SO MUCH AS HIS GUITAR SKILLS. JOHN DIDN'T REALLY PLAY GUITAR SO WELL—HE DIDN'T PLAY CHORDS—HE STRUMMED IT IN MORE OF A BANJO STYLE. HE HADN'T LEARNED TO PLAY THE GUITAR PROPERLY AT THAT TIME. PAUL ALSO TAUGHT HIM HOW TO TUNE A GUITAR. HE WAS CHARMING WAY BEYOND HIS YEARS, AND VERY HELPFUL.

Paul's bicycle trip to the church included what appeared to be a mini-audition. His charm had already impressed John, but the turning point was his rendition, so electrifying, of a song cowritten by Richard Wayne Penniman, aka Little Richard. Yes, that same Little Richard idolized by Joe Ankrah and millions of Americans. It was "Long Tall Sally" and, coincidentally, it would become the final song in the Beatles' dynamic set of their 1964 American concerts. I was amazed at Paul's rhythm and energy on the song during those concerts, which began with John on the lead on another rock 'n' roll giant, "Twist and Shout," originally recorded by the Isley Brothers. It is fascinating that the two most prolific songwriters in recorded history opened and closed their historic North American concerts with two contemporary classics written by others. It was always unique that John and Paul were never afraid to shine the light on other top performers, but also an irony that, because of their knockdown stage performances, the Beatles were credited with making songs hits—Paul with "Long Tall Sally," John with "Twist and Shout."

So, on the night of the meeting at the church, if Paul's style, helpful nature, and embracing personality had already impacted on the always skeptical John Lennon, it was his version of "Long Tall Sally" later that did the trick.

Hanton stayed with the band through late 1958, eventually being replaced, after alternating with a series of part-time drummers, by Pete Best. He continued with his studies, and had no regrets when John and Paul recruited Pete to take over. The master upholsterer, and obsessive football fan, remembers, "No, I wasn't good at all. Very amateurish. I was the bottom of the pile. I really wasn't very good at all. I think McCartney knew it. But he was too nice to say anything to me."

That humility is shared by most of the Quarrymen, especially Rod Davis, the banjo man, who has the distinction of saying he was actually replaced by Paul McCartney.

Davis played at both concerts at the church, but amazingly, he missed "the moment."

"I must have gone for a pee. The vital moment in rock 'n' roll history, and I went for a pee and missed it all, you see. . . . Paul remembers what happened because for him it was important. And he tells people [he] played either on Eric [Griffiths] or John's guitar, that way, left-handed, and he had to play the chords upside down. That would be pretty amazing, but so is everything about the guy.

"It was on the platform in a field outside the church hall. I missed it. A few weeks later, Paul was in, I was out," the affable Davis remembers. "I didn't know him well, but he made himself liked very quickly in the band.

And John's mum and Aunt Mimi seemed to really enjoy being around him."

So did Sam Leach. An active early promoter of the Beatles, Leach saw the Quarrymen playing at the Hamilton Club. As would happen many times in Merseyside events, fighting broke out on the floor. But that night something else happened—a first. The fighting stopped when the boys started playing. And Leach stopped in his tracks.

"Couldn't believe it, Larry. All of them—they all stopped fighting. It made me look a lot closer at the band," Leach recalls. He was especially impressed with Paul and John. In a classic first meeting, Leach, a gregarious and personable man—a few years older than the band members—recalls following the boys to a dressing room that had been converted from a toilet, and how Paul lit the flame, mostly with his personality.

SO, I'M IN THIS "DRESSING ROOM" AND I SAY TO THEM, "YOU WILL BE BIGGER THAN ELVIS." THEY JUST STARE AT ME LIKE I'VE LOST MY MIND. JOHN LOOKED AT ME LIKE I WAS MENTAL. THERE WAS SILENCE. THEN PAUL GOT UP, SMILED THAT TOOTHY SMILE OF HIS, AND SAID, QUITE VIGOROUSLY, "YOU HAVE WORK FOR US, MR. LEACH?" JOHN'S EYES ROLLED. I ANSWERED, "YES," AND IMMEDIATELY BOOKED THEM AT MY NEW PLACE, THE CASANOVA CLUB. PAUL WAS SHREWD. HE KNEW I WAS OPENING A NEW CLUB. HE TOOK ADVANTAGE OF THE MOMENT. HE BELIEVED IN THE GROUP.

Paul was as savvy as a teenager could be.

John's sister Julia Baird remembers the early duets between John and Paul at her mother's house, and Paul's undaunted optimism. She recalls little of the reported petty jealousies between the boys, but Paul's determination was clear and present. She says of Paul,

HE WAS JUBILANT AND BUOYANT, HE PLAYED THE MAJOR ROLE IN BUTTRESSING JOHN, BUT HE WASN'T THE ONLY ONE INFLUENCING JOHN. THERE WAS ROD DAVIS. ROD LEFT THE BAND BECAUSE OF PAUL, BUT ALSO BECAUSE HIS PARENTS PULLED HIM OUT TO GET READY FOR HIGHER EDUCATION. JOHN LOVED ROD. THERE WAS LATER STU SUTCLIFFE, WHOM JOHN LOVED. PAUL UNDERSTOOD THAT AND LET

THAT FRIENDSHIP PLAY OUT. ALTHOUGH PAUL WAS PRESENT, HE STAYED
AWAY FROM THAT AND FROM JOHN'S OBSESSION WITH CYNTHIA. IT WAS
LIKE A LITTLE MÉNAGE À TROIS WITH CYNTHIA, STU, AND JOHN. PAUL
WAS SMART; HE KNEW WHEN TO DISTANCE HIMSELF.

Baird, younger than John, was smitten with his friends.

"You can imagine what it was like when Jackie and my mother would
watch them practice. Paul was handsome even then, and John was so determined. You had this feeling from the chemistry that something special was
going to happen, and please don't forget my mother's role in being so present for that."

The observations Sam Leach had of the teenaged boys seems to put Paul
in the leadership position, not John.

EVEN WHEN WE WENT TO SHOWS, [PAUL] HAD THE IDEAS, MADE THE
DECISIONS—ABOUT WHAT CLUBS TO PLAY IN, FOR EXAMPLE, NEW THINGS
TO TRY ON STAGE. HE WAS THE IDEA MAN. JOHN WAS A BIT LAZY WHEN
IT CAME TO DOING STUFF. PAUL [WROTE] "CAN'T BUY ME LOVE" ALL ON
HIS OWN WITHOUT JOHN. . . . THEN JOHN CAME BACK WITH A REBUTTAL
IN "YOU CAN'T DO THAT." A RETALIATION, IF YOU WILL, TO PAUL.
THE NEXT ONE WAS BY PAUL, "I SHOULD HAVE KNOWN BETTER." AN
APOLOGY BY PAUL TO JOHN. AND SO ON—THEIR RELATIONSHIP GOT
PRETTY TEMPESTUOUS.

That recorded controversy could seem a stretch, but the fact is, the relationship was always on the edge, even in the beginning, the very beginning.
Paul managed to test the limits of John's patience, without blowing anything
up at first. Eventually, of course—twelve years after they came together—
their differences proved insurmountable and finally led, quite sadly, to the
breakup of the Beatles.

Rod Davis, who never had any real contact with Paul McCartney in the
early days, did have an accidental encounter with him in the beach town of
Brighton in the summer of 2005.

I WAS THERE FOR [A] WINDSURFING [COMPETITION]. A FRIEND SAID, "I
JUST SAW PAUL MCCARTNEY WALK BY WITH A BIG DOG." AND I SAID,

"You're joking." And he said, "No. . . . " So I walked around and there he was, talking to the officials of windsurfing—he had a hoodie on and a big scruffy dog. So, they knew me, and said, "Hey, look who this is," so I walked over, shook hands, and he said, "Who are you, then?" And I said, "I'm the guy you replaced in the Quarrymen in 1957." And he said, "Good God, that's going back a bit, isn't it? What happened? Did I elbow you aside?" And I said, "No, it was no big deal." And I was a banjo player, and you can't have a banjo in a rock 'n' roll band, and it was becoming more rock 'n' roll. And I should have said at the time, but I didn't think of it, "They weren't going anywhere, anyway!" But I didn't think of it at the time. And he said, "Oh, you must've been there in the photograph on the stage [at the Rose Queen concert]." And I said, "Yeah, I was standing behind John's right shoulder. I'm in the photograph." So we chatted a bit and they were trying to get him to present prizes for the windsurfing, and he said, "I'm not gonna be there tomorrow when it finishes," blah blah blah, and the dog got restless and off he went. So that's the only time I remember speaking to Paul.

I can just imagine Paul's face as he said, "Did I elbow you aside?" as if he were concerned about ending Davis's career. Paul, who is so amazingly private, has this ability to charm and please, a trait apparently embedded early by a soothing mother and an inspirational father. Davis, who missed the Woolton meeting in 1957 because he was "taking a pee," seems excited that he finally met the man, ever briefly, who quickly replaced him in John's band, freeing him up for a career in much higher education, and intellectual, if not hugely financial, success.

There is much to be learned in the ensuing pages about Paul McCartney, his agenda and manipulations, and, of course, ability.

James Paul McCartney, admired as he is today, is many things to many people, but in the early days that shaped the life of a young and starving band, he offered talent, a creative edge, and unswerving commitment to excellence. But there was another contribution—his role as a leader. He cheerfully learned to endure and persist with his mission, along with his new friends, while they jointly faced the indignity, humiliation, and conditions of life as a band without a home. That vacancy would soon take them to the land of the unexpected.

WHEN THEY WERE BOYS

PART TWO:
FEVER

M eet me at the Jac. It was the Toilet Bowl. Heavy scents of paint and lipstick, coffee and jealousy. Allan W. ran the day, but John, Paul, George, and Stu captured the night. Underground was really underground. Bill Harry, a man with two first names, and a promotional giant. George emerges, and he's got a free ride, on the bus. The hormones are raging, and so are the boys, hungry for a chance, facing rejection, not-so-sizzling in Scotland. Rory arrives on the scene, stormy Rory, and gives the boys a hot shot. And a young boy remembers the hormones raging.

There were long pauses in the Quarrymen's transition from adolescent dreamers to genuine music makers. In the Quarry Bank days—at the primitive concerts in the neighborhoods, on the backs of trucks, and wherever they managed to find a crowd—the seeds were planted for the bloom that would follow.

In the very beginning, it was just a matter of attention-getting, like John's escape from the angry and jealous boys, remembered by Rod Davis, at the bandstand concert. But even then, in the rickety days of skiffle, as Colin Hanton wildly beat the drums and John's lips enveloped the microphone as if he would swallow it altogether, there were stirrings, especially in the girls. But the boys eventually hit a wall, finding it hard to hit their stride without larger audiences. By the fall of 1959, they were desperate but determined to find even a small break, and willing to do anything to get some attention. Their music, much of it covering of the day's hits, was not unique, but as time would tell, their style was recognized, and not for the reasons that would make their success ingenious and universal in scope.

Before the frustrated genius of Paul and John would surface, ahead of the eventual harmony of style and range that would explode anywhere a radio was present, the Quarrymen were beginning to radiate an animated sexuality.

It was, in the early stages, a stirring. And it was so contagious that by the end of 1960, it was and would remain forever simply out of control. But before the new decade began, there were humble beginnings.

Very humble.

CHAPTER FOUR

SEE YOU AT THE JAC

"They were coffee-shop layabouts . . . just hanging around.
I never looked at them as a group but truants from school.
I became their manager; isn't that amazing?"
—Allan Williams, the Beatles' first manager

"What's all that bloody racket in the basement?"
—Cheniston Roland, photographer and member of the Jacaranda Club

A FORMER WATCH REPAIR SHOP AT 21 SLATER STREET IN LIVERPOOL IS, IN THE CURRENT DAY, THE POPULAR PUB THE JACARANDA. The club closed in 2011, but new owners have been trying to revive it. It certainly is a historic landmark by anyone's definition. The site was reconstructed by promoter Allan Williams in the fall of 1958 as a coffee bar and live-music venue. The geography was an excellent match for the boys, just blocks away from John and Stuart's studios at the Liverpool College of Art, and Paul and George's classrooms at the Liverpool Institute. They discovered the Jacaranda in the early part of October 1959 but had no real knowledge of its mythical qualities at first.

The jacaranda, for the record, is an exotic species of ornamental flowering tree native to South America but widely planted elsewhere for its beauty. Its scientific name is *Jacaranda mimosifolia*. Argentine author Alejandro Dolina immortalized the tree by describing a mythical jacaranda in Buenos Aires that could whistle songs on demand. Songwriters have even dedicated tracks to the blossoming blue jacaranda. Was this musical connection between the venue and the flowering tree a "sign"?

For Allan Williams, the Jac, as it came to be known, was also a transition. The man had a flair for enterprise, along with a Liverpudlian love for alcohol, and a cool command presence about him. Once an expert of drain cleaning and leak plugging, the former plumber morphed into a young, handsome, clever, and creatively devious promoter and club owner. And he would soon meet the boys who would turn him into a band manager, of sorts.

Williams, unlike most of the prudish club owners of the day, made it known that he would accept rockers, and offered his facilities as a play-and-practice, live-and-learn laboratory. The result? The Jac started drawing teenagers at night. Groups would gather there. Some, like the Quarrymen, would offer menial labor in return for rehearsal space. For the crafty Williams, it was a grand bargain. And so it was that the boys, aware of the attraction, arrived at the Jac in October 1959.

Williams had a voracious appetite for working people cheap. The former craftsman of the pipes sensed the boys' determination and passion. He gave them odd jobs refurbishing and cleaning up the place. A keen observer of raw artistic talent, Williams "commissioned" Stu and John to paint a mural for the ladies' room; it was perhaps their first and only truly commercial art assignments. In retrospect, the gig was likely humiliating for a serious artist like Stu. But there was a mission at hand, and the boys were determined to do anything to convince Williams to let them perform at the Jac. If that meant cleaning up, painting, or just hanging out with Williams and the Jac crowd, so be it.

As John told me years later, "We worked at this place [the Jac]. Did everything, you know, but kiss the guy's ass, which, Larry, I might have done to get us a break."

And that break was not necessarily forthcoming. Sam Leach, entrepreneur and the then-"Prince of Mathew Street"—the nightlife hub of Liverpool—gave me his observations years later of the early relationship between Williams and the boys.

"Allan Williams was a super promoter, but he never saw what was really in John's band in the beginning. He didn't see what it would be. He was amused by the boys, but hardly committed," Leach said. "It took others to convince him, but in the beginning, he probably violated child labor laws."

Williams faces me head-on in the lobby of the Hard Day's Night Hotel in Liverpool in 2011. It is 11 a.m. on a crisp winter morning and his glass is full of red wine.

"You know, Larry," he says,

YOU KNOW I USED THEM TO DECORATE THE TOILETS, AND THEY DID A
PRETTY GOOD JOB. BUT I HAD NO IDEA WHAT TO DO WITH THEM NEXT,
BECAUSE THEY WOULD SKIP CLASS AND JUST BECOME COFFEE SHOP
LAYABOUTS, BUMMING CIGARETTES OFF THE GIRLS AT THE COUNTER.
HARD TO BELIEVE THAT I WOULD SOMEDAY BECOME THEIR DOCTOR, OF
SORTS, WHEN WE HAD TO DEAL WITH ALL THE ERUPTIONS OF DISEASE
DURING THE NIGHTS AND DAYS IN HAMBURG. HARD TO BELIEVE. SO, I
REMEMBER JOHN COMING TO ME ONE DAY AND SAYING, "YOU KNOW WE
HAVE A GROUP, AND WE'VE BEEN REHEARSING HERE WHEN WE CAN." AND
THAT'S WHEN HE ASKED ME TO BE THEIR MANAGER. I HAD NEVER BEEN A
MANAGER, AND I THOUGHT IT WOULD BE INTERESTING. AND I SAID YES. I
THINK THEY WERE RATHER ALL SURPRISED.

While the boys—especially John, George, and Stu—kept busy (Paul
abhorred the work), Williams, a devotee of the beat generation and jazz, was
creating a two-headed monster. By day, businessmen came to the Jac to listen to jazz. At night, it became an early favorite of Liverpool teens into rock
'n' roll.

"It was a strange place, but in all reality, it became a social melting pot. The
well-dressed businessmen eyed the teenage girls. The girls, still in that wide-
eyed gaze before the sexual revolution was taking place, enjoyed the surroundings and the chance to get away for a few minutes, a few hours," Bill
Harry remembers. "The girls wanted a smoke and some coffee, and the stories they took with them would fill their minds and their fantasies for days."

John, Paul, George, and Stuart—a band without a drummer—shadowed
the artists at the Jac, cuddled intimately with female customers (some older
than them), cleaned sinks, and continued relentless rehearsals in the Jac's
basement.

The rehearsal sessions did not go unnoticed. One day Jac patron and photographer Cheniston Roland, stunned by the sound coming from below,
queried Williams. "What's all that bloody racket in the basement?"

"I said to him, 'You're not the first to complain. . . . They have a sense of direction. . . . I will get them some work when they improve,'" Williams tells me.

"Did you really believe that?" I ask.

"I don't remember," he says, and laughs heartily.

But he did come through for the boys, although at times reluctantly. The wary promoter started arranging gigs for the young band, including one daring and unusual assignment. On this infamous occasion, the boys provided backup music for a local stripper named Janice at another Williams-owned club, the Blue Angel. When word reached Aunt Mimi, it is reported by neighbors that the great aunt was speechless—a rarity—if not visibly distressed.

From October 1959 to May 1960, before the arrival of Janice the stripper, the boys went to school, pored through their homework in late afternoon, arrived at the Jac in the evening, and toiled as barely paid gofers for Williams, waiting for a break. George, quiet and soulful, would drink tea and indulge in a few sweets. Bill Harry, the future journalist-promoter, would delight in the Jac, especially the eats.

Years later, Harry talked to me about the times at the Jac. "We were poor. In those days, some tasty jam spread over the toast would cost a penny. John, Paul, George, and Stu weren't making any real money, so that spread of jam was a real treat, Larry, along with the girl-watching, of course."

The girl-watching would prove fateful to the intense, handsome, and devoutly intellectual Harry.

A classmate of John and Stu's at the Art Institute, who played an unsung but powerful role in the boys' ascent, Harry found the Jac an interesting place to be. It was a refuge for good company and a delightful place to meet people. One night he met a young woman named Virginia Sowry. Born in Yorkshire, Sowry was a comptometer operator for Woolworths. She soon abandoned the comptometer, a mechanical calculator, for the love of Bill. Soon Bill and Virginia would make more than love—creating *Mersey Beat*, a magazine that became the most significant music-news enterprise of its time. Hanging around the Jac also brought Bill Harry closer to his friends Stu and John.

"I knew John was talented. I knew Paul was amazing. With real humility, I must add that I sensed that there could be a future," exclaims the lifelong scribe and promotion man.

If the young writer was so confident, his level of confidence was rising faster than the Quarrymen were. While the Quarrymen toiled in an extravagant sweatshop, the boss of the coffeehouse was making his own waves. Inspired by a similar show in London, Williams launched an ill-fated arts festival. The boys were not invited to play. They were, as George would say later, "pissed."

The Quarrymen were languishing in the basement, fine-tuning their sound, yet they truly felt that they would be unseen and unheard—just another band.

Allan Williams was on a faster track. Working with gifted London agent Larry Parnes, he produced a large rock show at Liverpool Stadium. The boys, again, were not included on the bill. Instead they helped create floats and rather ordinary backdrops. They also watched the show with great interest because one of their favorite local bands was in the concert. Enter Rory Storm.

Many evenings at the Jac, the boys watched Rory Storm and the Hurricanes. They were Liverpool's hottest band, and they had something that the Quarrymen did not: a drummer. The percussionist's given name was Richard Starkey.

Rory, whose real name was Allan Caldwell, lived the ultimate irony. He had a stammer so severe that it disarmed even the most relaxed observer. But while Rory's stutter was disarming, so was the reaction of his audiences when, miraculously, he started singing and the stammer vanished.

Rory and the Hurricanes were part of the Liverpool Stadium concert. Their performance with established star Gene Vincent excited the Quarrymen. A Liverpool group they respected was on stage. On a big stage. May 3, 1960—the date of the Liverpool Stadium concert—was a day that set in motion a series of key events. For John's boys, the appearance of Rory and his group at the stadium was a shining symbol that local boys could succeed. They admired Rory, and he returned the favor in just a few months by making a temporary detour that opened a door for the boys.

Finally spring came, and with it, a crack in Williams's shoddy treatment of the boys. The band, with the help of part-time drummers, and now rebranded as the Silver Beetles, auditioned for big-time London band manager Larry Parnes and pop star Billy Fury. After the session, John Lennon, infused with joy, asked Fury for an autograph. By the end of the day, the Silver Beetles learned that they would travel on tour in Scotland as the backup band for Johnny Gentle, a popular rocker. Parnes and Fury liked their energy. It was their first serious gig, but as in life, ecstasy is often accompanied by seeds of doubt, and golden boy Larry Parnes insisted that the group drop the bass player, referring to Stu.

Sutcliffe, always the mysterious man on the side of the stage with the movie idol face, eyes hidden by sunglasses, used a technique of seeming to turn away from the audience. Parnes, according to Williams, was insistent that Stu had to vanish. In the flash of a few seconds, John said, "We are all or none." In reality, Stu Sutcliffe never really looked away from the audience; he just turned his body around in a rhythmic movement. John knew that. He was angry and outraged, and didn't hesitate to let the big-time Londoner know how he felt, with none of his real feelings ever left to the imagination. But the truth is, according to Bill Harry and others, that Parnes was not unhappy at all with Stuart. Parnes was more upset about the drummer, Tommy Moore, who was late for the audition.

But whatever the real reason for it, John's defiance in the face of a contemporary legend in the music world was part of his fabric, a sense of his continuing ability to speak frankly, even if it meant flirting with danger. There was a cockiness that put his energy into overdrive, regardless of the consequences. I saw that on several occasions during the first Beatles tour of North America when he confronted powerful Kansas City businessman Charles O. Finley, owner of the local pro baseball team and promoter of the band's appearance in that city. Much to the chagrin of manager Brian Epstein, John stared down the millionaire and steadfastly refused his request that the band sing a "few extra songs." Finley quickly offered more money, and John immediately answered, "No, Chuck. Not enough [money], man. We won't do it." Finley upped the price again, and a horrified Epstein, flushed with embarrassment, saw John look the storied baseball owner in the eye and say, "Chuck, no fucking way." At that point, Finley left the room in anger. Epstein, his honor shattered by John's outburst, pleaded with the group to at least sing one extra song. That song, "Kansas City," was the only exception to their repertoire on the famous 1964 tour. On another occasion of John's directness, in 1965, I saw a young woman, a local reporter on the tarmac in Kansas City, shout out at him, "Are you cheating on your wife?" And I saw John turn and slap her in the face. A few minutes later I said, "What's wrong with you? That was stupid. Why didn't you just move on?" He answered, "Why not, Larry? She was stupid." But he did admit later that I was right. In Seattle, it was John who led the three others in urinating on the carpets of their suite, but only after discovering that someone had planned to cut up the rugs and sell them. Even Paul, the ever-polite, do-it-right statesman of the band, joined in the soil fest.

Along with his ability to rage, John had a great sense of loyalty and an intense pride in sharing the spotlight. It was, after all, John who welcomed young Paul McCartney into his band in 1957.

"He was an amazing guitar man," John reminisced to me backstage in 1965. "He also had this ability to play to the audience. Paul brought in George, who was much more serious than both of us about the guitar. And I brought in Stu, Larry. And we began the journey."

When John took his Three Musketeers, all-for-one-and-one-for-all stance against Parnes, he was nineteen years old. He risked the big break, the Scotland tour, to keep his group together. Although their future together would face insurmountable obstacles, on that fateful day in the spring of 1960, John Lennon wasn't even thinking about going without Stu Sutcliffe.

After John's display of outright loyalty, Paul nodded his head in agreement, and George quietly did the same. For that moment, at least, Stu was for keeps. Although accounts of this event are conflicting, John was always defending and supporting his merry band.

Not for keeps was the band's name, the Quarrymen. Hoping for just the chance that Parnes was providing, the boys had spent considerable time contemplating the moniker to accompany their act. There are many stories of how the boys came to be named "the Beatles," but despite myth and mystery, only two theories stand the test of time. Faced with the prospect of a real touring gig, the Quarrymen decided at that point to change their name. Led again by John, they considered a name. Stuart was obsessed with the 1953 movie *The Wild One*, starring Marlon Brando. The saga of motorcycle gangs included a rival gang known as "the Beetles." Ironically, the film was banned in Great Britain for fourteen years.

The second theory of evolution came from John and Paul's adoration of Buddy Holly and the Crickets.

Bill Harry—the high commissioner of the "keeping the record straight" bureau—remembers the steps that led the boys from the Quarrymen to the Beatles:

I THINK IT WAS JUNE 1960; THEY STARTED TOSSING AROUND "JOHNNY AND THE MOON DOGS." NO, THAT WASN'T GOING TO BE IT. THEN STUART AND JOHN AND ROYSTON ELLIS, THE BEAT POET, WERE SITTING THERE CHATTING [WHEN] JOHN AND STUART SAID THEY WOULD LIKE TO COME UP WITH SOME SORT OF NAME. STUART SAID, "HOW ABOUT SOMETHING LIKE BUDDY HOLLY'S 'THE CRICKETS'?" BECAUSE, AS THE QUARRYMEN, THEY PLAYED A LOT OF BUDDY HOLLY TUNES. SO, THEY THOUGHT, "OKAY, THAT MIGHT WORK—INSECTS. OKAY, BEETLES." THEN JOHN SAID, "WHY NOT BEATLES WITH AN 'A' FOR THE BEAT GENERATION?" "OKAY, THE BEATLES."

But, Harry remembers, it didn't stick right away.

"They still thought at the time this name, the 'Beatles,' was a bit too punchy because at the time there was a fad for longer names. So originally they went out as the Silver Beetles, the Silver Beatles, the Beatles, and the Silver Beats. But by August 1960, they said let's just be the Beatles. So this was confirmed—the Beatles—by John and Stuart as the official name of the band in August 1960."

And so, if Chubby Checker emerged after Fats Domino, and if Buddy Holly had the Crickets, why couldn't the Quarrymen be called the Beetles, or the Beatles? And the Quarrymen? The name would remain forever legendary as the name of John Lennon's original group.

There was other business to attend to, mainly figuring out a sneaky escape from school to get to the Scotland gig with Johnny Gentle. This would take some imagination. George had left Paul behind at school and was working as an electrician's apprentice. While George took his vacation early, John and Stu just decided to skip classes, declaring that no one would notice. Paul, on the other hand, opted for deception, advising his parents that his school had given students time off to prepare for testing. His charm and guile, adored by millions for decades to come, had worked on his own family. It was a difficult moment for young Paul, who was close to his dad, but in retrospect, it was an important, if fleeting, moment.

When the boys showed up for the Scotland gig to back up Johnny Gentle, they were nervous and poorly dressed. Shaken up by an accident in their van en route to the venue, a mishap that dampened their spirits, the boys moved on to their first out-of-town gig. Their performance was well received by the audiences, but not memorable, except by the star. Gentle was impressed and passed the word on to all of his friends.

The Silver Beetles returned to Liverpool, depressed at their lack of good gigs, but soldiered on by doing shows on the Wirral Peninsula, across the Mersey from Liverpool, at venues like the Grosvenor Ballroom, the Neston Institute, and Lathom Hall in Seaford. They continued accepting appearances for a handful of pounds. There was little gratification and a lot of internal strife. Paul and George were complaining to John that Stu was contributing little, but John, loyal to the bone, would have none of it. Despite the band's being limited to unheralded appearances in church and social halls after the Scotland tour, word was starting to spread about the underdressed, chain-smoking lads.

Yet the Silver Beatles (they inserted the "a" in July 1960) were unaware that teenagers in Liverpool were spreading the word.

Derek Taylor was working in Manchester when he first heard of the Quarrymen/Silver Beatles.

During the 1964 tour, the Beatles press officer told me, "There was talk of a bunch of boys, and a lot of talk from the girls. At first, the kids were talking about a dance band. They just couldn't get enough of them. These guys were turning on little teenage girls, just by being raw and, I might add, a kind of sexual sensation."

It would be years before Liverpool would see the Beatles as the world saw them. And in the beginning, the band had a purely physical impact. Professor Michael Brocken, the Beatles scholar at Liverpool's Hope University, says, "Before they had a record deal, the people that came to see them were from both north and south Liverpool, in the days when they played here and there and were regarded as a relatively good group to whom people could dance. They weren't necessarily fans, but they knew the Beatles could play."

Brocken, who is the preeminent scholar of the history of Merseyside music, says that even in 1961 and 1962, the Beatles were not the favorite musical group in Liverpool, but they were stirring up feelings like few people could—not as great composers or writers yet, but as musicians with an animalistic instinct for the power of dance.

ONE OF THE PARTIALLY MISCONCEIVED HIDDEN NOTIONS IN THE DAY WAS THAT, TO THE LOCAL PEOPLE, THEY WERE A DAMN GOOD BAND IN 1961–62, BUT THEY WERE GOOD, NOT NECESSARILY BECAUSE THEY TURNED EVERYONE INTO BEATLES FANS—WHAT WE REGARD AS BEATLEMANIA NOW—BUT THEY WERE REGARDED AS A BAND THAT WOULD GET THE PEOPLE UP AND DANCING. AND THEY TOOK REQUESTS. . . . IT WASN'T LIKE YOU GO TO A CONCERT AND SEE A BAND LIKE PINK FLOYD, AND JUST SAT AND WATCHED. PEOPLE WENT TO DANCE, TO MOVE. THE ATMOSPHERE WAS USUALLY FAIRLY INTERACTIVE WITH THE BAND. YOU HAVE TO REMEMBER, DANCERS RULED IN THOSE DAYS. THE BEATLES FAN BASE WAS FORMED, INITIALLY, ABOUT THE PRAGMATIC POTENTIAL OF GETTING PEOPLE UP [ON THEIR FEET].

Colin Hall, a young teenager, witnessed firsthand the band's power to rouse the internal stirrings of young girls and boys. Hall, who would fatefully become the curator of Mendips, the Lennon home on Menlove Avenue, went to an early concert at the Empire Theater. He remembers the fever, and mostly, the girls:

"I had been hearing about them. I was shocked but kind of excited. It was with wild abandon. They [the girls] were just out of it with no inhibition. They were beside themselves with hysteria. I grew up thinking that girls didn't get dirty and climb trees, etc., and so to see such unbridled ecstasy was pretty much life-changing as much as the music for me."

To Hall and his friends, it was an awakening.

IT WAS THE THRILL OF THE MUSIC AND THE ENERGY THEY RELEASED IN YOU. IT WAS A CELEBRATION OF BEING YOUNG. I CAN SEE THAT THE GIRLS WENT CRAZY BECAUSE IT IS THE KIND OF MUSIC THAT ELEVATES. IT WAS THAT KIND OF MUSIC THAT MADE THEM STAND OUT FROM THE CROWD. THE MUSIC HAD SUCH A STRONG BEAT AND IT WAS SO POWERFUL . . . COMPELLING ALMOST. THE PROXIMITY TO THE MUSIC IS SUCH A STRONG PHYSICAL AND INTIMATE EXPERIENCE. IT WAS THE MUSIC THAT TOLD YOU THAT YOU WERE YOUNG. IT WAS THE MUSIC THAT MIRRORED SOMETHING WITHIN YOU, THAT DRIVING THING THAT YOU HAVE WHEN YOU'RE YOUNG—YOU CAN DO ANYTHING, YOU'RE INVINCIBLE. IT OPENED A WHOLE NEW WORLD; IT WAS SOCIAL AT A TIME WHEN EVERYTHING WAS SUPPRESSED.

So, that animal-like craving of the fans would be the initial attraction—not the music—that remains the band's primary legacy. When the physical, the musical, and the sexual combined to create stardom, the greatest band in history would never be remembered as a dance band that started "getting people up," as Professor Brocken would say.

Bob Bonis, the Beatles' tour manager in America from 1964 through 1966, would stand by the stages with me, taking pictures and marveling at their appeal. We would watch Paul flirt with 20,000 fans. He would smile and look adoring, while John hugged the microphone, and George put his head at an angle, listening to the music. Partially hidden by the drum set, Ringo bounced up and down. Along with Paul, he grinned from ear to ear. So many of those fans truly believed that each one of them, their favorite, was singing to them.

"You know," Bonis would say in his New York accent, "these guys are amazing. They are electric. I mean, look at those girls. I think the girls want them, if you know what I mean, but what makes it so unstoppable . . . is the music. You mix the music with the men, and what have you got? Hysteria."

The music would be discovered. But first it was the dancers who began to notice the passion of the newly named Silver Beatles in 1960. But it should be noted that, even on those North American tours, some of the obsessed girls and boys staring into the eyes of the Beatles were also dancing feverishly to the rhythms. The kids tried to hide their naked emotions, at first in the small clubs, and later on the big-time tours, but they rarely held back. But it was always a two-way deal. The boys, even before Pete Best, before Ringo, before Brian Epstein, and in the flush of close-up contact with teenagers just like them, felt the love and responded in kind, mostly with smiles and sexual body language.

The man this author calls the Prince of Mathew Street, Sam Leach, felt the stirrings. He saw them, and acted as quickly as he could.

In January 1961, he was trying to find a band to open a new club, the Casanova. He decided to check out the boys, who were playing at a low-rent location, the Hamilton club. As they were known to do, the kids, dancers all, broke out in fistfights on the dance floor. Much to Leach's surprise, the fists stopped pounding when the boys started playing,. Leach, ever the promoter, decided to act quickly.

Leach, his eyes staring straight ahead, breaks out in a smile. The memories make him even more animated. His head rocks up and down as he recalls the patrons at the club.

"I wasn't going to miss this. . . . First time I ever saw that happen. I literally followed them into the converted-toilet dressing room and started up a conversation with them, directed at Paul and John, as I recall. I offered them eight pounds, about twelve dollars, a day to play at the Casanova. I told them they were going to be as big as Elvis. John looked at me. His eyes rolled."

Leach, a man who loved being part of the Merseyside music revolution, declares that he knew inside, just by watching them, the fame that lay ahead for the boys.

Bigger than Elvis? That was impossible, wasn't it? Even the publicly confident John Lennon was incredulous at the statement.

Leach says, "He turned his head around, grimaced, and looked at me like I was mental."

John, and especially Paul, talked to me in 1972 about the probability of their success, which in those days looked like an impossibility. But unlike their first full-time drummer, Pete Best, and his eventual replacement, "Richie" from Rory Storm's group, and the loyal but otherwise free-spirited Sutcliffe, the two were anxious optimists.

"We always thought we had a chance, but we had to grow, get bleeping better," John said. "Back in 1960, it looked bleak, my friend, fucking bleak until a door was opened. And even then, who knew? I didn't."

Paul was more hopeful.

"The thing is, you know, that our families, even our friends, were happy, but, you know, we were just another band. But I felt we were getting a little better."

So, in the summer of 1960, depressed, almost deflated, John, Paul, George, and Stu did not know what was happening around them. They didn't even know that the kids who saw them perform in church halls and community centers and all those long-ago venues were starting to spread the word, and that mild fever was spreading. The boys could feel the tension in the rooms, but they were still waiting for a break that would set them free. Discouraged and hoping for that opportunity, they continued waiting for a door to open.

Meanwhile, Allan Williams had been scouting out the scene in the music-starved city of Hamburg, Germany. What he saw was a red-light district, flooded with prostitutes and a few nightclubs reverberating with a heavy beat and the words of fifties rock sung in German and English.

Williams will readily admit that he had no thoughts of bringing the painters of the ladies' room at the Jac to Hamburg. But again, a door would need to open.

And ironically, it was Rory Storm and the Hurricanes, with their sad-faced but enthusiastic drummer, "Richie," who opened it.

CHAPTER FIVE

PEN PAL #1—BILL HARRY

"'The Beatles are the stuff that screams are made of. . . .'
That's what Bob Wooler wrote. . . . I don't think
anything like this will ever happen again."
—Bill Harry, recalling a famous quote from *Mersey Beat*

THE NEXT CENTURY WOULD HAVE THE INTERNET, FACEBOOK, AND TWITTER, but in the early 1960s, during the cloudy dawn of the boys' march to greatness, there was Bill Harry—the inventor of social networking for the boys in the bands.

Bill Harry was all about dramatic journalism and exciting writing, and was also a master of promotion. It was quite a package for a young kid who really never had a chance, or so his neighbors and the kids who bullied him thought. Now in the twilight of his life, Harry knows what lives he shaped, even if some of the stars he made have a very short memory. At the 2010 salute to John Lennon in Liverpool, Bill Harry received an invitation, only to be sent away at the stage door into the general-admission crowd. Bill Harry? Impossible. No one did more to accelerate the path of the Beatles. But Harry, a philosophical man with a keen photographic memory, passed it off as a slight of time and ignorance, for in reality, he knows the truth.

Destiny called him, or was it the other way around? The record is there, even if the surviving Beatles don't remember, or respect it. After all, it was Harry who arranged for Brian Epstein to go to the smoky Cavern to meet the Beatles for the first time.

He savored his many talks, some of them under a mild buzz of alcohol, with the Art Institute's version of the beat generation. He nursed and nourished his ambition to publish the music scene, but did he know that he would awaken not just a city, but the entire planet?

His ambition and determination had allowed him to rise up from the poorest of neighborhoods near the Liverpool docks, where he was beaten to a pulp by classmates, and received routine corporal punishment from the priests at his school. His father died young, and his mother, mired in poverty, scraped for the money to send him elsewhere; scholarships provided the rest. Yet, through his young learning years, the boy had no electricity in his home. He read comic books and sketched by candlelight, and became an avid fan of science fiction. His life would later resemble a work of fiction. This diminutive and soft-spoken young boy, with an immense vocabulary and a gift for writing, would travel the world with the movers and shakers of rock music. But first, with the power of the pen and a rare insight into human nature, he would propel the boys to international fame.

Many individuals will gladly and convincingly credit themselves with aiding and abetting the boys' ascent, but very few can claim a major piece of their rise. Bill Harry is the real deal, and an unlikely one at that.

Bill Harry could smell it, even in the dark wood panels of the eighteenth-century pub, Ye Cracke. He could see it in John Lennon's conviction; in Cynthia, sitting next to John, with admiring glances; in the gentle face of Stuart. Few people really can sense history being shaped, but like all teenagers, Harry was fixated on a dream, and the dream master was sitting across from him.

He would soon come to know George and Paul, who went to school next door to the art school at the Liverpool Institute. He viewed them as less articulate than the semi-Bohemian John, yet intense in their desire to break through. But in the beginning, and through his life, there was always a fierce public loyalty and private dedication to John. And Harry loved the talking part.

Back in the art school days, John Lennon—poet, guitar man, and general troublemaker—held forth in a side room of Ye Cracke, also known as a public house, or watering hole, for the school's young elite. Dubbed the "war room," the space was transformed into John's version of a Churchill-like command center. After all, John was in command as he held forth with a pint in hand, maybe something stronger, discussing the state of the world and reading his poetry to the young journalist and friend, Bill Harry. John's future wife Cynthia would share in the conversation. It is an interesting contrast that while American teenagers gathered at drive-ins for milk shakes and Elvis music, the future cultural leaders of Britain gathered in pubs.

Harry smiles wistfully as he remembers the first meeting with the young and brazen John. It was 1958.

"I was sitting in the college canteen. I looked up and saw this guy stride in. I said, 'My God, who is that?' He had a DA haircut."

The DA, or "duck ass," haircut was famously popular in the fifties. If you want to try it now, comb your hair back around the sides of your head, then make a part down the middle of the back. The look, favored by Elvis Presley and many of this author's high school classmates, resembled the rear end of a duck.

Harry continues,

HE WORE TEDDY BOY–TYPE CLOTHES. ALL THE ART STUDENTS WOULD WEAR DUFFER COATS IN GRAY, FAWN, OR BLACK. THEY ALL HAD TURTLE-NECK SWEATERS, EITHER BLACK, GRAY, OR NAVY BLUE. I SAID TO MYSELF, THE ART STUDENTS ARE SUPPOSED TO BE THE BOHEMIANS, YET HE IS THE REBEL. I'VE GOT TO GET TO KNOW HIM. HIS WHOLE PRESENCE WAS LIKE, "WOW!" SO I GOT TO KNOW HIM AND INTRODUCED HIM TO STUART. AFTER THAT, THE FOUR OF US WOULD DO EVERYTHING TOGETHER. WE WENT TO PARTIES, PUBS TOGETHER. WE SPENT A LOT OF TIME AT YE CRACKE.

"The four of us" included Rod Murray, Stuart's roommate and best friend at the time. Harry enjoyed Rod's company. The renegade four formed the nucleus of what would become a powerful teenage speaking and drinking club. The pub was the heart and soul of their conversations.

Ye Cracke is a few steps up Rice Street, just off of Hope Street, near the Liverpool John Moores University (formerly the Art College) where Colin Fallows is a professor of sound and visual arts. Fallows is no ordinary professor; he's a man who studies the past and weaves its fabric into the future. It is Fallows who brought Stu Sutcliffe's girlfriend Astrid Kirchherr's amazing photo retrospective to Liverpool in 2010–2011. It is Fallows who points out the physical nuances of the art school, such as the actual chair that John sat in during classes where he would glance over at Cynthia, sometimes with a nervous smile, other times with the bravado of a hunter. Fallows notes the small courtyard through which Paul and George would travel quickly from their school, the Liverpool Institute for Boys, into the lower level of the Art Institute.

Fallows is a man who understands the Art Institute's physical insides, and the real meaning of art to the artists' world of popular music.

He beams with pride when he remembers the work of Stu Sutcliffe, the young artist and writer Bill Harry, and the direct connection between his institution, the Beatles, and so much of the popular music that preceded and followed them.

"In that day," Fallows remembers, "British art schools were an incubator for many rock stars. Almost all of them, almost all the big ones, were artists. Rock and art, a very significant connection."

Harry, an artist on canvas as well as the artist of one of the world's greatest verbal tapestries, agrees: "You can follow the beat generation. You can remember the days at Ye Cracke. All of it tied together. Rock and art. Art and rock."

Bill Harry remembers the makeshift rehearsals when George and Paul would join John in the art school canteen; Stuart often stayed behind, drawing.

As life model June Furlong confirms, "Young Mr. Lennon was very talented, but the real student of art was Stuart Sutcliffe. He was the man with talent."

Bill Harry even suggested, not too subtly, that Stuart was a better artist than a bass guitarist. His advice to Stuart: paint, and paint more. Harry is a real gadfly when it comes to making a point. Through the years, he has caused tremors in the minds of journalists, serving as the ultimate proofreader and arbiter of truth and fiction in the early life of the Beatles.

Harry's humble beginnings, his rise from poverty to worldly knowledge, may have disguised his ability to seek out and know people just like him.

After cultivating a warm and relaxed relationship with Stuart and John, and a good one with Paul and George, young Harry, inspired by the Dissenters, the group that met at Ye Cracke and other watering holes, began to survey the scene. By 1959, there were five hundred bands playing skiffle, jazz, and emerging rock in Liverpool. But there was little coverage in the established media of John's young band, and the other troubadours. Harry had an idea.

"I wanted to do a magazine that was part traditional jazz and modern jazz, called *Stories of 52nd Street*. I knew Sam Leach from Storyville Jazz Club, so I asked Sam if he would front the money, and he said he would get me the money I needed through the people from the club. So [my girlfriend] Virginia and I went up there. He was not there, and this happened four times. And I got dismayed. Now it was 1960."

The relationship with Bill Harry and Sam Leach has been strained for years, but never was it so intensely troubled as in 1960.

Leach forgot to connect. Leach would later tell me, "What a mess that was. I would have tripled my investment. Who knew what would happen?" A lot of people still ask that question in Liverpool today.

Harry *knew*. Although he had the greatest respect for Leach, he decided to look elsewhere and expand his outlook.

"I also wanted to do a rock magazine," Harry explains. "I wanted to [cover] other bands, too, like Gerry and the Pacemakers, Buddy Holly. I also wanted to do a music newspaper. So Virginia gave up her job and she lent me fifty pounds to do the magazine, newspaper, whatever. At that time, I finished the art-design course and I was supposed to travel to Europe, but I used the money as part of the startup."

The loan was repaid with decades of marriage, a partnership of love, long nights at the office, insightful news gathering, and ink-stained hands. The name of the newspaper/magazine became *Mersey Beat*. It was a catchy name, based on Harry's view of a policeman "on the beat."

The couple's *Mersey Beat* launched on July 6, 1961. Five thousand copies were printed. Five thousand copies were sold. Among the first distributors (and columnists) was Brian Epstein, the music merchant. Epstein's fascination with the music scene, sparked by *Mersey Beat*, would lead him to uncharted worlds of excitement. In a way, with its up-to-the-minute reporting, lively articles, and recurring themes of teenager entitlement to love, dance, and rock 'n' roll, *Mersey Beat* was the early-sixties version of social networking.

For the boys, *Mersey Beat* was, as they say in the record business, solid gold. Bill Harry soon realized that his friend John's band was ascending, and he covered that ascent with wild abandon. Yet, despite his love for Mersey music and the boy Beatles, Harry often let others sing their praises.

Bill quickly became a reporter's editor. Overwhelmed by John's poetry and creative writing, he commissioned John to write the first autobiography of the Beatles. These are the founder's words in the piece, titled "Being a Short Diversion on the Dubious Origins of Beatles (Translated from the John Lennon)":

ONCE UPON A TIME THERE WERE THREE LITTLE BOYS CALLED JOHN, GEORGE AND PAUL, BY NAME CHRISTENED. THEY DECIDED TO GET TOGETHER BECAUSE THEY WERE THE GETTING TOGETHER TYPE. WHEN THEY WERE TOGETHER THEY WONDERED WHAT FOR AFTER ALL, WHAT FOR? SO ALL OF A SUDDEN THEY GREW GUITARS AND FASHIONED A NOISE. FUNNILY ENOUGH, NO ONE WAS INTERESTED, LEAST OF ALL THE THREE LITTLE MEN. SO-O-O-O ON DISCOVERING A FOURTH LITTLE EVEN LITTLER MAN CALLED STUART SUTCLIFFE RUNNING ABOUT THEM THEY SAID, QUITE "SONNY GET A BASS GUITAR AND YOU WILL BE ALRIGHT" AND HE DID— BUT HE WASN'T ALRIGHT BECAUSE HE COULDN'T PLAY IT. SO THEY SAT ON HIM WITH COMFORT 'TIL HE COULD PLAY. STILL THERE WAS NO BEAT, AND A KINDLY OLD MAN SAID, QUOTE "THOU HAST NOT DRUMS!" WE HAD NO DRUMS! THEY COFFED. SO A SERIES OF DRUMS CAME AND WENT AND CAME.

SUDDENLY, IN SCOTLAND, TOURING WITH JOHNNY GENTLE, THE GROUP (CALLED THE BEATLES CALLED) DISCOVERED THEY HAD NOT A VERY NICE SOUND—BECAUSE THEY HAD NO AMPLIFIERS. THEY GOT SOME. MANY PEOPLE ASK WHAT ARE BEATLES? WHY BEATLES? UGH, BEATLES, HOW DID THE NAME ARRIVE? SO WE WILL TELL YOU. IT CAME IN A VISION—A MAN APPEARED ON A FLAMING PIE AND SAID UNTO THEM "FROM THIS DAY ON YOU ARE BEATLES WITH AN 'A.'" THANK YOU, MISTER MAN, THEY SAID, THANKING HIM. AND THEN A MAN WITH A BEARD CUT OFF SAID—WILL YOU GO TO GERMANY (HAMBURG) AND PLAY MIGHTY ROCK FOR THE PEASANTS FOR MONEY? AND WE SAID WE WOULD PLAY MIGHTY ANYTHING FOR MONEY.

BUT BEFORE WE COULD GO WE HAD TO GROW A DRUMMER, SO WE GREW ONE IN WEST DERBY IN A CLUB CALLED SOME CASBAH AND HIS TROUBLE WAS PETE BEST. WE CALLED "HELLO PETE, COME OFF TO GERMANY!" "YES!" ZOOOOOM. AFTER A FEW MONTHS, PETER AND PAUL (WHO IS CALLED MCARTREY, SON OF JIM MCARTREY, HIS FATHER) LIT A KINO (CINEMA) AND THE GERMAN POLICE SAID "BAD BEATLES, YOU MUST GO HOME AND LIGHT YOUR ENGLISH CINEMAS." ZOOOOOM, HALF A GROUP. BUT BEFORE EVEN THIS, THE GESTAPO HAD TAKEN MY FRIEND LITTLE GEORGE HARRISON (OF SPEKE) AWAY BECAUSE HE WAS ONLY TWELVE AND TOO YOUNG TO VOTE IN GERMANY; BUT AFTER TWO MONTHS IN ENGLAND HE GREW EIGHTEEN AND THE GESTAPOES SAID "YOU CAN COME." SO SUDDENLY ALL BACK IN LIVERPOOL VILLAGE WERE MANY GROUPS PLAYING IN GREY SUITS AND JIM SAID "WHY HAVE YOU NO GREY SUITS?" "WE DON'T LIKE THEM, JIM" WE SAID, SPEAKING TO JIM.

AFTER PLAYING IN THE CLUBS A BIT, EVERYONE SAID "GO TO GERMANY!" SO WE ARE. ZOOOOOM STUART GONE. ZOOM ZOOM JOHN (OF WOOLTON) GEORGE (OF SPEKE) PETER AND PAUL ZOOM ZOOM. ALL OF THEM GONE. THANK YOU CLUB MEMBERS, FROM JOHN AND GEORGE (WHAT ARE FRIENDS).

John was always a man who enjoyed intriguing his audience. So in the interest of curiosity and history, Bill Harry offers an interpretation of the first Beatles biography:

"The man with the beard cut off is Allan Williams, he of the Jacaranda Club, who first booked them in Hamburg [at slave-labor rates and conditions]. . . . The Casbah was a club . . . in West Derby . . . run by Mona Best, Pete's mother. It was truly the first residence of the Quarrymen/Beatles, their first club."

Smiling, with a sense of great nostalgia, Harry remembers some other Lennon signals, which caused an editorial nightmare.

JOHN'S PECULIAR SPELLING OF PAUL'S NAME [MCARTREY] MADE ME BELIEVE IT WAS HIS REAL NAME, SO I USED IT IN *MERSEY BEAT* FOR A WHILE. AS FAR AS THE "GESTAPO," IT WAS A REFERENCE TO THE GERMAN ALIENS

POLICE WHO FORCED GEORGE TO GO HOME TO LIVERPOOL BECAUSE HE WAS NOT YET EIGHTEEN. "GREY SUITS" WAS A HIT ON THE OTHER LIVERPOOL GROUPS, SINCE THE BEATLES, POST-HAMBURG, WERE IN BLACK LEATHER. ONE OTHER THING, IT WAS A THRILL FOR ME TO SEE THAT THIS PIECE, IN *MERSEY BEAT*, INSPIRED PAUL MCCARTNEY FOR HIS 1997 ALBUM, *FLAMING PIE*.

WHAT HAPPENED IN THE SECOND EDITION [OF *MERSEY BEAT*] WAS NOTHING SHORT OF AMAZING. THE CAVERN'S DEEJAY, BOB WOOLER, WROTE A LANDMARK PIECE ON JOHN, PAUL, GEORGE, AND PETE. SEVERAL WORDS STAND OUT, WORDS THAT REFLECTED THE GROWING FEVER. "THE BEATLES," HE SAID, "ARE THE STUFF THAT SCREAMS ARE MADE OF. . . . I DON'T THINK ANYTHING LIKE THIS WILL EVER HAPPEN AGAIN."

Wooler's article, along with coverage of so many of the Merseyside bands, helped establish *Mersey Beat* as the publication of record for the music fanatics of the early 1960s. The paper became a twice-a-month chronicler of local music history, with a heavy accent on the Beatles. *Mersey Beat* clearly helped propel the Beatles, and the Beatles fueled the sales of *Mersey Beat*. It was a marriage of press and public relations rarely seen in England, or any other country. And Harry's provocative readers' polls would make big news for the Beatles, as Harry explains in a startling admission later in this book.

News manipulation? Puffed-up journalism? No question about it. But Harry was also careful, despite being the Beatles' biggest cheerleader, to promote as many bands as possible. And when it came to the Ye Cracke crowd, he had exclusives. Did you know that Paul McCartney was a "reliable source"?

Harry remembers, "Yes, it was Paul that was the perfect PR person for me when he went to Paris with John, and to Hamburg, and he would write me all about it. He sent me all the stuff for *Mersey Beat* that was always so helpful to me. Although I was publishing all John's stuff, I now had Paul's stuff, as well. I was so pleased."

"Was his stuff detailed?" I ask.

"Yes," Harry replies. "But he put a good spin on everything, especially the crowd reaction." This author has always believed that Paul would have been a great journalist. In fact, he probably is, considering the uncommon talent he has had for creating his own imagery and controlling the message.

Paul was such a great "foreign correspondent" for *Mersey Beat* that Harry and Sowry were covered on every Beatles trip. Like George Harrison's ghost-written columns from North America in 1964 for a London newspaper, Paul's "reporting" was invaluable to Harry and his staff.

Mersey Beat was published through 1965. In 1964, Epstein bought a piece of the magazine, tried to turn it national, and partnered with Harry, but Harry resigned when he lost editorial control. It was a falling-out, no question about it, and it precipitated the end of the publication.

Bill Harry continued as a writer for national publications but remained in close touch with his friends from Ye Cracke and the Art Institute. He and Sowry then moved to London, where this child of poverty emerged as one of the most successful promotion operatives in music history. His clients included Pink Floyd, Jethro Tull, Procol Harum, David Bowie, and Led Zeppelin, among many others. In 1994, the British Academy of Songwriters, Composers, and Authors presented him with its Lifetime Achievement Award.

From the youthful sessions at Ye Cracke to the dark and sometimes primitive night spots of Merseyside, Harry left his mark. He also wrote twenty-three books. Mostly, though, he will be remembered for his guile and marketing genius in producing *Mersey Beat*, and for providing a bigger stage for his friend John and his Beatles.

Like most good reporters, he could sense news happening before anyone else. In 1962, he wrote a piece titled "Take a Look Up North," urging A&R (artists and repertoire) men to come to Liverpool and check out the spectacular music scene. It was a spirited piece, with the statistics and brief history to back up his claims.

Not one of London's record companies took his advice.

To the fans of popular music, Harry's books are a treasure. To the young people of the Art Institute, Harry was known for two talents: writing science fiction and looking east to the beat generation in New York City.

As part of my preparation in writing this book, I recorded numerous long interviews on tape that I quote throughout, wherever specific lines fit with a particular subject. The following interview with Bill Harry, however, so authentically and completely describes the time, the place, and the people of Liverpool, that I want the reader to have the opportunity to read his complete story, unedited:

My own involvement with the scene began in 1958, while I was attending Liverpool College of Art. I was asked to contribute to a magazine produced by the local music store, Frank Hessy. Mr. Hesselberg, the owner, insisted on the rather uncommercial title, Frank Comments, but gave complete editorial freedom in all other respects. I designed the covers and produced interior illustrations, reviewed local events, wrote about jazz legends such as Bunk Johnson, and even penned a science-fiction jazz serial.

In the meantime, Stuart Sutcliffe and John Lennon were amongst my closest friends and we used to spend a great deal of time together, mainly discussing the subjects young people discuss—what the future held, the latest books and films, art, academic life, and so on.

John had a group and two of its members, Paul McCartney and George Harrison, were pupils of Liverpool Institute, which was situated next door to the college. They used to come to our canteen during lunch breaks and also rehearsed in the life rooms. Stu and I were members of the Students' Union Committee and put forward the proposal that we use students' funds to buy a PA system, which John's group could use when they appeared at our college dances.

I referred to them as the "college band" at the time, and they were booked regularly for our dances as support to headliners such as the Merseysippi Jazz Band.

Skiffle music had been popular for the last couple of years, and I used to study the history of American folk music and railway songs at Picton Library, in addition to producing a duplicated magazine at the college, simply called Jazz.

WITH THE EXPERIENCE OF EDITING A NUMBER OF FAN MAGAZINES BEHIND ME, MY INVOLVEMENT WITH *FRANK COMMENTS*, MY ASSOCIATION WITH THEIR PRINTERS, JAMES E. JAMES, AND STUDIES IN TYPOGRAPHY, PRINTING, AND NEWSPAPER DESIGN AND LAYOUT AT THE COLLEGE, I HAD VISIONS OF PRODUCING A MAGAZINE CALLED STORYVILLE & 52ND STREET.

ONE EVENING, WE ALL WENT ALONG TO LIVERPOOL UNIVERSITY TO HEAR A POETRY READING BY ROYSTON ELLIS. LATER, AT THE LOCAL ART COLLEGE DRINKING HOLE YE CRACKE, IN A DISCUSSION WITH JOHN, STU, AND ROD MURRAY, I POINTED OUT THAT ELLIS, IN COMMON WITH A LOT OF OTHER POETS, WAS INSPIRED BY THE AMERICAN BEAT POETS SUCH AS LAWRENCE FERLINGHETTI, ALLEN GINSBERG, AND GREGORY CORSO. MY FEELING WAS THAT PEOPLE WERE MORE LIKELY TO STRETCH THEMSELVES CREATIVELY BY EXPRESSING THEIR OWN ENVIRONMENT AND EXPERIENCE RATHER THAN BY COPYING SOMEONE ELSE'S. I SUGGESTED THAT WE SHOULD USE OUR CREATIVE TALENTS TO EXPRESS WHAT WE WERE PER-SONALLY INVOLVED IN, THAT WE SHOULD TAKE A VOW TO MAKE LIVERPOOL FAMOUS: JOHN WITH HIS MUSIC, STU AND ROD WITH THEIR PAINTING, AND MYSELF BY WRITING ABOUT THE CITY. I EVEN SUGGESTED THAT WE CALL OURSELVES THE DISSENTERS.

AT ONE TIME, STU AND I WERE GOING TO PRODUCE A BOOK ABOUT LIVERPOOL. I WOULD WRITE ABOUT INTERESTING AND UNUSUAL FACETS OF THE CITY AND ITS PEOPLE, AND HE WOULD ILLUSTRATE IT. WE NEVER DID THE BOOK, BUT THE SEEDS OF *MERSEY BEAT* WERE SOWN.

IN ADDITION TO YE CRACKE, THE COLLEGE CANTEEN, AND VARIOUS STUDENTS' FLATS, WE WOULD ALSO HANG AROUND THE JACARANDA COF-FEE BAR, RUN BY A GREGARIOUS LIVERPOOL WELSHMAN, ALLAN WILLIAMS. IT WAS HERE IN MAY 1960 THAT I MET VIRGINIA. SHE WAS SIX-TEEN YEARS OLD, WAS WEARING BLACK BARATHEA TROUSERS AND A GREEN SWEATER, AND HAD FLOWING AUBURN HAIR.

THE LADS WERE PLAYING DOWNSTAIRS IN THE "COAL HOLE," WHILE THEIR GIRLFRIENDS HELD BROOM HANDLES TO WHICH THEIR MICS WERE ATTACHED. IN THOSE DAYS WE WERE ALL SKINT, YET MANAGED TO GET BY,

EVEN WHEN WE DIDN'T HAVE THE PROVERBIAL "TWO HALFPENNIES TO RATTLE TOGETHER."

VIRGINIA BECAME MY GIRLFRIEND AND THE VISIONS OF CREATING A MAGAZINE GREW. I'D INITIALLY BEGUN THINKING IN TERMS OF A JAZZ MAGAZINE BECAUSE THERE WAS A HUGE TRAD JAZZ BOOM AND LIVERPOOL WAS A THRIVING CENTER. THERE WERE CLUBS SUCH AS THE CAVERN, THE LIVERPOOL JAZZ SOCIETY, AND THE TEMPLE JAZZ CLUB, AND PROMOTERS SUCH AS ALBERT KINDER REGULARLY BOOKED ARTISTS OF THE CALIBER OF CHRIS BARBER AND LONNIE DONEGAN AT THE EMPIRE AND PAVILION THEATRE.

ONE LOCAL PROMOTER SAID HE'D ADVANCE ME TWENTY-FIVE POUNDS TO LAUNCH THE JAZZ MAGAZINE, BUT HE NEVER DID.

BY THIS TIME, MY THOUGHTS WERE DEVELOPING IN A NEW DIRECTION. MY EXPERIENCE WRITING FOR *FRANK COMMENTS* HAD TAKEN ME TO PLACES AROUND LIVERPOOL SUCH AS WILSON HALL, WHERE LOCAL ROCK 'N' ROLL GROUPS USED TO PLAY. I BEGAN TALKING TO MEMBERS OF GROUPS WHO DROPPED BY THE JACARANDA AND SENSED THAT SOMETHING UNIQUE WAS HAPPENING IN LIVERPOOL. THE ROCK 'N' ROLL SCENE WAS LARGER THAN ANYONE—EVEN THE GROUPS THEMSELVES—REALIZED.

THE LITTLE RED NOTEBOOKS I CARRIED AROUND WITH ME BEGAN TO FILL UP WITH INFORMATION ON VENUES, PROMOTERS, AND GROUPS.

I DECIDED TO WRITE TO NATIONAL NEWSPAPERS, SUCH AS THE *DAILY MAIL*, TO INFORM THEM THAT WHAT WAS HAPPENING IN LIVERPOOL WAS AS UNIQUE AS WHAT HAD HAPPENED IN NEW ORLEANS AT THE TURN OF THE CENTURY, BUT WITH ROCK 'N' ROLL GROUPS INSTEAD OF JAZZ.

NO ONE TOOK ANY NOTICE. LIVERPOOL, IT SEEMED, WAS ISOLATED. IT DIDN'T HAVE ANY MEDIA THAT COULD REACH OUT NATIONALLY.

HISTORICALLY, LIVERPOOL HAD LOST A GREAT DEAL OF POWER AND PRESTIGE WHEN THE MANCHESTER SHIP CANAL WAS BUILT, ALLOWING A LOT OF TRADE TO BYPASS LIVERPOOL AND GO STRAIGHT TO MANCHESTER. MANCHESTER BECAME THE CAPITAL OF THE NORTH AND WAS HOME TO

BOTH GRANADA TELEVISION AND THE BBC TV STUDIOS, IN ADDITION TO RADIO STATIONS AND THE NORTHERN EDITIONS OF THE NATIONAL NEWSPAPERS. MOST NORTH-WEST NEWS ON TV, RADIO, AND IN THE PRESS HAD A MANCHESTER BIAS. IN COMPARISON, LIVERPOOL SEEMED TO BE ALMOST A BACKWATER. AS A RESULT, WHAT WAS HAPPENING THERE DEVELOPED WITHOUT ANYONE REALIZING IT AND WITHOUT ANY UNDUE OUTSIDE INTERFERENCE.

HAVING RECEIVED NO REACTION TO MY APPEALS TO THE PRESS TO COVER WHAT WAS HAPPENING, I DECIDED TO DO SOMETHING ABOUT IT MYSELF. INSTEAD OF A JAZZ MAGAZINE, I'D WRITE ABOUT THE LOCAL ROCK 'N' ROLL SCENE.

ALTHOUGH I'D RECEIVED MY NATIONAL DIPLOMA IN DESIGN, I WAS STILL AT THE ART COLLEGE, HAVING BECOME THE FIRST STUDENT OF THE NEW GRAPHIC DESIGN COURSE AND LATER WINNER OF THE SENIOR CITY ART SCHOLARSHIP. JOHN LENNON HAD HOPED TO ENTER THE GRAPHIC ART DEPARTMENT WITH ME, BUT THE LECTURER, ROY SHARPE, WOULDN'T ACCEPT HIM.

MONEY WAS STILL A PROBLEM, BUT DICK MATTHEWS, A FRIEND FROM THE JACARANDA, INTRODUCED ME TO A CIVIL SERVANT JIM ANDERSON, WHO OFFERED TO LEND VIRGINIA AND ME THE FIFTY POUNDS WE NEEDED TO LAUNCH THE PROJECT. BY THIS TIME, I'D DECIDED ON A FORTNIGHTLY NEWSPAPER, COMPLETELY DEVOTED TO THE MUSIC OF MERSEYSIDE, WHICH WOULD ALSO BE A "WHAT'S ON" OF EVERY MUSICAL EVENT DURING THE FORTNIGHT.

VIRGINIA'S SUPPORT IS WHAT REALLY KEPT ME GOING AND ENSURED THAT THE VISIONS IN MY HEAD BECAME A REALITY. SHE GAVE UP HER JOB TO WORK FULL TIME ON THE PROJECT, AND JIM FOUND US AN OFFICE ABOVE A WINE MERCHANT'S SHOP IN RENSHAW STREET. JIM, DICK, VIRGINIA, AND I ENTERED THE TINY ATTIC OFFICE ROOM CARRYING A TYPEWRITER, A DESK, AND A COUPLE OF CHAIRS, WHICH JIM HAD PROVIDED US WITH. DICK ALSO TOOK OUT HIS CAMERA AND PROMISED TO COVER THE LOCAL MUSIC SCENE FOR THE NEW PAPER.

Sitting in the Jacaranda with John and Stu, I'd tell them of our progress. By that time they'd left the college and were about to go to Germany. I asked John if he could write a biography of the Beatles for the new paper, which I could run in the first issue. When the Beatles returned from Germany, John gave me the biography, written in his own inimitable style, which I entitled "Being a Short Diversion on the Dubious Origins of Beatles (Translated from the John Lennon)."

By this time, of course, I was friendly with all members of the group. As well as knowing Paul and George from college days and attending their early gigs, I also got to know Pete Best, who joined them at the Jacaranda. They were the group I was closest to and were the ones I was obviously going to promote the most.

Sitting alone in the office at about two in the morning, I was attempting to think of a name for the new paper. Having decided that I'd cover the entire Merseyside region—Liverpool, the Wirral, Southport, Crosby, St. Helens, Widnes, Warrington, Runcorn, and so on—I suddenly visualized it as a policeman's beat. The image of a copper walking around a map of the surrounding area came into my head, along with the name, "Mersey Beat."

The reaction to *Mersey Beat* was literally phenomenal locally, and all five thousand copies of the first issue sold out. The three main wholesalers, W. H. Smith, Blackburn's, and Conlan's, took copies; I delivered copies personally to another two dozen newsagents, in addition to the main local venues and musical instruments and record stores.

At North End Music Stores (NEMS), when I asked to see the manager, Brian Epstein came down from his office. I showed him the publication and he agreed to take a dozen copies. He phoned me soon after to tell me how surprised he was that they

SOLD OUT ALMOST IMMEDIATELY. HE ORDERED MORE, AND MORE, AND MORE. FOR THE SECOND ISSUE, HE PLACED AN ADVANCE ORDER FOR TWELVE DOZEN COPIES, AN INCREDIBLE AMOUNT OF COPIES FOR A SINGLE PUBLICATION IN ONE OUTLET.

THAT ISSUE, PUBLISHED ON 20 JULY 1961, DEVOTED THE ENTIRE FRONT COVER TO THE BEATLES' RECENT RECORDINGS IN HAMBURG UNDER THE HEADLINE "BEATLES SIGN RECORDING CONTRACT!" THERE WAS ALSO A PHOTOGRAPH OF THE BEATLES BY ASTRID KIRCHHERR, WHICH PAUL MCCARTNEY HAD BROUGHT BACK FROM GERMANY FOR ME, TOGETHER WITH ASTRID'S PERMISSION FOR ME TO USE ANY OF THE BEATLES PICTURES SHE'D TAKEN AS PUBLICITY FOR THE GROUP.

BRIAN EPSTEIN INVITED ME TO HIS OFFICE FOR A SHERRY, AND WANTED TO DISCUSS THE GROUPS HE'D READ ABOUT IN *MERSEY BEAT*. HE WAS INCREDULOUS THAT SUCH A THRIVING MUSIC SCENE EXISTED ALL AROUND HIM, WHICH HE'D BEEN UNAWARE OF. HE WAS ALSO AMAZED AT THE NUMBER OF YOUNG PEOPLE WHO CAME INTO HIS STORE JUST TO BUY COPIES OF THE PAPER.

BRIAN ASKED ME TO DESCRIBE THE LOCAL SCENE, AND WAS PARTICULARLY INTERESTED IN THE BEATLES' COVER STORY AND THE FACT THAT A LOCAL GROUP HAD MADE A RECORD. HE IMMEDIATELY BOOKED ADVERTISING SPACE AND ASKED IF HE COULD REVIEW RECORDS. I APPOINTED HIM RECORD REVIEWER, BEGINNING WITH ISSUE NO. 3, AND HIS COLUMN WAS HEADED "STOP THE WORLD—AND LISTEN TO EVERYTHING IN IT. BRIAN EPSTEIN OF NEMS."

HIS ADVERTISEMENTS AND REVIEWS SHARED THE SAME PAGES AS THE ARTICLES AND PHOTOGRAPHS ABOUT THE BEATLES, AND HE WAS PARTICULARLY IMPRESSED BY BOB WOOLER'S ARTICLE ABOUT THE GROUP IN THE 31 AUGUST ISSUE. OVER THE MONTHS, HE LIKED TO DISCUSS THE STORIES IN *MERSEY BEAT* WITH ME AND THEN ASKED IF I COULD ARRANGE FOR HIM TO VISIT THE CAVERN TO SEE THE BEATLES. I DID THIS AND HE VISITED THE CLUB, LESS THAN A HUNDRED YARDS FROM HIS STORE, DURING A LUNCHTIME SESSION ON THURSDAY, 9 NOVEMBER.

WHEN HE PUBLISHED HIS AUTOBIOGRAPHY, *A CELLARFUL OF NOISE*, IN 1965, HE CLAIMED THAT HE FIRST HEARD OF THE BEATLES WHEN A YOUNG MAN CALLED RAYMOND JONES CAME INTO HIS STORE ON 28 OCTOBER 1961 AND ORDERED A COPY OF THE BEATLES' SINGLE (THE ONE WHICH WAS THE SUBJECT OF THE FRONT COVER IN JULY). THE STORY IS SO NEAT THAT WRITERS WHO HAVEN'T REALLY EXAMINED THE FACTS CHRONOLOGICALLY LOVE TO CITE IT. IT'S THE OLD STORY OF HAVING TO CHOOSE BETWEEN THE TRUTH AND THE LEGEND, AND OPTING TO GO FOR THE LEGEND. I'M WELL AWARE THAT *MERSEY BEAT* READERS WENT TO NEMS TO ASK FOR COPIES OF THE BEATLES' SINGLE, BUT THIS WAS ONLY AFTER *MERSEY BEAT* PRINTED THE COVER STORY IN JULY.

THE FACT THAT RAYMOND JONES AND OTHERS WENT INTO NEMS TO ASK FOR THE RECORD OR NOT IS BESIDE THE POINT. I HAD BEEN DISCUSSING THE GROUP WITH EPSTEIN FOR MONTHS AND HE HAD READ ALL ABOUT THEM IN *MERSEY BEAT* AS THEY WERE THE GROUP I PLUGGED MOST IN THE PAPER.

AT LEAST PAUL MCCARTNEY RECOGNIZES THE TRUTH, AND IN HIS OFFICIAL BIOGRAPHY, *MANY YEARS FROM NOW*, HE WROTE, "BRIAN KNEW PERFECTLY WELL WHO THE BEATLES WERE—THEY WERE ON THE FRONT PAGE OF THE SECOND ISSUE OF *MERSEY BEAT*, THE LOCAL MUSIC PAPER. BRIAN SOLD TWELVE DOZEN COPIES OF THIS ISSUE, SO MANY THAT HE INVITED THE EDITOR, BILL HARRY, INTO HIS OFFICE FOR A DRINK TO DISCUSS WHY IT WAS SELLING SO WELL AND TO ASK IF HE COULD WRITE A RECORD REVIEW COLUMN FOR IT." HE IS UNLIKELY TO HAVE MISSED THE "BEATLES SIGN RECORDING CONTRACT" BANNER HEADLINE, REPORTING THEIR SESSION WITH TONY SHERIDAN FOR BERT KAEMPFERT.

ON THE GROUP'S RETURN FROM GERMANY, PAUL GAVE ME A COPY OF THE SINGLE IN QUESTION. THE ONLY OTHER SPARE COPY HE GAVE TO BOB WOOLER, WHO BEGAN PLAYING IT AT THE LOCAL VENUES. I STILL HAVE THE RECORD, PERSONALLY SIGNED BY THEM ALL (PROBABLY THE FIRST RECORD THE BEATLES SIGNED PERSONALLY), BUT THERE IS NO INDICATION THAT THEY ARE ON IT.

There is a photograph of Tony Sheridan on the cover and the only words are: "Tony Sheridan. My Bonnie. The Saints (When the Saints Go Marching In)."

There is no mention whatsoever about the Beatles, and it would have been impossible for Epstein to trace the record, as he said he did, on this information alone. Even if he had the catalogue number, he would have been told this related to a single by Sheridan only.

Mersey Beat became a catalyst for the scene, and groups, managers, and anyone connected with the music took to visiting the office. Initially the Beatles were the most frequent visitors, helping Virginia out on the typewriter or phone; even Ringo used to drop in when he was visiting the nearby dole office in Renshaw Street.

Soon, groups began calling themselves Beat groups instead of rock 'n' roll bands, and venues which had been advertising "Twist sessions" and "jive sessions" began calling them "Beat sessions," while the "jive hives" were now being called Beat clubs. Once the Beatles had achieved their initial success on record, and the papers were looking for a tag to identify the movement, they first began to call it the "Mersey Sound" and "The Liverpool Sound." Some years later they adopted the name of the paper and "Mersey Beat" became part of the English language.

As the world's first alternative music paper, the first "What's On," *Mersey Beat* introduced many innovations which were later adopted by the national music press. It also created a wonderful range of early photographs of the Beatles for posterity. No other group achieving their initial success would have had such a large photographic record of their early career.

Initially, Dick Matthews took all those wonderful shots of the Beatles at the Cavern for me. I made arrangements with

VARIOUS PROFESSIONAL PHOTOGRAPHERS AND PAID THEM WITH ADVER-
TISEMENTS, PUBLICITY, AND RECOMMENDATIONS IN EXCHANGE FOR
EXCLUSIVE PHOTOGRAPHS FOR *MERSEY BEAT*. I DID THOSE DEALS WITH THE
PROFESSIONAL STUDIOS OF PETER KAYE, HARRY WATMOUGH, AND
GRAHAM SPENCER.

AS THE POLICY OF *MERSEY BEAT* WAS TO INTRODUCE INNOVATION, THE
PHOTOGRAPHERS WERE ENCOURAGED TO DO WHAT THE LONDON SHOW-
BIZ PHOTOGRAPHERS DIDN'T DO—LEAVE THE STUDIO AND TAKE SHOTS
ON LOCATION OR DURING PERFORMANCES ON STAGE.

THE BEATLES HAD ORIGINALLY BEEN PORTRAYED BRILLIANTLY IN
GERMANY BY ASTRID AND JURGEN VOLLMER, AND *MERSEY BEAT* CREATED
A WHOLE RANGE OF UNIQUE PHOTOGRAPHS OF THEM PERFORMING
IN LIVERPOOL.

THERE WAS AN UNDOUBTED EDITORIAL BIAS IN THEIR FAVOR, AND
THIS CAUSED BOB WOOLER TO COME TO THE OFFICE ONE DAY TO COM-
PLAIN ON BEHALF OF THE OTHER GROUPS. HE SAID THAT *MERSEY BEAT* WAS
PLUGGING THE BEATLES TO SUCH AN EXTENT THAT WE SHOULD RENAME
THE PAPER *MERSEY BEATLE*, AND IN FACT I LATER INTRODUCED A SPECIAL
SECTION CALLED JUST THAT.

WHEN WE DECIDED TO RUN A POLL TO ESTABLISH THE NO. I GROUP
IN LIVERPOOL, WE RECEIVED A HUGE RESPONSE. VIRGINIA AND I SPENT
MANY HOURS SORTING OUT THE VOTES. WHEN WE'D FINISHED, RORY
STORM & THE HURRICANES HAD MORE VOTES THAN ANYONE ELSE.
HOWEVER, WE NOTICED THAT A LARGE BUNDLE OF THEIR VOTES HAD
BEEN WRITTEN IN THE SAME HANDWRITING IN GREEN INK AND POSTED
FROM THE SAME AREA AT THE SAME TIME, SO WE DISQUALIFIED THE
GREEN-INK BATCH, WHICH MADE THE BEATLES NO. I AND RORY STORM
& THE HURRICANES NO. 4.

OUR FAMOUS COVER OF ISSUE NO. 13 WITH THE HEADLINE "BEATLES
TOP POLL" ESTABLISHED THEM ONCE AND FOR ALL AS THE TOP GROUP IN
THE NORTH OF ENGLAND—A FACT THAT BRIAN EPSTEIN WAS QUICK TO
CAPITALIZE ON.

THE PAPER'S CIRCULATION KEPT INCREASING ISSUE BY ISSUE AND BEGAN TO STRETCH THROUGHOUT THE COUNTRY, COVERING GROUPS IN MANCHESTER, BIRMINGHAM, SHEFFIELD, AND NEWCASTLE. WE WERE ALSO TO CHAMPION THE ROLLING STONES.

WHAT GAVE *MERSEY BEAT* THE EDGE WAS THE "BULGE," WHICH AMERICANS REFER TO AS THE "BABY BOOM." THERE WERE MORE BABIES BORN IN THE FEW YEARS TOWARDS THE END AND IMMEDIATELY FOLLOWING THE SECOND WORLD WAR THAN AT ANY TIME IN HISTORY. THOSE BABIES BECAME TEENAGERS IN THE 1950S.

IN PREVIOUS DECADES, THERE WAS NO REAL AWARENESS OF "TEENAGERS" (A TERM WHICH ONLY EMERGED IN THE 1950S). IN LIVERPOOL, FOR INSTANCE, YOUNGSTERS WERE MINI REPLICAS OF THEIR PARENTS. FATHERS WOULD LOOK ON WITH PLEASURE WHEN THEIR SONS REACHED A CERTAIN AGE AND STARTED TO ACCOMPANY THEM TO THE LOCAL PUBS FOR THEIR FIRST PINT. SONS WOULD ALSO FOLLOW FATHERS INTO THE BUSINESS OR UNION THEY BELONGED TO, AND YOUNGSTERS WOULD DRESS EXACTLY LIKE THEIR PARENTS.

SUDDENLY, THERE WAS AN AWARENESS OF BEING YOUNG, AND YOUNG PEOPLE WANTED THEIR OWN STYLES AND THEIR OWN MUSIC, JUST AT THE TIME THEY WERE BEGINNING TO EARN MONEY, WHICH GAVE THEM SPENDING POWER. ON MERSEYSIDE, *MERSEY BEAT* WAS THEIR VOICE. IT WAS A PAPER FOR THEM, CRAMMED WITH PHOTOS AND INFORMATION ABOUT THEIR OWN GROUPS, WHICH IS WHY IT ALSO BEGAN TO APPEAL TO YOUNGSTERS THROUGHOUT BRITAIN AS ITS COVERAGE EXTENDED TO OTHER AREAS.

THE NEWSPAPERS, TELEVISION, THEATRES, AND RADIO WERE ALL RUN BY PEOPLE OF A DIFFERENT GENERATION WHO HAD NO IDEA WHAT YOUNGSTERS WANTED. FOR DECADES THEY HAD MANIPULATED AND CONTROLLED THEM [SEE THE SCENE WITH GEORGE HARRISON AND KENNETH HAIG IN *A HARD DAY'S NIGHT*], BUT NOW THE YOUNGSTERS WANTED TO CREATE THEIR OWN FASHIONS.

Bill Harry remains the most credible reporter of that early period. The story of *Mersey Beat* as a major force in pushing the Beatles to early success is more than just legend. At the level of the Beatles' talent and ability in those early years, Bill and Virginia Harry helped catapult them to prominence. But as the story unfolds to you, it becomes clear that the band, with all the competition and hurdles ahead, may have never moved forward without the power of the printed words in *Mersey Beat*, required reading for the music-hungry kids of Liverpool.

The period of 1958 to 1964 was exciting, energetic, and unique, a magical time when an entire city danced to the music of youth.

And Bill and Virginia Harry were the chroniclers, not just for the Beatles, especially in those lonely early days when the tight path between success and failure lived for a while in the basement of the Jacaranda.

CHAPTER SIX

HE WAS JUST SEVENTEEN

"He was a bit younger than the rest of us. But he was a great guy—
would just do anything for you."
—Colin Hanton

"George was so sweet. My family, especially my mother, loved him."
—Pauline Sutcliffe, sister of Stuart Sutcliffe

"You have no idea what George would give to just be able to walk down
the road to a pub and have a drink."
—Louise Harrison, sister of George Harrison

George Harrison: A Boy with Dreams and Soft Laughter

George was on a journey in 1960. And it ended in failure. Did he know when he joined the rickety band that he would literally be ejected from a country? Did he realize that before the age of eighteen he would be treated like a criminal, become dejected beyond despair, and consider quitting the band?

Like his future bandmate Richie Starkey, George Harrison was not a great student. Also like Richie, George came from a loving family, and despite the warm radiance of father Harry and mother Louise, George seized on a bit of deception to make his way through school—at one point asking the parent of a friend to sign a grim report card so his affectionate parents would not discover his educational deficiencies. Despite this problem, the future guitarist and songwriter scored well on standardized tests and made it into the prestigious Liverpool Institute, adjacent to the Art Institute famously attended by John Lennon and his pack, including John's closest man friend, Stuart Sutcliffe. At the Liverpool Institute, and on many bus rides, his relationship with a fellow student and future bandmate flourished.

Getting into the Liverpool Institute brought him in continuous contact with James Paul McCartney. In the long run, this would be a good thing, for it was Paul who pushed hard in 1957 to get George into John's band.

At first, John seemed to resist taking such a "young guy" into his band, but Lennon "got over it," as he said to me in 1964, seven years after first meeting George.

"He had a real kind of wild style on the guitar. It's as though . . . you know, that he and the guitar were joined together. He also looked like a Teddy Boy, but as you know, Larry, he was hardly that."

Hardly. Sensitivity to others was George's great talent as a human being. On the aircraft and in the hotel suites, it was George who was always asking, "Everything all right, Larry?"

I remember George's "Scouse" accent. When I first interviewed him, his accent was much thicker, and stronger. George was supposed to be the quiet Beatle, but that's not quite accurate. He just didn't talk unless he had something to say, as I remember. Some suspect that he was difficult to communicate with. But was this true?

Colin Hanton says, "Oh, I had no problems. He was a bit younger than the rest of us. But he was a great guy—would just do anything for you. They [the Beatles] all were, and I didn't have problems with any of them."

Julia Baird, John's sister, loved George's presence and his attitude.

"Larry, you had to love George. He was such a lovely person, so family-oriented. When we first met him, he seemed to be a boy reaching out to find what life was all about. My mother admired him. I think Mimi did, too, although I can't say for sure. I know John really loved him and his uncomplicated way."

George was warmly welcomed by Millie Sutcliffe, Stuart's mother. Pauline Sutcliffe, Stuart's sister, recalls, "He had a quiet kinship with Stu, and our mother felt he was the most courteous of the boys. Of course, Stuart was always protecting his sisters from the 'menace' of John and Paul. George in many ways was more centered than all of them. Much like Stu, he had an inner spirituality."

During a BBC interview, Astrid Kirchherr recalled how sweet he was to her after her boyfriend Stuart's death, and described a special moment in her studio:

WELL, FIRST OF ALL, I TOOK ONE PICTURE AFTER STUART'S DEATH OF GEORGE AND JOHN IN THE ATTIC [WHERE] STUART USED TO PAINT.

AND . . . IF YOU COULD SEE THE PICTURE, JOHN LOOKED SO VERY LOST AND
LONELY AND SAD. AND GEORGE IS STANDING BEHIND HIM. HE WAS ONLY
EIGHTEEN YEARS OLD, AND HE LOOKED SO WISE. AND, TO ME, HE HAD AN
EXPRESSION ON HIS FACE JUST SAYING, "I WILL LOOK AFTER YOU, JOHN."
YOU KNOW, SO THAT IS ONE OF MY FAVORITE PICTURES OF THE TWO OF
THEM. AND I TOOK SOME MORE PORTRAITS OF JOHN AND GEORGE THEN,
AND THEY LOOKED SO GROWN UP ALL OF A SUDDEN, ESPECIALLY JOHN, YOU
KNOW. BUT YOU COULD SEE HIS SADNESS, BECAUSE HE HAD GONE
THROUGH SO MUCH PAIN AND LOSSES IN HIS LITTLE LIFE, THEN.

Several early cues suggest George's leadership qualities but have gone unnoticed
by most writers. After Stuart's sad death in Hamburg, it was George who worried
most about the impact on John's emotional well-being. When John and George
made that visit to the apartment that Stuart shared with Astrid, the young photographer remembers, George displayed a sense of almost brotherly love.

"He had so much respect for John. And he always treated me with so
much sweetness. I think he understood real love, deep love, more than the
others. Professionally, I always remember how serious he was . . . how determined he was to make sure that I received the creative credit I deserved.
George was a sweet man, who, despite reflections on him by others, was
really the least complicated of the Beatles . . . at least to me."

John paid him back. What an irony that John, in his very devilish and
confused years of 1970 through 1975, offered constant attention to George
as the younger ex-Beatle launched both his solo music career and his long
journey searching for the meaning of life.

There is also evidence of the well-meaning but sometimes indifferent attitude
that Paul, and even John, had toward the sublimated creative side of George.

In the acclaimed 2011 documentary by Martin Scorsese called *Living in a
Material World*, there is an older film interview with Paul McCartney. The
discussion is about the art of songwriting. And Paul says, quite calmly, "Even
our guitarist, George Harrison" is writing songs now. In his using the term
"our guitarist" the question remains: Is that the way Paul viewed George, as "our
guitarist"? Because in the musical makeup and legacy of the Beatles, George is
much more than merely the guitarist. In recent years, and especially during live

concerts from 2010 on, Paul definitely cherishes George's memory and contributions, with a poignant and quite emotional tribute to his friend from Liverpool. Paul's rendition of George's sensitively written and performed masterpiece "Something" is enough to bring you to tears.

On the Beatles' tours, George was the most uncomplicated of the four, enjoying the ride and providing an extraordinary sense of humor in times of turmoil, like during the emergency landing of the chartered Electra airplane in Portland, Oregon, during the 1965 North American tour. While John and Paul were sweating nervously, George yelled out to me, "Remember, Larry, if anything happens, it's Beatles and children first!"

As a reporter who spent so much time with the boys in those early years of success, I was deeply impressed by George's willingness to express his feelings, many times with the sense of humor he expressed in that "special landing" in Portland. His composure during that event is even more compelling when you consider that airplanes were George's least favorite form of transportation. On another occasion, in August 1964, astrologer Jeanne Dixon had forecast that our airplane would crash on the flight from Philadelphia to Indianapolis. In the dressing room at Philadelphia's Convention Hall, George told me how upset he was at the prediction.

"Will you go on the plane tonight?" I asked.

"No, I'm going to ride a bicycle," he declared, laughing.

Just for the record, the flight, white knuckles emerging as people grasped their seats, was uneventful and ended with a safe touchdown and loud applause, led by George.

Fears aside, George was an excellent traveler, and was even more amazing to watch on stage. He developed an onstage habit that began at the Casbah and the Cavern, and continued on from there, that was always fascinating to watch. He would gently nod his head downward, as though listening to his guitar, although, frankly, at most locations, with the roar of the crowd and the high-pitched screaming, I couldn't imagine that he could really hear anything.

Quite the contrary. During a noisy flight on the Electra that carried us across North America, I quizzed him about the noise level in the arenas. Could he hear the music?

"I can hear everything," he said. "I know when it's right, and I know when it is not good."

Promoter Sam Leach recently offered me his early take on George from 1961.

"Very quiet—not an introvert like Pete, but very quiet and shy. He had more of a boyish immaturity. He said only what he had to say—he was not a talker, but when he did say something it was usually funny. He had a dry sense of humor and a quick wit."

Leach lamented George's early career, and the circumstances that laid a professional straightjacket around his abilities:

WHEN GEORGE DIED, I WAS IN CHICAGO DOING A SHOW WITH A LOT OF BIG ARTISTS—SPENCER DAVIS AND ABOUT TWENTY OTHER REALLY BIG STARS. GEORGE HAD DIED THE DAY BEFORE. I DID AN INTERVIEW WITH THE PRESS AND IT WENT WORLDWIDE. I TOLD THEM THEN THAT GEORGE WAS NOT USED PROPERLY WITH THE BEATLES. HIS TALENT WAS OVERLOOKED. NOT DELIBERATELY, THOUGH. PAUL AND JOHN WERE SO POWERFUL THAT GEORGE GOT SHOVED INTO THE BACKGROUND BECAUSE HE WAS QUIET, I THINK. I AM A LITTLE DISAPPOINTED WITH PAUL MCCARTNEY'S OUTPUT IN RECENT YEARS; IT'S ALL THE SAME. I THINK GEORGE'S ALBUM *BRAINWASHED* WAS THE BEST SINGLE SOLO ALBUM FOR TWENTY YEARS. HE WAS OVERLOOKED AND SO UNDERRATED.

That sentiment is echoed by author and world-class Beatles researcher Ron Ellis, who was also a witness to the very early concerts, and a regular supplier to the boys of American records:

MCCARTNEY, EVEN AT THAT YOUNG AGE, FELT LIKE HE WAS THE BUSI-NESSMAN. I THINK HE WAS THINKING LIKE, "'WE'VE GOT A GOOD THING GOING HERE, I WANT TO BE IN CHARGE OF THIS. . . . "

GEORGE'S AMBITIONS WERE, I THINK, HELD IN CHECK FROM A SONG-WRITING STANDPOINT. I WOULD SAY GEORGE WAS AS GOOD AS MCCARTNEY AND LENNON, YET . . . HE WASN'T ALLOWED TO DO IT. . . . LENNON AND MCCARTNEY WERE CONTROLLING WHAT WAS SAID. "WE'LL GIVE GEORGE A SONG, WE'LL GIVE RINGO A SONG." I THINK THEY PUT

GEORGE IN THE CATEGORY OF RINGO—THEY WERE THE TWO PEOPLE
WHO COMPLETED THE MAKEUP OF THE GROUP, BUT NOT RUNNING IT.

From the beginning, and consistently, George Harrison was a wonderful friend who believed in performing little kindnesses. It's a quality he seems to have gotten from his upbringing. Beginning in 1963, his parents felt obliged to answer thousands of fan letters, which brought them a lot of joy but also caused them to lose many hours of sleep.

The guitar man himself liked Sundays, especially the times when he would drive his new Ford Anglia, the first car he purchased, over to Tony Bramwell's house.

"He would drive up," Bramwell remembers, "and ask my mum and I to take a ride. We had such fun, and George loved making other people smile. He would drive up and say, 'Hi, Mrs. Bramwell, want to go for a ride?'"

Family was always on George's mind. After the initial success of "Love Me Do," and when money started to arrive in larger quantities, the Harrisons moved into a nicer home in Hunts Cross, not far from the Bramwells.

The house was soon overrun by fans who offered to wash the dishes, iron the shirts, and perform other chores and activities. As Bramwell remembers it, these fans became part of the Harrison family.

But the family, especially the parents, never really treated George as a star. George's sister, Louise Harrison, who lived in North America before and during the Beatles' ascent, brings real history to life when she reads letters from her mother from that time period: "I was reading one of the letters and someone said, 'You know, there's nothing glorious about the way that they are talking.' They were astounded by the matter-of-fact, non-adulation way that my parents were talking about my brother."

From the perspective of pressman and Beatles advocate Bill Harry, George really didn't need to stay in the background, but Harry thinks he may have been overwhelmed.

HE WAS QUIET LIKE THAT WITH THEM. WHEN I PUT THEM ON THE COVER
[OF *MERSEY BEAT*] INDIVIDUALLY, IT WAS GEORGE WHO WAS PORTRAYED
AS THE QUIET BEATLE. I SAID TO GEORGE ONE DAY, "LISTEN, GEORGE,
HOW COME IT'S ALWAYS LENNON AND MCCARTNEY'S NAMES ON EVERY-
THING? WHAT HAPPENED TO YOUR SONGWRITING?"

DID YOU KNOW THAT THE ORIGINAL NUMBER THAT MADE PRINT HAD GEORGE'S NAME ON IT? THE VERY FIRST SONG AS THE BEATLES, ORIGINAL COMPOSITION, AS DEPICTED IN ISSUE NUMBER TWO OF *MERSEY BEAT*, [WAS] "CRY FOR A SHADOW" BY GEORGE HARRISON. IN PRINT, THAT WAS THE FIRST MENTION OF A BEATLES COMPOSITION AND GEORGE WAS THE AUTHOR. SO I SAID TO HIM, "IF YOU CAN'T WRITE WITH JOHN AND PAUL, THEN WRITE A SONG WITH RINGO." HE WROTE A SONG WITH RINGO, AND I WROTE ABOUT IT IN *MERSEY BEAT*. I DON'T REMEMBER WHAT HAPPENED TO THAT SONG. THEN AT A LATER TIME, ONE NIGHT, I SAW HIM AS HE WAS COMING OUT OF THE CABIN CLUB ON WOODS STREET. I ASKED HIM ABOUT HIS WRITING. I SAID, "AREN'T YOU WRITING SONGS AGAIN?" HE MUMBLED. THEN I SAW HIM AGAIN IN 1964 IN THE ABC BLACKPOOL, AND I WAS SITTING WITH THEM, AND GEORGE SAID, "I WANT TO THANK YOU." "THANK ME FOR WHAT?" "YOU JUST MADE ME SEVEN THOUSAND POUNDS." AND GEORGE SAID THE REASON WAS THAT HE THOUGHT OF ME AND SAID TO HIMSELF THAT HE HAD BETTER WRITE SOMETHING BECAUSE HE WAS GETTING NERVOUS THAT HE WAS GOING TO RUN INTO ME, AND I WAS GOING TO GET ON HIS BACK ABOUT NOT WRITING, AND THAT HE WAS REALLY WORRIED. SO HE WANTED TO THANK ME BECAUSE HE ALREADY HAD ACCUMULATED SEVEN THOUSAND POUNDS IN ROYALTIES FROM A SONG CALLED "DON'T BOTHER ME."

"Was he as sweet and pleasant as everyone says, in those days?" I ask.

"He was very nice, very polite and refined—the Beatle who was most stretched," he says.

LIKE RINGO . . . GEORGE WAS LESS EDUCATED, LESS INTELLECTUAL. ALTHOUGH GEORGE WENT TO LIVERPOOL INSTITUTE WITH PAUL, HE WASN'T THAT INTERESTED IN EDUCATION OR AS KEEN ON GETTING AHEAD AS THE OTHERS. HE AND RINGO WERE NOT AS INTELLECTUAL, LIKE JOHN AND PAUL. GEORGE WASN'T INTERESTED IN BOOKS AND OTHER CULTURAL PURSUITS LIKE JOHN. BUT LATER ON, WHEN HE GOT TO MEET MONTY PYTHON, THE MAHARISHI, AND RAVI SHANKAR, THIS STRETCHED GEORGE . . . [AND] HE EXPANDED HIS HORIZONS. FROM WHAT HE WAS TO

WHAT HE WOULD BECOME, THIS I WOULD SAY WAS THE BIGGEST EVOLU-
TION, THE BIGGEST STRETCH IN ANY ONE MEMBER OF THE BAND. JOHN
ALREADY HAD IT. PAUL DID TOO. IT WAS HARDER FOR GEORGE AND HARD-
EST FOR RINGO.

Even as a boy, George cherished peace and quiet. The limelight was not his
intended destination as a teenager. Quarryman Rod Davis shared a wonderful conversation with me that relates to George Harrison and fame:

WE WERE DOING A GIG ONCE, AND LOUISE HARRISON WAS ON THE SAME
QUESTIONS-AND-ANSWER PANEL, AND SOMEBODY SAID TO US, WOULD WE
HAVE LIKED TO HAVE BEEN THE BEATLES? AND WE SAID, WELL, THE
MONEY WOULD HAVE COME IN HANDY NOW AND THEN, BUT WE CAN
WALK DOWN THE ROAD TO THE SUPERMARKET, WALK INTO THE PUB,
NOBODY'S THREATENING US AND ASKING FOR MONEY. AND LOUISE, SIT-
TING NEXT TO ME, SAID, "YOU HAVE NO IDEA WHAT GEORGE WOULD GIVE
TO JUST BE ABLE TO WALK DOWN THE ROAD TO A PUB AND HAVE A DRINK."
SHE SAID, "YOU KNOW, YOU DON'T REALIZE UNTIL YOU MISS IT HOW
IMPORTANT IT IS."

In my career, I've interviewed presidents and public figures from all indus-
tries. George was one of the most self-deprecating public figures I've ever met.
On one occasion in 1964 in an Atlantic City penthouse ballroom, George
and I and the others watched a private showing of the final cut of the Beatles'
first movie, *A Hard Day's Night*. He seemed to curl up and shrivel in embarrassment. He was shy, but not overly so—just in a very charming manner.
You would like the guy instantly. George was a person who reached out. He
was a perfect listener, but he was not a man of bullshit, or superficial charm.
Yes, he was an amazing performer, but not in the style of John and Paul,
rather as the keeper of the guitar, the finesse man who tickled the strings and
looked for a better sound than the night before.

Paul McCartney liked the guy from the beginning. The two would share rides
on the bus to the Liverpool Institute, and it was there that an excited George told
Paul about his first and last gig with George's very own group, the Rebels,
founded just a month before the Woolton meeting between Paul and John.

The Rebels were hired as a replacement band to perform at a British Legion Club near his home. George and his brother Pete handled the guitars. A few other friends provided what they could, which was two songs—the same two songs played over and over again. The crowd, George said, was pleased. Paul loved the story, but even more than that, he admired George's low-key but obvious enthusiasm, and the look on his face. Paul was enthused; his own day was not far away.

It was his sessions with the musically obsessed George, and George's determination to learn more and more about the guitar, that eventually convinced Paul to bring George into the Quarrymen.

The early days were frustrating, especially for the youngest player. But he had his own special support network, parents Harry and Louise, who were loving, caring, and willing to go with the flow.

George's sister, Louise Harrison, describes the parental dynamic of the Harrisons:

THEY WERE TOTALLY, TOTALLY, SUPPORTIVE, RIGHT FROM THE VERY VERY GET-GO. THIS IS SOMETHING THAT I WRITE A LOT ABOUT IN MY BOOK . . . WHAT AN EXCEPTIONAL COUPLE THEY WERE. I FEEL THAT ALTHOUGH THEIR STORY ISN'T KNOWN, I FEEL THAT IT'S A VERY IMPORTANT STORY AS THE FOUNDATION AS TO WHY THE BEATLES HAD SUCH A SOLID OUTLOOK ON LIFE. YOU SEE, BACK IN THEIR TEENS, BOTH PAUL AND JOHN LOST THEIR MOTHERS, AND MY MOM WAS THE ONLY . . . UNTIL, OF COURSE, RINGO CAME ALONG LATER. OF THE THREE OF THEM, MY MOM WAS THE ONLY MOM LIVING. GEORGE WOULD ALWAYS SAY, "BE CAREFUL, BE CAREFUL," BECAUSE THEY ALL SHARED HER. I'VE GOT LETTERS FROM HER, AND AT ONE POINT I HAD SAID SOMETHING LATER ON ABOUT HOW LEVEL-HEADED THEY WERE, AND SHE SAID, "PARDON ME, BUT I THINK I CAN TAKE SOME CREDIT FOR THAT."

Was George the nicest Beatle? There is no question about that. His sister claims that title for her kid brother, but my experience and the combined and cumulative impression of the major players also confirms that.

While in the busy days of their adult lives, Paul and Ringo rarely looked back (although Paul has been philanthropically involved in education in

Liverpool). George, meanwhile, always did the right thing. He was, indeed, the man who remembered people's needs in life and death—the family of Mal Evans, whose own story remains ahead, the legacy of his good friend Derek Taylor, his kindnesses toward almost everyone connected to his family, his lasting friendship from unknown to superstar with Tony Bramwell, and his benevolence and sense of concern for John and Ringo in their days of waste and addiction post-Beatles.

Beatles researcher Ron Ellis, who carries the title of football writer to his assorted credits, views George as the ultimate team player, whose respect for the group originally was enormous.

"George Harrison was a nicer person compared to the rest of the guys, and it was from the beginning. John could always be edgy and difficult. Paul was determined to gratify himself. Pete was moody but pleasant. And Ringo started out kind and innocent, but got jaded very quickly. George Harrison was a nice respectful kid in the beginning, and a nice respectful man at the end."

For his sister, Louise, there are vivid memories of a man who cared only about one kind of love.

SO MANY TIMES HE TALKED ABOUT UNCONDITIONAL LOVE. UNCONDITIONAL LOVE IS MUCH BETTER THAN "I'M IN LOVE WITH YOU" KIND OF LOVE. UNCONDITIONAL LOVE—THERE ARE NO CONDITIONS ON THAT LOVE. NO MATTER WHAT THAT PERSON DOES TO ME, "I LOVE YOU" . . . BUT IT'S NOT NECESSARILY ROMANTIC OR SEXUAL LOVE. IT'S LOVE. SIMILAR TO THE KIND YOU HAVE WITH A PARENT. IT TRANSCENDED THE SEXUAL LOVE. WHEN [FIRST WIFE PATTI BOYD] FOUND THAT SHE WANTED TO BE WITH SOMEBODY ELSE [ERIC CLAPTON], GEORGE JUST WANTED HER TO BE HAPPY.

The author believes that George, in his early years, was the happiest of the boys—just thrilled to be playing music on any stage.

Optimistic. Loving. Almost undaunted. His vision was enhanced, perhaps blurred, through the prism and dreams of hope. But in the late fall and early winter of 1960, the buoyancy of his confidence was seriously challenged when he returned wounded from an overseas incursion to the inner layers of hell and deprivation.

WHEN
THEY
WERE
BOYS

PART THREE:
ACROSS THE SEA

Far away. There are no comforts of home. Sleeping with a flush for an alarm clock. The girls who looked like girls but, wait a minute, why were they so willing? Going "all the way" from the art school and institute to the school of real life. The language was different, but the sex was the same and the Jacaranda man played "pox doctor" every few days. The boys paid a price for sowing their seeds. The so-called keepers of the flame—Paul and Pete as pyromaniacs? Angry thugs force them out as young George gets the boot, and Horst comes to the rescue. John stays under the radar; that's a change. And Stu chooses love over fate.

Rock 'n' roll lives, and the pills keep a-poppin', with a trio of friends on hand to give food, ideas, fashion, and the best four-letter word ever: hope. In the dark alleys and bright stages, they get to know Rory. Rory, who set the pace, and whose own sadness parallels their early triumphs.

Things are sloppy, but so is life among the ruins of drugs, insomnia, and sex, more of the latter than the former.

The music? The boys and girls who wander under the glow of the red lights keep coming back. It's a good sign, but life turns quickly and scary fists and truncheons are close by. The lights go dark for the young Beatles, but fate follows them like an invisible guardian.

When they come back home in self-imposed disgrace and depression, Mama Mona and a curious promoter help save the bitter-cold days of early winter with a trip to a place called Litherland, which can only be remembered as the boys' dramatic and scintillating December Surprise.

CHAPTER SEVEN

HAMBURG PART 1—THE WILD SIDE

"In truth, Allan Williams smuggled us into Germany. No papers.
Nothing legal. And that's the way the first trip ended."
—Pete Best

"George described it like 'the black hole of Calcutta.'"
—Louise Harrison, George Harrison's sister

HOME IN HAMBURG WASN'T PRETTY. So once again, fate and timing enter the boys' world. Fearing the unknown and yet deciding to hurtle toward it, they left school, left their jobs, and made a creaky, pothole-filled journey to Germany. Once again they would soon be convinced that they were failing. But in reality, they were quietly creating a juggernaut—they just didn't know it.

The world is filled with cities that project the sinister aspects of life, and neighborhoods that have little subtlety in their efforts to satisfy sexual appetites. Paris has Montmartre; New York City had 42nd Street; and Hamburg has St. Pauli. The red-light districts of the world have always been a sideshow, and in many cases the show includes drugs and violence and other dangers to the mind and body. It's an irony that the most clean-cut of bands in the British Invasion of 1964 cultivated its raw talent in the seedy surroundings and hostile environment of Hamburg. It is also, as you will learn, somewhat of a minor miracle that the boys survived Hamburg at all.

It was there, also, that they met "the Enforcer," the "dynamic trio," and many forgotten lovers. And through long hours and unfathomable conditions, the Beatles, talented and frightened, turned their desperation and their hunger into something that had until then eluded them—an electrifying act. They just didn't know it at the time. In fact, they didn't have a clue. They were too busy playing music, eating sparingly, smoking their lungs out, whoring into the morning hours, and popping prelude [Preludin] pills, washed down with beer, to keep themselves awake. There was plenty of violence, an occasional fistfight between Paul and Stu, and some later attacks by goons. In fact, if you look at the Beatles in 1960, you might surmise that with all the sex, drinking, and fighting, they may have been the world's first punk rock band. They were so involved in human degradation that it was only when they returned to Liverpool in the late fall of 1960, depressed and disoriented, that they discovered the seedy Hamburg nights, with all the muck and madness, had helped them create a real "act."

And this discovery came after an intense period of soul-searching, where the very survival of the group was being discussed, and aggressively at that. Think what might not have occurred if the Beatles had not played and grown in Hamburg. Think where the boys might have wound up if not for the experience of their first performances in Germany, and the love/hate dynamic they developed toward the city offering the wildest of opportunity, as they ate, slept, and played in surroundings of mediocrity with such alacrity.

When Rory Storm and the Hurricanes decided to stay and play in the UK for the summer, Allan Williams took the Beatles to Hamburg instead. This first trip was exciting and scintillating because, while the boys were experiencing more work and stage time than they expected, they also traveled a parallel life of dirt, daring, and risk-taking that most ordinary people would find not just breathtaking, but dangerous. Storm would eventually join them in Hamburg in the fall of 1960, but he got top billing, and in comparison, much better lodgings. The sleeping quarters ranged from primitive and creaky beds to lounge chairs, not to mention a close proximity to bathrooms, odor and all. It was hardly the stuff that dreams are made of.

As in all stories of adventure, there are heroes and villains. The primary villain in this case is Bruno Koschmider, the smart and somewhat sinister owner of nightclubs and porn theaters. The hero is "the Enforcer," a man with much experience—sailing the world at the age of fifteen, becoming featherweight boxing champ of the Hamburg region at the age of twenty, and by his twenty-first birthday, spending nine months in jail for the unintentional killing of a sailor on the streets of the St. Pauli quarter. There is also Allan Williams, a most unlikely manager. And three young

Germans you will meet, a trio better fit for existentialism and the free-wheeling beatnik culture than they were for five boys from Liverpool who took a daring, devilish trip into life's ugly underground, and a most outlandish neighborhood.

Today St. Pauli is a thriving neighborhood of homes and condominiums, with an invigorated restaurant district, but it remains synonymous with the sex stores and prostitutes on the Reeperbahn, its most infamous street.

The Beatles made five trips to Hamburg, the last one a brief stop in 1966, several years after they had taken over the music world. Their second through fourth journeys had the greatest impact on their music, but the first, in the summer and fall of 1960, changed their fortunes. They came and they played music, and they played in other ways, and in retrospect they were lucky to get out in good health—or even alive.

Allan Williams describes the boys' first trip to Hamburg as a journey to remember. The king of the Jacaranda had graduated from small-time promoter to hard-drinking darling of the big London talent bookers. After early success in Hamburg with the group Derry and the Seniors, Williams was asked to send over a second group. With Liverpool's hottest group, Rory Storm and the Hurricanes, temporarily engaged at Butlin's, a well-known and friendly family campsite back in the UK, he took a risk. He would instead book his self-proclaimed "coffeehouse layabouts," the Beatles.

As the morning sun shines through the windows of Liverpool's Hard Day's Night Hotel in present day, Williams sips his red wine and recalls how, in the beginning, he decided to help them out. After all, the coffeehouse regulars who painted the bathrooms and cleaned up after hours deserved a break.

But in those days, the Beatles were that hard up. . . . They hadn't got the train fare. . . . So I thought when I came back that I'd take them there myself in the minibus—that was a journey to remember. . . .

There's actually a famous photograph, I think it's in my book, but it's been produced many times. It was the first time the Beatles had ever been abroad. The van broke down after we got

OFF THE FERRY. IT WAS A HORRIBLE TRIP. AT ONE POINT, THEY ALL BURST OUT LAUGHING AND I SAID, "WHAT'S THE JOKE?" REMEMBER, THIS IS THE FIRST TIME THAT THEY'D EVER BEEN ABROAD. IT SEEMS THEY WERE LAUGHING SO HARD BECAUSE LENNON HAD STOLEN A MOUTH ORGAN FROM A MUSIC SHOP, A MUSICAL INSTRUMENT SHOP. I THOUGHT, CHRIST, THE WAY THEY'RE BEHAVING WE'RE NOT EVER GOING TO MAKE IT TO HAMBURG; WE'RE GOING TO FINISH UP IN JAIL WITH THIS. THESE THIEVES.

John once told me that he loved playing the harmonica, especially at the Shea Stadium concert in 1965. At the time, I never knew that he loved the "mouth organ," as he called it, enough to steal one and risk arrest on that first minibus journey to Hamburg. Williams, who would later warn Brian Epstein about the alleged dishonesty of John's group, seems even today to have a love-hate emotional connection to the boys. But this author sees it more as love, and an affectionate nostalgia for the rough-and-tumble Beatle boys. If he didn't love them then, Williams certainly loves them now.

When Allan Williams's van finally arrived in Hamburg, nightclub owner Bruno Koschmider brought them to the Indra club, not the larger Kaiserkeller, as planned. Williams was furious.

IT WAS A STRIP CLUB. THE BEATLES HAD ALREADY PLAYED IN A STRIP CLUB OF MINE IN LIVERPOOL AND I THOUGHT, "I DON'T KNOW. WE DIDN'T COME ALL THE WAY TO PLAY FOR STRIPPERS IN HAMBURG." I EXPLAINED THIS TO THE GUY WHO OWNED IT, [WHO SAID] "OH NO, THIS IS THE LAST NIGHT OF STRIPPERS; TOMORROW IT WILL BE A ROCK 'N' ROLL CLUB." SO THEY WERE A BIT PLEASED. SO WE GOT AN ACCOMMODATION, WHICH WAS ATROCIOUS. HE OWNED A CINEMA—KOSCHMIDER—WHICH HE TURNED FROM A CINEMA INTO A NIGHTCLUB. YOU CAN IMAGINE WHEN IT WAS A CINEMA OR A THEATER, THE DRESSING ROOMS WERE AT THE BACK OF THE STAGE AND, OF COURSE, HE HADN'T CLEANED IT IN, OH, TWENTY OR THIRTY YEARS. THE DUST WAS ABOUT AN INCH THICK EVERYWHERE. THEY WERE SO GRATEFUL THAT THEY WOULD HAVE SLEPT ON THE FLOOR. SO THEY WERE SETTLED IN.

"Settled in" might have been an exaggeration. In the ensuing four months, the boys, including newcomer Pete Best, slept near bathrooms, stages, rodents, and sheer filth. The place was called "Bambi Kino." It remains to this day the Beatles' filthiest memory.

"I never really slept anywhere so horrible," Pete Best exclaimed to a crowd at the Fest for Beatles fans in New Jersey in 2005.

"You felt dirty, always," Pete remembered.

"George described it as like the 'black hole of Calcutta,'" recalls his sister, Louise Harrison.

Promoter Koschmider's "accommodations" resembled the squalor-filled surroundings of child labor in a Dickens novel.

Paul has assorted memories of the storeroom that they called home. "It was awful . . . you might say. No heat . . . some basic beds with no sheets. We were . . . frozen . . . and the room was at the toilet. . . . You could always smell them."

George was stunned and unhappy. "We did most of our washing in the washbasin in the bathroom. I think that's why we always felt dirty."

John shared this grotesque memory with me in the mid-seventies: "Knowing that we had to go back to that fucking little house was enough to make you stay and work. Sometimes, after all those little pills, I would be wide awake staring around, wondering if the dirt would cake up inside of me. Sleep was an escape. You shoulda been there, Larry."

Daily life was a combination of little food, lots of drink, and the obsessions of the boys: rocking hard and sexing hard, not necessarily in that order. There were scenes of decadence that stayed around, for hours and for years, in the vivid memory of one's own flight to danger. In *Fifty Years Adrift*, Derek Taylor's amazing memoir, "editor" George Harrison remembers the perils and sheer terror of life in Hamburg with John Lennon.

"John would go out in Hamburg for nights without sleep. And then we'd be trying to get to sleep and he would come in. One night, he came in and some chick was in bed with Paul and he cut up all her clothes with a pair of scissors and was stabbing the wardrobe. Everybody was lying in bed thinking, 'Oh fuck, I hope he doesn't kill me.' A frothing mad person, he knew [how to] have 'fun.'"

Stuart had less of a problem with the vagaries of an unleashed, undisciplined John Lennon, although he would experience his love-hate dynamic later on. Stuart fell in love in Hamburg, real love, which also had some real benefit for the boys. It is no wonder that Stuart's early romance with Hamburg photographer Astrid Kirchherr helped provide an escape from life in the Bambi Kino.

As Astrid remembers, "The Beatles smelled awful. . . . They had to wash where the Kino customers were having a wee. When they came to my house they would want to have showers."

A visit to the Kirchherr household also offered hot meals, and a family atmosphere that was missing in the booze- and drug-filled lives of the four Beatles. They would routinely visit, clean up, eat home cooking, and return to the club, where they would alternate with Rory Storm and the Hurricanes when that band finally arrived in Hamburg.

And besides the dirt, drinking, and drugs, there was another problem: sex. Too much, and with the wrong crowd. For Allan Williams, the readily available sex was less a distraction, in his view, than a real medical threat. Williams was no doctor, but by the time the first trip was over, he might have qualified for status as a nurse.

"They had a lot of fun," Williams recalls.

ALL THE GIRLS WHO WENT OUT WITH THEM . . . MOST WERE PROSTITUTES. IT WAS A RED-LIGHT DISTRICT AND THE GIRLS USED TO SIT IN THE WINDOW AND YOU JUST PICK A WOMAN AND YOU KNOW THERE'D BE A BACK ROOM WHERE YOU'D DO YOUR SHAGGING. AND THESE GIRLS, OF COURSE, LOVED THE BEATLES. MOST OF THE GROUPS CAME BACK FROM HAMBURG WITH A DOSE OF GONORRHEA. . . . I WAS CALLED THE POX DOCTOR. THEY USED TO COME AND SAY, "LOOK, I'VE GOT A DOSE; YOU KNOW, THE CLAP." SO I'D MAKE THEM PISS INTO A GLASS AND LOOK AT IT, AND IF IT WAS LIKE SHREDDED WHEAT, I'D SAY, "YOU BETTER GET DOWN TO THE DOCTOR; YOU'VE GOT A DOSE. . . . " ONE SHOT IN THE ASS AND THEY WERE OKAY.

Williams, who has the most joyful laughter you will ever hear, laughs out loud when he talks about his so-called medical career.

"Truthfully, the prostitutes in the windows loved the boys. I mean, it wasn't a real problem, though it could be troubling."

He howls again.

"The truth, Larry? In the red-light district of Hamburg, [getting an STD] was like catching a cold."

While the Beatles got their medical "protection" courtesy of Allan Williams, they found an unusual protector of their bodies in the form of ex-boxer, and ex-con, Horst Fascher, who was also, coincidentally, a lover of rock music. Fascher, "the Enforcer," was a bouncer for club owner Koschmider at the Indra and the Kaiserkeller. He protected the boys from the violent thugs of St. Pauli, and also from themselves. One dramatic night, the Enforcer noticed that John was missing from the stage. He looked and looked and found young John in a restroom, where he was locked in an embrace with a woman. Never one for displaying a gentle touch, Fascher poured water over both lovers and demanded that John get on the stage, "even if he was stark naked." John did appear with only his underpants on, along with the covering guitar, and according to Fascher, the "toilet seat hanging around his neck."

But despite the sleep deprivation and sanitary disasters, the boys managed to rock their way to a limited sense of self-worth and gratification.

What Williams and Fascher couldn't do was protect the boys from Koschmider's fighting goons, who punished them for abandoning the Kaiserkeller for another club. The Beatles' sudden arrival at a third club, the Top Ten, set off a rampage against them by the furious club owner, leading to a disgraceful exit from Hamburg. The only bright spot of the attacks against the boys was the courageous defense by Fascher, whose presence was menacing to the gangsters, who enforced their own brand of martial law. Fascher's protection was a courageous defense, but he couldn't cover every attack, and the boys were constantly being beaten up.

"I tried to protect them, Larry, but it didn't always work," Fascher says. "I did my best against the bastards. When they left, I was really down. I really liked these boys."

Much like the trio of friends who will soon enter this story, Fascher would make a difference later on.

The Beatles were finished with the filth, sex, violence, and short-lived hope of Hamburg. They were done with Hamburg, after a humiliating exit.

They would be happy to never go back, but "going back" had a much different meaning when the boys returned to Liverpool, unknown and ready to consider blowing it all up.

CHAPTER EIGHT

BREAKTHROUGH AT LITHERLAND

"I had never seen anything like it. . . . It was a near fucking riot."
—Tony Bramwell

"I was completely knocked out by them . . .
pounding, pulsating, overwhelming."
—Brian Kelly, music promoter

"People didn't go to a dance to scream. This was news."
—Pete Best

"I was flabbergasted."
—Bob Wooler

Direct from Hamburg—The Beatles!

Isn't it amazing how one moment in time, like a flash, can change the direction of our lives—a meeting, a chance encounter, a walk into the unknown, a look, even a glance, and perhaps also the timing of such things. Is it fate? Whatever it is, it just kept showing up for the boys.

There were so many emotions for the boys when they returned from Hamburg in mid-December 1960. George was already at home sulking, embarrassed that he, the underage Beatle, had actually been deported from Germany. The deportation was not received well in the Harrison household. Harry Harrison was livid, but as always, supportive and concerned about his son's dreams. Pete and Paul were accused by the nightclub owner, Koschmider, of starting a fire at the famous, odorous Bambo Kino, as they were packing their suitcases. Paul and Pete were arrested. After the embarrassing episode, the boys were released and no charges were filed, evidence that the accusations were questionable in the first place. After this unseemly finale in Hamburg, they came home shortly thereafter, arriving without luggage or money. Paul, pressured by father Jim, applied for work and labored briefly as an assistant to a truck driver; he was soon laid off. Pete, with the help of his mother, scheduled a concert for the boys at the Casbah. This was a welcome break in what seemed like endless days and nights for the exalted yet emasculated and ejected Hamburg rockers. John, the man who'd told the nightclub owner to "get stuffed," left on his own, without incident, wishing a brief farewell to Stu, who stayed with Astrid in Hamburg. John was visibly distressed when he returned to Menlove Avenue. He was moody and down-beat, and rarely left home unless it was to see his girlfriend, Cynthia Powell.

It is ironic that Pete, the most positive Beatle in terms of the band's possible fate at that juncture—even more than Paul—eventually would find his loyalty and optimism unrewarded. But before that happened, Pete's fast effort to put together the Casbah concert, after the humiliating return from Hamburg, was an attempt to revive the boys' spirits. His mother, Mona, also knew that getting the boys on stage again would be a tonic. At the same time that Mona scheduled the Casbah concert, there was talk among the Beatles of breaking the entire project apart—dissolving the band entirely. These were serious conversations, especially between John and Paul.

George Harrison, in particular, was beginning to doubt his future with and his place in the band. At this point, he was also sensing that his friend, Paul, was trying to push him into the background. His feelings may have been overreaction, but that's the way he felt at the time.

"George would tell me stories about that on so many different occasions," the late press master and writer Derek Taylor shared with me in the sixties. "At first, he thought he was just overreacting, but it was a sore point, a sensitivity about his role, and his feeling that Paul, even at that young age, was trying to diminish it, that would stay with him for a long time."

Paul brought George into the band and was generally supportive of his younger friend, especially during the days after Hamburg when everything was falling to pieces. It was, after all, George who suffered the greatest embarrassment when he was ejected from Germany.

"Paul can be Paul because Paul is Paul," said longtime friend Tony Bramwell, in a conversation in 2010. "In those days it was all about survival, and maybe by being just upbeat and looking confident. But the truth is, Paulie always loved George and loves him today."

One aspect of life inside the Beatles was the fear factor. Age played a role. How stable were all of us as teenagers? George Harrison was seventeen years old in 1960—*just seventeen*—and none was over twenty-one. Can you imagine the insecurity suffered by all of them, especially after the highs and lows of Hamburg?

The boys had toned up their act in the sweat- and smoke-filled Kaiserkeller, living hard, drinking harder, and loving the working women in St. Pauli. They stirred the crowds, but in their minds had nothing to show for it, absolutely nothing. Or at least that's what they thought.

"The project did not seem to benefit from all their trying," remembers Stuart's sister, Pauline. "Our family was a little nervous about Stu staying behind with Astrid, but he seemed happy; the other boys were not. They had taken their shot, and felt down about it. At least Stuart had the gift of love."

The damp winter weather had arrived in Liverpool. The boys were a mess. Shame. Depression. Hopelessness. By Christmas there were more whispers of ending the experiment. Yes, it is true. The Beatles came this close to disbanding forever in the winter of 1960. And if they had, who could have questioned the decision? By any standard, their conduct in Hamburg was dubious, considering they got involved in contract-jumping, out-of-control drug use, a lack of organization, and Allan Williams's humorous yet constant issue: visits to the doctor—a payment, you might say, for unprotected adventures in Hamburg. In truth, this was not a band of sophisticated troubadours, but rather five young people, ranging in age from seventeen to twenty, who still had some maturing to do. What could you expect, really?

That absence of direction, mixed with youthful ignorance of real-life challenges, would open the door for a daring young manager to enter the scene in late 1961. The question in December 1960: Could they hold on? In life, ignorance of the unknown is an absolute killer of dreams. For that moment, in the days after Hamburg, the doors were shut. Shut tight.

For teenagers there are always consequences, and the earlier episode of immaturity might have cost them. Their lack of maturity had surfaced nine months before when John snubbed London agent Larry Parnes, in the famous conversation when Parnes insisted on dropping either Stu or their part-time drummer, months before Pete Best joined the group. John's angry attitude toward Londoner Parnes had not exactly endeared the group to the London agents.

So, over six months later, Johnny's boys were given the most famous second chance in music history. And they didn't even know it.

Christmas Day 1960 was challenging for Brian Kelly, a young Liverpool promoter. He was one group short in his lineup for a dance at the Litherland Town Hall, north of Liverpool. The town hall, today a health center, was huge, with a capacity of 450. Kelly was eager to fill the bill when he got a surprise call from Allan Williams's associate, Bob Wooler, who offered the Beatles for the slot. Wooler—who saw something early on in the four lads—plays a key role in the Beatles' rise, and was even victimized by it, as you will learn later. The promoter, Kelly, had no knowledge of the Beatles at the time. He remembered a group called the Silver Beatles, though not fondly, and was hesitant to book them. But Wooler intervened, and along with Kelly, made the deal.

In an interview with Gillian Gaar of *Goldmine* magazine in 1996, Wooler explained how it came about. Wooler had met up with the boys again after they returned from Hamburg,

RATHER IN DISGRACE, BECAUSE THEY WERE BOOTED OUT. I WAS THEN WORKING FOR A NORTH END LIVERPOOL PROMOTER WHO HAD A STRING OF DANCES, AND THEY HAD NO WORK, AND I FIXED THEM UP WITH WHAT TURNS OUT TO BE A MEMORABLE DATE. AND IT'S NOT JUST ME SAYING THAT. IN *WHO'S WHO*, THE BRITISH EDITION, IN MCCARTNEY'S ENTRY, OF ALL THE BOOKINGS AND APPEARANCES THEY MADE AROUND THE WORLD, LIKE SHEA STADIUM OR THE CAVERN DATES, IT SINGLES OUT AS THE MOST SIGNIFICANT DATE THAT THE BEATLES PERFORMED THE ONE I GOT THEM ON TUESDAY, THE 27TH OF DECEMBER, 1960.

FOR SIX POUNDS, BY THE WAY, THAT'S ALL THE PROMOTER WOULD PAY THEM. NOT SIX POUNDS PER PERSON, BUT FOR THE WHOLE GROUP. I'D SAID, "LOOK, I'M DOING THE SHOW, I'LL PUT YOU ON JUST

FOR HALF-AN-HOUR, AT A VERY GOOD SPOT IN THE MIDDLE OF THE NIGHT. PLEASE DO IT." AND THEY HAD NO OTHER WORK, SO THEY DID IT. AND THAT'S THE DATE LISTED IN *WHO'S WHO* AS BEING THE MOST SIGNIFICANT DATE. A TURNING-POINT DATE. A LANDMARK DATE.

THEY JUST WOWED EVERYBODY. AND IT WAS SO BEWILDERING WHAT THEY WERE DOING. BECAUSE THEY WERE DOING NOTHING SPECIAL, EXCEPT THERE WAS A CERTAIN ENERGY THAT NO OTHER GROUP RADIATED.

Money was not an issue. Wooler had asked for eight pounds. He got six, but also got something bigger. Kelly, like most local promoters, had heard about the Silver Beatles' decision to break a deal with Parnes, the London promoter, for a gig the previous May and go off on that raggedy tour with Johnny Gentle in Scotland. There is one thing to know about promoters: they have long memories. But Kelly had an open mind, along with a hard press by Bob Wooler, who proved persuasive. Kelly also needed a band, quickly. It was the first time Wooler took up the cause of indecisive teenagers who showed *some* talent but, although hard-driving, also showed naïveté when it came to personal relationships. Still, Wooler took up their cause. He liked what he saw and was convinced that the boys' performance would more than make up for their no-show back in the spring. Wooler was mad, other promoters thought, to entrust his young career to the boys from the Jacaranda, the former cleaners and toilet painters.

Did he know that it would became the "stuff that screams are made of," his later description of Beatlemania? It was unknowingly the turning point, that special moment that can only play out unrehearsed, when the senses are unaware of what's happening around you.

The show happened December 26, 1960, Boxing Day, a secular holiday that occurs the day after Christmas (or the first or second weekday after Christmas). It was, and remains, a bank holiday, another day of freedom for workers and students.

Tony Bramwell read an advertisement about the show and decided to go. Bramwell grew up near George Harrison and Paul McCartney. He boarded the number 81 bus, the bus that Harry Harrison drove on most days. Tony had not seen George in some time, and was always wondering what was happening in George's life. And suddenly there was George, sitting on the number 81 bus, guitar case in hand, looking directly at Tony. (For those who, like John, exalt the numerological power of the number 9, it should be noted that both the 8 and 1 from the number 81 bus, and the numbers of the date, 2 and 7, add up to 9. Numerology enthusiasts aside, the various coincidences of the number 9 in the boys' lives are amazing.)

Wearing a black leather jacket and jeans, George explained to Bramwell that he was also headed to Litherland Town Hall. Tony, impressed by the shiny jacket, smiled. But he was a little nervous and his voice was a bit shaky.

"So you are headed to the dance?" Bramwell asked.

"We're playing there tonight," George said.

Bramwell was stunned. Shocked. He replied, "*You're* the German group?"

George nodded and said, "Yes, direct from Liverpool!"

So George, Bramwell thought, was now part of the Beatles, who were in fact advertised for the show as: "The Beatles—Direct from Hamburg."

And then Bramwell, who would eventually do business with the boys for five decades, made his very first deal. He arranged to carry George's guitar into the Litherland Town Hall in return for free admission. It was, in the long run, a bargain. George also found his first "personal assistant." Bramwell got a free backstage pass and the youngest Beatle would find a lifetime friend.

"It was my first job, Larry," Bramwell exclaimed to me with pride fifty-one years later.

Litherland was a popular dance hall for teenagers. Alcohol was banned, and there was a strict dress code forbidding jeans, which in those days were viewed as working clothes. It turns out no one needed alcohol to get a buzz on that night.

When George stepped off the number 81 bus at Litherland with his valet, Mr. Bramwell, promoter Brian Kelly did a double take. George and the others had longer hair, tight-fitting jeans, and black leather jackets. At that moment, the veteran promoter had no choice but to go with the flow. The flow was unpredictable, jeans and all.

With Stu still in Hamburg, the Beatles needed a bass guitar player.

But Paul, until then a guitarist, would not play bass guitar that night. A friend, Chas Newby, filled in.

Their first song, a song that would find its way into their repertoire a year later, was Little Richard's famously electrifying "Long Tall Sally." The kids of Litherland were dancing, but after a while, the dancing stopped. There was a surge, followed by a continuing onrush of the fans, toward the riser. In a preview of things to come, some of the girls screamed for the drummer, Pete Best, who was impressing the dancers with his so-called atomic beat—his very loud use of the kick drum. The boys and girls became frenetic. It was, Bramwell would tell me fifty years later, as if "someone had found a new source of energy, pulled the switch, and turned it on."

Even Bramwell couldn't control the beat of his heart, the adrenaline flowing through his body.

THEY WERE FUCKING BRILLIANT, LARRY. . . . THEY WERE SO LOUD AND ENERGETIC. THEY WERE ROUGH, CRUDE, AND THEY WEREN'T DOING THE RUN-OF-THE-MILL STUFF. THEY WERE DOING B SIDES, MOST OF WHICH I NEVER HEARD BEFORE BUT STUFF WHICH I REALLY LIKED. THEY WEREN'T DOING THE CLIFF RICHARD AND THE SHADOWS KIND OF STUFF LIKE EVERYONE ELSE WAS DOING. THEY WERE JUST BRILLIANT. A TOTALLY NEW SOUND . . . A NEW THING. IT WAS MAGIC. I HAD NEVER SEEN ANYTHING LIKE IT. . . . [IT] WAS A NEAR FUCKING RIOT. I MEAN, THESE GUYS WHO WERE MY FRIENDS, SEARCHING FOR SPENT BOMBS AT THE MILITARY AIR BASE NEAR OUR HOMES, WERE *THAT* BAND FROM HAMBURG. IT WAS THRILLING AND EXCITING AND I COULDN'T STOP TALKING ABOUT IT.

"What made it so special?" I ask.

Bramwell smiles broadly.

"Picture this. Usually a band gets people dancing. But they were loud, a bit raucous, and in perfect, well almost perfect, harmony. They made the kids, including me, all hyped up. They were together, really together, and I'll never forget Paulie screaming into that microphone on 'Long Tall Sally.' It was music perfection. The Beatles were sweating, the kids were sweating; it was like a riot that shattered the senses. . . . I couldn't sleep that night . . . thinking about it, and I was part of the riot."

The "riot," he explains, forced promoter Kelly to send some bouncers around the back of the stage. Bramwell thought they were placed there to keep the fans out. In truth, Kelly was protecting not the Beatles, but rather himself.

With great nostalgia, Kelly later told *Mersey Beat,* "I stationed the bouncers on the floor of their dressing room to stop other promoters who were in the hall from entering."

But he missed one.

A protégé, Dave Forshaw, was at Litherland that night at Kelly's invitation. Forshaw was just seventeen, but he was already a promoter of dances. The minute the show was over, he raced backstage and signed the Beatles to five Thursday and Saturday concerts at St. John's Hall in the Bootle. The offer was for seven pounds and ten shillings per concert.

A half century has passed, but Forshaw describes it as if still in the thrill of the actual moment.

"I knew I had to get them, Larry. They were so different. Instead of people just dancing, people were in a passionate, eye-popping, mind-blowing trance. The Beatles set the trap. In the first appearance at St. John's, their boots on, their black jackets shining, their rocking even harder, an extra 192 fans showed up. I remember. My 'gate,'" he says with backward-glancing humor, "was the biggest I ever had. And since I worked on such a narrow margin, I took home a few extra pounds. In the meantime, I was having a ball. I booked them constantly, but then the Cavern took over. And I had to watch them from afar."

The man who put them in the Cavern, deejay and visionary Bob Wooler, colorfully describes the Litherland performance.

"I have a word for the occasion," Wooler recalls, "if you'll pardon me: I was flabbergasted!"

One of the people who watched them at the pulse-pounding Litherland concert was John's passion, Cynthia Powell. In her memoirs, she recalls the special moment that was Litherland.

"The boys did [in Litherland] what they did in Hamburg, throwing themselves around the stage, playing numbers that went on and on. . . . The . . .

energy, humor, and wild pounding music packed such a punch . . . it left Liverpool's teenagers crazy with excitement."

There was a boy in the crowd who was fascinated, almost breathless, by the performance. At the time, he was just seventeen, training to be an apprentice for British Railways. His name was William Howard Ashton. Is the name familiar? He lived in Bootle, a blue-collar neighborhood of Liverpool, one that he describes as "tough but respectful." He had gone to the concert on the number 61 bus. When he got inside Litherland, he became inspired, shocked, and very shook up.

LET ME TELL YOU ABOUT THIS, LARRY. THERE WERE ABOUT 150 PEOPLE. THEY DIDN'T KNOW WHAT TO EXPECT. I WAS ALL HEATED UP. I HAD NEVER SEEN A BAND LIKE THIS. THEY DIDN'T PLAY THE USUAL COVER SONGS. I THOUGHT PEOPLE WERE GOING TO EXPLODE WHEN THEY SAW THE JEANS AND THE BLACK LEATHER. SOME OF THE GIRLS IN THE CROWD STARTED SCREAMING WHEN THEY STARTED SINGING REALLY HARD ROCK AND MOVING AROUND. . . . THERE WERE TWO SONGS I REMEMBER—"MONEY" AND ESPECIALLY PAUL SINGING "LONG TALL SALLY." I HAD NEVER HEARD A WHITE GUY SINGING 'LONG TALL SALLY.' I HAD NEVER HEARD ANYBODY SING IN THAT WAY—RAW AND SCREAMING. I HAD NEVER SEEN ANYTHING CLOSE TO THEM IN PUTTING AN ACT TOGETHER.

It was a night that would change young Ashton's life. He walked home, unable to sort out what he had just seen.

"I thought they would be bigger than Elvis. I had never seen anything so good. It was so memorable."

William Howard Ashton would someday look in a phone book and randomly pick a stage name, Kramer, as in "Billy J. Kramer." The boy in the crowd at Litherland would soon receive a gift from the boys—a song, a musical legacy. But on that night, a chilly December night, he walked home just a dreamer, a kid possessed by the band and the music. Like the boys, he too had a date with fate.

For the Beatles, still down-and-out, needy, and insecure, there was at least a shred of hope that night. Walking quietly out of Litherland, the roar of the crowds now a distant thunder in their ears, there was a renewed air of optimism. Tony remembers boarding the bus with John, Cynthia, Paul, Pete, and George. Pete remembers that they had a van that was dirtied up by the crowd, forcing them all to take the bus instead. One thing was certain: whatever the mode of transportation, there was a gleam in their eyes.

"They were so up, it was amazing," Bramwell recalls. "I didn't know they were even upset after Hamburg. I asked John if he was happy to be back in Liverpool. In what would be remembered as typical John Lennon fashion, he said, 'Fucking fabulous.'"

Bramwell will never forget that ride home. Pete got off first, then John, Cynthia, and Paul.

"Later, I rode quietly back to Speke with my employer for the night, George Harrison. We stared into space, wondering if all around us was about to change. George smiled that crooked smile of his, and in the middle of a cold winter night, we walked to our homes."

The best was yet to come. News accounts would describe the Litherland appearance as an "explosion" of emotion. Dave Forshaw, maybe the youngest promoter in Liverpool history, calls it a moment of change.

"It was raw, animalistic, even somewhat unreal that five people could make so many others so charged, so delighted, so on fire."

The Beatles would play thirty-five more concerts at Litherland, but as they say in Hamburg's St. Pauli sex district, "You always remember the first."

The timing of the "first" was impeccable.

"The music of that period was dominated by Cliff Richard and the Shadows, the first really successful rock enterprise in Britain," remembers rock music historian Ron Ellis.

"Richard was the UK version of Presley; he was magnetic and exciting. But the boys' style showed a new aggressiveness, a wilder stage presence, more of a reckless abandon. Eventually, their music dominated. But like they did to Lonnie Donegan, they eclipsed Richard, who was one of their standards."

Although eclipsed by the Beatles, Richard, born five days later than John Lennon, has had an enduring career. He was the first rock star to be knighted, in 1995, two years before Bramwell's friend "Paulie" became Sir Paul.

"Richard was really good, but by the time the boys came back from Hamburg, a crescendo was building for something new," Ron Ellis remembers.

"The old jazz groups were dying out. Hundreds of bands were doing rock all over Merseyside. When they showed up at Litherland, it was simple—they were just better than anyone else around. They were so much more professional. Combine that with John's acerbic wit coming out more and more, and it was an amazing unfolding of a new sound, a new look. The legend of Litherland spread."

But how quickly, and is the focus appropriate? I fully accept Litherland as an important moment, mainly for the spirit of the boys. But there is a question: When do legends become legends? Rarely do legends become legends in real time; it usually evolves years later.

Freda Kelly, who would work with Epstein and the boys for many years, and the woman I call "Freda the Believer," did not see the boys in their first appearance at Litherland, but she attended later gigs at the town hall.

"Interestingly, word spread about that first event, but it wasn't like a tidal wave, just whispers among some of the kids. Was I excited? There is no way to explain just how excited I was."

Liverpool Hope University's respected Beatles and pop scholar Dr. Michael Brocken sees Litherland as a mythological moment—not really seminal, but rather just a step.

I SUPPOSE ONE MIGHT SAY THAT IT WAS IMPORTANT FOR THOSE WHO ATTENDED, AND ALSO FOR THE GROUPS [THE SEARCHERS, THE DEL RENAS, AND THE DELTONES] WHO HAD TO PLAY ALONGSIDE THE BEATLES. . . . SO, WHILE WE MUST NOT CALL PEOPLE LIARS WE SHOULD ACCEPT THAT THIS WAS VERY SMALL BEER AT THE TIME [AND] HAS BEEN MYTHOLOGIZED, BUT STILL HOLD HISTORICAL SIGNIFICANCE, OF COURSE. EVEN IF WE ACCEPT THAT A WHISPER WENT OUT AFTER THE GIG . . . ONE WOULD HAVE TO SAY THAT EARLY 1960S LIVERPOOL WAS FULL OF PREGNANT SILENCES ABOUT POPULAR MUSIC AT THE BEST OF TIMES BECAUSE OF ITS PAROCHIAL NATURE.

Brocken refers to the jazz and skiffle ideals of the city, and the general antipathy toward the ascent of rock.

Always on target in his historical analysis, Brocken seems to put things in perspective. The Litherland appearance became well known, in the beginning, to a small group of Merseyside people. But it was, to the *smallest* group, the direct-from-Hamburg Beatles, much more than just a show that created "buzz."

Whenever, and however, the lore of Litherland made its way into the Beatles' history, there was and remains a very good reason for it: the boys themselves.

Three years and seven months later, in a dressing room at the famed Montreal Forum, I asked John Lennon what the real turning point was in their evolution from unknown to fame, from boys traveling on a snowy night on the number 81 bus to budding celebrities in their hometown and beyond.

WELL . . . YOU COULD LOOK AT MANY EVENTS . . . OUR PERFORMANCE BEFORE THE QUEEN MUCH LATER . . . THOSE *MARVELOUS* HAMBURG NIGHTS [HE SAID WITH SARCASM], THE CAVERN. . . . BUT TO BE TRUTH-FUL, IT ALMOST ENDED AROUND CHRISTMASTIME IN 1960. . . . WE WERE DOWN AND OUT . . . AND WE PLAYED AT THIS PLACE . . . LITHERLAND TOWN HALL . . . AND ALL OF A SUDDEN WE GRABBED IT BY THE HORNS . . . AS YOU AMERICANS WOULD SAY, WHATEVER THAT MEANS . . . AND WE STARTED TO MOVE FORWARD . . . GOT MORE DEALS . . . BEFORE EPPY [EPSTEIN] . . . AND ON THE BACKS OF SEVERAL HUNDRED KIDS, JUST LIKE US, WHO THOUGHT WE WERE GOOD . . . AND LET ME TELL YOU, LARRY [HIS GESTURES SUDDENLY CHANGED FROM HUMILITY TO HUBRIS] . . . LET ME TELL YOU, *WE WERE GOOD*. . . . WE JUST WEREN'T SURE WE WERE GOOD ENOUGH. DID WE KNOW THAT IT WOULD CHANGE EVERYTHING? NO, LARRY, WE REALLY DIDN'T, BUT WE FELT A BIT BETTER AFTER OUR SO SAD AND PAINFUL RETURN FROM HAMBURG. AND LARRY, IT WAS VERY, VERY PAINFUL," HE CONCLUDED, CHUCKLING WITH FOND REMEMBRANCE.

Litherland was, as Professor Brocken describes, "small beer" in the big Liverpool scene. But to the boys, it was a jolt, a shot of hope in the midst of a dark period of despair. They survived December 1960. There were new bookings ahead, and they would earn pocket change. But not far away, before the young music retailer walked into their lives, before Bill Harry exploded on the scene with tabloid music genius, and despite internal feud-ing, their pockets would be a little less empty.

After genuine depression, the humiliation of being booted from Hamburg, and internal debate about whether they should split, the Litherland Town Hall experience transformed the young men from gloom to optimism. That in itself, the transfusion of hope, makes the Litherland concert a meaningful event in saving the boys from possible destruction at their own hands.

All this came on the heels of the first trip to what appeared to be a forbidden city. They had barely escaped Hamburg. Despite their ambivalence, there would be more trips to the city of the night, but along the way, a personal tragedy, one that left a lifelong imprint on the founder of the band.

CHAPTER NINE

THE LIFE AND DEATH OF STUART SUTCLIFFE

"It may be something John Lennon regretted for the rest of his life, not that he struck the blows that killed, but that he thought he might have, a bit like everyone comes to a crime scene and every witness is unreliable."
—Ron Ellis

"Most mothers believe their children are the most brilliant and the most beautiful—but it happened to be true about Stuart."
—Martha Sutcliffe (aka "Millie"), mother of Stuart Sutcliffe

THE STORY OF THE STRIKINGLY BEAUTIFUL BOY IS THE CENTERPIECE OF THE BEATLES' FIRST MOMENTS IN HAMBURG. It is also a story of deep love—man to man, and man to woman—portrayed as a romance for the ages, yet one that lasted so briefly.

If Hamburg was on the cutting edge of art and pop culture in 1960 and 1961, then the most forgotten Beatle, Stuart Sutcliffe, was in the right place at the right time. An inspiration to his best friend, John Lennon, and a startling sex symbol on stage, Stuart, in the Hamburg days and nights, arrived at the confluence of three driving forces: music, art on canvas, and love. Mostly love.

Yoko Ono talks of Stuart's friendship and its impact on John, and then wistfully, she remembers her talks with John about Hamburg.

"He told me *everything*. He loved to talk about Hamburg. There were no secrets. It was the kind of life I never knew. . . . It meant total freedom. At his side always was Stuart, sweet Stuart. There wasn't a time in John's life when he didn't think about Stuart. He spoke always of his love and respect for Stuart."

Stuart joined the group because of John. All those meetings at Ye Cracke, all the soul-searching between them, had created a bond that few men have in a lifetime. Was Stuart the brother John never had? Maybe. But mostly the boy Paul McCartney once described as a "typical pimple-faced art student" was just a wide-open conduit for John's innermost feelings.

John worshipped Stu as a confidante, a brother almost, a best friend in a life of seeking real and genuine friends. Their journey to Hamburg, that fateful first trip in 1960 during which they lived in near-poverty conditions, ended badly. But in life, living in a certain moment and trying to understand what that moment means, can be a mystery that, in time, can unlock abilities never before considered. What the young Beatles accomplished in Hamburg in 1960 seemed irrelevant in the moment, but became strong and durable when the moment was over. Stuart played a powerful role in that moment. With Astrid Kirchherr by his side, his talent for fine art and her extraordinary view through the lens of a camera not only strengthened his bond with John, but also led to the creation of a revolutionary look and style that would define the early Beatles—with the dark suits, thin ties, and mop-top haircuts. They would later embrace their acid and spiritual period in 1968 with longer hair, freakier clothing, and a new look that was more compatible with their contemporaries who were in the same funk of drugs, protest, war, and revolution. But it was the original look that will always endure, and the beautiful son of Millie Sutcliffe was a certifiable originator of it.

Along with that enduring style, there was an energy between John and Stuart that outlived Stuart.

"They were like soul mates," says Yoko, who adds that she wishes she could have met Stuart. In my earlier book, *Lennon Revealed*, Yoko emotionally recalled, "There was not a period in our lives, daily, weekly, or whenever, that John did not remember Stuart."

What Stuart brought to the table—especially the wooden table at Ye Cracke in a post-beatnik environment of great social debate—was a vision of life that John might never have experienced. Stuart, unlike the young John Lennon, was spiritual—not in the religious sense, but in the curious and empathetic way he looked at people, the environment, and the joys of everyday life. Stuart, remembered fondly by Bill Harry as a member of the beatnik-like Dissenters, was often the conscience of the debating group. Although John would do most of the talking at the pub, he freely gave the platform to his close friend.

"We were plotting for a better society, and we thought we had all the answers for our generation," Harry says. "The interesting thing was that, while we were wide-eyed with large hopes, Stuart, in general, had what I would say was a larger view of his canvas of the world. Unlike most rebellious teenagers, he had a worldview and was quite ready at seventeen or eighteen to make his point with art."

Colin Fallows of Liverpool's John Moores University (formerly the Art Institute), and an expert on Stu's work, revels at the talent and the connection between art and the rock and pop revolutions of the fifties and sixties.

"Many people will point out that the art schools of England were the incubators of a generation of musicians, but in Stuart's case, the Art Institute was the incubator of his own brilliant career in art itself. He enhanced the Beatles' early life, but at the same time, in Hamburg, escalated his art to a higher level."

Fallows shows me the interesting little courtyard through which Paul and George would sneak into the Art Institute from their own school, to jam with John and Stuart. There is probably no single expert more versed on Stuart's art work than Fallows.

"You have to understand that Stuart, so influential in John's life, is not a footnote able to bridge the interface of sound, music, and visual arts. He was a very serious student. His and Astrid's [art] should not be viewed as Beatles memorabilia, but rather interesting art on its own. It's also interesting that at the time Stuart and the Beatles came to Hamburg in 1960 and 1961, the world was turning to Hamburg not just for music, but its burgeoning art scene. The timing was fascinating."

Unfortunately, Stuart is not around to crow about his influence. One would guess he probably wouldn't boast about his impact. He was much too busy painting his canvases and looking, along with his love-mate, Astrid, and his best friend, John, for the real meaning of life.

But there are many survivors still here to explain the magical being of Stuart Sutcliffe.

George Harrison, in his special comments in Derek Taylor's rambling and revealing autobiography, *Fifty Years Adrift*, offered his always-candid view: "Stuart Sutcliffe was like our art director. In a mysterious way, Stuart in conjunction with the German crowd [not just Astrid] was really responsible for that certain look we had. . . . I had a lot of fist fights with Stuart, but I really liked him and we were very friendly before he died."

Life model June Furlong still talks about how sweet Stu was, yet so serious about his work—much more serious than his friend John, also an artist but a great and funny mischief-maker in class.

"Now, there was a talent," Furlong remembers. "He couldn't wait for their makeshift rehearsals, when Paul and George would sneak over from the Institute. But I always felt, you know, that for Stuart, the art was everything. He put his heart into it, with a passion."

An artist he was. His paintings are the object of desire here in the twenty-first century. A "very good rock 'n' roll bass guitar player," says Bill Harry. Certainly a physical presence, as well. But his sister Pauline wants people to know that Stuart was much more than eye candy.

He was, she says with endless love, "a man of supreme spirituality who was preoccupied and completely fascinated with the questions of life and death. He was a trusted friend with a solid moral base. Yes, he could be naughty and wild, but there was in Stuart a morality that few his age would ever under-stand. And also, more than anything, he was so interesting to be around."

He was also a talented musician, although the fading truth of time, always the enemy of telling the real story, has distorted his talent. Witnesses from Klaus Voorman to Bill Harry and many others still remember Stuart's talent on the bass guitar, and his brief but alluring stardom and appeal to the crowds in Hamburg. Perhaps, though, his most significant contribution was his impact on the former milkman.

Bill Harry sees Stuart's own life as a prism in which John could see joy, despite so many moments of indecision, distrust, and hurt inflicted on him by his splintered early life.

JOHN WAS SMITTEN WITH STUART'S COOL AND INTRIGUING WAY. . . . STUART WAS NOT A MAN WITH SUPERLATIVE WORDS OR DEMONSTRATIVE PROCLAMATIONS. HE WAS A QUIET, SENSITIVE THINKER WHO BROUGHT A SPECIAL INTELLECTUAL ACCENT TO THE GROUP. I THINK GEORGE HAD A SPECIAL ATTRACTION TO HIM. GEORGE WAS ALSO A THINKER, ALWAYS

TRYING TOO HARD TO FIND LIFE'S TRUE MEANING. IT IS NO SURPRISE, TO ME, THAT IT WAS GEORGE WHO ACCOMPANIED JOHN ON THOSE VISITS OF CONSOLATION AND REFLECTION TO ASTRID AFTER STUART'S DEATH. JOHN NEEDED GEORGE TO HELP HIM COPE; HE NEEDED THAT TIME.

Stuart's impact on the group, especially John and Paul, was never premeditated or calculated. He was in the forefront of the group's early rise because he *was* so understated. His actions were spoken in looks, appearances, and a genuine concern about the inner workings of people. He had an inner warmth that radiated in his eyes. He was a fascinating young man. His avant-garde personality reflected so many aspects of the group's evolving success: a cleaner look, yet an appearance of modernism; a step ahead of current fashions; a daring, reflected in Stuart's most sexual and stirring movements on stage. Stuart and his young love Astrid Kirchherr mesmerized the group—he, merely with his presence, and she, with her beauty, photographic art, and themes that corroborated their music with a futuristic style that reverberated throughout the world of pop culture.

Yet, with all due credit to Ms. Kirchherr, it was, according to Stu's sister Pauline, "less Astrid and more Stuart" that changed Johnny's boys into a first-class physical attraction.

"Astrid deserves so much credit, but Stuart was the inspiration," Pauline says. "It was her love, her dedication to him, and his for her, that led them to this amazing collaboration of art, photography, and ideas."

No one who testifies in this story will deny that. But also, no one can deny that the eye and spirit of the photographer brought alive the boys' youth and vitality. As the decades have passed, Kirchherr's photographs have provided a vibrant retrospective of that time in the boys' lives, and behind them is a backstory of her influence, Stuart's lasting legacy, and the two love stories that shaped the Beatles in Hamburg.

The first is a story of young love: Astrid and Stuart.

One privately held photograph is proof of the endless affection of this love story. In a rare contemporary interview, Kirchherr told colleague and fellow Lennon biographer Tim Riley that a photo of Stuart remains at her bedside, a picture she acknowledges each and every night.

She told the *Woman's Hour* program on the BBC during the opening of her photography retrospective at the Victoria Gallery and Museum in late 2010, "I still love him up to now, and he is my first and last love, in my life."

As the other boys scrambled to the safety of home, three of them disgraced by the law, Stuart decided to stay in Hamburg. Astrid emphasizes that their relationship was one reason, but she adds, "Don't forget the art. Well, he had the chance to get a scholarship in the University of Hamburg, the Art College. So that was something brilliant for him. And he always wanted to become a painter. He loved the idea of being a rock 'n' roll musician, and, you know, all the behavior that came with it. But in his heart, he was just an artist, and when the opportunity came up to stay in Hamburg, and his teacher was Mr. Paolozzi, he just couldn't resist not to do that. So . . . that's why he [eventually] left the band."

The second love story—between Stuart and John—was not romantic, as far as we know. Although Pauline acknowledges it was possible.

"They were experimental boys. So anything was possible, but their friendship was deep in another way. . . . He was a man, a young boy of huge integrity, and I also remembered the quote John Lennon said about him—that he looked up to him, he trusted him, he respected him because he always told him the truth, and that's what he was like as a brother as well. So it echoes to me in the same way that it did—so it has the same authenticity—when John Lennon said that, because he was like that with everybody."

Beatle buddy Tony Bramwell was privy to the friendship in its earliest days.

"Stuart Sutcliffe was his closest friend. They shared secrets, women, and their influence on each other was incalculable."

All the time, watching on the sidelines, was Paul McCartney, who along with George, was not impressed with Stuart's musical talents. Still, the musical record shows how powerful and memorable Stu's solo rendition of "Love Me Tender" was to Hamburg audiences.

Horst Fascher and others were eyewitnesses to Paul's open jealousy of Stuart. Yet George, who cared little for Stuart's music, was fond of him on a personal level. Pauline Sutcliffe, who has fond memories of George, believes that Paul wanted Stuart to leave but was not prepared to take action.

"Paul knew that he and John were going to be something special, so when Stuart decided to leave the band, it sort of cleared the deck, so to say," she says. "Paul was a bit jealous of Stu's good looks, and he didn't appear too impressed with his musical impact, which I believe was totally underrated in the day. George, on the other hand, was sensitive to John's eventual guilt and grief, and his own as well."

Was Paul jealous? Jealous, perhaps, of Stu's good looks, but also a bit envious of his relationship with John—"as close as two men could be," according to Pauline. There were tensions on stage, and a few fistfights between Paul and Stu. There was a double-edged sword for Paul—a feeling that Stu was not up to the task musically, and Stuart's closeness to John.

The legend of John and Stu's relationship is also confirmed by John's sister, Julia Baird, who says, "He was a lovely boy. He moved with grace, and John was so dependent on him."

Paul, who today is bounded by his own code of silence regarding anything that may reflect a tad of controversy (certainly his right), will not comment on his suspected jealousy of Stu or, for that matter, anything else in this body of work. But unlike the overt and covert eventual moves toward ousting Pete Best, there doesn't appear to have been a coordinated effort to push Stuart out. To the contrary, it was the other factors that contributed to his departure: his love of Astrid, and his passion for art. His departure from the band was voluntary. About that fact there is no dispute.

Allan Williams, the man who brought the boys to Hamburg, knew that in his heart Stu was devoted to the canvas.

"He was more a friend of John's; he wasn't really a musician. John persuaded him to come to Hamburg, which upset Paul, because Paul wasn't stupid and he knew that Stu was no guitarist and he wanted to be the bass player."

John's loyalty to Stu was amazing and unswerving. In fact, there were times, not all the time, mind you, when John had his back and conspired a bit to cover up any of Stu's musical shortcomings.

One memorable episode was at Sam Leach's Casanova Club on February 11, 1961.

First Leach complained to Stuart that he was turning his back to the audience. Stu didn't seem to care. Then Leach noticed something else. In his book *Birth of the Beatles*, and a subsequent conversation with his American friend John Rose, Sam explained how he almost gave a secret away:

NOTICING THAT THE LEAD FROM STU'S GUITAR WAS DETACHED FROM THE SPEAKER, I THOUGHT I COULD HELP BY PLUGGING IT IN. UNNOTICED BY THE REST OF THE BAND, I SLIPPED ACROSS THE BACK OF MY STAGE, PICKED UP THE LEAD, AND INSERTED IT INTO THE SPEAKER SOCKET. AT ONCE, THE MOST DISCORDANT RACKET EXPLODED IN THE ROOM AND ALMOST BLEW THE ENTIRE AMPLIFIER APART. THE AMOROUS DANCERS SMOOCHING IN A WORLD OF THEIR OWN JUMPED SEVERAL FEET INTO THE AIR. HANDS WERE CLASPED OVER THEIR EYES. STU HAD BEEN HAPPILY PLUCKING AWAY AT THE STRINGS, SAFE IN THE KNOWLEDGE THAT NOBODY COULD HEAR WHAT HE WAS OR RATHER WASN'T PLAYING. . . . PAUL LEAPED ACROSS THE STAGE AND YANKED THE OFFENDING LEAD FROM THE SPEAKER, WHISPERING HARSHLY, "WHY DID YOU DO THAT SET? YOU KNOW HE CAN'T PLAY." . . . TO MAKE MATTERS WORSE, PAUL'S STAGE WHISPER CAME OUT OVER THE ENTIRE SPEAKER SYSTEM. . . . I SEARCHED FOR THE NEAREST HOLE. LENNON GAVE ME A SLY SMIRK.

In later years, Paul offered compliments to Stuart. In 2001, in an article published in *Beatlefan* magazine, Paul said, in a 1964 quote referring to guitar talent, that "Stuart . . . was a great bass man." George Harrison, back in Liverpool after the first disastrous trip to Hamburg, pleaded with Stuart to come back to Liverpool and pick up where he left off, on the bass guitar.

If there truly was a shortage of talent, the fans never complained, especially when Stu sang "Love Me Tender."

But musical issues aside, Stuart Sutcliffe was the all-time male best friend of John Lennon. Stuart and John were hard to separate—their conversations about life and love, anxiety, promise, and fear of failure would last for hours. They both loved art as well as music.

Stuart's artistic acumen rubbed off on John in more ways than one. Yoko Ono smiles warmly when she talks about John's recollections of Stu Sutcliffe. In some ways, she tells this author, it was Stu's influence as an artist that led John to her.

In the early days I think he really had a very deep kind of exchange and got a lot out of Stu Sutcliffe. . . . He said that Stu was somebody that he really cared for . . . he was into Stu. He was kind of feeling that artistic kind of thing for Stu, and then he had to be a rocker. So you know, in some ways he was thinking, "Oh yeah, well you know, actually, I'm an artist," or whatever. You know, in his soul he was thinking he was doing something that was not as classy as what he should, he could be doing, you know. So then, you know, he came to the gallery and I'm doing an art show. . . . It was like a bit like that.

When asked if Stu may have played a subconscious role in John's attraction to Yoko, she replies, "Well, Stu was an artist, I was an artist, you know? There's a bit of a connection there."

Stuart Sutcliffe in his art and heart was anti-establishment. He titillated John and inspired him to become a better artist, and in return, John heated up the fire against all forms of authority. Eventually the respect turned to mutual and deep affection and love. They told each other the truth, sometimes painfully. And Pauline Sutcliffe witnessed it up close.

I think they both absolutely loved one another for very obvious reasons, you know, and we're not talking about same-sex relationships now—more about that later. We're talking about intimacy between men. Stuart was the personification of everything John wanted to be, and John was the personification of that part of my brother that he was uncomfortable with. My brother was a very, very sophisticated anarchist as a painter. He had anti-authority issues that came out in the most effectible way—like when he was told that art students can only produce work from thirty-by-sixteen-inch canvases, he would paint on six-feet-by-five-feet canvases. That's a form of anarchist. That's not going with the rules. It's clear from the manuscript that I've shown you before [Stuart's personal writings about John] that he also found John's way of expressing his anarchy, uh,

WORRYING, PUZZLING, NOT PARTICULARLY ACCEPTABLE, AND WHEN YOU READ ON IN IT, YOU CAN SEE THAT HE'S TRYING TO CHANNEL HIM INTO USING HIS CREATIVE ENERGY IN A CREATIVE WAY RATHER THAN A DESTRUCTIVE WAY.

The destruction of Stuart Sutcliffe is still one of the greatest mysteries in the history of the boys. And the exact reason for his physical demise remains one of the great controversies in the life of John Lennon.

Stuart's problems began on the night of January 30, 1961. The group was playing at Latham Hall, Seaforth, Liverpool, when a group of toughs attacked Stuart as he helped load equipment in the rear of the hall. He was kicked and punched so hard in the stomach and head that he was covered with blood before Pete Best arrived to battle the roughnecks, with John Lennon soon joining in. It was not uncommon for the boys to face the wrath of so-called Teddy Boys, the slick blue-collar street boys who made it their business to threaten artists and performers, especially the good-looking ones who vied for the attention of the girls. This beating was especially brutal, but the only real casualty was John, who broke a finger The impact on Stuart's long-term health is really unknown.

A few months later, another beating would allegedly come at the hands and feet of the man he respected most. It was a late night in Hamburg during the band's second visit to Germany. John was extremely frustrated by demands by George and Paul that Stuart leave the group. He was also pressured by Stuart's obsession with Astrid and his disenchantment with performing. That night, Stuart told John he would leave the band and study art, a mission he would begin in July. In a drunken rage, John Lennon beat Stuart Sutcliffe to a pulp, punching and flagging at him and kicking him repeatedly in the head. As Stuart lay there in pain, Paul McCartney tried in vain to break it up, but did manage to get him home, even as John ran from the scene. The description of the beating was relayed from Stuart to his sister Pauline, who notes that doctors say Stuart's death was caused by an indentation in his skull, the result of a trauma like a punch or a kick.

Paul's attempt to save him seemed to work, at least for a while. But in time, the headaches increased, and he suffered greatly.

Conflicts abound over the events leading to his death, and the uncertainty remains today. Some historians, such as Bill Harry, insist that Stuart's injuries resulted from a fall down the steps of Astrid's house.

Harry believes that there was no such beating. "John Lennon never beat up Stuart Sutcliffe or had a fight with him," Harry insists. Others say the Teddy Boys' beating was a key factor, while some believe John's beating contributed as well. But whatever the cause, the loss of Stuart was, in truth, less impactful to the others musically than artistically. The exception was John, who never quite got over it.

Stuart's death cast a brief pall over the Beatles' rise to fame. He died on April 10, 1962, the victim of a brain hemorrhage. The Beatles did not learn of his death until Astrid met them at the airport as they arrived on April 13 for their triumphant third visit to Hamburg.

Although the Beatles praised Stuart in Hunter Davies's biography of them in 1968, it would take decades for the potential causes of his death to surface. The story, so many years later, remains a mystery. But it also took decades for people to understand the real story of his impact on the group's success: a lesson in raw sex appeal, a progressive, forward-looking perspective of life in the moment, the talent of a gifted artist, and a stylistic personality that accented modernism. He is, in this corner, a most underrated influence on their overall success. Like his dramatic oil on canvas that has infatuated the contemporary art world, Stuart's influence on the future stars was emphatic.

I never met the man, but scores of people I spoke with on the Liverpool scene did. Like Astrid Kirchherr, they fell in love with his quiet grace and boyish charisma.

His death may have also left behind an unsolved mystery in the remaining eighteen years of John Lennon's life.

Like others, researcher and author Ron Ellis wonders what impact Stuart's death had on John in his remaining years.

"It may be something John Lennon regretted for the rest of his life, not that he struck the blows that killed, but that he thought he might have."

Whatever the real cause of his physical demise, the young and beautiful

Stuart Sutcliffe left behind treasures of art, and a real living legacy. Like others after him, he gave the Beatles a sense of knowledge about the world around them, especially the forms of art, and the dimensions of extra-modern fashion, that Brian Epstein added to their look later on in his historic makeover.

In 1961, though, still in their jeans and leather jackets, they carried on in Hamburg, where other influences were ever present, and unlikely friends provided bountiful gifts.

CHAPTER TEN

HAMBURG PART 2—"LOVE ME DO"

"Sometimes they had loose tongue. I was so strict . . .
that's why Lennon, the leader, called me a 'Nazi bastard.'"
—Horst Fascher, the Beatles' friend and protector

"'Love Me Do,' Larry, wasn't the best song we ever wrote.
But it really put us out front."
—Paul McCartney, to the author, three years after the song was recorded

With the exception of George Harrison's attempts to care for John's grief, the Beatles, as a group, filed away Stuart's death as they continued their Hamburg journeys.

The boys were fresh and invigorated when—already well known in Britain—they were greeted as celebrities upon arrival back in Hamburg for a third visit, this time at the Star Club, in April 1962, primarily because of the guile and energy of Horst Fascher.

During a visit to Liverpool, the sometime bouncer, club manager, and rock enthusiast convinced Brian Epstein, now the Beatles' manager, that the Star Club would be the most famous club in Hamburg. "The Enforcer"—the man who had shielded them and protected them when they escaped Bruno Koschmider on the first trip—was waiting with open arms, not to mention rules.

Horst Fascher was now the boss at the Star Club, an arrangement that had sent him to Liverpool to make the deal with Epstein, one of his big contributions as part of the "Fearsome Foursome," coming up in the next chapter. Sitting in his home today, not far from the Reeperbahn, Fascher, proud of his friendship with the boys, shows me the picture of the Fabs at the Star Club, and remembers the mood as he brought them to the Star.

"They still were not confident and wild. I had been given a chance to run a club that booked a thousand people a night, so I told them, 'No drunken musicians on stage.' I told them, 'Don't go on the stage with street clothing; I want you not drunk. . . . ' Sometimes they had loose tongue. I was so strict . . . that's why Lennon, the leader, called me a 'Nazi bastard,'" Fascher recalls, laughing.

He may laugh now, though at the time the slur hurt a little. But Fascher had a thick skin. He never told John that his parents had helped hide some German Jews in Hamburg during the war. His attitude was, as he says now, "Keep the boys happy, to a point."

But today, as yesterday, he is fascinated about the dynamics of the group, how much better they were on stage in their return to Hamburg in 1962. Remember, this was the same Horst Fascher who had wrangled John and a young woman off of their transformed love sofa, a toilet seat, on their first visit to Hamburg. He loved John, even his brashness.

IT WAS JOHN. HE HAD THE BIGGEST MOUTH. WHEN JOHN SAID SOMETHING, PAUL ALWAYS AGREED. HE NEVER SPOKE AGAINST JOHN WHEN WE WERE THERE . . . MAYBE LATER ON WHEN THEY WERE BY THEMSELVES; I DON'T KNOW. NEVER IN FRONT. NEVER ARGUMENTS BETWEEN THEM ABOUT HAVING DECISIONS MADE. GEORGE WAS A YOUNG GUY, HE HAD NO MEANING AT THAT TIME. SHY. [HE] WAS A GREAT PLAYER . . . HAD LITTLE TO SAY. PETE, THE DRUMMER, HAD NOTHING TO SAY. IT WAS ALL JOHN. BUT PETE WAS THE MOST-LIKED GUY IN THE BAND. HE WAS SO GOOD-LOOKING, YOU KNOW WHAT I MEAN. THE GIRLS REALLY LIKED HIM, ALTHOUGH HE NEVER HAD MUCH TO SAY.

So, from Horst Fascher we get more confirmation that Paul McCartney laid low in 1962 and even later, in 1963, when the band members were sleeping in beds and not close to the aroma of toilets. But we also get a glimpse of Paul's constant need to be writing, to be creative, and to seek validation for his work.

Paul was eager for a man like Fascher to listen to a new creation. With deep respect and affection for the former boxer and big music fan, Paul approached Fascher one night.

ONE DAY PAUL CAME TO ME AND ASKED ME, "HORST, WE WROTE A NEW SONG. DO YOU MIND TO LISTEN TO IT?" BECAUSE THEY GAVE VERY MUCH

OF MY POSITION. THEY WERE ASKING, "WAS THE SHOW GOOD?" THEN I WAS SAYING, "I LIKE YOUR SHOW, GUYS. GOOD. FANTASTIC." I SAID, "YES, I DON'T MIND TO LISTEN TO IT," AND PAUL TOOK HIS ACOUSTIC GUITAR AND SAT DOWN ON A BACKSTAGE CHAIR SOMEWHERE AND WAS PLAYING "LOVE, LOVE ME DO." . . . I INTERRUPTED HIM BEFORE THE SONG WAS FINISHED AND SAID, "PAUL, IT'S BETTER YOU STAY TO ROCK 'N' ROLL; I DON'T LIKE THAT." AND HE WAS DISAPPOINTED. I SAW HIS FACE, NEVER AGAIN LIKE THAT. IS IT POSSIBLE THE HORST SAYS THAT? IT WAS ALL TOO SOFT.

Paul looked devastated. He graciously thanked Fascher and thankfully didn't take the advice to stay with the raw rock 'n' roll that the Enforcer loved.

Paul was disappointed, but he and Lennon decided to bring "Love Me Do" to a recording studio at some point anyway. It was a decision they would never regret.

"'Love Me Do,' Larry, wasn't the best song we ever wrote. But it really put us out front," Paul told me on the 1965 Beatles tour.

"Out front" was an understatement.

"In Hamburg we clicked. At the Cavern we clicked. But if you want to know when we *knew* we'd arrived," John Lennon told me, "it was getting in the charts with 'Love Me Do.' That was the one. It gave us somewhere to go."

"Love Me Do," released on October 5, 1962, was the Beatles' first single. It carried with it some unusual history. It reached number seventeen in Great Britain. It fared better in the United States later, where it was a number-one hit in the glory year of 1964. But in 1962, it was the song that kick-started the Beatles. And most of it was penned in Liverpool and Hamburg.

While Fascher interacted with Paul, his relationship with John was much more intense, filled with moments of laughter and friction, but also trust.

"Yes. He played the leader for me; in my face he was the leader," Fascher explains. "That's why he recorded his record in '62 live at the Star Club, which was recorded by Kingsize Taylor and our stage manager, Adrian Barber. I was singing on that record. You know that?

"After we recorded it, we would go back to the Beatles, the three of us, and ask them, 'What can we do with the tape?' John was saying, 'Go ahead, you do what you want.' So I made a record out of it."

The recording of the Beatles playing "Love Me Do" live at the Star Club was done on a low-fidelity home tape recorder. Ted "Kingsize" Taylor, one of England's giants of rock 'n' roll, recorded several other Beatles' performances around that time, but it would take him fifteen years to get past legal issues and release the recordings as a double album in 1977, with the title *Live! at the Star-Club in Hamburg, Germany; 1962.*

It is coincidental that Taylor, who was swept away by Epstein and the Beatles, would have recorded their early performances in Hamburg. Did he know then that, fifty years later, the musical pundits would compare the groups side by side?

Curiously, remembering their first trip to Hamburg and Fascher's gravitating toward them, protecting them at the Star Club, they constantly asked for reinforcement—but not just physically. Even though Paul and the others rejected Fascher's critique of "Love Me Do," they also always wanted to know if he liked their show, and the music. He was a wonderful muse to the group, a man who never allowed his affection to stand in the way of his honesty.

In fact, Fascher was not afraid to give his opinion, and he may have been one of the influences, along with Klaus Voorman, to encourage the Beatles to abandon their skiffle roots.

"When they played at the Indra in those first concerts, everything they did was a mix. They played too much 'scrammel' music," Fascher says.

"Scrammel?" I ask.

"Yes. Scrammel. Skiffle. They thought Lonnie Donegan was Elvis. All that washboard stuff. Yes, they liked Lonnie Donegan. Lonnie Donegan was like Elvis in America. Every English boy that bought a guitar followed Lonnie Donegan. Then he came to Hamburg, and I had already heard some rock 'n' roll bands like Derry [and the Seniors], Tony [Sheridan], and things like that. I was saying, after listening to five, six, seven songs of them, this is too much washboard."

The Liverpool days of washboards and banjos and antique drum sets, with the Quarrymen, so innocent-looking staring sheepishly at a crowd of kids, were over. The halls were getting bigger in Merseyside, thanks to promoters like Brian Kelly and Sam Leach, and the first months of Brian Epstein's reign. And once again, the boys seemed to grow with bigger crowds. They worked the long, grueling hours, but like any artist, the more they played, the more they accelerated their growth process.

Allan Williams believes that Hamburg, at all levels, was a finishing school for the Beatles.

"Oh, yes. Hamburg was their schooling for the future," Williams says. "You used to work seven nights a week, and the playing time was between six and eight hours a night. You ask a group now to play six hours and they can't even play an hour. Groups still say to me, 'How do you become a Beatle?' I said, 'Go to Hamburg, go work in a club for six or seven nights a week, and see how you last.'"

If the Kaiserkeller was a rude awakening for the Beatles, the work at the Top Ten and Star Club were the real finishing schools that Allan Williams is talking about. Changes in dress and professionalism did not come quickly in Hamburg.

The boys returned to Hamburg later in 1962, this time with Ringo Starr on the drums. The new drummer's arrival was another major element, for better or worse—at first, most definitely, for worse, with the drummer still adapting to life without his old band, Rory Storm and the Hurricanes.

But even the promising Beatles needed help along the way.

So in between the first visit to Hamburg in 1960 and the fourth visit in 1962, there was a cavalcade of friends who left their imprint on the Beatles in many unusual and striking ways—some with art and style, and another, as you already know, with fists. Their individual stories, and how they relate to the boys, are almost as interesting as the ascent of the tough and untested boys from Liverpool.

CHAPTER ELEVEN

THE FEARSOME FOURSOME

*"Larry, so it is one day and I passed a club, and it was an American group,
and I listened and it [was] really good, even though, at the time,
I didn't understand the words."*
—Horst Fascher, on the first time he heard the Beatles

Rock, Roll, and TKO

Fate on a razor-thin margin continues to dominate our story. In retrospect, it is clear that the Beatles' experiences in Hamburg formed a major building block in their road to ultimate success. Without Hamburg, the world may never have known the Fab Four. And their visits were given an exclamation mark by four people, not as "fab" in the mood of the time, but certainly quite fabulous. And without these four key players in Hamburg—who became supporters, friends, influences, and in one case, a lover—the Beatles may never have gotten out of Germany with their hopes alive.

In fact, they may not have gotten out alive, period, if not for one of the four: Horst Fascher, their friend, fighter, and true fan:

I ENJOYED WHAT I HEARD IN THE NIGHTCLUBS IN ST. PAULI, IT WAS MUCH MORE EXCITING THAN ANY GERMAN MUSIC THAT I HAD EVER HEARD BEFORE. I FELT, I HAD THAT RHYTHM IN ME. THE BOXING AND THE ROCK 'N' ROLL WAS VERY CLOSE. WHEN WE WENT TO TRAINING, I TOLD MY TRAINER [I WANT] TO BOX TO ROCK 'N' ROLL MUSIC. JUMPING AND DOING SHADOW BOXING AND THINGS LIKE THAT. WE STARTED TO TRAIN SOMETIMES TO ROCK 'N' ROLL MUSIC—ROCK 'N' ROLL MUSIC ONLY ON RECORDS, WHICH YOU COULD BUY, BUT ONLY A FEW. MAYBE FROM BILL HALEY, LITTLE RICHARD, AND THINGS LIKE THAT. SO WHEN I SAW THE [BEATLES] AT THE KAISERKELLER NIGHTCLUB, I REALIZED, YOU KNOW, THAT THIS COULD BE SOMETHING SPECIAL. I WAS, WELL, YOU MIGHT SAY, A BOXER, WITH A HAND AS A HAMMER AND ROCKING FEET.

And so Horst Fascher tells his story, a story of triumph and trauma, a tale so bizarre that it includes a case of manslaughter, time in prison, and years on the run, plus a tour with British musical great Tony Sheridan in South Vietnam during the escalation of the Vietnam War.

Although he had been to sea and worked odd jobs before the age of eighteen, Fascher's parents urged him not to go across the river to the Reeperbahn red-light district. But he did anyway, to train as a boxer and to satisfy his obsession to see "naked ladies." There were plenty around. But the diminutive and handsome young athlete was drawn in by American rock 'n' roll, at first from the British Forces Network, broadcasting near Hamburg for the occupying Allied forces, and later, from several eye-opening nightclub experiences, one of which is carved into his memory.

LARRY, SO IT IS ONE DAY AND I PASSED A CLUB, AND IT WAS AN AMERICAN GROUP, AND I LISTENED AND IT [WAS] REALLY GOOD, EVEN THOUGH, AT THE TIME, I DIDN'T UNDERSTAND THE WORDS. A WHILE LATER, I THINK 1958, IT CAME THE DAY WHEN [BILL] HALEY CAME TO HAMBURG AT THE ERNST-MARK-HALLE [HALL], WHERE HE ALSO PLAYED LATER ON AND WE WENT THERE, OF COURSE, WITH MANY OTHERS. AFTER TWENTY MINUTES THE SHOW WAS OVER, BECAUSE THEY START HAVING A RIOT THERE. THEY START DANCING. WANTED TO DANCE, ROCK 'N' ROLL. THE POLICE CAME AND TRIED TO PUT IT BACK IN THE SEAT AND OTHERS WENT AGAINST IT, BECAUSE THE POLICE WERE STOPPING OTHERS FROM HAVING FUN. THERE WAS A BIG RIOT GOING ON AND TURNED THE WHOLE PLACE INTO PIECES. THE CONCERT ENDED IN TWENTY MINUTES AND I WAS SO MAD ABOUT IT, BECAUSE I CAME TO LISTEN TO THE MUSIC AND NOT HAVE A RIOT WITH THE POLICE.

As Fascher's love for rock flourished, his father was angry that he was a fan of what was called "hot and tot" music. Fascher ignored his parents' warnings. "Hot and tot" would ring in his ears forever.

When the Beatles came to Hamburg in the summer of 1960, Fascher was already a rocker at heart. He and the boys, including Pete Best and Stuart Sutcliffe, clicked right away. In a period of a few short months, the young and wild boxer hung out and became a real friend. And when the boys left late in their gig at the Kaiserkeller club to briefly play at the Top Ten Club, and were threatened with physical harm by Koschmider's thugs, it was Fascher who became an enforcer and protected them, except, of course, from themselves—a destructive story still to come.

But the unusual alliance with the boxer lasted for all of the group's five trips to the Reeperbahn, even when Fascher was not available due to incarceration.

The fate that brought Fascher into their lives is a story stranger than fiction, but it is true: Horst Fascher, defiant, devoted, and unpredictable, found the time and place where the boys would graduate to a much higher plane of success.

By 1959, Fascher had become featherweight boxing champion of Hamburg and the region, making the music lover a qualifier for the German national championship. Fascination with a girl, and raw emotion, stopped his march to the amateur title.

"I had a fight on the street with a sailor," he tells me, shrugging his shoulders, his eyes seeming to well with regret. "I had a fight because I liked a girl. . . . I knocked the guy out. He fell down on his head and broke his head. . . . He went back to his ship and he died overnight there."

Fascher's promising boxing career was done. He spent nine months in jail, and upon emerging he almost immediately fell in love with a woman, a prostitute. He was so much in love he even brought her home. It was a serious relationship, but one thing led to another, and the man who would later be remembered as a driving force for the Beatles in Hamburg became, for a while, a pimp.

Fighter, rock fan, jailbird, pimp—all prerequisites for his future career as a nightclub guard and, eventually, nightclub manager.

Creatively maneuvering his way through the red-light district, Fascher managed the Top Ten Club, quit the place, worked at another club in the interim, and was drawn to the Indra and Kaiserkeller. He was "turned on" by their music, and his good graces and outgoing personality provided a one-man support team for the disbelieving and doubting young musicians.

Fascher had graduated from security chief to a man with a concept for his friends from Liverpool. His concept: performing in a new nightclub with multiple bands and shorter performances. The boys' belief in him, and his in them, would bring them to a place called the Star Club. Now, in a genuine way, his support would give their career an undeniable boost.

There was and remains between Fascher and the Beatles an emotional component, a respect and love nurtured in nightclubs, amid an air of mutual respect.

Pete Best told the original Beatles scribe Bill Harry about that friendship. Harry quotes Pete in a vintage edition of *Mersey Beat* as remembering that when the boys were about to leave Hamburg on their ill-fated first trip in 1960, Fascher was shedding tears, wondering if he would see them again. Fascher and the boys had become that close.

Eventually Fascher had his chance for a special reunion. He was determined to bring the boys back to a venue where they could really break through. So, he traveled to Liverpool, caught the Beatles in one of their daily concerts at the Cavern, and through the influence of his pals, the boys set up a historic meeting for Fascher with their new manager, Brian Epstein.

"[At] that time, I met Roy Young. Roy Young was an English musician. He was the English Little Richard. He could sing like him. He came into the Top Ten. So Roy became a friend of mine. So one day I said to Roy, 'Would you come with me to England? I have to book some bands and my English is not that good to discuss contracts, so come with me and you can start working at the Star Club.' He was a piano player."

"So you started the Star Club?" I ask him.

YES. MOST ROCK BANDS WERE BASS GUITAR, DRUMS, AND RHYTHM GUITAR, AND HE WAS A PIANO PLAYER, AND PIANO ALWAYS FITS WITH A ROCK 'N' ROLL BAND. SO WE WENT TO ENGLAND. YES . . . AND THERE WE SAW SOME YOUNG GUY WALKING IN THE STREET AND ASKED HIM WHERE IS THE PLACE WHERE ALL THE ROCK 'N' ROLL BANDS ARE PLAYING. HE SAID THE BEST PLACE IS YOU GO TO THE CAVERN. SO WE WENT THAT NIGHT TO THE CAVERN AND MET THE BEATLES. I MET PAUL, JOHN, AND ALL [OF] THEM. WE HAD SOME DRINKS. THEY SET UP A MEETING AT THE NEMS OFFICE OF BRIAN EPSTEIN. ROY CAME ALONG AS . . . WELL . . . MY INTERPRETER.

Although this meeting was unnoticed in the early history of the Beatles, it turned into a major moment.

WE CAME TO THE NEMS ENTERPRISE OFFICE, UPSTAIRS. DOWNSTAIRS WAS THE RECORD SHOP. HE WAS VERY SMART-DRESSED AND HE SPOKE VERY FUNNY, LIKE, "YES, MR. FASCHER," AND THINGS LIKE THAT. HE SAID, "YOU ARE INTERESTED IN BOOKING THE BEATLES?" AND I SAID, "YES, WE HAVE A NEW CLUB IN HAMBURG AND WE'D LIKE TO HAVE THE BEATLES, BECAUSE I KNOW THE BEATLES ALREADY FROM BEFORE AND I THINK THAT THEY WOULD BE THE RIGHT BAND TO OPEN IN APRIL." THEN HE SAID, "I THINK WE CAN'T DO IT. . . . THE BEATLES ARE BOOKED ALREADY AT THE TOP TEN." I SAID, "MR. EPSTEIN, THE BEATLES CANNOT GO BACK TO THE TOP TEN. IF THE BEATLES COME BACK TO HAMBURG . . . THEY'LL COME TO THE STAR CLUB, BECAUSE THERE IS NO TOP TEN ANYMORE." HE SAID, "HOW DO YOU MEAN THAT?" I SAID, "LIKE I SAID, MR. EPSTEIN," AND HE SAID, "WELL, I HAVE TO TALK TO THE BOYS FIRST. IS THAT OKAY?" "I COME BACK TOMORROW."

"Tomorrow" would be the date of the pivotal meeting at the old and grand Adelphia Hotel. Fascher was stunned, thrilled at the outcome.

"Epstein says to me, told me, 'Mr. Fascher, I spoke to the boys, and the boys were saying, "If Horst say so, there will be no club, then it will happen," and the boys decide to go with you.' That was his words. Then we signed a contract. The Beatles got more money. At the Top Ten they earned fifty max."

The money was an afterthought. It was the place and the atmosphere that moved them into a new league. It was in the Star Club that the Beatles emerged as world-class rockers on two visits in 1962 that changed their world, and ours. It was during these visits that they recorded music, tested the waters, cleaned up their act, and began to soar. These two trips, in the spring and fall of 1962, also featured a changing of the drummers: Pete in the spring, Ringo in the fall. The differences in the 1962 visits were noticeable: The boys were more serious on stage, less sloppy. Their shirts were no longer hanging out. They wore jackets, sometimes with ties. The makeover was not complete, but it was beginning.

Fascher briefly performed with the Beatles during their New Year's Eve show, which was recorded by another Liverpool musician, Ted "Kingsize" Taylor. Years later, in 1977, the tape was released commercially as *Live! at the Star Club in Hamburg, Germany; 1962.* One song from the album, "Hallelujah, I Love Her So," includes Fascher on backing vocals. And on another song, "Be-Bop-A-Lula," his brother Fred's vocals can be heard.

Fascher remained friends with the band long after they became famous. Some of his stories about the Beatles' Hamburg days have been published in other works, and he published his own memoir in 2006.

In 1966, triumphant and rising toward superstardom, the Beatles returned to Hamburg. But Fascher could not attend their shows; he had been sentenced to another year in jail for violating his parole.

"From '62 to '65, I had eight fights. . . . The hardest fight was somebody broke his chin."

The boxing cost him plenty. He had sworn not to fight, in the ring or out, and his parole violation was another painful moment in his life.

Though Fascher could not make it to the Star Club, he was honored in absentia.

"When the Beatles came here [in 1966] and played the same hall where Bill Haley played . . . my brothers went there and they also went backstage. They had a few words and [my brother] Freddie was saying, 'Horst can't be here because he's still in jail. But give him a song tonight,' and John said, 'Yes we [will].' So during the show, John Lennon was saying to the audience through the mic, 'Ladies and gentlemen, our friend Horst Fascher can't be here tonight because he's still, uh, in jail.'"

The Beatles returned to Britain. Fascher finished his prison stint and then, as usual, went where the trouble was. Where was Fascher headed? Vietnam, where he accompanied Tony Sheridan on a visit to entertain the troops. The rest of his life has included stints at resurrecting the Star Club, and remaining an icon in St. Pauli, where people still remember him as a man who helped bring quality shows to a neighborhood known for other forms of entertainment.

And the Beatles remembered. Ringo and George were there when he opened a new version of the Star Club a couple years later in December

1968. Once again, Tony Sheridan was the top bill. At a difficult time in his life, Fascher had lost a child. His baby girl, with a rare heart problem, could not be saved. But when the girl was still fighting for her life, Paul McCartney flew a team of heart specialists to London to seek options for the little girl, including special surgery. Fascher and his girlfriend were flown to London. Paul arranged the trip.

Fascher tells me about the story, fifty years later, tears welling in his eyes.

"I will never forget. Never forget them. The music. What they did for me."

Nor will they.

In 1965, without having any knowledge of Horst Fascher, I asked George, "Who were the people who helped you the most?"

"Well, our parents, of course. Our families, you know. Honestly, all of them," George replied. "Then there were people like Tony [Barrow], [Tony] Bramwell, Mal [Evans], Neil [Aspinall], Derek [Taylor], Brian [Epstein], and many people. George Martin. Oh, there is so much to remember. A woman, Astrid Kirchherr. And . . . a really fascinating guy . . . a bouncer . . . promoter and manager. His name was Horst. It was in Hamburg."

The Beatles encountered many interesting characters in Hamburg. There were the prostitutes, the doctors who fixed their problems from the prostitutes, the sinister nightclub owner, the German alien police, and the beautiful and devoted Astrid Kirchherr, who lit up their look and design and, in the case of Stuart Sutcliffe, a heart. But it is true; none was as multifaceted as the hard-punching Fascher, who protected them, adored them, and watched them grow into emerging stars at the Star Club. He was an unlikely friend in the unusual city that showed off the most exclusive neighborhoods of northern Germany, and in contrast, the worst.

"I will never forget them," Fascher says as he stares at this author, who finds it hard to believe that this kind, older man has lived so much, and lost so much. But, as he says, "My soul is still beating, my mind clear, of the days when music from the inside drew me into the nightclubs, and my meeting them. Remember, I loved them, the Beatles . . . before they were stars, and when they were boys. And I love them now."

The Talented Trio—Style and Substance

The Beatles were rousing the Hamburg crowds to a near frenzy almost nightly. And the males, in the beginning, were as fascinated as the females. During their first trip to Hamburg, a young artist, shaking off depression after an argument with his girlfriend, wandered into the Kaiserkeller. Eventually he lost the girl, but he gained something else: a lifetime of high drama, creativity, and lasting friendship within the Beatles universe.

Klaus Voorman was a young student and artist who, at the time, was dating Astrid Kirchherr. That night he walked into the Kaiserkeller, his inner curiosity was sparked. The first band he watched was Rory Storm and the Hurricanes. The Beatles followed, and Voorman caught the fire—the sound, the gyrations, the entire mood. He convinced his girlfriend, Astrid, to return with him to the seedy neighborhood, along with a friend, Jürgen Vollmer, a student at the Fashion Institute. Kirchherr had never seen a "live" rock concert. Vollmer would later tell friends he was "incredibly loving the music." By the end of that first night, the trio was ecstatic, even though Kirchherr's presence would soon cost Voorman his romance with the young beauty. In time, the Fab Four's life and times would graduate from raw and raucous to refined and respected, thanks in part to the talented trio, and their love and input. And it started way before young and sensitive Brian Epstein arrived on the scene.

Soon after they met at the Kaiserkeller, Astrid Kirchherr and Stu Sutcliffe fell in love. Voorman maintained his friendship with Kirchherr, and together with Vollmer all three developed a close relationship with the band.

Their impact would be monumental.

Kirchherr remains emblematic of a different time, the recovery of her nation from the devastation of World War II, as her generation, born during the 1930s—in her case, 1938—struggled to empower the people of what was once a militaristic dictatorship to the postwar search for modernity and the road to civil and social justice. To that end, Kirchherr, a young student of photography, became quite a liberal activist, a role she has played all of her life.

Colin Fallows, professor of sound and visual arts at Liverpool's John Moores University, was coeditor of an extraordinary book of photographs that accompanied the show *Astrid Kirchherr, A Retrospective* at the Victoria Gallery and

Museum in Liverpool in 2010–2011. The book offers a startling photographic collection of the moods of the young boys. The photographs in this book and collection are haunting and revelatory. You look into the eyes of the boys, and you can sense the times, feel their innocence, view their moods.

Recently, in a coffee shop across from the school, the devoted researcher and veteran art historian talked about Kirchherr's work with tenderness and joy.

"This is so definitive," Fallows said. "She studied under Reinart Wolf, a master in his time, a man who understood lighting and mood and the power of simple black and white. The photographer uses a machine, but it's what the great photographer sees that makes it special."

From Fallows's perspective, Kirchherr was intuitive, especially when John and George came to the studio where Stuart had lived and worked. It was after his death, and the two boys were in mourning. They had calmly asked Astrid to take a picture in Stuart's space, in Stuart's light.

Fallows's interpretation of that one picture speaks to the extraordinary intuition of the twenty-four-year-old photographer. In his book, Fallows offers his view:

A PORTRAIT PHOTOGRAPHER, KIRCHHERR POSSESSES A RARE FUSION OF ACUITY AND COMPASSION. IN THE PHOTOGRAPHS OF THE INDIVIDUAL BEATLES, SHOT IN THE ENTIRELY BOHEMIAN VENUE OF THE KIRCHHERR LOFT [WHERE STU WOULD LIVE AND PAINT], THE YOUNG MUSICIANS APPEAR BOTH WARY AND YOUTHFULLY VULNERABLE. . . . THEIR PERSONALITIES ARE CAPTURED PHOTOGRAPHICALLY AT A REMARKABLE STAGE IN THEIR DEVELOPMENT AS YOUNG MEN AND ARTISTS. KIRCHHERR, AS THOUGH WITH FEMININE PSYCHIC INSIGHTS, SHOOTS THEIR PORTRAITS IN A MATTER THAT IS ONCE UNDERSTANDING OF THE BROODING TOUGH IMAGE EXPECTED OF YOUNG MALE ROCK 'N' ROLLERS, YET ACKNOWLEDGING A PROFOUND AND ISOLATING INDIVIDUALISM THAT SEEMS TO EMANATE FROM THE GROUP THEMSELVES. THESE EARLY PORTRAITS APPEAR TO BE DOMINATED BY MONOCHROMATIC DARKNESS: BLACK PREVAILS—IN THE CLOTHING, THE JACKETS AND THE SHADOWS IN WHICH THE GROUP MEMBERS ARE SO OFTEN POSED. THEY APPEAR PREMATURELY AGED, AND

THERE ARE FEW SMILES—EVEN THOUGH THE TRANSPOSITION TO WORLD CHARMING "MOP TOP" WAS IMMINENT.

In Kirchherr's world, the Beatles have remained a powerful life force. Perhaps to Professor Fallow, she opened up more about that first moment she saw them, before the pictures, before Stuart, before she ever knew what fate and timing had sealed for her.

I SAW THESE WONDERFUL FIGURES ON A LITTLE STAGE MADE OUT OF JUST LITTLE PIECES OF WOOD AND THEY WERE JUST SCREAMING THEIR HEADS OFF. . . . WHEN THEY USED TO SING THEIR HARMONIES IT WAS SO PERFECT AND BEAUTIFUL THAT I COULDN'T DESCRIBE HOW I FELT . . . AND THEN SINGING IT AND PERFORMING IT WITH SUCH BEAUTY AND SUCH INNOCENCE WAS ABSOLUTELY AMAZING FOR ME. . . . BUT THE FIRST ONE I REALLY ADORED FROM THE FIRST MINUTE I SAW HIM WAS STUART, BECAUSE HE HAD THIS WONDERFUL DELICATE LOOK AND THESE BEAUTIFUL EYES, AND THE WAY HE WAS STANDING ON STAGE—THAT REALLY KNOCKED ME OUT.

Their romance is the stuff of legends. But beyond everyone else's description of the young lovers' personal relationship is their impact on the boys' lives and career.

"John was stunned that Stuart stayed in Hamburg to study art, and love this woman," Bill Harry remembers. "Along with the early photographs, her continuing work made them look inwards. In some ways, they saw her pictures as the real thing, a portrait of how they really were, scared to death but ready to take on the world."

Beatles historian Denny Somach says, "The photographs of Astrid Kirchherr will always be viewed as the way people 'see' the Beatles in the beginning."

In fact, the perception of the Beatles when they played the famous show at Litherland Town Hall, billed as "The Beatles—Direct from Hamburg," was a reflection of the early Kirchherr work that captured the boys as slim, adorned in leather, and raw with eyes mysteriously haunting and sexy.

Kirchherr also helped supply, along with Horst Fascher, the Preludin pills to help the Beatles stay awake during those long Hamburg nights. She was close to all of them, but had what she described as a "sweet bond" with George, who wrote more letters to her than the others. Once again, as he has throughout this work, George stands out as the compassionate one. It was George who accompanied, along with Brian Epstein, Stuart's mother on the airplane to Hamburg to console Kirchherr, and bring Stuart home.

Kirchherr's perspective on the Beatles seems oriented toward them more as people, rather than as rock stars. George's sister Louise has met her several times. She recalls,

> SHE HAD A SPECIAL FONDNESS FOR GEORGE, ESPECIALLY HIS SENSITIVITY AFTER STUART'S DEATH. WE WERE GUESTS AT A NUMBER OF BEATLE CONVENTIONS TOGETHER, AND IT WAS FUNNY BECAUSE INEVITABLY WHEN THE PANEL WOULD ASK QUESTIONS, SHE AND I WOULD INEVITABLY ANSWER WITH EXACTLY THE SAME ATTITUDE TOWARDS THE BEATLES. WE BOTH HAD A SLIGHTLY MOTHERLY, SISTERLY ATTITUDE TOWARDS THE BEATLES, WHILE OTHER PEOPLE SAW THEM AS A PRODUCT. WE TALKED ABOUT THAT TOGETHER. IT'S AMAZING HOW ALL OF THESE OTHER PEOPLE ARE NOT LOOKING AT THEM AS REAL HUMAN BEINGS. THEY SEE THEM AS A COMMODITY. . . . ASTRID AND I FELT, WELL, OBVIOUSLY I HAD THE BIOLOGICAL CONNECTION, BUT SHE HAD ALMOST AS CLOSE AS A BIOLOGICAL CONNECTION. . . . SHE WAS STILL SEEING GEORGE AND THE OTHERS AS REAL, VULNERABLE, DECENT, CARING, HUMAN BEINGS.

Kirchherr's impact on the boys did not end in Hamburg. She gladly worked with the Beatles through the years, a quiet inspiration on film, albums, and design—quiet, that is, until the mid-seventies, when stories of her impact started to emerge.

In the field of photography and design, Astrid Kirchherr had some welcome and warm support, if not competition.

Her ex-boyfriend, Klaus Voorman, practically became an unofficial member of the band. He was a power on bass guitar, and accompanied the individual Beatles in the post-Beatles era, his most notable appearance being on his friend John Lennon's legacy song, "Imagine." He also won a Grammy for his design of the cover of the epic Beatles album *Revolver*.

Kirchherr and Jürgen Vollmerr together produced early photographs of the boys that inspired the band, and the fans. And Vollmerr was the inspiration for the boys' famous early haircuts, although, as you will learn, there are several viewpoints on that.

But on the Beatles' first trip to Hamburg, the "dynamic trio," as I will call them, was an inspiration to the young musicians from Merseyside.

Style was the centerpiece of the trio's lives, and a great influence on others.

Kirchherr was the love of Stuart Sutcliffe's life, a soul mate who intimately defined a daily life of love and work. She shaped Stuart by designing his clothing, and doing his hair much like hers. The boys laughed at Stu's newly coiffed locks, a bit longer and sculptured, but they didn't laugh for long.

The young woman's observations of her man and the Beatles, and the dynamic between them all, was fascinating: "John would taunt Stuart, but he loved him."

She told Beatles biographer Philip Norman, "When Stu and John had a row . . . you could still feel the affection that was there. But when Paul and Stu had a row, you could tell Paul hated him."

Of course, in those days Paul wanted to be bass guitarist, and Stuart was an irritant to him. Although Paul may have had his misgivings about Stuart, about one thing there was general agreement among them all: Kirchherr, through her art, photography, and sense of style, was a force.

Even Stuart's sister Pauline will concede her influence, although she wants people to know that this "sweetheart" of a brother had his own powerful convictions about life, love, and art. "He was," she says, "his own man who made a decision to leave the band, the only early band member who was not pushed out."

Jürgen Vollmer, who was along on that first visit by the trio to the Kaiserkeller, was also influential in a way that secured an unusual niche for the original "Fab Five": John, Paul, Stu, George, and Pete. It was all about the hair.

Like all Beatles "legends," there is disagreement and controversy about the hair. Liverpool's cultural ambassador and Brian Epstein's friend Joe Flannery insists with great emphasis that John, visiting the Flannery house late one night after a gig, saw a picture of Joe's mother as a young woman in the 1920s, and that was the pivotal moment. The picture was colored by hand, as was the custom in those days. His mother's hair, Flannery tells me, "resembled a helmet. . . . The bangs were rather large, and deep down on her forehead."

To this day, Flannery, who shared so many moments with the group as Brian Epstein staged their transformation in the early days, is convinced that it was his mother Agnes's picture that inspired the haircuts.

"Larry," he says, looking directly at me. "Larry, the picture was the inspiration. There is no question. It was more than a loving picture of my mother— it was the inspiration. At my flat, John picked up her picture. He looked at it. He admired it and said, 'That's the way I want my hair to look.'"

Flannery adds, "The fact is that Brian took them to Horne Brothers [barber shop] in Liverpool, and one of the barbers created the look. Astrid herself has told me several times that she did not create the cut."

In pre-Epstein days, the boys toyed around with various hairstyles, especially Stuart, with Kirchherr occasionally styling his hair in a longer look— a cut that was so ridiculed by the other Beatles that Stuart would sometimes try to flatten down his hair with water. It is ironic that John and Pete, who laughed uproariously, would one day have a stylish cut that would actually change the world.

The style of their hair was certainly not top of mind when, without telling George and Pete, John used some gift money to travel on vacation to Spain with Paul. They never reached Spain, instead deciding to go to Paris following a letter from Stu, who was living in Hamburg with Kirchherr, stating that Jürgen Vollmer was also headed to Paris. They liked Vollmer. He liked them. There was something adventurously romantic about the avant-garde Vollmer.

It was the summer of 1961, and Paris was steamy, filled with existentialists like Vollmer, who bedded down in the bohemian Montmartre district, where he cheerily greeted Paul and John. They hung out in an atmosphere of artists, writers, and so-called beatniks who were trying to illuminate the real meaning of life's existence.

They were also fascinated by Vollmer's French hairstyle, asking him to cut their hair in the same style.

"It was a very popular style with the young in France those days," remembers Bill Harry, describing a flattened-down hairstyle with a fringe in the front.

Vollmer has his own distinct confirmation. "I gave both of them their first 'Beatle' haircut in my hotel room. I gave them the haircut. It was their idea to have it the same as mine. They left Paris, and never brushed their hair back again. That's the real story of the haircut. Don't let anyone tell you different."

And in an interview later, when George Harrison was asked how the Beatles haircut came about, he said, "I only brushed my hair forward after John and Paul came back from Paris."

John and Paul enjoyed the trip to Paris, but at a price. George and Pete were angry. After all, they had caused the band to miss several scheduled gigs. The 1961 summer vacation flap almost split up the band. Again, there were talks about dissolving, and in retrospect, a breakup would have happened only months before Brian Epstein entered the scene. But although destructive in one way, the excursion to France cemented a relationship with Vollmer, whose early photographs of the Beatles live on as some of the pictures that helped develop their legend.

During a 1975 visit to Philadelphia, John discussed his solo album, *Rock 'n' Roll*, with me.

"That is Jürgen's picture on the cover, Larry. He was the first photographer to capture . . . I think . . . to show what we were all about. No one else [comes] quite as close to what we were all about. I think the photographs tell the story of the kind of attitude we had. And also, I might add, the look in Hamburg."

"The look in Hamburg." It was so critical to the future success. Hamburg brought the boys unbearable conditions, a grotesque setting that allowed them to scream their lungs out and take onstage risks, without worry or concern that they were going over the top, which they did, and quite spectacularly.

But in the end, it was the relationships that affected them the most—Stu's love for Astrid, the boys' fascination with Vollmer, and most of all, the lifelong association with Klaus Voorman, not to mention the protection and friendship of Horst Fascher.

Voorman could not have known how his stop at the Kaiserkeller that one fateful night would change his life. In their visits to Hamburg, the Beatles and Voorman became inseparable. As time progressed, Voorman designed album covers for them (*Rubber Soul* and *Beatles Anthology*), joined them on stage through the decades, and even lived in London with George and Ringo. Inspired by the Beatles, he took up bass guitar and appeared with the individual Beatles at concerts and on records, and most notably played bass guitar on the recording of John's "Imagine." Later he became a key member of John and Yoko's Plastic Ono Band, continuing a close legacy friendship with John. There were even reports after the band's breakup that Voorman would replace Paul and join the others in a new band. It was pure speculation and juicy gossip—that's all.

In addition to his talents and drive, Voorman was "always there," as John would say, for three of the Beatles—John, George, and Ringo—even during the insecure days.

Yoko adds, "Klaus was a close friend to us. He is a very sincere man, who John always felt was one of us."

During an extended interview with me in May 1975, John talked about his musical friends: "[Harry] Nillson, Klaus [Voorman], George, Elton [John], the Beatles, and so so many more, along the way."

Artist. Rocker. Writer. Entrepreneur. Voorman was a renaissance man, but there is one aspect of his life that cannot be measured by levels of performance. In a time of uncertainty, from 1960 to late 1962, Klaus Voorman was a friend, pure and simple, a young man who inspired the five Beatles to stay the course. He gave them a high-spirited lesson in learning how to be more confident, even when they were disheartened and inclined to walk away. That, in itself, was the most important contribution of the dynamic trio.

CHAPTER TWELVE

FORGOTTEN FRIEND– HURRICANE RORY

*"He was athletic, thin, and dynamically physical. His act made Elvis look
tame. For a while, he owned Liverpool and almost all Merseyside.
But he had a problem."*
—Jim Turner, legendary Merseyside manager and agent

"He was very sensitive. A very caring man."
—Allan Williams

"Rory Storm was Rod Stewart before Rod Stewart was Rod Stewart."
—Ron Ellis

THE INIMITABLE RORY STORM. HE GAVE RINGO A HOME.

Ringo eventually left for the Beatles.

Allan Williams insists that Storm's decline began when Ringo left. "He was
making progress on his stammer. But when Ringo left, the stammer came
back."

Along with the Ringo factor, Rory Storm's life story intertwines with the
Beatles in different ways, including a brief but critical interlude, a time when
he gave them an important lesson in the art of stage charisma.

It was just a momentary decision, because, he told friends, the money was
better. In a few months he would join up in Hamburg, but in the summer
of 1960, the leader of the Hurricanes would take his successful young group
to perform at Butlin's family camp. So, Allan Williams, faced with a brief
vacancy, took the Beatles to Hamburg instead. Storm opened the door to
Johnny's boys, who grew to adore him, and to look back at his decision with
the minds of individuals who had defied fate, and all of its uncertainty.

Rory Storm. He was a star who helped pave the way for the biggest stars,
but he really didn't know it at the time.

Alan Caldwell was his real name. Like Jim Turner, the manager and operator of a large talent and entertainment agency who helped develop his career, he was a "steeplechaser" in his youth, a runner, with slick moves. In fact, the two competed, and vigorously. Caldwell was a definitive athlete. His legs could move on ground, and in swimming competitions. In the water, he glided through the lanes to victory. Although he had a speech communication problem that was barely tolerated during his time, young Alan Caldwell betrayed his disability by expressing himself with his extraordinary physical ability. Speed was his power, and breathless, he took home trophy after trophy.

The charismatic Storm used his physical attributes well, and sometimes dangerously. In Hamburg he competed with the Beatles to see who could crack a precarious wooden stage at the Kaiserkeller. Jumping up and down, the uproarious Storm caused the stage to collapse. Along with Richie Starkey's drum set, Storm vanished below the stage. Engaged in unbridled laughter, the Hurricanes and the Beatles joined together for a morning meal, interrupted by Bruno Koschmider's goons, who beat them up. Storm also was a man of daring delights—jumping into a swimming pool at the end of a song, falling once through a glass skylight, and fracturing his leg when he fell near a balcony at the famed Majestic Ballroom in Birkenhead.

From the time he joined the rock revolution, his verbal limitations, marked by a bad stutter, were quickly overshadowed by a gyrating, scintillating body that would make the girls moan and the boys scream for more. Given his physical abilities, he was a perfect onstage tutor to the boys, both at the Cavern and in the dirty nightclubs of Hamburg. They played on the same stages, and his influence on their animalism and sense of the audience was unlimited.

Friend and former manager Jim Turner sentimentally recalls two people in one body. "He had this stage panache . . . he out-Elvised Elvis. His eyes were James Dean blue. . . . He was daringly handsome and he reeked sex appeal. The music was pure dynamite, and he was electricity personified in a body. As long as he was singing and dancing and shaking, he was okay. But when he began a conversation, his personality changed. He became a second personality, filled with fear, and terrified of the reaction."

Allan Williams fondly remembers Hurricane Rory.

"He was very sensitive . . . a caring man. But he didn't show it on stage. There, he seemed fearless."

Fellow rock man Billy Kinsley of the Merseybeats thought that if there was fear, Rory Storm never showed it.

RORY STORM DIDN'T HAVE THE BEST VOICE IN THE WORLD, IT WAS A BIT RAW, BUT AS A SHOWMAN THERE WAS NO ONE LIKE HIM. IN THE SIXTIES, HE WAS SO DYNAMIC, THE WAY HE MANEUVERED ACROSS THE STAGE. HE WAS SO ATHLETIC AND TRIM AND HE HAD MORE GYRATIONS THAN ELVIS OR JERRY LEE. IF YOU WANT TO TRY TO PICTURE, THINK OF ROD STEWART. ACTUALLY OVER THE YEARS, ROD STEWART HAS REMINDED ME SO MUCH OF RORY. DID HE AFFECT ALL OF US? NO QUESTION. HE MADE US MORE DARING, OR WILLING TO BE MORE DARING. IT'S JUST HIS SPEAKING THAT POSED A PROBLEM.

Stuttering or stammering, still difficult, remains out in the open in the modern day. It is a disability. But in the fifties and sixties, it was difficult to overcome. Rory could sing without hesitation, but speaking was anguishing, especially in his later careers as a deejay, salesman, and water-skiing instructor, all three jobs where clear communication was a prerequisite.

Former manager Turner, a Liverpool regular who at one time managed the Odd Spot Club, a local favorite, remembers the dilemma: "He was so confident, but the confidence went away when he started talking. It was so much of a contrast. Either way, he was likeable, and loved by his loyal friends, but it was difficult to connect with strangers, so difficult. It's one of the saddest things, Larry, because although he was insecure, he brought so much joy to people."

"Rory was a favorite, after the group disbanded, as a deejay at bar mitzvahs and school events. I booked some of them," recalls Southport's Ron Ellis. "He was easy to work with and the kids loved him. So did the parents. But, internally, he was a sad man. It is an irony because in his day, he was so electric on stage, his voice was so unique, he took so many physical risks, that, in effect, Rory Storm was Rod Stewart before Rod Stewart was Rod Stewart."

Above: The early Beatles in a Liverpool studio in March 1962, five months before drummer Pete Best (second from left) faces the unthinkable.

Left: The "boys," now with Ringo Starr as drummer, on a Liverpool street in February 1963.

John Lennon with mother Julia outside of Mendips—the home of Julia's sister, Mimi—a residence he called home until early adulthood.

Mary McCartney with sons Paul (left) and Michael. Along with father James, the McCartneys rose from humble roots to join the middle class.

Richard Starkey (a.k.a. Ringo Starr) with mother Elsie, at home in the late 1940s. Elsie worked long hours to support her sickly son.

Twelve-year-old George Harrison with his favorite companion, the guitar, at home in Liverpool in 1955.

Proud parents Harry and Louise Harrison help George pack for the Beatles' first trip to America in February 1964.

John Lennon's first band, the Quarrymen, in the St. Peter's Church Rose Queen procession, July 6, 1957, the day of the historic first meeting between John and Paul.

Above: Paul McCartney (second from left) is photographed for the first time with the Quarrymen, performing at the New Clubmoor Hall in Liverpool, November 1957.

Left: Paul (left) and John perform with the Quarrymen at Mona Best's Casbah Club on August 19, 1959. The young lady to the right is Cynthia Powell, who would marry John in 1962.

The Beatles at the Indra Club on August 17, 1960, their first night in Hamburg. (L-R) John, George, Pete, Paul, Stu Sutcliffe.

Stu (left) and John onstage with the Beatles at Hamburg's Top Ten Club in 1961.

The glow of love surrounds Stu Sutcliffe and Astrid Kirchherr in April 1961,
photographed in Hamburg by another influential Beatles friend, Jürgen Vollmer.

Above: *Mersey Beat* publisher Bill Harry (right) presents the boys with their very first award, the *Mersey Beat* Popularity Poll Shield.
Below left: Lovebirds Bill and Virginia Harry. She gave him the loan to start *Mersey Beat*; he gave her the ring.

Above: Mona Best, a powerful force in the Beatles early years, is photographed with her son Pete in December 1961, the day the Beatles signed a contract with Brian Epstein.

Above: The *Mersey Beat* edition featuring the controversial poll results declaring the Beatles the Number One band in Merseyside.

Above: Flashing his signature smile, early Beatles promoter Sam Leach reunites with Paul McCartney and wife Linda in Liverpool, 1984.
Below: Beatles' manager Brian Epstein in his London office, 1965. The handsome chief executive propelled the Beatles to success while hiding a complex personal life.

A personal hero to each of the Beatles, Lonnie Donegan, "The King of Skiffle," was a superstar in Great Britain whose impact was felt for decades.

Billy J. Kramer and the Dakotas. John Lennon was so fond of Billy that he urged Kramer to record several Lennon and McCartney compositions. (Clockwise from top left) Mike Maxfield, Billy J. (center), Robin MacDonald, Ray Jones, Tony Mansfield.

Rory Storm and the Hurricanes, with Ringo Starr on drums, at the Tower Ballroom in 1961. Storm's gyrating, athletic, and magnetic stage presence greatly influenced the Beatles and brought him praise in Merseyside and Hamburg. (L-R) Johnny "Guitar" Byrne, Rory, Ringo, Lou Walters, Ty O'Brien.

Above: Gerry Marsden has been loved in Northern England for decades. (L-R) Gerry, Les Chadwick, Les Maguire, Fred Marsden.

Right: Unheralded in most accounts of the era, Johnny Kidd and the Pirates were emulated by the Beatles. (L-R) Johnny Spence, Frank Farley, Johnny Kidd, Mick Green.

The Merseybeats, pictured here in 1963, often shared a stage with the Beatles and were among the boys' biggest supporters. (L-R) Aaron Williams, Tony Crane, John Banks, Billy Kinsley.

Stylish and filled with drama and excitement, writer and promoter Derek Taylor (left) was a critical force in the Beatles' takeover of the world's music in 1963–1964.

Paul McCartney and Mal Evans in Boston, 1964. Evans spent most of his early adult life serving the Beatles in various ways. His death in 1976 was shocking, and his true impact on the Beatles' success was never fully recognized.

aul with Freda Kelly, secretary
o the Beatles and Brian Epstein.
reda's stories of the boys are
lled with admiration and respect.

Described by the author as the most talented press
officer he ever met, Tony Barrow (right) shares a
moment with Brian Epstein in 1966.

Photographer Albert Marrion's famous studio photo of the Beatles, with Pete Best on drums and the boys all in leather, taken on December 17, 1961.

The makeover continues. The contrast in the band's look from just a year earlier is striking at this October 1963 Palladium concert.

Collarless and coiffed, "Mod" style takes over as the former leather-and-denim boys startle the fashion world, 1963.

Poised to embark on their first American invasion, the Beatles pose for a close-up in this October 14, 1963, photo.

The boys perform on February 19, 1963, at the famous Cavern Club in Liverpool, where they would make nearly three hundred appearances.

For the Beatles, Rory Storm was a model for success. They were addicted to success, and not shy about learning. The sometimes inhibited boys learned so much about stage presence from Storm. After all, they played on the same programs from Liverpool to Germany over a period of three and a half years.

Was Rory Storm bitter over his mentoring of Johnny's boys? "You never saw bitterness," says Jim Turner.

Bill Harry says that Storm was touched that the Beatles, wanting to return the favor, convinced Brian Epstein to produce Rory's rendering of the song "America" from Leonard Bernstein's *West Side Story*. The record was released with little success.

The Beatles felt close spiritually and professionally to Rory. They watched his stage antics, helping them emerge as more raw, taking more risks. They enjoyed his camaraderie, his daring, his loyalty. They played so much with Rory Storm and the Hurricanes that John and Paul became friends with and admired the band's drummer, Ringo Starr, the erstwhile Richie Starkey. Even Pete Best enjoyed Ringo's company, to a point.

For the man, the performer, the blessings of his earlier career were in marked contrast to his later pursuits. As the Beatles soared, Storm, whose earlier band was called the Raging Texans, began a decline. After the death of a band member, the Hurricanes were disbanded in 1967. Storm took on deejay work, and eventually taught and hosted dance parties in Jersey and Amsterdam.

Then Storm's father died, prompting a return to his mother.

September 1972 was not a good month, as Storm was experiencing a severe chest infection. On most nights, to get through the night, he would take sleeping medication, and a touch of scotch. One morning his mother found him dead. The bodies of both Storm and his mother were found on September 28. Police ruled his death an accident. But speculation remained that his mother took her own life after finding him, although that has never been proven.

The funeral cortege occurred on October 19, the two caskets side by side, the ex–band members playing as his friends sang his favorite song, "You'll Never Walk Alone."

Ringo Starr did not attend, later saying, in the sardonic Liverpool style of dark humor, "I wasn't there when he was born, either."

Ringo's quote should be taken with a grain of salt. He did everything possible to arrange recording work, and sessions, for Storm, but Storm declined. Too proud? No. Content in his early success? No doubt.

Going through notes of my earliest contact with Ringo Starr, I had asked in 1965 who his greatest influences were. He said, "There were some—Hank Williams, and of course, Buddy Holly. And there was a guy named Rory. He's still around."

But, as it turned out, not for long.

His closest friends in this era tell me that today, when he tells the sad story of Rory Storm, Ringo's eyes turn moist.

And it was indeed Storm's decision to play all summer at Butlin's summer camp in 1960 that convinced Allan Williams it was time to take the young Beatles to Germany. It didn't change the course for Storm; he later played on to success in Hamburg. But it began an uncertain journey for the boys, including the chance to watch the young star, up close and personal, and learn his almost magical command of the stage and the audience.

WHEN
THEY
WERE
BOYS

Part Four:
Where Were You in '61?

Still lonely, still desolate, but rescuers await. The Prince makes an entrance with the Tower of Power. Climb down the steps to the filthy grit and choking smoke where the Cavern waits, and so does deejay Bob with a bag of tricks. Later, pulverized, the trick's on him. He says, "Can you dig it?" Bill Harry's magic survey is out. Billy Kinsley sees energy through the haze of chaos. Merseyside is alive with everything from Flamingoes and Undertakers to a Terry and a Jay, a Jerry and a Derry, plus Pete, John, George, Paul, and sometimes Stu. As the leaves fell, so did Brian, aka "Eppy," the man with those silky-soft whispers. He traveled to his "Cellarful of Noise." He walked in as a skeptic, climbed out in love. And as '61 approached '62, he took the risk of a lifetime—and mind you, his own lifetime was not an ordinary one.

CHAPTER THIRTEEN

NINETEEN STEPS TO HEAVEN

"It was not the Hollywood Bowl."
—John Lennon, on the Cavern

"It was hot . . . a horrible odor . . . sweaty . . . I was breathless."
—Joe Ankrah of the Chants, on his first visit to the Cavern

"It was wild, very much alive!"
—Billy Kinsley of the Merseybeats, on the Cavern

IT WAS LUNCH HOUR ON FEBRUARY 9, 1961, WHEN THE FIVE BEATLES descended the steps for the first time as "the Beatles," the first of what would be hundreds of lunchtime and other concerts at the Cavern—the storied and gritty home of the Beatles' early exploits.

It almost didn't happen. The Cavern's owner, Ray McFall, had forbidden jeans (or, as they would say in the States at the time, "dungarees") from the club. McFall had even been *opposed* to rock 'n' roll in the beginning, but Sam Leach's success with the boys at a nearby club had changed all of that. The Prince of Mathew Street's opening of the Iron Door club nearby forced McFall to rethink his format. Once again, Leach paved the way. But the Cavern was still off-limits to jeans of any kind. McFall was just following tradition, a precedent set by the Cavern's original owner. Bill Harry says the Cavern was always concerned about propriety, and image. The truth is that propriety and image always vanish when father time and his powerful force sets the pace. Harry says,

ALAN SYTNER WAS THE MAN WHO CONCEIVED THE CAVERN IN MATHEW STREET, AFTER VISITING A FRENCH JAZZ CLUB CALLED LE CAVEAU FRANCAIS. HE WAS STRICTLY A JAZZ MAN AND WOULDN'T ALLOW ROCK 'N' ROLL TO BE PLAYED AT THE CLUB. HE BOOKED SKIFFLE GROUPS TO SUPPORT THE JAZZ BAND BILL TOPPERS. THE QUARRYMEN WERE AWARE

THEY WEREN'T ALLOWED TO PLAY ROCK MUSIC, BUT WHEN THEY
APPEARED THERE AS THE QUARRYMEN ON 7 AUGUST 1957, JOHN LENNON
COULDN'T RESIST AND BURST INTO THE ELVIS NUMBERS "HOUND DOG"
AND "BLUE SUEDE SHOES"; ALAN SENT A MESSAGE UP TO THE STAGE,
"CUT THE BLOODY ROCK!"

On the very first day, it was almost a non-story. The no-jeans directive
forced doorman Pat Delaney to try to turn away the Beatles because bass guitarist Stu Sutcliffe was wearing jeans. The Beatles were on the bill, but the
directive applied to paid entertainers and paying customers alike. Delaney, a
former police officer, relented and let them in, but owner McFall wasn't
happy, delivering what was described as a "stern" message to the boys in their
dressing area. In due time, the Beatles, who would become such a sizzling
draw, would never be stopped at the door again. So much for the original
bans on rock and denim.

In truth, the Beatles should have arrived in wet suits or fancy bathing
attire, or at least something, anything, to keep them dry. The inside of the
original Cavern was not environmentally sound.

Sir Ron Watson, the Southport man who saw so many of those concerts
as a break from his office job nearby, reminisces about the feel of the club,
more pleased about the music than the atmosphere: "It was so hot, Larry, so
steamy, and tremendously uncomfortable, but the beat of their music,
believe me, made up for all of that. It was the music that kept bringing me
back, day after day."

Joe Ankrah, he of the wonderful collection of singers known as the
Chants, remembers feeling all closed in, claustrophobic, even as his group
jammed with the boys. It was a sweat-dripping mess, with healthy breathing
a rarity.

"My God," he says. "The cigarette smoke and the moisture created a horrible odor. The walls had drips of moisture on them. The walls had sweat,
the people were sweating, the bands were dripping with sweat. Smoke from
the cigarettes was forming a moving cloud over the room. You might say I
was breathless."

Ankrah, whose group, facing intense racial barriers, was given an enormous break by Paul and the boys, will never forget the opportunity, or the impact of the human traffic jam.

"Everybody was so close. Many people were standing. There was little room to stand, or to breathe."

Mick Jagger first took the Rolling Stones to the Cavern in late 1963. In a brief conversation afterward, he described the in-close excitement: "Was it hot! We almost sweated away. They've had so many big groups at the Cavern that you've got to prove yourself; they asked us back, so they must like us."

The Merseybeats' Billy Kinsley has spent "nearly a lifetime" at the old Cavern (and the new one), and he says the conditions were much worse than described. "Remember, 130 years ago the building was adjacent to the water, so quite often the toilets in the old building had a problem. . . . Drains in the bathrooms were flooded over the top. . . . It was not pretty. As far as hot, it was hotter than hot. . . . You could walk in and start sweating profusely."

Famed music historian Spencer Leigh, through his always careful research, says in his book *The Cavern* that the "Beatles walked on water." He further explains that "when the cavern was excavated in 1982, the builders stumbled upon an old shaft that led to a huge hole . . . a cavern underneath the Cavern, as it were. It was filled with water and, bravely, the architect and the site agent investigated in a rubber dinghy. The lake was one hundred twenty feet deep and seventy feet long . . . they could tell the site was man-made."

In my conversation with Leigh, the BBC broadcaster and prolific author says, "There was a theory that there was a slave hole there once, but that's unlikely."

For Leigh, the Cavern is mostly about the Beatles, but also the home base for all of the great Merseyside groups.

"Remember," he tells me, "although the Quarrymen played there in the fifties, the Beatles' first appearance as the Beatles didn't happen till February of 1961. They were preceded by other bands that could have been headed to greatness, notably Kingsize Taylor and the Dominoes. But in the end, it will always be known for the Beatles, and as the most famous club in the world."

Even in the new location, you can feel the closeness, the intimacy of the Cavern with its small stage and the reverberation of the sound through the thick walls. But today, unlike 1961, alcoholic beverages are served, and jeans are accepted! Even Julia Baird was dressed in jeans when she met with me recently for a long interview at the Cavern.

Eventually the boys embraced and owned the place, although their first appearance was, according to one witness, not so fine at all.

"When the Beatles first came to the Cavern, I thought [they] were absolutely dreadful, and musically awful," says Ray Ennis, lead vocalist with the Swinging Blue Jeans. "Stuart was on bass and making a horrendous noise. They were smoking on stage, and Stu was sitting on the piano, facing Pete Best on the drums and not even looking at the audience."

Stu did have a habit of turning away from the audience, especially in Hamburg, but it seemed to make him all the more intriguing and mysterious.

There was no mystery about the effect of the intimate Cavern on musicians and fans.

Billy Kinsley, whose own band was first called the Mavericks, named affectionately after the popular American TV western, would not have traded the experience for anything. "I was just a wee teenager and there I was with Bob Wooler and all the bands that I idolized. We began working there for about six pounds a night for *all* of us . . . not a lot, mind you, but it was as though they were paying us to have fun, which we did quite intensely."

For young writer Bill Harry, the descent of nineteen steps into the unknown brought him into several cellar areas that combined to create the Cavern, which for years was a jazz club. Harry's visit was a reunion of sorts of the young art-school students who gathered after school at Ye Cracke, the charming pub where John Lennon, Stu Sutcliffe, Harry, and friends gathered in the "war room" to talk of their role in shaping the future of mankind.

Bill Harry had arrived at the Cavern at the suggestion of Stu, the bass guitarist, who, along with John, was friends and classmates with Harry at the art school. It would be the first of countless visits to the Cavern for Harry, who played a role later in the year in getting Brian Epstein into the club for the first time.

"It was unusual," says Harry. "Mona Best, who was still developing the allure of the Casbah, and who was doing everything possible to promote the boys, had talked Cavern owner McFall into booking the group."

Once again, the forgotten Beatles advocate Mona Best gets the credit for getting them in, not to the biggest, but to the most memorable of all their venues. On that day, in 1961, the modern legend of the Cavern was born, although no one knew it till years later, when it was celebrated, like Hamburg, as the place that drove the Beatles to fame. In reality, it all could be reversed—the Beatles put the Cavern on the map.

In all, the Quarrymen/Beatles played a total of 292 gigs at the Cavern, if you include the Quarrymen's first appearance in 1957. The Beatles' first appearance in February 1961 was supposed to be another big hit, following the Litherland Town Hall surprise success where they were billed as "The Beatles—Direct from Hamburg."

While not everyone in attendance was impressed, word spread quickly about the simple raw energy of their performance, and in a matter of days the "Fab Five" would be rocking the city.

The group's final appearance was on August 3, 1963, so the record runs at the Cavern spanned a period of six years. But just like Litherland, it was the early appearances that had the most impact.

Young Billy Kinsley remembers the word-of-mouth messages that were spreading through the area: "The Cavern experience was a sudden cultural flash. It wasn't pretty, not comfortable, but being there was the fun, and it was wild and very much alive."

And cheap. Admission was a shilling; in those days, that was worth a few American pennies. For the lunchtime crowd, cheese rolls and Coke were available. But liquor was not served, in contrast to the new Cavern, a replica of the original, which was demolished in the seventies.

Chances are the young women and men, dressed to the hilt, would have paid more to be there for the group's heralded arrival. In the end, most of them walked out in a "trance," according to Bill Harry, who was just a few years older than most of them, and only a year older than John. So when you read the quote of what the music did to *him*, remember that these are the thoughts of a twenty-one-year-old, not the mature writer-legend of Merseyside and beyond. With flair, and his eyes wide open, his head thrust forward almost like a TV news anchor who wants to get his message across with strong body language, the Bill Harry of the twenty-first century explodes with emotion as he recalls the scene.

"What I remember the most, Larry, about the lunchtime gig, was the startling and quite savage blast of sound. There is no exaggeration when I say that the moment they started playing, the hair on my neck stood up. [What I] recall most about that Thursday lunchtime performance is how the hair on my neck stood up."

In a commemorative column written on the anniversary of that first Beatles concert for the *Daily Express*, pen pal Harry confirmed an earlier story that some "borrowed equipment from the art school played a significant role in the group's history."

Harry explains, "We had used students' union funds to buy PA equipment that the band could borrow, but somehow it had never been returned and I noted that the group was using it at this gig."

And about the drama he had witnessed, he says, "What became apparent from the moment the band took the stage was how they had been transformed by the experience in Germany between August and December 1960, when they had played night after night in a Hamburg *bierkeller* and honed their act."

At the time, the curious young reporter knew very little about the despair, accusations of criminal activity, and the wild life of Hamburg. In time, he would be the first to report on the grimy life in Hamburg, but on that chilly February day, Bill Harry was all smiles and proud of his art-school compatriots.

Quietly, he thought to himself, "Is this the way we were destined to change the world?"

A Cellarful of Noise was Brian Epstein's 1965 memoir on his beginnings with the Beatles. Coauthored by Derek Taylor, the book recalled Brian's experience at the Cavern in a different manner than the screams and "hair-raising" experiences of most of the kids who were ten years his junior, but with similar emotional investment.

Three years after he first set eyes on the boys, "in a haze of smoke,"

Epstein, in his always fine-tuned English, said to me, "To say I was impressed was an understatement. Obviously the real discoverers of the Beatles were the intuitive young people of Liverpool who found them quite a long time before my awareness . . . but it was in the cellar . . . the Cavern, where I saw all things coming together . . . the music, the noise, the facial expressions of the customers. It was quite impressive."

Over the years, until it was closed down in 1973 to make way for a rail line, the original Cavern saw the likes of Gene Vincent, Billy Kinsley, the Big Three, Kingsize Taylor and the Dominoes, Gerry and His Pacemakers, the Rolling Stones, Billy J. Kramer, Epstein's find Cilla Black, and so many others.

But the spark that became a raging inferno, a steady flame of sound, the real transition from the jazz age to the rock age, began nineteen steps below Mathew Street.

"What was the Cavern like?" I asked John Lennon during the North American tour.

"You would have liked it. Little light, lots of people, very noisy, hot, like me [laughs] . . . but it was not the Hollywood Bowl. It was, for all of us, at the time, pure heaven."

CHAPTER FOURTEEN

THE PRINCE OF MATHEW STREET

*"I remember 'Pike the Mad Axman'. . . curious eyeballs looking ready to pop
out of the sockets. . . . Pike used to walk around with [a] meat cleaver
and whack people out."*
—Tony Bramwell, on one of the violent "Teddy Boys"

*"January 25, 1961. I needed a new band for the new club that was opening,
the Casanova Club. So I picked the five Beatles. Yes, the original five.
Not a bad choice, eh?"*
—Sam Leach, the "Prince of Mathew Street"

THE GHOSTS OF JOHN AND GEORGE ARE PROBABLY SITTING ACROSS FROM
HIM, HOLDING A RUM AND COKE—or in John's case, a touch of Brandy
Alexander—watching the Prince with great glee, and maybe a touch of
empathetic laughter thrown in.

The Prince arranges his hair, still wavy with silver shine, and he smiles that
toothy smile that made him a teen idol in those heart-gushing early days,
when girls became young lovers and boys didn't have to search far for undying affection.

He sits in the corner at the usual table at The Grapes, a small, cluttered,
and charming bar, with a stream of live entertainment, located in the heart
of Mathew Street, the quaint and sometimes grim-looking walkway that sits
adjacent to the new Cavern, as well as the spot of the original Cavern, which
was unceremoniously destroyed by the city fathers of Liverpool in the seventies. The Prince is there every Thursday, Friday, and Saturday, remembering the many afternoons he spent with the boys, drinking and talking about
their favorite subjects: melodies and maidens, not necessarily in that order.
His contemporary companions are a cold beer, a bag full of books, and the
tourists in Liverpool, never far away and always eager to hear the legacy of
his most unusual life. The Prince is a storyteller. He tells his stories with

gracious panache, that stirring Liverpool drawl, the spectacular pauses, so touched by the Irish impact that remains so much a part of the fabric of England's third-largest city.

Yet there were warnings about the veracity of these stories. Warnings are a way of life among the memoirists, the group of the living who claim a piece of the Beatles' legend. In many cases, owning a chapter of the folklore surrounding the boys becomes more important than the accuracy of the story. There is joy in Liverpool, but the surviving storytellers warn that only *their* story is the true story. This author has experienced this more than once, but when it comes to the Prince, there are no warnings, just a heavy dose of affection, and sadness—affection for his dreamlike vision for the boys, sadness that he was preempted by another young dreamer, Brian Epstein.

"Remember his last name, just remember," said a close friend of three of the Beatles.

I do remember. His name is Leach, Sam Leach, and although like many others he profits from his place in time and history, he doesn't deserve the moniker of the last name. Not at all. Despite the fading memories of time, he was definitely there, and to have been there, to have assembled the memories, and to be equipped with the talent of a superlative storyteller makes Sam Leach one of the premier voices of those left behind.

The Prince offers a selfless view of the beginning, and his history is filled with that greatest of all Liverpudlian requisites for great storytelling: irony with a touch of fate, not just for the boys but for the thousands of teenagers enraptured in the ascension from skiffle music to rock 'n' roll. In his early days as a renegade promoter, the Prince fought off the assault of Teddy Boys, a peculiarly English brand of what fab-fifties Americans would call "juvenile delinquents." The Beatles would have their fill of Teddy Boys, but the fast-punching Leach would be a pioneer in the fight for good and justice in the small and cheap nightclubs of rock and sock in Liverpool.

The Teddy Boys, unlike their dungaree-clad American counterparts, were thugs dressed as dandies, Brylcreem helping to place a shine on their hair, draped coats hiding their weapons of destruction, mainly a well-developed muscle group and a spare knife thrown in, but used cautiously. Teds didn't want to kill, because once put away, they were rendered useless by society in their ability to destroy. Like most anarchists, they had no real cause to fight except the ultimate litmus test of nihilists: conformity. They were perhaps the best-dressed rioters in contemporary history, with Edwardian frills in their shirts and "winkle-creeper" shoes; dangerous in their creeping silence, they made life miserable for random victims who dared dress routinely or demurely. With their sometimes-ruffled high collars, the Teds looked elegant; their message was not. The Teds were somewhat attractive to young John Lennon, not for the fisticuffs but because of their tight trousers and "winkle-picker" shoes, also called "wrinkle pickers." At first he was enamored of the fashion. Alan White, he of the immortal rock band Yes, and the drummer on John Lennon's track "Imagine," remembers that the Teds even spiked fashion interests throughout Britain.

"I remember wearing those kind of shoes when I was a teenager; they were called wrinkle pickers because you could pick wrinkles out of clothes with a pointed toe. The soles of the shoes were lined with crepe, and were famously known as 'brothel creepers,' because that was the recommended footwear, the legend said, when you crept into brothels, or so they said."

For all their style issues, many of which were romanticized by the teenagers of England, the Teds were truly and masochistically violent. Beatle buddy and promotional icon Tony Bramwell laughs out loud when he speaks about the Teds, but there is no question that, back in the day, he was terrified.

"I remember 'Pike the Mad Axman,'" Bramwell says, curious eyeballs looking ready to pop out of their sockets. "Pike used to walk around with [a] meat cleaver and whack people out.

"Ray Sutherland. Now there was a danger. He had razor blades hidden in the lapels of his jacket and if you grabbed him, well, you would, well, cut, pretty bad."

The Teddy Boys fought often. Prince Sam Leach, the deejay and later publicity manager of the Blue Diamonds Club, fought back, in 1958 and 1959. Prince Leach also was eyewitness to history, even though he rejected an opportunity both in 1957 and 1958 to book a well-regarded group, known as the Quarrymen. It was a colossal misstep, but after all, the Prince was riding a thrill-a-minute roller coaster, except, that is, when the Teddy Boys arrived on the scene, one of them on a motorbike, in 1958. That was the night the Teddy invasion forced Barbara Burroughs through a plate-glass window and into the body of a policeman a floor below. The policeman survived. But fate would have its day, wouldn't it.

Sitting in the semicircle booth of a waterfront restaurant, slamming Sam, sipping a Guinness draft, erupts in laughter.

"Barbara," he says. "Barbara was daft for the Blue Diamonds. Years later, she married the Diamonds' chief guitarist, Frank Campbell. I've always said that the night of the Teddy attack [when she smashed through the window] was the night Barbara 'fell' for Frank."

While Derek Taylor developed his writing skills, Brian Epstein shaped the bottom line, and Tony Bramwell looked in adoration at the wild mini-club scene and stole free rides from George Harrison's bus-driver father, and high schooler Bill Harry carefully chronicled his friend John Lennon with the future newspaper already in his head, Sam Leach began adoring his role as a young Colonel Parker, a novice P. T. Barnum, and above all, a charmer with a fantastic smile and the passion to back it up.

It was with that backdrop that the Prince plotted day and night to find venues for the boys, bigger and financially more attractive. Frankly, he knew that the Beatles had not yet matched in their hometown their early successes in Hamburg.

Leach gleefully remembers:

JANUARY 25, 1961. I NEEDED A NEW BAND FOR THE NEW CLUB THAT WAS OPENING, THE CASANOVA CLUB. SO I PICKED THE FIVE BEATLES. YES, THE ORIGINAL FIVE. NOT A BAD CHOICE, EH? I MET THEM AT HAMILTON HALL, A HORRIBLE CLUB, A REAL DIVE WHERE THERE WAS ALWAYS LOTS OF FIGHTING. THEIR DRESSING ROOM WAS A CONVERTED LADIES' TOILET. SO WHEN I CAME IN, EVERYONE WAS FIGHTING, AND WHEN THE BAND CAME ON, I NOTICED ALL THE FIGHTING STOPPED AND ALL EYES WERE FOCUSED ON THE BAND. . . . YES, THEY ALL STOPPED FIGHTING TO WATCH THE BEATLES. THAT IS HOW GOOD THEY WERE. FIRST TIME I EVER SAW THAT HAPPEN. I KNEW I HAD TO HAVE THEM FOR THE OPENING OF THE CASANOVA CLUB.

So the Prince went looking, and what he found was several venues, like the Hamilton Club and the big one, the Tower Ballroom, that helped secure their future, even at a time in 1961 when the band members were arguing and, at different times, talking about splitting up. As Leach found bigger venues, the internal issues were escalating. There were simmering disputes between John and Paul, even months after Stuart Sutcliffe left the band, John still upset that Paul's disappointment in Stuart's music may have accelerated the bass guitarist's departure, even though Stuart *did* leave on his own to study art full-time. Money was always a point of contention, and Paul was quietly beating the drums to replace Pete, even as Mona Best continued playing a major role in the boys' lives.

Sam Leach, with his wide grin and never-say-die attitude, came into the picture with a transfusion of optimism, but the truth was, as he confirms, that he was really a promoter, not a manager.

And then along came Brian Epstein. The date, in December 1961, is etched in Leach's memory.

ON THE WAY BACK FROM ALDERSHOT, A SUNDAY, DECEMBER 10, 1961, THEY MADE THEIR DECISION TO GO WITH BRIAN EPSTEIN AS MANAGER. I WILL ALWAYS REMEMBER THAT DATE BECAUSE THE ADVERTISING DIDN'T GO IN THE PAPER FOR THE FIRST NIGHT AND THEY ONLY GOT EIGHTEEN PEOPLE TO COME TO THE VENUE. ON THE WAY BACK, THAT IS WHEN THEY DECIDED TO GO WITH EPSTEIN. THEY HAD CONVENIENTLY FORGOTTEN THAT THE WEEK BEFORE THEY HAD OVER FOUR THOUSAND AT THE TOWER THEATER IN NEW BRIGHTON, ON A FRIDAY NIGHT. ANYHOW, THEY DECIDED TO GO WITH EPPY. HE ALSO HAD THE MONEY, THE POLISH, AND THE CONNECTIONS. AND HIS ACCENT WOULD HAVE GOTTEN HIM INTO DOORS, WHERE I MIGHT HAVE GOTTEN THROWN OUT. ACTUALLY, THEY CAME TO TELL ME ABOUT BRIAN AFTER THEY GOT BACK FROM ALDERSHOT IN LONDON, AND THEY LOOKED VERY NERVOUS. THEY SAID, "WE HAVE A MAN THAT WANTS TO MANAGE US AND HE IS A MILLIONAIRE, LOTS OF MONEY." I SAID, "NO, I AM GOING TO MANAGE YOU." THEY SAID, "HE'S GOT MONEY. WE'LL STILL INVOLVE YOU, BUT JUST GO AND HAVE A LOOK AT HIM AND TELL US WHAT YOU THINK." I WENT TO TALK TO HIM,

SUMMED HIM UP IN FIVE MINUTES, SAW THAT HE WAS GENUINE, THOUGHT HE HAD MONEY, AND REALIZED MAYBE I COULD DO BUSINESS WITH HIM. MAYBE HE WOULD BACK MY RECORD LABEL. I HAD THE INDEPENDENT TROUBADOUR RECORD LABEL AND RECORDED GERRY AND THE PACEMAKERS' "YOU'LL NEVER WALK ALONE." THAT WAS GERRY'S BEST SONG. WHEN I WAS WALKING BACK, I DECIDED I WOULD TELL THEM HE WAS NO GOOD FOR THEM. BUT WHEN I SAW THEM LOOKING SO TRUSTING, I COULDN'T TELL LIES, AND I SAID, "YOU WILL MAKE IT WITH THIS GUY. HE'LL BE GOOD FOR YOU. YOU'LL BE FAMOUS. GO WITH HIM AND IT WILL WORK FOR YOU." THIS IS WHAT I SAID TO THEM. POLISH, MONEY, ACCENT—ALL OF IT WAS A VERY ATTRACTIVE PACKAGE.

If Leach had recommended against Brian, would the boys have listened? The bigger question is whether John, Paul, George, and Pete asked Leach to "check out" Epstein merely as a courtesy.

As Epstein began to remake their image, Leach continued promoting events.

I CONTINUED TO DO SO UNTIL AUGUST 1962. WE MADE A LOT OF SHOWS TOGETHER AND I GOT THEM A LOT OF MONEY. THE TOWER BALLROOM WAS A BIG VENUE—HUGE. BRIAN APPROACHED ME TO GO IN ON A PERCENTAGE OF PROMOTING GIGS. HE CAME UP WITH LITTLE RICHARD, JERRY LEE LEWIS, AND BEATLES AS THE NUMBER-TWO BAND. HE WANTED TO GO IN WITH ME. I SAID FIFTY-FIFTY AND HE SAID, "CAN'T DO THAT, BUT I'LL DO HALF." THEN IT WAS DOWN TO 12.5 PERCENT, AND THAT WAS THE END OF THAT. I HAD TOO MANY MOUTHS TO FEED TO ENTER THAT MEASLY CONTRACT. AS JOHN LATER WROTE, "LIFE IS WHAT HAPPENS WHEN YOU'RE BUSY MAKING OTHER PLANS." EPSTEIN HAD NO INTENTIONS OF ANYONE BUT HIMSELF TAKING THE CREDIT.

Leach carried on and promoted other groups during the years, never taking his eyes off the Beatles. He had hits and plenty of misses.

I TURNED DOWN HERMAN'S HERMITS, THE HOLLIES. ONCE I WAS WORKED OUT [BY EPSTEIN], EVERYTHING ELSE IN THE BUSINESS SEEMED HOLLOW TO ME. THERE WAS NO MORE IN ME FOR THAT. MY WIFE WANTED ME TO COME

OUT OF THE BUSINESS AND LOOK AFTER THE FAMILY. WE HAD THREE KIDS IN THE FIRST FOUR YEARS. I DID END UP COMING OUT AND HAVE NO REGRETS AT ALL. SO AFTER THAT I LEFT AND WENT INTO A STATE AGENCY FOR A COUPLE OF YEARS AND THAT DIDN'T WORK OUT TOO WELL. THEN I WENT INTO DRY PROOFING AND HAD ABOUT TWENTY, THIRTY PEOPLE WORKING FOR ME AND THAT WORKED WELL UNTIL ABOUT 1990, WHEN THE BUSINESS FAILED. THEN I MORE OR LESS RETIRED, DECIDED TO WRITE MY BOOK. MY WIFE DIDN'T WANT ME TO, AND WE DRIFTED APART, AND ENDED UP GETTING DIVORCED, BUT WE ARE STILL GOOD FRIENDS.

It is historical irony that his huge success, "Operation Big Beat," a big show at the Tower Ballroom, came the night after Brian Epstein walked into the Cavern to see the Beatles up close. And inevitably, that visit would be a bad omen for the future of Leach and the boys.

"Operation Big Beat was Sam's greatest success," recalls former Beatle Pete Best. "It was thorough, and as promised, big, with so many bands."

Best has warm feelings toward Leach and Allan Williams, two men who have carried on a competitive battle of words since the early sixties: "Sam is a wonderful man, but he made some mistakes along the way. Allan is mercurial. People here either love him or hate him."

Like his mother, who "wanted to bring live music to the kids of Liverpool," Pete respected Leach's desire to create new ideas, such as Operation Big Beat.

Like some from the arena of Liverpool music in the sixties, Leach, the Prince of Mathew Street, is hard not to like. He has a wonderful glow about him, proud of his place in history. He is hardly sad, irritable, or bitter about what happened, but very happy to share his story about one of the people left behind who made giant steps possible for the fledgling Beatles.

In the end, the gig at the Tower Ballroom was a key turning point, and Leach made it happen.

Has Leach ever gotten the credit he deserves?

There was a time when Paul McCartney called the period during 1961 and part of 1962 "the Sam Leach era." Leach's accomplishments have been noted by select authors, but not all. There are times when the omissions of history may be more important than the inclusions. An example: Some authors have practically written May Pang out of John Lennon's life story. She was, through her eighteen-month relationship with him, a powerful force in John Lennon's life. The same incredulous historical revision has happened to Sam Leach. There are those biographers who have not even mentioned him, and others who give his historic bookings and love for the group a brief mention, if that.

Few people report John Lennon's uncharacteristic tears when the Beatles and Leach parted ways, after Brian Epstein maneuvered him out of their lives. John had said, "Sam Leach was the pulse of Merseybeat. What he did, the rest copied."

And that is true. The concert dates, and the amount of tickets sold, prove that in the early, pulsating rise of Mersey Beat, fans of the music would start buying up tickets whenever Leach's name was connected to a concert.

And the biggest omission of all?

The most thorough accounting ever of the Beatles, biased but important nevertheless, was *The Beatles Anthology*, in print and on video. In its accounting of the Liverpool years, there is not one mention of Sam Leach.

The anthology was produced and edited by the organization representing the surviving Beatles.

Sam Leach, often copied, was always loyal, creative, and hopeful. Like others left behind, the Prince of Mathew Street is often forgotten as the enemies of history prevail—foggy memories and omission making the real truth elusive.

CHAPTER FIFTEEN

THE POLL

*" . . . when I discovered that there were around forty votes for Rory Storm
written in green ink in the same handwriting, I decided to disqualify them.
This made the Beatles number one."*
—Bill Harry

*"And by the way, Larry, forget about the counting method.
The guys were the most favorite in Merseyside."*
—Tony Bramwell

LESS THAN TWO MONTHS AFTER SAM LEACH'S TOWER BALLROOM SUCCESS,
Bill Harry unleashed a crafty piece of journalism, backed by a public opinion survey that struck a raw nerve on the music scene. Was it a "scientific"
survey?

There was a buzz on the streets—*Mersey Beat* was becoming "Mersey
Beatles," or so they said. It was true that the Beatles were featured heavily in
Harry's popular new newspaper, but a look at most of the editions will show
that Bill and girlfriend Virginia Sowry spread the wealth with significant
coverage of all the big Merseyside groups, especially Gerry and the
Pacemakers, Rory Storm and the Hurricanes, and Kingsize Taylor and the
Dominoes.

The survey, though, became a catalyst.

When the January 4, 1962, edition of *Mersey Beat* hit the newsstands, its
cover featured the headline "Beatles Top Poll!" and the tagline "Full Results
Inside." The cover story listed the boys as the number-one Merseyside band in
a poll of readers, and the Beatles were elated. They thought, for sure, that the
people at Decca would view it as another affirmation of their coming success.

In the meantime, with a heavy schedule at the Cavern, the Tower, and
other assorted venues, the boys became even hotter after the *Mersey Beat* poll,
which Harry carefully conducted.

"The survey was indeed a significant moment, signaling a local supremacy, but not necessarily a predictor of their rise to the top," recalls Harry, who then describes the methodology. "We had a coupon inside each issue. When the completed coupons were filled in and sent to our office, Virginia and I counted them."

But hold on. It's not that simple. Bill Harry says good-natured trickery was afoot. "Rory Storm and the Hurricanes [with drummer Ringo Starr], had the most votes. With my Beatles bias, I decided to go over the coupons again, and when I discovered that there were around forty votes for Rory Storm written in green ink in the *same* handwriting, I decided to disqualify them. This made the Beatles number one and Rory dropped to number four."

There was more to it than that. Harry and Sowry launched their own investigation, of sorts.

"The news agent at the corner of Castle Street contacted me to tell me that someone had bought his entire stock of *Mersey Beats* and his description matched Joe Flannery, at that time manager of band leader Lee Curtis. Curtis is Flannery's brother. I realized that groups and their managers must have bought copies, and it later emerged that Paul McCartney admitted to doing the same. It was simply a case of keeping it honest, and fair."

So how did the Beatles finish at number one?

"Considering the amount of votes we received and our knowledge of who was really popular, due to the fact that Virginia and I were out virtually seven nights a week going to various venues, I reckon that the poll results were the accurate mirror of the popularity of local bands."

Was there a "margin of error," as we now see in surveys? No. But Harry and Sowry were comfortable that the Beatles were really number one, even though Bill's confessed "Beatles bias" made it into the mix.

Young Tony Bramwell, who couldn't wait for each *Mersey Beat* copy, has distinct memories of the January 4 cover.

Soon to join Team Epstein, the future big-time promotion man understood the meaning of the story. "Let's face it; the guys had been struggling," Bramwell says. "Even with their local successes, there wasn't yet an image of 'owning' the territory, so to speak. This was a really big deal for me and my mates to see them on the front cover of *Mersey Beat*. And by the way, Larry, forget about the counting method. The guys *were* the most favorite in Merseyside."

Freda Kelly, Epstein's secretary, was just "totally blown away."

She recalls, "All of a sudden the success that we saw at the Cavern was right there. . . . I mean . . . number one in Merseyside. How could you top that? Unfortunately, the people in London didn't get it. Yet. I'm sure they were thinking, 'Who cares about those simpleton fans in Liverpool.' They didn't realize how perceptive and brilliant we were in discovering talent."

Years later, John Lennon, joining me for a 1975 charity radio marathon in Philadelphia, shared some stories of 1962, and an audition from hell. When the poll was published, Epstein and the Beatles were waiting for the answer on an audition for Decca Records, an important milestone that you will soon experience. In retrospect, John understood that, at the time, the London musical geniuses were biased.

"The Decca thing was rubbish, although we thought we did well. There was bias against Liverpool. But in the meantime, we were doing quite well everywhere and at the Tower Ballroom, and then . . . *Mersey Beat* proclaims us number one. That was the best press we ever got, even better than you, Larry [makes a funny face]."

Bill Harry remembers the edition and the poll results. "In reality, all the groups were happy to be on the list, but there were jealousies, a lot of that. There might still be today, but the poll was fair, considering all the discrepancies that Virginia and I discovered."

Here are the printed results from the poll:

> 1. The Beatles
> 2. Gerry and the Pacemakers
> 3. The Remo Four
> 4. Rory Storm and the Hurricanes
> 5. Johnny Sandon and the Searchers
> 6. Kingsize Taylor and the Dominoes
> 7. The Big Three
> 8. The Strangers
> 9. Faron and the Flamingos
> 10. The Four Jays

11. Ian and the Zodiacs
12. The Undertakers
13. Earl Preston and the TTs
14. Mark Peters and the Cyclones
15. Karl Terry and the Cruisers
16. Derry and the Seniors
17. Steve and the Syndicate
18. Dee Fenton and the Silhouettes
19. Billy J. Kramer and the Coasters
20. Dale Roberts and the Jaywalkers

In all fairness, Billy J. Kramer, soon to be a star, was just beginning, but Kingsize Taylor and the raucous Big Three were doing quite well, along with Rory, Ringo, and company, and of course, Gerry and his Pacemakers. In a twist of irony, these groups, as you will learn soon in the chapter "Bands on the Run," contributed mightily to the boys' success.

CHAPTER SIXTEEN

TOWER OF POWER

"Yes, I hold the record for largest attendance in England in 1961:
Tower Theater in New Brighton—Operation Big Beat.
That is where and when Beatlemania began."
—Sam Leach

IF ALLAN WILLIAMS WAS THE MAN WHO GAVE AWAY THE BEATLES, then Sam Leach was definitely the man who had the Beatles taken from him. Right up to the present day, Leach has never lost his love for the boys, and it all traces back to a night of nights, in New Brighton, England. The date was November 10, 1961.

New Brighton is a resort on the Wirral Peninsula; its beaches are charming, with a view of the Irish Sea. And its Tower Ballroom was a huge venue.

"It was massive, like a cinema or two mansions pushed together," recalls Leach. "Larry, when I thought of putting the Beatles there—and remember, it was the fall of 1961—my friends thought I was crazy. Maybe I was."

The Tower Ballroom, in various formations, lasted from its opening in 1900 until 1969, when a fire ended its run. Its demise was soon followed by the breakup of the Beatles.

Leach was having a very good year in 1961. In March he helped open a place called the Iron Door Club, a stone's throw from the Cavern. On March 11, a concert featuring Gerry and the Pacemakers, Kingsize Taylor, and the Big Three drew over 1,800 people into the early morning hours. Around the corner, the Cavern had just fifty people.

The Beatles played the Iron Door later in the month, but on that early March night, the Iron Door changed history. The owner of the Cavern, Ray McFall, took the cue. The Cavern began allowing rock 'n' roll bands at night, and would become legendary. Without that decision, the Beatles' temporary home would have given way to other venues, and Mathew Street would have lost its luster.

Leach loved themed events. He called the big Iron Door concert "Rock Around the Clock."

A little later in the year, the excited showman began "Operation Big Beat," a big show held at the Tower. But the ballroom's operators had no interest in the Beatles—in fact, they didn't even know them. Leach recalls,

LARRY, I WENT THERE AND SPOKE TO THE OWNER, WHO HAD NEVER HEARD OF THE BEATLES AND DIDN'T WANT TO HAVE ANYTHING TO DO WITH THEM AT FIRST. HE SAID, "IT'LL NEVER WORK," BUT I CONVINCED HIM TO GIVE THEM A TRY, AND BY THE TIME I LEFT, WE HAD A DATE. WHEN I WAS LEAVING, I ASKED HIM WHAT THE RECORD ATTENDANCE WAS AT THE TOWER. HE SAID SOME NUMBER LIKE 1,000. I TOLD HIM WE WOULD BEAT THAT. HE THOUGHT THAT WAS A RIOT, AND HE WAS LAUGHING AS HE WENT DOWN THE STAIRS. TEN DAYS LATER, I WENT BACK WITH THE TICKETS AND THE POSTERS. HE WAS VERY EXCITED AND WAS SHOUTING AT ME, "SAM, THE PHONE HASN'T STOPPED RINGING! WE KNEW IT WOULD BE SUCCESSFUL! WE KNEW YOU COULD DO IT!" WE GOT A RECORD 4,100 PEOPLE IN ATTENDANCE ON NOVEMBER 10, 1961—AND IT WAS FOGGY.

It was, until that point, the largest crowd for a rock 'n' roll extravaganza in England. Even some of the ivory-tower record producers in London were stunned when they heard the news.

In Hamburg, a proud Stuart Sutcliffe received a note from George Harrison, the most efficient letter-writer in the group.

George wrote, "Sam has done it again, he's got 6 bands, 11 bars, 4,000 people. No doubt next week he'll have 20,000 for us." Stuart, engrossed in his art studies and very much in love, was proud of his boys. He wrote back, thrilled.

A little-known fact in the modern era is that of the swift work that John, Paul, George, and Pete pulled off as performers and roadies, as it were. Bill Harry recalls their speed and agility: "Virginia and I were at the very first [Tower event] organized by Sam Leach. The Beatles took the stage at 8 p.m., then rushed to Knotty Ash Village Hall [another, smaller concert] and then returned to the Tower for their second appearance at 11 p.m. There were around 3,000 people in attendance, one of the largest groups of youngsters for a gig on Merseyside, as most of the venues only had a capacity for hundreds."

On the 1966 Beatles tour of North America, a wry and happy George Harrison told me, "That town hall [Litherland] was really special, you know, but when thousands of people showed up at this Tower Ballroom, once again, you know, it kept us going. We needed something to keep us going."

The Tower was the Beatles' venue of choice for big crowds through 1961 and early 1962. They played there, at Epstein's direction, with major American acts, the most memorable being Little Richard.

The Tower is the place that Paul McCartney brought Joe Ankrah, leader of the Chants, the most promising black group in Liverpool, to the dressing room. Joe met his idol, Little Richard, who had just broken the color barrier at the Adelphi Hotel by staying there. Paul invited Ankrah and his group to the Cavern, where the Beatles backed them up. The result, remembers Ankrah, was electric.

"We, the Chants, went to the Cavern for the first time. Paul was so gracious, but it was John who lost control during the jam session, and started jumping on the piano."

The session had affected the Beatles as much as the Chants. They were listening to the doo-wop sound that had so inspired them in their mid-teenage years. And it all began in 1962 at the Tower Ballroom, where the Beatles, surrounded by postwar racial and religious bigotry, went against the grain and gave a black group a break, even as they were pursuing their own dream.

The Tower was a turning point, but just around the corner, and after a few more dazzling concerts at the Tower, the boys got a break, a Valentine in the press, thanks to Bill Harry and his girlfriend, Virginia Sowry, in the form of the controversial readers' poll ranking Merseyside bands.

The other acts on that November 10, 1961, concert at the Tower Ballroom included, among others, Bill J. Kramer, Rory Storm and the Hurricanes, Gerry and the Pacemakers, the Remo Four, and Faron and the Flamingos—all of whom appeared below the Beatles in the *Mersey Beat* poll, another fortunate "moment" during the still-uncertain story of the boys.

CHAPTER SEVENTEEN

BOB WOOLER—"CAN YOU DIG IT?"

"Wooler explains in florid terms how the Beatles had become the toast of the rock scene by resurrect[ing] original-style rock 'n' roll music."
—Dr. Michael Brocken, Beatles historian

"I looked out of a window and saw Bob Wooler staggering about with blood all over his face. He was saying, 'Get Brian Epstein.'"
—Eyewitness to the beating

Busy, aggressive, charming, and devoted—even once bloodied by the one Beatle he loved the most—Bob Wooler had an unusual title, traced back to the early days of nightclubs. The first time I heard it spoken out loud was with Paul McCartney, when I talked to him about the Cavern many years ago: "We had a compere at the club. His name was Bob Wooler, you see, and he was quite instrumental in helping us, and . . . I might add, quite a few people."

Wooler, as compere, was a person who wore several hats: deejay, stage master, king of the club, host, and overall hometown booster for Liverpool. He also had another career, as a music writer, which paralleled the enthusiasm and encouragement by fellow history-making pen pal Bill Harry. And what Wooler did for the Beatles in print was memorable for the kids of Liverpool, who followed his every word.

What was he like? Billy Kinsley, the Beatles' contemporary who performed at the tender age of fourteen, speaks of Wooler in the modern day with a deep sense of endearing respect:

Bob Wooler was very generous, a mentor to all of us. He was a much older man, middle-aged man at the time. He had a wonderful voice, smooth and believable. He never made a lot of money, but he had a lot of time to give to all the hopefuls, like me, and Gerry, and of course, the Beatles.

He was a small guy with a big voice. I'll tell you, he got such a joy over talking up the bands all over the place. I think when Epstein saw the Beatles being introduced by Bob, he was determined to use Bob to do as many gigs as possible. Bob had a wonderful presence.

In the Britain of the early sixties, local radio outlets with star deejays did not exist. In his time, Wooler was as close to a local announcer or host "star" as you would find. He loved creating monikers for the music stars of the day, including the people who helped make them stars. Well-dressed to the hilt, Wooler would develop snazzy names. For Brian Epstein, he coined the name "Nemporer," including the letters "NEM" to highlight Epstein's NEMS record store that became famous in its time. He called his friend Bill Harry "the Boswell of Beat." It was that friendship, a mutual appreciation, that led to a magnificent gift for the young Beatles.

There is no question, after years of research, that Wooler, Harry, and Epstein's close friend Joe Flannery played a vital role in Epstein's actual first look at the boys. There is also no doubt, says Liverpool Hope University professor Michael Brocken, that the combination of Harry's *Mersey Beat* and Wooler's surprising writing style sparked the Beatles' local comeback after the grim finish to the first Hamburg trip in December 1960.

Brocken cites the importance of the narrative in *Mersey Beat*, and Wooler's writings within it: "*Mersey Beat*'s contribution to the milieu within which the Beatles found meaning and self-expression cannot be overestimated. . . . In 1961 . . . Wooler explains in florid terms how the Beatles had become the toast of the rock scene by resurrect[ing] original-style rock 'n' roll music."

Wooler's writing personally buoyed the five Beatles, and no doubt, according to Joe Flannery, was a catalyst for Epstein to seek out the young musicians. After all, says Bill Harry, "He [Brian] was writing his own reviews for the paper. There was no way in heaven he could have missed the stories and the excitement, especially 'The Piece.'"

"The Piece" Harry describes may have been one of the most important items at that juncture in the history of rock journalism.

The date of the *Mersey Beat* issue was August 31 to September 4, 1961.

"The Piece" was Wooler's long and wordy essay on *why* the Beatles were soaring in Merseyside. But keep in mind that Wooler's words were written before the entire British nation and the world noticed the boys. His words were prophetic, especially, as mentioned earlier in this book, his reference to the "the stuff that screams are made of."

"The Beatles are the biggest thing to have hit the British rock 'n' roll scene in years. . . . Here again, in the Beatles, are the stuff that screams are made of . . . the excitement both physical and aural that symbolized the rebellion of youth in the ennuied mid-fifties. This was the real thing. Here they were . . . human dynamos generating a beat which was irresistible."

Through "The Piece" and others, Wooler's words were able to translate his onstage style, and the kids were crazy about it.

Lennon House curator Colin Hall remembers, "What Bob Wooler wrote about the Beatles cemented, reinforced the growing legend. Everyone knew he was partial, and no one cared. . . . Such was the heartbeat of my generation of Beatles fans. It was somewhat like reading exactly what you were thinking or feeling."

Billy Kinsley, whose band the Merseybeats was on bills with the boys, read the twice-monthly newspaper. "Couldn't wait for it to come out. Bill [Harry] was so creative with it. And Wooler's pieces. He was so significant in the success of the Beatles. Outside of Bill Harry, maybe the most."

Bob Wooler also became good friends with the boys, and was respected by the entire organization.

Freda Kelly, our lifelong Freda the Believer (whose story is told later, in the chapter "Secret-Agent Girls"), remained close to all of those who stayed behind, and remains today the "Great Uniter" of all the people who played a role.

"Bob was an original member of the team who sent the Beatles on their way. He was classy, and respectful, and he loved them, especially John."

It was the closeness of that friendship between Wooler and John Lennon that stunned the Liverpool scene when one friend turned on the other. It happened during the magic year of 1963, when on June 18 Paul McCartney turned twenty-one. He was feted at a party, and there, in the celebration, the joy of Paul's celebration was shattered when John's holy-terror side surfaced in an ugly way, this time toward Wooler.

The headline three days later in the *Daily Mirror* read: "Beatle in Brawl, Sorry I Socked You."

Brian Epstein, who was at the party and drove Wooler to the hospital, was shocked and angry at the negative national press.

What happened?

In Wooler's own words: "I don't know why he did it. I was booted in the face. I begged him to stop. Finally he was pulled off by other people at the party.

"I have been a friend of the Beatles for a long time. I have often compered shows where they have appeared. I am terribly upset about this—physically as well as mentally."

Wooler suffered a swollen eye socket, rib bruises, and some hand injuries after John unloaded on him, presumably because Wooler made some remarks about John's visit to Spain with Brian Epstein.

The episode was witnessed by a large crowd, including Paul, George, and Ringo, and the Pacemakers.

An eyewitness said he would never forget the scene. "I looked out of a window and saw Bob Wooler staggering about with blood all over his face. He was saying, 'Get Brian Epstein.'"

Wooler, gracious and publicly cool, took months to get over it, even though John sent a telegram apology and did everything, month after month, to show his regret.

Fourteen months later, it was obviously still on John's mind, as well.

In an interview during the 1964 North American tour, I asked John about his greatest regrets, unaware of the 1963 episode. In honesty, how many twenty-three-year-olds can really classify their life regrets?

John said, "I beat up my best friend. I was so high. Still can't believe I did it. So fucking stupid." Was he referring to Bob Wooler or Stuart Sutcliffe? Since I didn't know what John was referring to at the time, I will presume now that he was talking about Wooler, simply because the Sutcliffe episode was something he never, ever referred to in public.

After the episode of violence, Bill Harry recalls that John never really apologized to Wooler, and that an apology was forwarded through Epstein. But he did recall that dark night a few years later.

During the 1964 and 1965 tours, my daily radio reports were syndicated nationwide. When our network of forty-five stations aired the tape of that interview, the profanity was edited out, but the quote was shocking to Beatle fans. Those who wrote in to my station and others were quite angry that we had run anything about this untold incident.

At the time of the quote, the legend of Bob Wooler had not yet reached the entire world. Over the years, he would finally receive recognition.

Bob Wooler died in February 2002. His name and his life have been connected to the Beatles. In later life, he joined Allan Williams in developing Beatles conventions in Liverpool. He was quoted often, most notably upon John Lennon's death, when he called John the "Ernest Hemingway of rock."

Along with his hosting, writing, and promotional expertise, Wooler was the man who brought the Beatles in for their first gig at the Cavern, was with them during their important meetings with Brian Epstein, and was always tied to them in one way or another. He also played a forceful role in getting them the December 27, 1960, gig at Litherland Town Hall, the "game changer," as most people call it.

Ironically, he would never share in their worldly and financial success, but his mark as a supporter, believer, journalist, and unapologetic promoter will never be forgotten.

Wooler's impact on the boys began in 1960, and surged in 1961, the year a shy, highly private, and proper English gentleman—the businessman with the record store—finally made his move.

CHAPTER EIGHTEEN

BRIAN EPSTEIN—SILKY SOFT WHISPERS IN THE DARK

"I was immediately struck by their music, their beat, and their sense of humor on stage—and, even afterwards, when I met them, I was struck again by their personal charm. And it was there that, really, it all started."
—Brian Epstein, on his first visit to see the Beatles at the Cavern

"I say to you, Larry, here in 1965, that the children of 2000 will be listening to the Beatles. And I sincerely mean that."
—Brian Epstein, during the Beatles' 1965 North American tour

"Brian Epstein was the first finely cut and beautifully polished diamond I'd ever met in the music business."
—Journalist Tony Barrow

THERE ARE MANY SECRETS TO THE BEATLES' SUCCESS, many anecdotes and theories. A common one is that Paul, playing his guitar left-handed instead of right-handed, could more easily lock faces with John as they sang their amazing harmonies.

The Beatles were particularly adept at this whenever Paul would use the same microphone as John, which produced a visual effect that drove fans wild and that most other groups couldn't imitate.

Watching every concert on the Beatles' North American tours, I marveled at the two of them, face to face, their guitars out of the way, looking like they were about to swallow the shared microphone.

That, of course, is a technical tidbit that has some merit. But in reality, the real igniters of the flame were the people who made the decisions, labored in their defense, and traveled the potholed road, literally, to fame and fortune.

At the head of the class is the man with the silky-soft voice and the very special demeanor. I always felt that I was about to attend a formal dinner at an English castle when I approached Brian Epstein on the plane, even though all of us were eating just plain airline food. The way he talked, dressed, and carried himself was, you might say, the secret to *his* success.

Our story begins with an invitation I received from this complex man.

I should have known better. After all, John had warned me, "He wants more than your long nose."

In the middle of an eventful stay in Hollywood during the 1965 tour, Epstein invited me to his private cottage in the tony Beverly Hills Hotel. I sat in an easy chair. He was planted in the corner of a sofa, his elbow resting on the edge. It was, at first, a bit awkward. After all, he was the interview subject, and I was the reporter. But he did like me, and I admired his seemingly unending panache. For the public side of Brian Epstein—the only significant music mogul still awaiting his place in the Rock and Roll Hall of Fame—was one of cool and calm, and belied the inner chaos that had ruled his life.

We chatted about the boys' meeting with Elvis, the concert at the Hollywood Bowl, and their unending energy. He was proud, offering a perspective of the future.

"I tell you, Larry . . . there is no other band, there will never be any band like them, ever, for eternity. They are . . . the best. . . . I say to you, Larry, here in 1965, that the children of 2000 will be listening to the Beatles. And I sincerely mean that."

He talked about the early days, not so far in the past, really, because his stewardship of the boys at that time was just over three years in duration.

"Much is said about my management," Epstein said, "but in a really focused perspective, it is my opinion that someone would have realized their potential. The truth really is that they discovered themselves long before I discovered what they would be."

Humility aside, Epstein's role in helping them help themselves was undeniably the key factor to their ascent.

Interviews over, Epstein reached for some records. The first album was a symphony. I wasn't paying attention when Epstein opened a bottle of red wine and poured two glasses. After a few seconds, he raised his, I raised mine, and he said, his eyes staring into mine, "Here's to you and me."

I don't remember what I said, but I made some small talk, sipped some wine, and maneuvered my way out of the cottage. I had no knowledge before that meeting that Epstein was homosexual. But now I knew. I didn't mention it to anyone, but I was really surprised. And it was the first time I realized that he was living a private life, beneath the public veneer.

That life would play a significant role in his mental state, but he never showed it during what Tony Bramwell always called "the *real* Magical Mystery Tours."

In Flight Aboard the American Flyers' Electra

He rarely took the luxurious suit jacket off, even in the heat of airline flight. The carefully folded handkerchief, usually silk, rose a quarter-inch from the breast pocket, accentuating the bicolor shirt. The collars were firmly starched, the tie rarely untied. From head to immaculately shined leather toe, he was the model of English gentleman, even down to the aristocratic accent, and his firm upper-class carriage. On the tours of America, he appeared in command, even though, I would later learn, he was as insecure as the rest of us. He had a way about him, and that way was elegant and at the same time eclectic. He loved classical music, the classics he played for me in the Beverly Hills Hotel cottage, on the night he made the brief but classy pass at me. When he forecast that the Beatles would be adored by the "children of 2000," I was doubtful. Since that juncture was thirty-five years away, it seemed an incredible forecast, but then again, nothing about the life of Brian Samuel Epstein and the making of the Beatles was not incredible and astonishing.

He loved the boys, and not just for business, constantly displaying an uninhibited appreciation for their qualities of grit and determination. It was an irony that in the years before and after his death, the boys gave him the credit due, but rarely with the same passion, the enthralled sense of excitement that he exhibited about them. Later in his life, though, Paul McCartney dubbed him the real "fifth Beatle."

His presence in those formative final months of the race to greatness was unquestioned. His flaws, never seen in public, were outmatched by his personal touch. Each night, on the chartered Electra during the American tours, he would carefully walk the aisles and, beneath the din of the engine, he would just talk. I will always remember his words as silky-soft whispers in the dark. He would gracefully lean over, at times on one knee in the aisle, and whisper.

"Is everything working all right, Larry?" he would ask. "Is there anything you need?"

"Thanks for asking, Brian."

"Were the boys just fantastic tonight?" he would ask.

He would negotiate the narrow aisle of the airplane and stop at the seat of Motown star Brenda Holloway, who opened for the Beatles in 1965. "Brenda," he would whisper to the energetic and unforgettable vocalist, "is there anything at all that you need, sweetheart?" She would smile back at him.

Cilla Black, former Cavern hostess, big-time rock star in the sixties and seventies, and TV host in her later years, would tell her friends over the years that if it was not for the boss and his gracious efforts to give her the chance to perform, she would never have had that career. In addition to his gracious manner with talent, Epstein had an ability to inspire performers he believed in. The four boys he began managing became his greatest leap of faith. Artists often practice their art in the quiet of their own insular world. Whether it is at a neighborhood drinking hole or a big venue, performers need constant feedback. Fans often find this hard to believe. After all, they may not view stars as "needy." But Epstein had an uncanny knowledge of the emotional tightrope that talented and sometimes already successful people can tread on.

Maybe he understood those needs from his own rough start in the professional world. Epstein traveled a shaky road in his early twenties. There were many disappointments, the kind of setbacks that would stop most mortals, all the while seeking a place at the table of the great artists of his nation. And then, in a flush of luck, and through unselfish intuition, he became a kingmaker. He was, in the words of many who came after him, a careless dealmaker. But in one area of expertise, marketing and skillful promotion, he had no equal.

Personality overwhelmed his shortcomings, and according to an early and close friend, his pedigree played well in the chambers of power.

"It was perfect, the situation was," says childhood friend and confidante

Joe Flannery. "Yes, it was. He was Jewish and he was gay and that played perfectly with the London musical powers at the time. So, even though he was naive in some of the ways of promotion and business, he came to the table with some empathetic vibes."

He discovered his homosexuality at an early age. Joe Flannery, whose parents worked for the Epsteins, talks carefully about their mutual affections, emphasizing that we "both found early on that we were attracted more to boys than to girls."

He was, more than a manager, in love with the Beatles, not in the romantic sense, although other self-styled experts will try to convince you that he had an intimate relationship with John Lennon. That story is one of the Beatle myths so carefully crafted by the fanciers of fantasy. But one thing is clear: his relationship with John was much more intimate and complex than with the other boys.

"There is no doubt that he was a father or even 'older brother' figure, especially in the early days, for John," explains Flannery.

But to Yoko Ono, who was married to John for twelve years and shared countless intimate conversations with him, there was no question that John felt that Epstein wanted more. A lot more.

Yoko, sharing an exotic health drink with me in the kitchen of her home at New York's Dakota building, remains sentimental yet pensive as she remembers their bedside conversations, saying that John knew "Brian was in love with him." But, she adds, "John was always straight, never gay, although he loved, in his performances, to act somewhat gay on stage to show his support for gays."

As for Epstein, Yoko says, "Brian showed his real love for John by respecting him. John understood Brian's 'crush' on him, but from 1962 on, John was impressed with Brian's professional manner. He liked the fact that Brian was so good. John [and the boys] felt so lucky that Brian had picked them up. But there was never any sexual connection to Brian."

Not everyone associated with Epstein in the early years agrees with that assessment, especially "the Enforcer." Horst Fascher, the German boxer, rocker, and nightclub legend who helped steer John and the boys through the sexual and sometimes drug-induced maze of Hamburg, has a different take. John had deep respect for Epstein, but he also "fathered" Epstein when the young business genius allowed himself to go to extremes, which was usually in secret, but not always. As Fascher remembers,

HE WENT FOR SOME DRINKS AND THEN HE WENT TO A BAR THAT THEY CALLED ZASCHA AND THERE HE STARTS GETTING TIRED AND SLEEPING WITH THE HEAD ON THE BAR. SO I GOT A PHONE CALL FROM THE BARTENDER. HE SAID, "HORST, THIS IS ONE OF YOUR ENGLISH MUSICIANS LAYING DRUNK WITH HIS HEAD ON THE BAR AND SLEEPING. CAN YOU COME AND PICK THAT GUY UP?" I SAID, "HOLD ON, I'M COMING OVER." SO I CAME OVER AND THERE WAS EPSTEIN SLEEPING. SO I SAID, "LET ME GET A MUSICIAN FROM HIS BAND, BECAUSE HE'S THE MANAGER OF THE BEATLES." SO I WENT BACK AND I SAID TO ONE OF THE BEATLES, "EPSTEIN IS LYING THERE DRUNK; HE'S SLEEPING ON THE BAR. CAN YOU COME AND HELP ME?" JOHN SAID, "YES, I'M COMING." THEN WE WENT THERE AND EPSTEIN WAS LAYING [HIS HEAD ON THE BAR] AND IN FRONT OF HIM WAS A BIG GLASS OF BEER THAT WAS ALREADY OLD. I SAID, "JOHN, WHAT DO WE DO?" AND JOHN SAID, "HOLD ON," AND HE TOOK THAT GLASS OF BEER OVER EPSTEIN'S SHIRT, DRESS, AND *SHHH* . . . THE FULL GLASS OF BEER DOWN HIS NECK. EPSTEIN WOKE UP. I SAID TO JOHN, "JOHN, HOW CAN YOU DO IT, MAN? THAT'S YOUR MANAGER." THIS RESPECT . . . WAS NOT THERE. LENNON SAID, "HORST, DON'T WORRY, MAN, I ALREADY KNOW HOW TO DEAL WITH HIM. WE ARE MATES."

Horst believes they were more than "mates," but that theory has already been investigated, and scoured, and investigated again, as if it really has anything to do with the Beatles' rise.

Whether Brian was ever physically involved with John, as scintillating a story as it appears to be, is secondary to the genuineness of their friendship, and to the synergy that was created over time—a coupling that was absolutely essential to the group's success. The suspected physical bond will always be debated. Brian Epstein developed a close personal relationship with John Lennon. There were benefits to that relationship—open lines of communication, and total unrestricted candor—but in the view of a former press secretary, there was also a downside. A lifelong journalist, Tony Barrow, who traveled more miles with the boys than anyone except Epstein, remembers vividly how the manager's closeness with John inspired many a confrontational experience.

"It was always John who did the heavy lifting when it came to the boys' issues with Brian. It was John who was elected to talk to Brian. Brian had enormous respect for John's intellect. As time progressed, the mentor, Brian, needed John's guidance as he maneuvered the minefields of negotiating and protecting the boys' interests. They were close. They understood each other. Those early conflicts were benchmarks for the successful days ahead."

So Lennon respected Brian, and Brian respected John. That revered and symbiotic pairing, essential to the critical first years, was also noted from the grave.

Yoko, with great pride, notes that in his last will and testament, Epstein left two very valuable paintings of British artist Laurence Stephen Lowry to John. (Lowry achieved fame and fortune for his paintings of grim urban landscapes, and their impact on modern life.) John, she says, was honored that Epstein had thought so much of him, remembering him in that way. Considering that Epstein had no inkling that he would die young, it is therefore an extraordinary act of respect and love for John that he would bequeath some of his most prized possessions to him at such an early point.

His impact on John, challenged by John's insurmountable excesses of early success, and the parallel world of forced marriage and fatherhood, was impressive. Sensing the potential for collapse of his bright young star, Epstein provided a home for the newlywed John and Cynthia, a house on Gambia Street.

Four months before his demise, a letter arrived at my door. The language and style were typical of Epstein, formal with a touch of kindness. The letter was dated April 9, 1967. It was a response to a note I had sent him with my change of address.

Dear Larry,
Thanks for the letter. The reason for such a delayed reply is the fact that I
was in the States up to a week ago. As it happens, I had heard that you had

moved to Philadelphia. Thanks for letting me know, and I hope it won't be
too long before we are associated again.
  With all best wishes,
  Brian

I folded the letter, put it away. I would never see him again. On August 27, 1967, I opened the letter again. That was the day the coroner reported that Brian Samuel Epstein had died accidentally from a drug overdose, although self-styled experts called it a suicide, as if they really knew what only he would know.

"He was hanging with a rough crowd in London," says Barrow. "There were abuses of him, total confusion, and a constant identity crisis."

In 1968, before I made a trip to see the Beatles in London, I chatted on the phone with writer Derek Taylor about the loss.

"What someone does in private is their business, but the boys, and the people around them, were starting to see him a bit more erratic than he usually was," Taylor said. "The public never saw that. I had a bit of separation from him when I helped manage the Byrds. But we stayed in touch. There's no question, Larry, that in the spring of 1967, Brian was troubled."

The letter that I received in 1967 offered no clue to any depression. His writing was crisp, formal, and majestic, much like the articles he wrote for *Mersey Beat.*

Taylor, who became a lifelong devotee to the boys, and ghostwriter of Epstein's colorful early autobiography, *A Cellarful of Noise*, stood in awe of Epstein's miracle act. The journalist, who was my main conduit to the boys on their first American tour, and remained a friend through the decades, was respectful if not sometimes resentful of Epstein, who was four years younger.

"Larry, let me tell you, Brian can be difficult and painful to be with, but how can anyone take away from him the fact that he signed a contract with the boys on January 24, 1962, [and] within nineteen months, they owned the world. They were simply the best, and Brian knew it. While their music will outlive Brian and all of us, his contribution, his understanding of the nuances of getting publicity, and staging, and all that, was a wonder, an amazing intuitive sense."

Part of that intuition was a rarely understood fact that Epstein, in most of 1963, limited the boys' appearances to small venues, where there was never a chance for an empty seat. Although the Beatles were climbing the charts and building a rabid fan base, Epstein, with only a few months of entrepreneurial expertise, refused to risk playing them at bigger venues. In that critical beginning, Brian sought and received the press imagery he wanted: packed houses, dynamic and intimate performances, and the priceless photos of screaming fans in hysterical poses, tears streaming down their faces. Taylor, Barrow, and others engineered the visuals.

Epstein, it turns out, had plenty of help, including the powerful words of Taylor, whose reviews of the Beatles in Manchester catapulted the boys to stardom there. There was prim and proper Tony Barrow, whose reporting in the *Liverpool Echo*, and later, crisp and businesslike management of the boys on tour, was invaluable. And there was that teenage journalist Bill Harry, who along with a special love interest named Virginia Sowry literally invented the world of rock journalism, with an accent on the bands of Liverpool, and especially on the boys. They are all players in this story. But in truth, the most powerful player in the story is the one no longer around to tell it, which is a dreadful irony.

What Derek and many of his confidantes didn't know at the time of the deal made with the future "Fabs" is that Epstein never signed the contract with the boys, a show of faith and confidence. In reality, that gave John, Paul, George, and Pete the chance to opt out of their association with him at any time. It also, in a selfish sense, gave Epstein his own out. The boys never dreamed of opting out, nor did he. But the events of August 27, 1967, would, tragically, end their association and perhaps—who's to say?—be the beginning of the end for the boys.

The cause of his death has long been debated, but it's very clear to friends and family that Brian Epstein would never have taken his own life. Boyhood friend Joe Flannery says there is no doubt that his mix of pharmaceuticals was deadly, but it was not intentional.

"Brian had just lost his father," Flannery explains. "There was no one closer to him than his mother, Queenie, and there is no way in hell that he would have taken his life, knowing that he would have left her with the mountains of paper that took so long to clear up his estate. I had helped the family sort out all the transactions. I know what an ordeal that would have been."

He adds, "I knew Brian inside and out. He never would have inflicted that kind of punishment [his own suicide] on his family. Never ever, even though his life was filled with conflicts. He loved his mother so much."

Freda Kelly, the former personal secretary, aide, and fan club coordinator, says, "Brian was a lot of things. There is no Beatles without Eppy. He was a tough boss. He wanted perfection. He was a man who could be self-destructive, but he was not a man who would ultimately self-destruct. His love for his mother was so intense that he would never have committed suicide."

Brian's earlier life was a series of frustrations. He experimented with different jobs, in the mid-fifties, with limited results. Family lawyer Russ Makin watched the awkward transition from teenager to young adult, and although troubled by Brian's anxiety, found his emerging personality to be refreshing.

"He certainly wasn't conventional . . . and wasn't usual. It was as if he was trying to break out of himself and take an uplift. He had enthusiasm and sudden bursts of flights of fancy, but he really wasn't very stable . . . rather like a butterfly. Butterflies are very colorful, as well as floating, and don't settle for very long at any one object."

Makin's description magnifies the years of searching, longing for direction. After a stint in the army as a draftee, Epstein attended three terms at the Royal Academy of Dramatic Art in London. His classmates included Peter O'Toole, Albert Finney, and Susannah York. Although he was enamored of theaters, acting would not suit him, although his sense of drama played out very well in his negotiations for the boys' early record contracts.

Returning to Liverpool from London, and impacted by the broadcasts of rock 'n' roll on Radio Luxembourg, Epstein became a director of the family business NEMS (North End Music Stores). He was an active seller of records, and although a fan of classical music, he became more and more interested in the pop-music scene. There are conflicting stories of what led to his meeting with the Beatles. The most common is the visit by a young man, Raymond Jones, on October 28, 1961, asking for a copy of "My Bonnie," a song the Beatles recorded with Tony Sheridan in Hamburg. That visit, it is said, caused Epstein to inquire about the Beatles.

But the truth is simple: Epstein had been selling young Bill Harry's *Mersey Beat* in the NEMS store, a publication that had lionized the Beatles. The contradiction between his sudden "discovery" and the much earlier notice of them remains today. Harry, *Mersey Beat*'s publisher, is convinced that Epstein had to know about the band when the fever was spreading.

"I mean," Harry insists, "I mean, he was selling records and there was absolutely no way he could not have heard of the Beatles."

Harry's truth is confirmed by real events. When he came around to Brian's record store, Harry convinced Epstein to buy a dozen copies of *Mersey Beat*. That was issue number one, July 6, 1961. By issue number two, Epstein ordered twelve dozen. In a few weeks, Brian Epstein began working, freelance of course, as a record reviewer at *Mersey Beat*. It was great for business.

"He was aware of every group in town," Harry says.

The sequence of knowledge is undisputed. And *Mersey Beat*, which owned the collective minds of the fans and hundreds of would-be stars, holds the real story.

In the famous issue number two, a photo of the Beatles was featured on the entire front cover. Epstein did indeed purchase 144 copies of the publication to sell in his store. Issue number three featured deejay Bob Wooler's dramatic eyewitness account of the Beatles, plus an advertisement for NEMS, Epstein's business, on the same page.

By August 1961, Epstein, an avid reader of *Mersey Beat*, would have had a difficult time ignoring the decisive column written in those early days.

Bob Wooler, the deejay at the Cavern, waxed poetic about the young, raw Beatles. He reported, "I don't think that anything like this will ever happen again."

In the 1970s, John Lennon set the record straight. He told me, "It is rubbish that Brian didn't know who we were. We were in *Mersey Beat*. People were talking. The first Hamburg stories were all around. He knew us. But he had yet to see us."

John had to be correct. Was Epstein oblivious to the buzz about the sexy boys with the amazing backbeat, or just indifferent?

The stories of Epstein's "discovery" will no doubt persist. But one thing is certain. Brian Epstein first *watched* the Beatles at noontime in the Cavern on Mathew Street on November 9, 1961. He visited them backstage, enjoyed a lunch with his assistant, Alistair Taylor, and is quoted by Taylor as calling the Beatles "tremendous" that day. Taylor was not impressed, but Epstein didn't care.

The contract offer for Epstein to manage the Beatles came in two months, but in the meantime, Epstein called Allan Williams to make sure they were, indeed, free to sign. Williams was frank. He told Epstein not to "touch them with a fucking barge pole." Williams was angered that some money, earned in their performing dates in Hamburg, had been held back from him.

"I'll tell you," Williams says, looking at me with intense eyes and a flash of sarcastic anger, "we had a commission dispute. I was happy to be rid of them. Then and now, the Beatles were users, and once they used a person, they discarded them."

It didn't bother Epstein, who was leery of Williams's attitude toward the group, that Williams claimed to have discovered them. One thing you have to give Williams: he did indeed give them their first break. He did take them to Hamburg. He did watch for their health, and he proudly, in a book and throughout the decades, has proclaimed that he was the man who gave them away. And Epstein seemed happy to take them off his hands. Like all of history, versions pile up quickly, especially in a town where one's turf is sacred and protected ground.

In characteristic Liverpool fashion, where one rarely holds back one's feelings, Sam Leach proclaims Williams less of a manager than a promoter.

"Brian Epstein was the first real manager," Leach states. "Allan Williams was an agent. He was almost a manager. Allan got them to Hamburg. The six-hour shifts held the band together. Hamburg is what made them. But Brian Epstein was the first real manager. And although he could be unlikable, what he did for them . . . was . . . I would say . . . truly amazing."

Leach looks across the St. Albert's dock, as the waters from the Mersey, mere ripples, splash rhythmically. He sips his beer and wistfully says, "I taught Epstein a lot."

"You did?" I ask.

"Yes."

Then his expression changes from wistful to gloomy. He looks at me and adds,

I WAS THE ONE WHO GAVE THEM AWAY. TRULY, I KNEW. THEY PLAYED FOR ME IN 1961. MY ROLE WAS PROMOTING SHOWS. EVENTUALLY I WANTED TO MANAGE THEM . . . AND WAS TRYING TO. IT WAS CLOSE BETWEEN ME AND EPSTEIN. I TOOK THE BEATLES TO LONDON, TO THE ALDERSHOT. THE SHOW BOMBED, AND THAT DAY ONLY EIGHTEEN PEOPLE CAME IN BECAUSE THE ADVERT NEVER WENT IN THE PAPER. ON THEIR WAY BACK THE FOL-LOWING DAY, I BELIEVE, IS WHAT MADE THEM DECIDE TO GO WITH BRIAN AS MANAGER. THEY FIGURED THAT WOULDN'T HAPPEN WITH HIM. I SHOULD HAVE SIGNED THEM. BUT BRIAN DID. FOR THAT, HE DESERVES THE CREDIT. BUT HE HAD SOME ASSETS THAT I DIDN'T HAVE.

"Assets?" I ask.

THE LIVERPOOL IRISH ACCENT IS WHAT I HAVE, WHICH DIDN'T GO TOO WELL IN LONDON. BRIAN HAS THE ACCENT OF MICHAEL YORK, THE ACTOR. IT WAS VERY DISTINCT, POLISHED. VERY CONTROLLED, VERY MEASURED, AND VERY SUAVE. HE WAS EDUCATED AND REFINED, ALL OF THAT. ALSO, HE WAS JEWISH AND GAY, AND THEY WERE TWO BIG INS IN LONDON. AT THAT TIME THERE WAS SO MUCH SNOBBERY IN LONDON AMONGST THE ASIANS, AND THAT'S WHAT GOT HIM IN. IT WORKED FOR HIM, WE'LL JUST SAY THAT. HE WOULD HAVE TO HIDE THE GAY THING IN LIVERPOOL.

As Epstein moved quickly on the Beatles, there were those who tried to talk him out of it.

Allan Williams, a newcomer to Epstein, had punctuated his bad review of the boys by calling them "poison." But Epstein, trusting his own instincts, went into fast-forward with aggressive intensity.

There were barriers. More than three sources, who wish to remain anonymous for obvious reasons, have quoted Jim McCartney telling his older son about his concern for doing business with a Jewish businessman. That would be so unlike Jim McCartney that it remains unbelievable to many who knew him. But the mood of the day and the times suggested that a blatant anti-Semitism was part of Liverpool society, as much as the bitter and sometimes emotional divide of Catholics and Protestants in Liverpool.

Paul McCartney, for his part, was uncharacteristically subdued at the boys' meeting with Epstein that sealed the deal. But in subsequent years, his admiration and respect for the boss was clear and vocal. His assertion that Epstein was the "fifth Beatle" was repeated on many occasions.

The deal meeting was on December 3, 1961. Paul was taking a bath and arrived seventy minutes late—his nonchalance about that first business meeting was never explained. But after calling Paul at home, and Paul telling Epstein he was in the bath, the sometimes intensely serious businessman replied, "He is quite late."

George responded, "Yes, but he is clean."

George's humor, in my time with him, and throughout his career, was always a relief in tense situations.

That meeting and two subsequent sessions—on December 6 and 10—sealed it. And it was the leader, John Lennon, who nodded in favor of Epstein and said, "Give me the contract. I will sign it."

So three years and six months after the rendezvous at Woolton, the first real Lennon-McCartney connection, Brian Epstein inherited the rough-and-tumble foursome. Epstein's prediction that the children of the millennium would be enjoying the Beatles came true. He never lived to see that, but the time he spent with the boys, a mere five and a half years, would pave their road with gold and glory. No, he never witnessed the blessing of the Beatles to cultural immortality. But the failed actor, nervous soldier, socially conflicted young businessman, and delightful fantasist would find his date with destiny, his true calling: the twenty-three-month race that would propel them to the top.

And how did Epstein succeed? The once-shy, introverted young man had somehow developed a talent that is, for the most part, difficult to define—a sense of understanding of what people want. Maybe it was the experience on the stage, or the contact with music fans at NEMS. But he was, in the words of early and lifelong Beatles friend and world-class record promoter Tony Bramwell, a master, by the age of twenty-seven, of personal communication.

Bramwell's mother was so impressed with Epstein that she looked the other way when her mid-teen son traveled with the band, at Epstein's request, in a van for hours, returning from concerts a hundred miles away in the middle of the night. She admired Epstein, and so did he.

"He was classy, well dressed, knowledgeable, and educated. Brian would talk to you like you had something to contribute," Bramwell remembers. "He didn't belittle you. He had a way about him.

"He was very intelligent in dealing with people—a consummate business-man. People paid attention when he walked into the room. But they liked him, respected him. He didn't evoke fear, just respect."

Epstein had the respect of the boys and their faithful, but his management prowess, never challenged in those special early days, was tested by flawed contracts and inadequate security that led to great dangers on the American tours. But in the first flush of success, his leadership was incalculable. And more than any one factor, his belief in their potential was a driving force.

That absolute belief was always part of Epstein's message, which, while sitting next to me on that awkward evening at the Beverly Hills Hotel, he made very clear.

"Although I had never had anything to do with pop artists, and this was a new world to me, I never thought that they would be anything less than the greatest stars of the world."

Epstein's business acumen mirrored his view that, in the young Beatles, he was managing the best of the best. But in hindsight, he may have made some errors. In the early years, he asked the record label for 10 percent of all mer-chandise; in later years, business experts would say his cut of merchandise was far too low. He did scrimp on security down the road, putting the boys close to unnecessary danger. His personal life was at times a mess, threatening to blow wide open. But despite these issues, Brian Epstein had one thing going for him in those years of unthinkable success: a belief in the boys, an unshakable love for them as individuals, and a personal adoration.

Even Allan Williams understands the meaning of mutual respect. When I ask Williams about the importance of Brian Epstein to the boys' career, he says, "Dedication really comes into it. If you are going to manage a group, you've really got to believe that you have the faith and you've got to pass it on to the group and never let them down. Your main object is the group and you must promote them and look after them as best as you can."

Williams becomes sad as he continues. "When he died, I think he was depressed that his boys may not have needed him anymore. I once was at some function—Jewish, King David's in Liverpool—and I remember going to some sort of parents' meeting, and his mother came over and thanked me profusely, and I said, 'Why?' and she said, 'Because you always treated my son with respect.' Which I said, 'He deserved it.' And she said, 'Well, you know, most people knocked him because he was gay. He was a gentleman.'"

Whether the Beatles were tiring of him is a matter of controversy. John Lennon was devastated at the loss, and one thing was certain: Epstein's 1967 death was a trigger that began the unraveling of the group, because he was more than just a manager; he was also a guardian and a protector.

The Beatles' welfare and daily happiness were paramount to Epstein. He was dedicated, and he loved showing it. Several months after he became their manager, opportunity struck. With an advertised band calling out sick, Epstein managed to get the Beatles a fill-in gig, way down on the bill, at the Empire Theater in Liverpool. The meticulous Epstein decided to put on a show. With assistants Beryl Adams and Freda Kelly accompanying him, he sat down in an elevated box, stage right, to watch the boys. Kelly was all aflutter:

"The hired box was very private. Just the three of us. He stared at the boys, proud, his smile was so broad. He was 'doing it up' for them," Kelly remembers. "I was looking down at the darkened stage with a light shining on Paul, as he sang 'Besame Mucho.' I had heard it at the Cavern, but that night, it was majestic. It gave me the chills, and Eppy was a delight to watch. I had never been in a box before. I was so excited. He was beaming."

While "Eppy" was the consummate protector, he was also an unflinching boss, and somewhat of a micromanager. Kelly remembers a time when she left a comma out of a date on a letter. "He put a big circle around it. . . . I couldn't fit the comma in . . . I would have to type the letter over. I looked at him with hatred in my eyes. . . . He got the message . . . and said, 'You learn from your mistakes.'"

Although Epstein could be cold and hostile, Kelly knew very well that he was the right man for the boys. "I was beginning to believe that he believed he could take them anywhere. Anywhere."

Beatles contemporary Tony Crane of the Merseybeats shared his private thoughts with our filmmaker friends, John Rose and Tony Guma, who have been working on a film on the life of Sam Leach: "Brian had no real experience in managing a band, the things you need to do . . . but he took to it like a duck in water. . . . It was amazing."

Just as stargazers puzzle over infinity, one could think of the thousands of people with raw talent who never find their way, the hidden gems of music, art, and literature, people who are never discovered, who never find a break. Could that have happened to John, Paul, George, Pete, and Ringo? Could their genius have been marginalized? Perhaps. But raw talent may not have been enough. For the invisible artists of the world, quietly toiling, their talent and the beauty of their art, writing, and music rarely emerge without some individual or individuals who can "see" the art and transcend the natural barriers, helping them emerge from their quiet and lonely work. Epstein recognized the talent, loved the work, and had the determination, if not the guile, in the beginning, to fight for the boys.

There is no question that Brian Epstein believed that not even the sky was the limit for his boys. Gazing at them at the Empire Theater, watching them in the Cavern, drinking with them late at night, harnessing their behavior, and carefully dreaming of and plotting their future, the man of confusion and contradiction had finally met his calling. It was a spiritual and personal commitment. That was the difference between flesh-eating managers looking for a quick buck and the carefully plotting and visionary young Brian Epstein.

His was not an easy road. His relationship with John Lennon was erratic.

His boyhood friend Joe Flannery remembers that Epstein was often distraught when John could be insulting, and even threatening, with questions about his plan for the group. "He would be in tears, and confess to me how troubled he was by John's tirades and his wickedly nasty sense of humor. Brian was easily rattled, but he would overcome those moments by demanding order and consistency. I must say, though, that John did upset him."

Nowhere was that demand for excellence challenged more than when Epstein began the incredible "makeover," still ahead in this story. Once again, the young and mostly selfish boys would have a decision to make: listen to some wisdom, or perhaps fade into obscurity.

The fact remains that talent prospers among talent. Brian Epstein was an emotional but talented visionary. He may have feared John Lennon, but John had commitment. And so did Epstein.

On the verge of signing the boys, Epstein visited Tony Barrow in the "Sleeve Department" at Decca Records where he was writing his liner notes, and at the same time freelancing at the *Liverpool Echo* newspaper as "the Disker," writing about recorded music. Epstein wanted him to write about the Beatles, but Barrow reminded him via letter that he wrote only about groups that had *recorded* music.

Epstein decided to confront him in person. What Barrow saw resulted in one of the greatest descriptions I have ever read about Brian Epstein. No one has ever written or said anything close to Barrow's account of what he saw on his first meeting.

I WAS MORE IMPRESSED BY THE MAN THAN THE MUSIC HE BROUGHT FOR ME TO HEAR. VISIBLY, HE MADE AN IMMEDIATELY FAVORABLE IMPRESSION. HE WAS EXPENSIVELY GROOMED, WITH CAREFULLY CUT, SLIGHTLY WAVY HAIR AND POLISHED AND MANICURED FINGERNAILS. HIS SUIT WAS HANDMADE, HE HAD A COSTLY AND WELL-TAILORED CAMEL COAT WORN WITH A DARK BLUE SILK SCARF WITH WHITE POLKA DOTS, AND SHINING BLACK SHOES. . . . HE SPOKE LIKE A CONTEMPORARY BBC ANNOUNCER, REVEALING SCARCELY A HINT OF A LIVERPUDLIAN ACCENT. . . . AT THE TIME, MOST OF THESE [RECORD PEOPLE] I WORKED WITH WERE ROUGH DIAMONDS WHO TENDED TO CHEW ON WORN-OUT CIGARS AND STANK OF

STALE TOBACCO. BRIAN EPSTEIN WAS THE FIRST FINELY CUT AND BEAUTI-
FULLY POLISHED DIAMOND I'D EVER MET IN THE MUSIC BUSINESS.

Barrow, who would play a role in two dramatic auditions, and in the boys'
career, was impressed as well by Epstein's passion and belief in them. But as
their working relationship continued, he was disturbed by Epstein's private
life, which seemed to diminish at the same time his Beatles were accelerating.

"Brian was so confident in public, but he is unfortunately the perfect
example of the fact that money really can't buy you love."

Talking to Barrow is a pleasure, but reading what he writes is a lesson in
profound journalistic wisdom. In his book, *John, Paul, George, Ringo, and
Me,* Barrow gives the most incisive view of Brian Epstein's adult life:

"His inability to form any lasting and loving relationship left him miser-
ably unhappy. Instead, his lust for rough sex led him into brief sexual
encounters with dangerous characters, heartless men and boys who took
advantage of him, hurt him, robbed him and left him helpless."

Like the other Tony, Tony Bramwell, Barrow revered Epstein as a friend
and a good boss, but he regretted the path that Epstein's life had taken. Make
no mistake about it, his personal life was sad. But in five short years, he had
helped transform four young men into a force for their era, and for decades
to come.

That commitment, along with his professional style, allowed Brian to
develop into an agent of change. In the two years following Brian Epstein's
first association with the boys, his delicate balancing act became a script that
he created for decades of future managers. Without him, and despite the
amazing talent, individually and collectively, of the Beatles, there is a good
chance that the greatest band in history might never have been.

WHEN
THEY
WERE
BOYS

Part Five:
Turning Points

Drum beaters Richie and Pete—Pete was there first; Richie lasted. While Pete had the "atom" beat, Paul, George, and John sought the nuclear option, and Pete took a backstabbing for the team. Fate and timing won out, or was it fear and loathing? Back in London, the so-called musical elites tell Brian to pack it up. John gets the jitters. Eppy fights on. Decca loses, and Gentleman Tony the pressman lends a hand. Hello, George Martin. Goodbye to the old guard. Turning points? The points are turning. The boys snatch victory from the heartless jaws of defeat.

CHAPTER NINETEEN

"MEAN, MOODY, MAGNIFICENT"– PETE BEST

"America had Elvis; Britain had Pete Best."
—Tony Bramwell, on Pete's popularity

*"The original sound, the powerful sound of raw drumming,
was really not there after the change was made."*
—Tony Crane, cofounder of the Merseybeats

IT IS ONE OF THE MOST INTRIGUING STORIES OF THEIR RAW BEGINNINGS, the story of a talented and extremely good-looking young man who helped the Beatles make it, and then was unceremoniously dropped. It's a story with so many versions that it's hard to tell who is telling the truth. Obviously someone is lying. Maybe more than just one someone.

When you meet Pete Best today, you encounter a warm man who has, after many decades, embraced his legacy as the first full-time drummer for John's boys, and at the same time, a somewhat unlucky musician who sadly and for many years was reported as an afterthought—the man the Beatles left behind, the answer to a trivia question, the exiled "asterisk" of music history.

Pete is far more than an asterisk. In reality, before and after Brian Epstein's arrival, Pete Best was the most popular Beatle in Merseyside, Manchester, and Hamburg. Although some historians, and the boys themselves, would revise his role in history, Pete was a catalyst to their early success, and can truthfully take much credit for the rise of the band that, unashamedly, left him behind.

Even in their own *Anthology*, which Pete was paid handsomely to assist with, the Beatles insisted that he was replaced because they found a better drummer. Decades after he left the band, Pete spoke with *Beatle Brunch* radio broadcaster Joe Johnson:

IT'S VERY MUCH A CASE OF, YOU KNOW, AS THEY WANTED IT TO BE. YOU KNOW, IT'S ONE OF THOSE ONES, THERE'S BEEN SO MANY DIFFERENT RUMORS AND ASSUMPTIONS AS TO WHAT THE DISMISSAL WAS. I THINK EVEN TO THIS DAY, THE REAL FACTOR TO WHAT'S BEHIND IT HAS NOT COME OUT. WHETHER IT EVER DOES, I MEAN, I DON'T KNOW, NONE OF US MIGHT BE ON THE PLANET WHEN IT DOES SURFACE. [LAUGHS] THEY KEPT VERY MUCH TO THE LINE, WHICH THEY'D ALWAYS SAID, WHICH WAS THAT THEY FOUND A BETTER DRUMMER. BUT TO ME, THAT'S NEVER HELD UP WATER BECAUSE I WAS ALWAYS REPUTED TO BE ONE OF THE BEST DRUMMERS IN LIVERPOOL.

Sitting with him, as I have on panels at the Fest for Beatles Fans, has been fascinating. He is shy and soft-spoken as he talks about the Casbah, his mother's coffeehouse in the cellar of their home in suburban West Derby near Liverpool.

"It was," Pete tells me, "the real beginning. It was where we rehearsed, entertained. . . . It was a very special place. Coffeehouse during the week, entertainment on the weekend; it never stopped moving with people, you know. . . . We had snacks, hot dogs, soda, and coffee, and a lot . . . a lot of smiling people. My mother, I called her Mo [for Mona], was in heaven. So was I. . . . It was a place for me to pound the drums."

The Casbah, a triumph in the life of Best, opened its doors on August 29, 1959, to a crowd of three hundred people, mostly friends of the Best family and some school buddies of the ever-changing Quarrymen. The cozy nightclub was really the first venue and rehearsal hall for the future Beatles, but it became known for who was in the audience as well as who was on stage. John, George, Paul, and local guitar sensation Ken Brown were on stage that first night, playing as the Quarrymen. Brown would inspire another future Beatle, Pete Best, to form his own group, the Blackjacks. Pete, of course, ever the trouper in helping his mother open the club, was also in the audience, along with Alan Caldwell and his band, the Hurricanes.

As Pete views it, it was an irony that Caldwell, aka Rory Storm, would entertain on Mona Best's stage in the beginning.

"True, Ringo was there for many performances with Rory. Who would know that I would become a drummer in a short while, and that someday he would replace me in the Beatles? It is amazing that Rory would be there with Ringo."

Caldwell had just renamed his band Rory Storm and the Hurricanes, and as of March 1959 they were backed by the quiet, sometimes solemn (in those days) drummer, Richie Starkey—Ringo Starr. Caldwell watched curiously; he was a good student from the beginning of his career. He watched the young Beatles and admired their spunk. He sat a few feet away from a young man named Neil Aspinall, who rented a room in the Best home. Fate would have it that Mona Best's lodger and eventual lover would spend all of an adult lifetime serving the Beatles first as a driver, then as a personal assistant, road manager, and chief executive of Apple Corps.

Once again, as it had been almost two years earlier the night John and Paul first met, "Long Tall Sally," Paul's eternal rock 'n' roll anthem, was a big hit. It was greeted with thunderous applause on opening night at the Casbah.

The boys were thrilled with the venue. It was truly their home, this Victorian house that Mona Best put together. They were so involved with its beginnings, they even helped paint the place, with their neighborhood buddy Tony Bramwell joining the paint brigade.

"We had so much fun helping to fix up the place," Bramwell recalls. "The house looked like something out of a gothic novel, a big stone wall on the outside, nine bedrooms. It was big for all of us anyway, and Mo was a kick. Everyone loved Mona. She was a real personality, very energetic."

Even though the boys had some conflict with Mona down the line, Bramwell is very quick to point out that she had all the makings of a professional organizer: "There wasn't much left to task. With Neil [Aspinall] by her side, it might have been the most organized voluntary cleanup ever. I loved it. She took part of a house and turned it into the Casbah."

It was also the place that the Beatles retreated to after their first significant and embarrassing trip to Hamburg.

Mona, or Mo, as she wanted to be called, was a hardworking incubator of young musicians. Everyone was invited to play at the Casbah, whether they had the goods or not.

Pete, in a film interview with producers John Rose and Tony Guma, said, "She was so helpful in getting any group in. If they were not good enough, then they were told to improve and come back."

That helping-hand attitude was music to the ears of the youthful musical aspirants of Liverpool.

The Quarrymen actually painted the place out of respect for Mona. That was twelve months before Paul reached out to Pete to ask him to join the band and go to Hamburg.

In some ways, Mona, with her direct yet welcoming personality, was Dick Clark without the TV program, an innovator who wanted all the bands to have a chance.

Although her relationship with the boys would come to an end, the respect for her cunning and instincts did not. When Brian Epstein became the Beatles' manager, he reached out to Mona for input. Pete remembers what she told Epstein: "My mother said, 'You have an unpolished diamond. . . . Polish it up right.'"

In the beginning, Epstein was a bit timid, but he understood what she was saying, and in due time he put the shine on the group. Like many observers in Liverpool, Epstein understood the role that Mona and her Casbah played, even if he rarely wrote or talked about it. It's interesting how time and memory revision has for the most part diminished Mona's and Pete's roles.

In a 2004 conversation at the New Jersey Fest for Beatles Fans, and before he sat down to meet admiring autograph seekers, Pete asserted, "The Casbah was the true home of the Beatles, the first place that embraced this group warmly, even before I was a real member. It never got as much attention as the Cavern, but there is no doubt, absolutely, that the rhythm and flow of the band was developed there. And I should add, Larry, that my mother really cared about all the boys."

That she did, although there were some conflicts along the way. Best is correct when he explains that the Casbah was a major early venue for John Lennon's Quarrymen/Silver Beatles/Beatles, a band still without a permanent drummer. The Quarry boys liked Mona Best and her son, and enjoyed the comfort of the Casbah. From the summer of 1959 to the winter of 1961, the Casbah remained their home venue. And it was there, with close prox-imity to the Best family, that Paul McCartney's mind started racing, as it always did. Paul, the ultimate realist even as a teenager, according to Bramwell and others, was obsessed with the details of performance. He espe-cially enjoyed the Casbah but was well aware that there was an important piece missing from the ensemble.

In August 1960, nervously facing their first visit to Hamburg, the newly renamed Beatles needed a backbeat. The Beatles had split with Ken Brown, a talented guitarist, in what Pete describes as a huff over money—"huff" in Liverpool means a serious argument. Pete was close to Brown, so it was a lit-tle awkward when Paul McCartney called him and made the invitation. He joined the band, along with the small entourage, on the ferry ride across the sea to Hamburg. As the first non-temporary drummer took his place with the vagabond touring group, mother Mona was already plotting concerts and special appearances for their return, with the promoter Brian Kelly. She was also trying to book them in the Cavern, but she came away frustrated. The owner of the Cavern had a strict jazz-only policy at the time. She called incessantly, but the policy remained intact, and that was that.

But in the B.E. era (before Epstein), their association with Mona helped kick-start the boys into high gear during a period of almost two years that would bring Pete instant fame, a fast demise, and the gift of a brother, Vincent "Roag" Best, who was conceived by Mona in her relationship with Aspinall, a man half her age, a story that is an unusual side event for the Best family. But while Roag would become a blessing to the Best family, the story of Pete and the boys themselves had an unhappy ending. Mona and Pete were truly, before Brian, the closest thing to real managers the boys had had. In later years, Mona told the Beatles' first biographer, Hunter Davies, "He'd [Pete] been their manager before Brian arrived, did the bookings, collected the money . . . looked upon them as friends. I had helped them so much, got them bookings, lending them money. I fed them when they were hun-gry. I was far more interested in them than their own parents."

The last statement in that interview is furiously contested by all those who remember the families' support for the boys, but in reality, Mona had a stronger understanding of the boys' craft—their music—than the mostly loving parents.

And then of course, there was her son.

The truth is that Pete Best was, and remains, an incredible drummer. There were 274 performances by the Beatles at the Cavern from 1961 through 1963. Sir Ron Watson, now of Southport, worked nearby and saw sixty-one of them.

"In the beginning," he says, "before their creative songwriting began, the Beatles were able to take American songs and put their own stamp on them. Pete Best was an integral part of that. I would munch on a hot dog or cheese roll, sip a Coke, and tried to ignore the thick cloud of cigarette smoke as I watched them, mostly at lunchtime, some of this in the pre-Richie [Ringo] days."

Watson, who worked at the nearby landmark Liver Building, was obsessed with the hard-rock sound, and the drummer's beat.

"Dynamic is an understatement," he recalls. "The place was always packed, boys and girls together. I will tell you, Larry, that the truth of the matter is . . . Pete was an anchor, although a shy one. They played two long sets each time, and the drumming energized them. Quite often the boys would mix with the crowd; Paul, of course, was the most talkative. Pete was friendly but unassuming. He appeared, I think, a little uncomfortable with the fact that he was the girls' favorite."

"The girls' favorite." That's an understatement.

Joe Ankrah, leader of the Chants—an all-black group that broke through, thanks to the Beatles—observed Pete from a distance, and what he saw was a most dramatic personality. "He was certainly different, you know, a bit of a throwback to the movie-star figures of the fifties, and the girls seemed to love his good looks, because much like the James Dean types that were so popular in the fifties, Pete's quiet nature seemed to telegraph that he was a reluctant idol."

Best had movie-star good looks, mixed with an unusual drumming style. From their very first appearance at the Cavern on February 9, 1961, a show arranged by Pete's mother, the Beatles, with John, Paul, George, Pete, and Stu, owned the Cavern. The real owner, Ray McFall, almost stopped their debut. McFall continued his strict ban on rock 'n' roll. It was, after all, a jazz club. The owner also banned the wearing of jeans. McFall eventually relented, and his nightclub, an underground venue nineteen steps down from the surface of Mathew Street, became legend.

Pete was a big piece of it. His beat was unique. He called it the "atom beat," what Bill Harry describes as a "driving thrust" of percussion. Pete's style was copied by many of the bands of Merseyside.

For frequent visitor Watson, Pete was getting better and better, along with his bandmates. In fact, Watson was there the day Brian Epstein came for lunch. "He looked out of place, a man with a formal business suit sitting there surrounded by people ten years his junior. He was looking at the band, but also looking at the people. Pete was especially 'on' that day, and the band, minus Stu, was on fire."

History has not always been kind to Pete, who until recent years has been reticent to discuss the real story, allowing his brother Roag to call the shots. Roag, as a gatekeeper for Pete, has modeled himself after his father, Neil Aspinall. Aspinall gave new meaning to the word "gatekeeper," and Roag, in his quite loving protection of Pete, has been a magnificent guardian of Pete's professional life, and of his story. Pete's story, though, is much more worthy than he might believe. And with great flair, half-brother Roag, along with Pete and his brother Rory Best, resurrected the story of the Best family's influence on the Beatles with the 2003 book *The Beatles: The True Beginnings*. After all, the Quarrymen, Silver Beatles, and Beatles played at least ninety times in Mona's refurbished basement.

The surviving Beatles have little, if anything, to say about Pete, but back in the day there was no question of Pete's popularity.

He was the first Beatle mentioned by name in the *Mersey Beat* newspaper. Fans like Freda Kelly (the original Beatles Fan Club organizer), Sir Ron Watson, and Lennon house curator Colin Hall witnessed firsthand the hysteria surrounding Pete. Hall was especially impressed by Pete's drumming.

"He was very good and worked well with the band. George and Paul brought him in, but eventually it was John who respected him the most," Hall says.

Sir Ron sees it a different way. "Pete spent many more hours playing with the band in those long Cavern sets. Ringo came in at the time when they were beginning those awful thirty-minute shows. That's when I stopped going to see them."

Most of the fans were impressed by Pete's drumming style.

Billy Kinsley—who was close to Pete even as his own band, the Merseybeats, was making headway—was more than impressed: "I saw him at the Cavern and elsewhere. He was a great drummer, dynamic in his style, and he took his work seriously. Watching him at places like the Tower Ballroom and Litherland early in 1961, there was no sense that there was any problem with him and the other guys. Quite the contrary."

During this time, Mona Best was playing a role, and it was a job contrary to the social mores of the time.

Bill Harry remembers, "She was a strong woman in a time when women were swept under the rug in Liverpool. It's always been amazing to me that John didn't respond to her in a positive way, considering that the Stanley sisters were so opposite the norm. It's very telling that John treated Cynthia abominably—he swept her under the doormat young in their marriage—but later revered Yoko, who like the five Stanley sisters was strong and in some ways defiant and unmoving on her key ideals. In the case of Mona, John appreciated her, as much as he personally enjoyed being around Pete, but he was not afraid of her, as he could be of Mimi."

As the group started taking off, so did the legend of the Casbah, home to other groups as well, including Gerry and the Pacemakers and the Searchers. Mona's cozy Casbah was significant to the boys. She was proud of all of them, but Pete was a budding superstar. No one, no journalist or historian, can ever challenge that. Unfortunately, his celebrity, coupled with his mom's strong hand, may have begun to hurt him. The Pete legend, fueled by the girls who adored him and the admiring boys, was in real life a "movement." Movements have a flow that can succeed one moment and fade in another.

"Pete was loved," Freda Kelly says, "but mostly by the fans, and not enamored of inside the group. He was and is a lovely young man, and a wonderful adult man, husband, father, grandfather. In the beginning, though, things got a bit rough."

Kelly is too nice to say what "rough" was. No doubt part of "rough" was raw jealousy, matched with a ton of resentment toward the mother and the son.

Paul McCartney was and is a charmer, but in the beginning, the animal attraction, the magnetism surrounding the early boys, was almost all Pete. *Mersey Beat* described him as "Mean, Moody and Magnificent." He wasn't mean. He could be moody. But he definitely was magnificent to his fans.

Too magnificent, at least on March 7, 1962, at the "live" concert in the Manchester Playhouse for the radio show *Teenager's Turn*. Years later, Roag Best would say that that performance, and what happened around it, was a lightning rod in the turn against Pete, especially for George, who didn't especially like Pete, and most especially for Paul and his usually mild-mannered father.

The appearance was marked by trouble from the start. Bill Harry remembers fans cutting out Pete's picture from concert posters, and others running to the stage trying to push John and Paul's legs aside to get a look at Pete. This onstage antic embarrassed the other members of the band. But what happened after the concert may have been even worse. The group had arrived in Manchester with members of their family aboard a motor coach. It was a pleasurable trip arranged by Brian Epstein to celebrate the rising profile, and the plan was for them to leave in the same coach, triumphant. But it didn't end on a pleasant note.

Bill Harry recalls the show: "When writing about the show in *Mersey Beat*, I commented, 'John, Paul, and George made their entrance on stage to cheers and applause, but when Pete walked on—the fans went wild! The girls screamed. In Manchester his popularity was assured by his looks alone.' After the show we all boarded the coach, but Pete was missing. We waited, but there was no sign of him; the coach went round the block."

What happened in those few minutes was frightening.

Because of security concerns, members of the playhouse staff tried to sneak Pete out of the theater in a large bin designed to carry laundry. The motor coach's driver had to circle around the area while everyone waited for Pete.

As the girls surrounded the exits, the staff quickly carried out the bin with Pete inside. In the desperation of the crowd, one fan tried to get a piece of Pete's shirt, and in the process, penetrated his skin with a pair of scissors. He was cut and bleeding when he finally trudged into the coach. The mood was icy. Paul's affable dad, Jim, went right up to Pete and said, "Are you happy with yourself?" According to Roag's account of the night, passed on to him as an adult, Pete was bleeding and terrified after the wild exit. And he was shocked and despondent about what happened next. There was silence on the trip back—a lack of concern for Pete, and what appeared to be a simmering jealousy.

Bill Harry says he and girlfriend Virginia Sowry, also invited on the trip and riding back in the chartered bus, were stunned.

"When [Pete] got aboard, Jim McCartney was furious and accused him of trying to upstage the other members of the band," Harry recalls.

OF COURSE, PETE HADN'T DONE THIS. THERE WAS NO DOUBT AT THE TIME THAT HE WAS THE MOST POPULAR MEMBER OF THE BEATLES. PAT DELANEY, THE CAVERN DOORMAN, TOLD ME, "PETE WAS INCLINED TO BE MORE POPULAR WITH THE GIRLS THAN ANY OTHER MEMBER OF THE GROUP." LOCAL PROMOTER RON APPLEBY COMMENTED, "HE WAS DEFINITELY THE BIG ATTRACTION WITH THE GROUP AND DID MUCH TO ESTABLISH THEIR POPULARITY DURING THEIR EARLY CAREER." WHEN BOB WOOLER WROTE HIS FAMOUS ARTICLE ABOUT THE BEATLES, THE ONLY ONE HE MENTIONED BY NAME WAS PETE, WHO HE CALLED "MEAN, MOODY, AND MAGNIFICENT," AND WHEN BRIAN EPSTEIN SENT ME THE TELEGRAM SAYING THE BEATLES WERE TO BE SIGNED BY EMI, I MADE IT THE COVER STORY—BUT ONLY USED A PHOTO OF PETE ON THE COVER—IRONIC!

There was extreme jealousy among his bandmates that Pete was getting all the attention, but it was a fact, chronicled in *Mersey Beat* and other publications. The legend of girls sleeping in his backyard to get close to Pete is true. It's also true that there was an overwhelming outcry by the Beatles' female fans when Pete was released by the band in favor of Richie Starkey. In the aftermath of his departure in the summer of 1962, on the cusp of extraordinary success, it is hard to reconcile what an impact Pete had on the band and easy to forget the momentum he gave them.

So what *really* led to Pete's departure and history's lost chance to view the band as John, Paul, George, and Pete? As it is in most of the seminal moments in Beatles history, it may all depend on whom you talk to. But there are some absolute truths to consider, the first being that Pete never accentuated his good looks and drumming talent with an outgoing personality—and by all accounts, he didn't. Would his supposed lack of personality have stopped the Beatles' rise? Perhaps not—especially when you consider that Ringo's sometimes sullen demeanor didn't bring the band down. But Pete's personality *was* used as a reason by the two people who wanted him out—both of whom had an agenda. It all began in late 1960, just before the Beatles' historic appearance at Litherland Town Hall, and it ended with immaculate timing.

Mona Best was a strong woman with a big heart, a bad marriage to her husband, John, and an unbroken and always forgiving love for her first two sons, Pete and Rory. She was also the de facto early business leader of the Beatles. On the evening of a scheduled Litherland appearance, Mona found George, apparently a bit intoxicated, slumped over. Outraged, she told him that he was "out of the band." George eventually was awakened with some hot, black coffee administered by John, and quickly driven to the concert. George never forgot the episode, and neither did a very angry Paul McCartney. Even John, growing close to Pete, was deeply upset.

Joe Flannery, Brian Epstein's friend and confidante, remembers that John had complained to Epstein that Mona was "quite bossy." Flannery, who talks of a close relationship with the Best family, remembers spending some time with John as the Beatles' bandleader dreamed of performing in America. Flannery told Professor Michael Brocken of Liverpool Hope University that John confided in him, "Joe, I'm not going to let Mona get in the way." The angst about Mona was further complicated after Epstein took over and, during a coffee with Beatles family and close friends, asserted that he was in control of their fates and fortune.

Flannery insists that Mona was fuming, angry that control of the group was being wrested away.

All this happened in the same period that Mona became pregnant in her quiet relationship with Neil Aspinall. Neil, seventeen years younger than Mona, had rented a room in the Best home. He became very close to Pete, and eventually closer to Mona, who was separated from her husband. Mona and Neil's baby, Vincent Roag Best, was born in July 1962. It was a joyful time for Mona and Neil and the Bests.

But not for long. The combination of Mona's power grab and the growing role of Brian Epstein in the boys' lives set the stage for what came next. Paul and George lobbied Epstein to get Pete out of the band, and the hammer dropped when Epstein called Pete to his office. Epstein told Pete, "The boys want you out." And on August 16, almost three weeks after Roag's birth, Pete was fired.

Pete, who is notoriously shy and unpretentious, told my colleagues, filmmakers John Rose and Tony Guma, that Epstein also told him, "George Martin wanted you out." Both Pete and Mona Best didn't believe that for one moment. When Mona confronted George Martin, Pete says his reply was, "Mrs. Best, I never said that. What I said was that, because his drumming sound was so big, we might have to bring in a session drummer. But I never asked that Pete leave the band."

Whatever the reasons, the moment that Pete discovered his firing, he was devastated.

As Pete left Epstein's office and navigated down the stairway, Epstein, tears flowing from his eyes, stood on the landing and watched Pete exit the building. John later described Paul and George as "cowards," but the deed was done. John respected Pete, and his ouster was a seminal moment—an aggressive action led by Paul, with George's consent, that would begin an era where Paul would begin to chip away at John's prior dominance. John, as it would turn out, remained the most loyal Beatle in the years ahead, helping his childhood friend Pete Shotten become a millionaire, and paying his respects always to the suddenly lonely roadie Mal Evans in the early seventies. It was also an irony, but not unexpected, that John, in his thirties, mentored Pete Best's replacement. Ringo, like John, dealt with alcohol and drug issues in the years after the Beatles' breakup. John stood by him like no other friend did.

Pete, who rarely socialized with the boys in Hamburg and Liverpool, was never really a confidante. But his sudden departure, and replacement by Ringo, left him crestfallen.

Billy Kinsley was walking into Brian Epstein's office on the day of the firing.

"Pete, being escorted out by Neil, looked at me with an empty look," Kinsley remembers. "He looked pale. I couldn't imagine what was going on."

Pete and Aspinall walked to the Grapes, the legendary early Beatles bar on Mathew Street, where Pete gave Aspinall the news, a play-by-play of the sad and grim meeting. In an act of enormous unselfishness, Pete urged Aspinall to stay on. Aspinall protested. He was so close to the family and insisted he would quit. But Pete told him, "Don't go. Stay with it. They are going to be very big."

That meeting sealed the fate of Neil Aspinall as road manager, confidante, and eventual heir to Brian Epstein as the guardian of the Beatles' interests through the rest of the century and into the next.

Mona tried unsuccessfully to get Epstein to change his mind. Epstein later wrote in his autobiography that John, Paul, and George thought Pete was "too conventional to be a Beatle, and though he was friendly with John, he was not liked by George and Paul."

The news broke in a flash. The fans were angry. Future Beatles press secretary Derek Taylor remembers the moment. He told me in August 1964, "People in Liverpool were devastated, you know. Brian insisted that Ringo was a great drummer, and Pete knew, in his mind, *he* was up to the task. It was a mystifying moment to the fans at the Cavern. But change was coming, and Ringo's fate was sealed. In the long run, the Ringo connection, a different look, another person to idolize out of the four, was magic."

But in that moment, the departure was problematic. Tony Bramwell, who had joined Epstein in the inner circle, was not surprised by the fan reaction. Pete was popular. Today, Bramwell philosophizes, "America had Elvis; Britain had Pete Best."

The timeline of these developments is amazing. The sacking of Pete Best came exactly two years and two days before the beginning of the boys' historic North American summer tour of 1964. I've often thought that it could have been Pete Best sitting there on the sofa at the San Francisco Hilton on August 18, 1964, during my first extensive interview session with the boys.

But it was not meant to be. Pete Best's life went into a tailspin. Although he did go on to work for twenty years in municipal government, and made a decent living, Pete often became depressed. In the eighties, mother Mona inspired him to get back into show business. The Pete Best Band was formed in 1988, and to this day he still travels around the world, brother Rory by his side, and with Roag a constant companion and super business manager, a composite of mother Mona and his dad, Neil Aspinall.

One of the first members of Pete's new band was Billy Kinsley. During their very first performance, he noticed Mona Best in the audience. "She was sitting there smiling broadly, happy that he was back on stage, but tears were streaming down her face," Kinsley says. "Three days later, after a lengthy illness, she died after suffering a heart attack. It was a sad time in Liverpool, where Pete and his family were and are still revered."

It was also an irony that Kinsley joined Pete's new band, because in the aftermath of Pete's firing, Epstein had urged Pete to join Kinsley's band, the Merseybeats. So, it took more than a quarter of a century, but Kinsley and Pete were eventually united in song.

And then there is the carefully woven story of Neil Aspinall. He never forgot his roots with the Best family. Of course, there was his son, Roag. That was always there. But the friendship endured with Pete, as well. In the beginning of this century, Aspinall, Apple's director, rewarded Pete and the family he loved with a lucrative contract to help prepare the book and video *The Beatles Anthology*, which included music with Pete on the drums, although in the Beatles' carefully crafted version of their lives, Pete is hardly given the due he deserves.

When Pete talks about his mother, who died in 1988, tears well up in his eyes. She was an amazing inspiration. Both she and Pete helped shape the band. The Fab Four rarely acknowledged that, but the facts are there.

Still, the nagging questions remain, as does the search for the whole truth.

Theories still abound that Mona Best's staunch control over the band's early activity prompted Epstein to fire her son. There is a major hole in that story. If Epstein was so intent on getting Mona out of the way by sacking Pete, why did Epstein work so hard to keep Best in his stable of boy bands? Besides, when Pete was sacked, Mona was the mother of a newborn, Vincent Roag, and was very busy with *that* special assignment.

The other theory for his abrupt departure was the music. But that also is apparently bogus. The genius producer George Martin had brought in a different drummer for one recording session. Session drummers were routinely brought in for purposes of more finite recordings, because of their expertise in understanding sound and recording techniques. In fact, when the newly anointed Ringo Starr arrived at EMI studios on September 11, 1962, he found himself replaced on the drums by Andy White, a session drummer. The session drummer was called after Ringo's performance on a September 4, 1962, session, a month after he joined the band. He has, on more than one occasion in his career, suggested that the group members were pulling a "Pete Best" on him.

Another rarely reported quote stands out, and sheds some light. In a 2002 interview in his *Wingspan* DVD, Paul McCartney discussed a change of drummers in Wings, and also mentioned the Beatles' drummer situation. He said, "In the Beatles, we had Pete Best, who was a really good drummer . . . wasn't quite like the rest of us . . . fine line between what is exactly in, and what is nearly in. . . . So he left the band, so we were looking for someone who would fit."

So there, in Paul's own words, is a clear rebuke of the theory that Pete was not a good drummer.

Michael Brocken reinforces doubts about one popular theory. In person, he appears very analytical. The professor is a man with no personal agendas, only obsessed with the truth: "Larry, there are so many agendas, but the facts are the facts." Brocken writes in his book, *Other Voices*.

THE EVIDENCE IS THAT PETE BEST WAS A DAMN GOOD DRUMMER. . . . THERE REMAINS VERY LITTLE EVIDENCE THAT PETE BEST WAS INFERIOR AS A PERCUSSIONIST. . . . IN FACT, BILL HARRY RECORDS THAT ONE OF THE

BEST DRUMMERS IN THE LIVERPOOL ROCK SCENE AT THIS TIME, JOHNNY HUTCHINSON (A.K.A. JOHNNY HUTCH), CONSIDERED BEST TO BE AN EXCELLENT DRUMMER. BILLY J. KRAMER WAS ALSO TO COMMENT, ACCORDING TO HARRY, THAT HE "DIDN'T THINK THE BEATLES WERE ANY BETTER WITH RINGO STARR. I NEVER DOUBTED HIS ABILITY AS A DRUMMER BUT I THOUGHT THEY WERE A LOT MORE RAUCOUS AND RAW WITH PETE."

Perhaps no one has spent more time researching Pete's story than Dave Bedford, the author of *Liddypool*, one of my favorite books on Liverpool and the Beatles, and his good friend Ed Jackson, from Buffalo, New York, who has assisted Pete Best on some of his recent US tours.

Jackson thinks, in general, that "it may [have] been all about Pete's being a fan favorite. After all, we all know now that Pete's drumming talents are considerable."

So, with Pete's ability, then and now, rarely questioned, why was he let go? Was it underlying jealousy, or something else?

Bedford's theory:

THE BEATLES WANTED TO SPREAD THE EARLY PROFITS THREE WAYS. IT WAS ABOUT MONEY, LARRY, AND RINGO WAS BEING HIRED ON A PROBATIONARY CONDITION, AND WOULD NOT BECOME A FULL-SHARE PARTNER UNTIL THE FOLLOWING YEAR.

WHILE I BELIEVE THERE ARE MANY CONTRIBUTORY FACTORS TO PETE'S DISMISSAL, THIS ALL CAME TO A HEAD WHEN GEORGE MARTIN TOLD BRIAN THAT PETE WOULDN'T BE DRUMMING ON THE RECORD. I BELIEVE THAT JOHN, PAUL, AND GEORGE MUST HAVE WONDERED WHY THEY SHOULD PAY PETE A QUARTER SHARE OF THE RECORD PROCEEDS WHEN HE WOULDN'T HAVE CONTRIBUTED TO THE RECORDING. IT WOULD THEREFORE BE BETTER TO GET RID OF PETE, HIRE A SESSION DRUMMER ON A FIXED WAGE UNTIL THEY KNEW IF THEIR RECORDS WOULD BE A SUCCESS. RINGO WAS THAT MAN, WHO JOINED FOR A FLAT FEE OF £25 PER WEEK, ON PROBATION, AND DIDN'T FULLY JOIN THE BEATLES UNTIL MAY 1963.

Bedford adds, "It wasn't just Ringo who was approached to replace Pete, as some have claimed."

According to Spencer Leigh's book, *Drummed Out*, John met former Quarrymen banjo player Rod Davis in March 1962. Davis told John that he had made a record and played guitar, banjo, fiddle, and other stringed instruments. John said, "You don't play drums, do you? We need a drummer to head back to Hamburg." Davis, who left Liverpool earlier for a distinguished academic record in higher education, admitted it may have been his second bad career move. Billy J. Kramer and the Dakotas' drummer, Tony Mansfield, recalled that Epstein also approached the band's manager, Rick Dixon, to ask about his availability.

Jackson and Bedford, close friends of Pete's, are sleuths who continue to look for clues, but in the background, Pete Best has proved his worthiness in another way.

In one area, Pete Best can always claim success. He has been married for over forty-six years. His wife's name is Kathy, and they have two daughters and four grandchildren.

Freda Kelly, the sensitive and respectful confidante, the girl who kept the "boys on track," reflects on Pete with a smile and sparkle in her eyes. "Maybe, maybe, in the end, he is the one who is enjoying the most stable and happiest of lives."

She adds, with a loving grin, "maybe."

About one aspect of post-Beatles life, there is also a question from most Beatle insiders: Why has there never been contact between the Beatles and their former drummer? In all the years since Pete Best left the band, now over fifty years, the late John and George, and the surviving Paul and Ringo, have not seen Pete Best. It would be pleasant and poignant to think that they would have tried, would have planned some sort of reunion, or at least reached out. Certainly there was a wonderful opportunity when funeral services were held for their most consistent and longest-serving friend and business leader, Neil Aspinall, on April 8, 2008, at the Church of St. Mary the Virgin in Twickenham, southwest London. Paul, who was said to have visited Aspinall a few weeks earlier at a New York Hospital, was out of the country. Ringo, who had paid his respects earlier, did not attend. In their places were Stella McCartney, Paul's fashion designer daughter, and his son, James.

Ringo's wife, Barbara Bach, was there, along with John Lennon's widow, Yoko Ono. The musical legend and architect of the Beatle's musical success, George Martin, attended.

The Best family was represented well. Pete, Aspinall's best friend, was there, along with his half-brother and Aspinall's son, Roag. Despite the lack of any reunion with Pete, the surviving Beatles had a thread to Pete through Neil and his son Roag.

If any occasion was appropriate for a reunion of the boys and the former Beatle who helped propel them to success, the farewell to Neil Aspinall was it—the seminal moment when the survivors could have looked him in the eye and embraced a man who was so influential to their real beginnings.

The revisionist historians, and some of the Beatles' friends, will continue to say that Pete Best was severed from the group because he lacked a sense of connection with the boys. There may be some truth to that, but it was never the stated reason.

The real history, the clippings, the memories of fans, the recorded music, and all the facts, will show that the young drummer was, in the early going, the most popular Beatle, and, along with his astonishing mother, had a potent and clear impact on the success of the group that he, sometimes painfully, witnessed climbing to the top only months after his unceremonious departure.

And what about the bottom line: the impact of the change from Pete Best to Ringo Starr?

"Technically it was a good move, but a part of the real Beatles sound was lost," Tony Crane, cofounder of the Merseybeats, explains, quite forcefully. The original sound, the powerful sound of raw drumming was really not there after the change was made. . . . They seemed to lose a lot of the sound. The feel wasn't as good, no better [in] the long run."

The Beatles became the golden megastars, universally admired, and by default history backs up the change in drummers. But a question remains: Would the Beatles have been just as successful with Pete?

The answer is obvious, isn't it? "John, Paul, George, and Pete" would have no doubt made it.

As a younger man, Pete talked about wanting to be an actor. He didn't get there, but he did play a singular role, a very significant but disputed one, that certainly helped put the Beatles on the map, just months before they rocketed to enormous success. And his life, although lacking in the nuances and frills of superstardom, has been a life well lived.

CHAPTER TWENTY
THE DECCA DISASTER

"The disaster at the record company could have killed the Beatles, stopped them in their tracks. But Brian forged on and had the most fateful meeting. But before that meeting, it looked dark, really dark."
—Chris Carter, Beatles historian and host of *Breakfast with the Beatles* on KLOS radio in Los Angeles, and Sirius XM satellite radio

IN POLITICS, AS IN LIFE, SOMETIMES YOU HAVE TO LOSE TO SEEK A SECOND CHANCE. In sports, an early loss sometimes helps the athlete grind on, perfect the act, and soar to victory.

In the world of music, there are few second chances. But in 1962, John, Paul, George, and Pete once again defied the limits of destiny and daring, with a lot of help from their friends, and with a high degree of misery and doubt along the way.

It began with Tony Barrow, Mr. Pressman, who was looking for a way to help Brian Epstein get some attention for the group. And it continued with the marketing department at Decca Records, where Tony wrote album-sleeve copy. When Epstein, trying to show the boys his devotion to them in the early days of his management, called Decca for an audition, he was surprised by the reception. Tony Barrow and the marketing people had recommended that Decca audition the boys, out of respect for Epstein's work as a major retailer for the music business in northern England. It was a courtesy call, but the usually provincial and proprietary record giants in London had also heard rumblings about the boys and, it should be noted, many of their counterparts. The boy bands of Liverpool were making news.

And so the date was set. But who would schedule an audition for January 1—New Year's Day? Was it a "blowoff"?

Certainly the date was a mixed message. Barrow had written an item, based on his conversations with his Decca cohorts, that noted the Beatles were viewed favorably at Decca, especially by the company's record producer,

Mike Smith. The item, in the *Liverpool Echo*, was published four days before the scheduled audition. At the same time, Bill Harry's *Mersey Beat* posted a similar item saying that Decca was big on the Beatles. Both notices were greeted with excitement by the boys and Epstein. But the excitement was short-lived.

January 1, 1962, was a most important day for what it *didn't* accomplish. Everything in the record industry was stacked up against the Beatles, even the weather.

The drive the night before was unbearable—two hundred miles of high winds and blizzard conditions. Neil Aspinall, the man who could get them anywhere, through any ordeal, got lost on the road. Aspinall was a master of preparation and execution. He would be considered, in this century, as a human global positioning system (GPS). The weather and the directional failure were frustrating. They got in late, had very little sleep, and were stunned the next day when Decca producer Mike Smith, actually excited about the audition, was late for it. They were also surprised that their new manager, Brian Epstein, had selected a very conservative group of songs for them to sing—staid older songs, and not the electric set that constantly turned on audiences at the Cavern and their other gigs in the North. At that time, John and Paul were involved in their most serious songwriting efforts, but even some of their crowd favorites, written by others, were "scratched" by Epstein.

What was he up to?

Epstein later would say that he wanted to show their range, their variety, the fact that they could transition from softer rock to a harder version, but there wasn't much chance to see the latter. In fact, George Harrison, who at the time was experimenting with his vocal skills (later quite powerful), was the lead singer for almost as many songs as John and Paul.

There were fifteen songs in the audition, including such standards, for that time, as "To Know Her Is to Love Her," "Crying, Waiting, Hoping," Chuck Berry's "Memphis, Tennessee," and three Lennon-McCartney originals, "Like Dreamers Do," "Hello Little Girl," and "Love of the Loved."

Bruce Spizer, the world's premier chronicler of Beatles contracts, music, and negotiations, with eight books on the subjects, understands where Epstein was coming from.

"He had a vision, and this date with Decca was the beginning of his work. He didn't want to take any chances, so he was cautionary with the music, perhaps too cautionary. But please remember that he was cunning, always weighing the risks of his decision. He thought it was important to display their reach."

Mike Smith, the producer with all that optimism, told Decca writer Tony Barrow that the Beatles did not do well. And Decca executive Dick Rowe, Smith's boss, gave him the directive that he could sign only one group.

Barrow, beginning to like more and more of what he heard from the boys before this point, was ultimately disappointed with their audition, but he was impressed with Epstein's passion to make something, anything, happen, especially after the big boss, Dick Rowe, gave his appraisal. Barrow remembers Rowe's words well.

"Not to mince words, Mr. Epstein, we don't like your boys' sound. Groups of guitarists are on the way out. You have a good record business in Liverpool. Stick to that."

Eventually Smith passed on the Beatles and instead signed Brian Poole and the Tremeloes, a band with strong voices and consistency. The group is still working, after a superb career, though they've been overshadowed by many groups, including, of course, the Beatles.

And what did Epstein do?

"Brian didn't 'stick to that,'" recalls Bruce Spizer. "In fact, he was relentless in looking for any opening. He kept visiting London in the months after the Decca disaster. He was determined to get a label, even made some headway at EMI Records, and most importantly, he stayed in touch with Tony Barrow, who helped him navigate the rough terrain of the London music scene. That connection with Barrow would really pay off. For a young man, and with the skills of a journalist, Barrow had all the right moves on making contacts."

There was also a learning curve. Bruce Spizer explains:

"Brian realized that letting the boys be the boys, just letting them do their wilder, more raw act, with that amazing harmony, was far better than doing a crooning, kind of older style. He had still not changed their appearance. That was to come. But first, he had to get a label, and with Merseyside groups coming out of the woodwork, time was his biggest enemy."

After January 1, the boys were nervous. Days passed, then a week, and they were waiting and hoping. They were devastated when they learned in mid-March that Decca had rejected them. But John, unlike during the post-Hamburg depression in late 1960, was more hopeful, especially with Epstein on the case.

Cynthia Lennon recalls the mood in her reflective book, *John*: "John was down about it—but he couldn't stay miserable for long. . . . In spite of lack of interest from the record companies, we all felt that change was in the air."

With Barrow advising him, and getting closer to the boys, Epstein was relentless.

Epstein's friend Joe Flannery emphasizes that Epstein was a bit nervous.

"He had yet to sign them to a formal contract as their manager. [That did happen later in January.] He was upset that Decca said no, and so indignantly at that. But he told me he was determined to get them recorded and recorded well in 1962. And he kept searching. Through this time, the band played on."

From January through the spring, even as tragedy struck Stuart Sutcliffe in Hamburg as the boys arrived for another German adventure, the excitement at the clubs in Liverpool helped buoy their spirits. People like Brian Kelly and Sam Leach got bigger and bigger crowds, even as they began working with Epstein.

But once again, irony ruled the day. And again, despite their own doubts, the relentlessness of Brian Epstein, his gut-wrenching determination, saved the boys, despite their burgeoning talent, from sliding into oblivion.

"They failed at Decca, but that also meant they were through with Mike Smith and Dick Rowe," says Bruce Spizer, emphasizing another fortunate break. "Rowe would never quite live it down that he passed on the Beatles, but of course, he would claim signing the Rolling Stones. Some people would call that a concession, but let's face it, the Beatles would be better and bigger, and history would always say that Decca passed up a fortune."

History would also show, with tremendous hindsight, that the Decca audition was really not that bad.

"In one way," says music researcher and satellite radio host Chris Carter, "the audition showed something that would emerge later—the boys had wide range, which would eventually mean wider appeal.

"The songs they covered were written by Carole King, Chuck Berry, Buddy Holly. They came from Motown [Gordy/Bradford], Phil Spector and many others. They had three of their own, but even though Brian was [in later years] criticized for not showing their own talents, it was, and remember this, it was the recording of the Decca session that got Brian in the door to meet George Martin."

That story is coming up. But Carter's point is valid: the Decca audition served its purpose, and one company's reject would become another company's elation.

"The disaster at the record company could have killed the Beatles, stopped them in their tracks," Carter explains. "But Brian forged on, and had the most fateful meeting. But before that meeting, it looked dark, really dark. How amazing, isn't it, that some people just couldn't feel what they could turn out to be. But that is what people are all about. They make judgments and sometimes those judgments are flawed."

So it was in spring 1962. Epstein was offering his young band to anyone who would listen. Despite doubts about him from the parents, notably Jim McCartney, who had expressed anxiety about his business skills as well as his faith, Epstein was doing well. The door that Decca had shut would soon be opened, and on the other side, with the help of friendly writers who would soon join them, a driven Neil Aspinall, and his own inner gut, the merchant from Liverpool was getting closer to a breakthrough—in fact, a lot closer than he thought—and once again, Tony Barrow was riding shotgun.

CHAPTER TWENTY-ONE

ON THE POOR SIDE OF TOWN— HURRICANE RINGO

"I am Ringo. When I was growing up I was just plain Richard Starkey.
Here I am, Ringo, but I will always be just Richie."
—Richie Starkey, aka Ringo Starr, during an interview with me
in the summer of 1965

RINGO STARR. HIS IS A STORY OF POVERTY, SICKNESS, SURVIVAL, A HEAVY
DOSE OF LUCK, AND THE MEANING OF A NAME. Of all the young men who
struck it rich in the Beatles, he was the most unlikely, not because of a lack
of talent, but because when he was a boy, he faced a luckless challenge to find
real opportunity. Yet, when he arrived, he maintained the standards of a boy
who had grown up in a working-class neighborhood.

Ringo is unique because when he was a boy, he found a place in the
Beatles. Throughout his adult life, he has repeated the words. He is, at times,
incredulous that people call him Ringo. In a year 2000 interview with me,
Ringo repeated, "I am just Richie, that's all." His feelings about identity go
back to the beginning, as you can see in the quotation above.

Joe Flannery, Brian Epstein's lifetime friend, onetime Beatles booker, former bouncer and manager of Hamburg's notorious Star Club, and
Liverpool's cultural ambassador, finds Ringo's attitude on his heritage loaded
with hypocrisy.

"Why do they call you 'ex-Beatle' Ringo? Because you are. You are you, liv-
ing in luxury in the South of France and in Los Angeles because you are
Ringo, and frankly none of this would have happened if John and Paul and
George had not asked you to join their band. That is true, isn't it?"

Flannery may sound harsh, but he has great pride for his city's cultural
contributions to the world. Ringo apparently thinks less of Liverpool,
according to recent comments, although he has backtracked on those senti-
ments. In 2008 he graciously opened Liverpool's Capital of Culture

Ceremony. During that visit, he was chastised in the media for refusing to sign autographs (not uncommon in a world where Beatles autographs sell for a small fortune). But that was the least of his problems.

A reporter asked him what he missed most about Liverpool. Ringo replied with a laugh and the words, "Er . . . no." Later, to his credit, he offered a more positive view of his childhood. But over the years his attitude concerning his city of birth has been vague.

The lack of support haunted him as he began a 2011 tour of Europe with a scheduled appearance at the Liverpool Empire Theater. When asked again about his earlier remarks, Ringo apologized, in a certain way.

"I apologize to those people [who were offended], as long as they live in Liverpool, not outside," Starr told a BBC interviewer. "No real Scouser took offence, only I believe people from the outside."

The truth was that some of the people who were outraged may have misinterpreted his unusual sense of humor.

It has been a long time since Ringo took the title of "Scouser," the nickname for a resident of Liverpool. Ringo's apology did not sit too well inside the city where he grew up, and the Scousers *did* take offense. Shortly after the 2008 comments, vandals cut off Ringo's head in a foliage sculpture of the Beatles. People on the street expressed anger at his remarks, although he went on in 2011 to express his fond memories of growing up in the Dingle neighborhood of Liverpool.

There is something you need to know about Ringo. He may be somewhat secluded in his later years, but in the prime time of his greatest success, there was no more engaged or friendly Beatle than Ringo Starr, because his was an early life of wonderment, gritty hard work, and a full appreciation in that time of where he came from, and where he came from was the poorest side of town. The houses were narrow and there was substandard plumbing, in some cases no indoor bathrooms. The Starkeys were forced to seek their relief in outdoor toilets. Imagine going to the bathroom in thirty-degree weather. The Dingle was bypassed by much of the middle-class expansion during the postwar years. Unlike John, Paul, George, and Pete, young Richie did not have any advantages, except for a loving, comforting mother who would do anything for her boy, even when he lost himself to drinking and drugs at a very young age.

Although he will always be Richie, Ringo became Ringo at the direction of a man who plays so many roles in this miraculous story of success, the scintillating bandleader Rory Storm.

Cynthia Lennon, John's first wife, reports that Ringo became Ringo in recognition of the rings he displayed on his fingers. But the name was not his choice. Ringo's name had a ring to it because of Storm, one of the most formidable figures in Liverpool, and in Richie Starkey's life.

Ringo became Ringo when he was the drummer for Rory Storm and the Hurricanes, the electrifying Liverpool band that the Beatles admired so much. Storm loved his players. Even though his own life was marked by insecurity and instability, Storm was quite paternal with his band members. He treated them with deep respect, and enjoyed featuring them, allowing them to stand out. Storm wanted all of his players to have stage names. Richie was known for his love of rings and American westerns. So Richard Starkey became Ringo Starr and the moniker allowed his idol, Rory Storm, to advertise "Starr Time" at his many concerts.

But the name game aside, Ringo was a man with three lives: a delightful young Beatle, a victim of addiction in middle age, and a healthy and mature multimillionaire later in life. As with the sheer poverty he was born to and the sickness he endured, Ringo was able to overcome the drug habit.

There are many stories about Ringo Starr, including the fact that, prior to his joining the Beatles, he was offered a job with Kingsize Taylor and the Dominoes. Ringo of course took the ensuing calls from Brian Epstein and John with great anticipation. While working for Rory Storm and the Hurricanes, Ringo shared many a stage with John, Paul, George, and Pete in Hamburg, at the clubs in Merseyside, and of course at the Cavern. He had developed relationships with all four of them, and especially a real chemistry with John, Paul, and George. By the time he joined the band, Ringo was an old hand at dealing with the boys. He respected John's eccentricities, adored George and his passion, and expressed great wonder at Paul's ability to remain cheerful, at least publicly, amid the chaos and uncertainty that followed the Beatles.

For me, getting to know Ringo was an absolute pleasure, and always news-worthy. On the Beatles' North American tours of 1964, 1965, and 1966, we had a wonderful rapport on the airplanes, in the hotels, and on the back stages of Beatlemania. My complete history with him covered the period from 1964 through 1970, and again for brief reunions in 1989, 2000, and 2001. What I learned in recent years about his earlier life was stunning, even shocking. Ringo was generous. He gave me the first news in the summer of 1964 that he would soon have his tonsils out. It was, in the world of the young Beatles, a "major breaking story." When his tonsils were removed on December 2 of that year, it was front-page news across the world.

No doubt the tonsil surgery was a grim reminder of the earlier challenges faced by young Richard Starkey. And there were so many of them that his mother, Elsie, was always scared about what would happen next. When you look at the history, you can't blame her.

The scene at 9 Madryn Street was narrow, quite bare, and missing an important piece of life: his parents divorced when he was a toddler. In the ensuing years, Elsie and Richie moved to 10 Admiral Grove so Elsie could be closer to her work at a pub. The primary reason for the move was an attempt to cut monthly costs.

Richie's early years in school were not productive, and were especially impacted by health. At six years old, he fell into a coma for two months. The diagnosis was peritonitis, a severe abdominal condition. After he emerged from the coma, he never caught up with his schoolwork. By the time he was twelve, truancy and a lack of interest had caused his educational options to degenerate. And then illness struck again, just as his mother remarried to Harry Graves, a man who would become a dedicated stepfather. This time it was a lung illness, pleurisy, and it cost him more time and less education.

By the time he was seventeen, Richie was ill prepared for the work life ahead, but he was engaged in a period of active self-education. Although invested in alcohol and smoking, young Richie developed a love for American westerns and anything closely resembling country music. His British favorite was Lonnie Donegan.

In daytime he worked at a number of jobs, and at night he drank a lot and listened to music wherever he could find it. But trouble was looming. In one of his jobs, waiter and bartender on the ferry across the river Mersey, he extended his love for alcohol by getting free and illegal access to the trove of liquor. Shockingly and candidly, he confessed and moved on.

Despite his comments about Liverpool, there is an aspect of Ringo Starr's existence that has stayed true over the years. As he got older, he became less loyal to his cadre of supporters, but in his youth he was an extreme loyalist. His life was also marked by a candor that is something to respect. For example, his remarks to me and others about the impatient nature of fans was always refreshing. "All I ask for is a little bit of respect and privacy," he would say. "People come up to you like you are not a person, not a human being."

When I would ask him a question about the earlier tours, in 1989 and again in 2000, he was not afraid to admit he didn't remember a lot about those days. "You tell me, Larry. You have it all written down, don't you? You tell me about what I've forgotten."

About one thing in Ringo's life, almost everyone who knew him, and knows him, concurs: he was always likeable and friendly and funny, and in the early years of 1964 and 1965, a man with great insights to the world around him. In fact, in the era of escalation of the war in Vietnam, he was the most outspoken Beatle. His intellectual curiosity was as deep as John Lennon's. But unlike John, he was gullible, hilariously gullible, back in the beginning.

One night a long time ago, Billy J. Kramer and the Dakotas were on the bill with Rory Storm and the Hurricanes, when Billy J.'s band members decided to hide Ringo's polo sweater. Ringo looked and looked, while the band members looked on trying desperately to cover their smiles. Finally, when he started crawling around the room, the Dakotas gave it back. He laughed, they laughed. They loved him.

Ron Ellis, a young fan in those early years and a future music researcher, remembers, "They really loved him. Back in the early times, everybody loved him. He was very honest, extremely hardworking, and always giving."

In the year that John and Paul got together, Richie was searching for a musical identity, and he looked to his workmates at Hunt and Sons, where he worked successfully as an apprentice to a carpenter. He found a few who toiled alongside him at the company, a successful creator of equipment for playgrounds. He formed a skiffle group—one that lasted all of one concert. The reader should remember, with deep respect, that hundreds of boy bands were started up every week, and hundreds quit very quickly. While Ringo's attempts to organize a band were limited in scope, there was no limit to his enduring love of music. The early Ringo band was denied, but Ringo's efforts to find the right band would not be.

And the journey was a hard one. On a typical concert day, Ringo would have to carry his washboard and tea-chest bass to a roundabout where he would board one bus, transfer to another, and hope beyond hope that one of his friends would pick him up from the second bus and give him a lift. He was, along with his friends, handler, mover, setup man, and finally, player. So getting into a group with genuine promise was a real priority.

Rory Storm's group was a natural. Storm, aka Alan Caldwell, met Richie in the early spring of 1959, and soon afterward he invited Richie to join his band, originally known as the Ravin' Texans. Ringo felt right at home with Storm, guitarist "Johnny Guitar" Byrne, Ty O'Brien on bass guitar and vocals, and Lu Walters on guitar and vocals. Ringo began playing drums for Storm and company; he loved the outfits and the Texas theme. Anything to connect him to the American West was an absolute delight.

Eventually Ringo gave up his apprentice job to join Storm's Hurricanes in the band's famed summer job at the Butlin's camp, the one that left an opening for the Beatles to take Allan Williams's invitation to the dirty yet hopeful scene in Hamburg. Before heading to Germany, the Silver Beatles, with John at the helm, left for a rough concert trip in Scotland with Johnny Gentle. The Beatles were envious of Storm's gig at Allan Williams's big stadium concert along with Gene Vincent and others. But they passed up on Butlin's to try Germany. Storm and his boys, including Ringo, would play many dates after the summer in Hamburg. Chemistry was forming between Ringo and John, Paul, George, and Stuart, but there was little interaction between Ringo and the Beatles' first drummer, Pete Best, although Best has claimed they were good friends in the days that Pete was a Beatle and Ringo played for Storm.

It would be three years of hard and devoted work before the Beatles came calling in the summer of 1962. By that time, Ringo Starr had become more self-assured, but not cocky. This lack of cockiness, along with his bouts of stage fright, and his look of vulnerability, made him popular with most of the area bands' members. He was frank about his feelings, but kind and friendly to almost everyone he met. Just as he had developed a real relationship with Storm, the drummer would also create a genuine friendship with John, Paul, and George. His illnesses and setbacks in school had caused tremendous suffering, and with Storm, and with his Beatle friends, he had found an extended family.

In fact, outside of his sparse family, Ringo viewed the bands as his main source of inspiration. Months after his famous tonsil operation, he shared with me the sense of community that he shared with the boys.

"When I was away [for the operation] I felt disconnected. A real band is like a family. When the family is separated, it feels very broken up. I was happy to see the lads again as we met here [in the Bahamas to film *Help!*]."

It was there, in February 1965, with Mal Evans by our side, that Ringo opened up even more.

"It was odd for them to be without me, and me without them. I had heard before what it was like for a band to break up. Even for my operation, I felt somewhat vacant, if you know what I mean, there."

"But you're already settled as a success with the Beatles," I added.

"Yes, Larry, but you've never been a band member. You see, the band becomes a permanent . . . sort of . . . extended family. Now we are back together again [in the Bahamas], and I feel good about it. Seems like things are really good now."

Keep in mind that Ringo's comments on band friendship were made a year and a half after the band became a success.

It is also not unusual that after the band *really* broke up that Ringo suffered the most, becoming awash in drugs and alcohol. During that period, it was the head of the family, John, who reached out to help Ringo even while dealing with his own problems of substance abuse.

There was also a mostly hidden leadership role for Ringo. During 1963, before they came to America, he was a team builder and a jolt of energy.

"He was a lovely boy becoming a lovely man," recalls fan club secretary Freda Kelly. "He knew there was controversy when he was chosen to replace Pete, but he kept his head up and just played on."

"Ringo Starr was the brother that everyone wanted back in those days," adds Billy J. Kramer. "Yes, he was gullible, but it made him just the more loved. I mean, how could you not like him?"

There is no question that Ringo changed as an adult, in some ways. But a man who spent more time in the studio with him than almost any other living person offers a portrait of a man who never forgot his genuine roots.

Marc Hudson, a musician, composer, and world-class arranger, spent ten years producing eight albums for Ringo Starr. As a result of his close proximity to the drummer, Hudson has a vivid account of Ringo's early days.

"There is no question that the young Rory Storm, prior to the Beatles, gave Ringo his biggest break. I mean, he not only loved his work—he loved the man behind the drums. And Ringo, until the Beatles came asking, was loyal to a fault. It was a deep sense of loyalty."

That loyalty was tested in later life when the former Beatle would walk away in a flash from longtime business associates, a prerogative of any successful person. But Hudson never saw that as a flaw. Rather, he deeply respects Ringo for rarely, if ever, complaining about the harsh living conditions of his growing-up years.

THIS WAS [A] SICK CHILD, A REALLY SICK CHILD. FOR A WHILE UNTIL HIS STEPFATHER ARRIVED, THERE WAS ONLY HIS MOM. HIS HOUSE DIDN'T EVEN HAVE PLUMBING. WHAT I LOVE ABOUT RINGO IS HE WAS A MAN WITHOUT PITY, A MAN WHO NEVER COMPLAINED ABOUT HIS CONDITIONS OF LIFE. IT WAS AS SIMPLE AS "THIS WAS THE WAY IT WAS" AND IT WAS TIME TO GO OUT AND WORK, TIME TO GET ON WITH IT. LIVERPOOL WAS HARD ENOUGH TO GROW UP IN. MUSIC WAS HIS WAY OUT, AND HE USED IT [TO GET] OUT OF THE MISERABLE CONDITIONS OF HIS CHILDHOOD.

Ringo, Hudson adds, has always had an obsession with Rory Storm.

HE LOVED RORY AND JUST ABOUT EVERYTHING ABOUT HIM. HE HAS THIS UNBELIEVABLE PHOTO HE GAVE ME OF RORY SITTING IN A LIVING

ROOM . . . NEXT TO HIM IS A JAMES BROWN ALBUM LEANING AGAINST A FIREPLACE. HE LOVED RORY STORM'S LOOK . . . HIS BURGUNDY COATS . . . THOUGHT IT WAS SO COOL.

AS FAR AS THE BEATLES, HE WAS SECRETLY IN LOVE WITH THEIR WORK. OF COURSE, HE DIDN'T SAY ANYTHING TO RORY, BUT WHEN THE BAND [THE HURRICANES] WAS FINISHED IN HAMBURG OR MERSEYSIDE, RINGO WOULD SIT DOWN AND WATCH THE BEATLES ALMOST AS A FAN. HE RESPECTED THEM, ADMIRED THEM.

Ringo may not have excelled in school, but in the observant, working-class "school of Ringo," he studied overtime. He listened to and tried to mimic country artists, and studied all the Liverpool groups, including the outstanding but volatile Big Three, and its drummer, "Johnny Hutch."

There are those who would say that Ringo Starr was lucky. But not Marc Hudson.

"Ringo worked at his craft from the beginning. I don't think he was lucky. Nobody I have ever met in forty-two years of arranging [Aerosmith, Ozzy Osborne, Seal, Pete Seeger] has ever done what Ringo has done on the drums. Most drummers can be selfish. Give them an inch and they steal the show. Ringo always plays the song, not just a solo act on the drums.

"Nobody ever plays a song like Ringo plays."

"Was he, and is he, the greatest?" I ask.

"He's one of the greatest drummers in rock history, if not the greatest, and he just kept getting better," Hudson says.

As a young reporter in those golden days of 1964–1966, just a few years separated from his days with Rory Storm, his idol, I was truly amazed to watch Ringo perform night after night. I am not and have never been a music expert, but I know a person's joy when I see it. And although John, Paul, and George had their good nights and bad nights, as we all do, Ringo, the man in the back with the nonstop smile, was the most consistent performer night after night.

As with all of them, I often wondered what their backup plans were, just in case they didn't get the breaks that would allow them to show their talents off to the world.

Back in the Bahamas, in 1965, I asked Ringo about a second career. Did he ever think of a backup plan?

"Well, Larry, I would like to be a deejay or newsman like you. But first . . . "

"Yes?"

"But first, Larry, I have to learn how to talk."

At this he laughed out loud heartily, and with that lovely and engaging smile, the same smile that engrossed passengers on the ferry across the Mersey where he worked as a bartender, the smile that energized Rory and his Hurricanes night after night, and the fearless laugh that he displayed at the Montreal Forum in 1964 when he shrugged off a telephoned death threat from Quebec separatists, and played on with his fellow Beatles, telling me on the airplane a few hours later, "There was so much noise that if there were a real threat, I would, you know, never heard it."

In many accounts of his early life, Ringo has been described as a sad-eyed little boy. I asked Ringo repeatedly about that "sad" label. He said, quite pointedly, in a Chicago dressing room, "It's just the face. I'm quite happy inside."

Yet, many writers and musical pundits still insist he was the "sad Beatle."

Perhaps it was his sickly nature, or the loneliness of having no siblings. But as life endured, he became a man of many emotions, some of them expressed with a daring bluntness, others with that unforgettable face of joy, which in public almost always lit up the back of the Beatles stage.

CHAPTER TWENTY-TWO

TRIUMPH AT PARLOPHONE

*"There was this huge north–south divide, which still exists in the UK, and
you've probably heard George quoted occasionally as having been told by
people, 'Oh, you guys from Liverpool, you're wasting your time down here in
London.' It was wonderful that a group from Liverpool went down to London
and knocked them sideways. And not only knocked London sideways
but knocked the whole world sideways. What this did for the psychology
of northern England was just immense."*
—Rod Davis

*"Although I told Paul it wasn't good, I am happy that I was wrong.
I hope he didn't hold it against me."*
—Horst Fascher, on his critique of the song that made history

MASTER PROMOTER TONY BRAMWELL ADMITS PROUDLY THAT HE WAS
CONNIVING AND DESPERATE FOR NEWS EVEN AS A TEENAGER. Bramwell
would hang around the NEMS record store to try to get a bead on what was
going on. What he found was that Brian Epstein and Epstein's just-signed
boys, whom he was friendly with, were down after the Decca disaster.

"I wasn't that close to Brian at that time," Bramwell says, "but he liked to use me
as a sounding board for new music and all that stuff. By early spring, in late March,
the boys were not aware that they had been rejected, but finally Brian pulled out
the letter from Decca and nervously told them about the failure at Decca."

John, ever the optimist, seemed helpless. But Bramwell, as a future
promotion man, was "impressed" when Brian put out a smart press release.

"It was a good 'cover,'" Bramwell explains. "It announced a European
tour, but it was really a month-and-a-half gig at the Star Club in Hamburg.
They would arrive with tragedy facing them, in Stuart's death. What they
didn't know, as I learned much later, that Brian, still relentless, was running
out of options. Facing loss, and back in the grasp of Hamburg, they needed

good news. As a fan and friend, I also felt helpless."

Once again, the "what-ifs" of life enter the picture. At play here was Epstein's steely determination, plus a sense by the manager that Tony Barrow from Decca was a good man to stay in touch with. Barrow, for his part, liked the boys and thought Epstein was first-rate. In truth, while working for Decca, Barrow had been quietly doing freelance jobs to promote the Beatles. Coupled with Bill Harry's efforts, Bob Wooler's singular promotion in person and in print, and Barrow's planting of timely reminders of the group's Merseyside achievements, the fires were still lit in the north of England.

London was a different story, until a chance visit.

The fact is that, near the end of spring 1962, despite his happy face and optimism toward the boys, Epstein was running out of options when he arrived in London at the Oxford Street offices of Ardmore and Beechwood, a publishing arm of the big EMI record conglomerate. Epstein was not selling the Beatles that day. He was simply looking for an engineer to make vinyl copies of the Decca recordings. The engineer made the duplicates, and in doing so seemed remarkably impressed by the songs. He urged Epstein to go to another floor of the building and meet one of the company's executives. The man's name was Syd Coleman. One thing led to another. Coleman listened to the recordings, offered to publish them as sheet music, and surprised Epstein with another offer.

"Now this was a dramatic turning point," Tony Barrow remembers. "This chance meeting changed everything."

Coleman referred Epstein to a young producer at Parlophone, an unusual label, not confined just to music, but owned by EMI. The man's name was George Martin. Epstein, all excited, phoned his expert pressman Tony Barrow that very day.

He was thrilled, so thrilled, but thought, "Parlophone?" That was an odd choice, but the door was at least opened.

At the time, Martin's stable included men of comedy and satire, with the biggest star being Peter Sellers.

Liking some of their tunes and finding a good chemistry with the young musicians, he set a test recording for June 6. The place was studio #3 at Abbey Road Studios. In several later interviews, Martin called it "love at first sight."

But there was work to be done. Martin, who impressed the boys with his regal bearing, was not speedy, but methodical.

"One of the untold stories of George Martin was how really detailed he was," says Tony Bramwell, "all the time he spent getting to know John, Paul, George and Pete. I watched in many later sessions and the man was classy and deep."

In 1962, before the Parlophone connection, the Beatles owned only one contract, with Polydor, for backing up Tony Sheridan's "My Bonnie" in Hamburg in 1961, thanks to the strong support of German songwriter Bert Kaempfert, a huge success in his own right.

Beatles business and contract expert Bruce Spizer thinks that Epstein made an initial mistake with the Sheridan record.

"He passed it off to everyone at EMI in the early months of 1962. But it was a backup performance and did not show their songwriting ability."

It turns out that the songwriting talent, which in the early days separated John and Paul, and to some extent George, from the other Merseyside groups, was hardly noticed, until George Martin showed up.

"Ironically," Bramwell muses, "if Dick Rowe of Decca was making the decisions, the Beatles might never have been the Beatles, so Brian's search for a recording studio and the link to Parlophone and Martin was extraordinary.

"In a way, he was going behind the same EMI people who rejected them in early 1962, since EMI owned Parlophone. People talk about missed opportunities all their lives, but Epstein's chance meeting with Syd Coleman, as he looked for a studio to simply make copies [of the demo], was the most powerful turning point. With all their talent, they still could have been ignored, or bureaucrats could have buried them in the waste bin."

George Martin was no bureaucrat. He was forward-looking and willing to take risks. After Epstein signed a basic artist's agreement with Parlophone, the boys performed an artist's test. It was in that session that Martin and another producer, Ron Richards, decided they needed a session drummer, a decision that had continuity when Pete Best left and Ringo came aboard. As the summer months arrived, there was also disagreement, a friendly dispute, between the boys and Martin over what single they should record. The Beatles wanted "Love Me Do"; Martin wanted "How Do You Do It."

Martin demurred. "Love Me Do" was recorded. Ringo played the tambourine while session drummer Andy White played drums, although Ringo later played drums on the album version of the song. Abbey Road was busy for the Beatles, George Martin, and Ron Richards, another significant producer. Both men insisted on recordings and re-recordings. They were regular drill sergeants on demanding the best the boys could offer.

It was a long road for "Love Me Do," and its history will show just how good timing and patience paid off. "Love Me Do" had been in the boys' bag of goodies for four years before it surfaced as a hit, thanks to the chance meeting with Syd Coleman; and thanks to Syd Coleman's referral to George Martin, who technically worked for EMI, which had rejected the Beatles in the first place; and thanks to the carefully crafted words of Tony Barrow, Bob Wooler, Derek Taylor, and the venerable Bill Harry. The truth is that Paul McCartney wrote most of it, back in 1958 and 1959, and John wrote the so-called middle eight, or bridge.

So, it took four years, constant revision, help from friends and writers, and two masterful producers, plus the addition of John Lennon's mouth organ (harmonica) to make it work.

There are many myths and disagreements about the Beatles' first single, notably that Epstein bought up thousands of copies to help the record make the charts. That has never been verified, but the following stats have.

"Love Me Do," the very first Beatles single, with "PS—I Love You" on the flip side, hit the market on October 5, 1962. Its highest ranking in the United Kingdom was seventeen, in the fall and winter of 1962. Total sales were 17,000. In fourteen months, it would be number one in America. In 1982, twenty years later, after an official reissue, it hit number four on the UK charts, with sales totaling 150,000. While not totally accepted in the beginning, the song was the linchpin of the Beatles' roar to greatness, and the biggest hit as the Beatles began their iconic era following John Lennon's death.

"Love Me Do"? Remember the early test when Paul played the song for boxer–bouncer–star maker Horst Fascher in Hamburg? "Love Me Do" survived Fascher's review of it.

The rollout for the song was classic Epstein. Location was very important to him. He arranged for the Beatles to play supporting act for Little Richard at the Tower Ballroom. In fact, a full-page NEMS ad purchased for *Mersey Beat* emphasizes Little Richard, with the Beatles as first supporting act, but never mentions "Love Me Do."

For press genius Tony Barrow, one of the invigorating pen pals, the Beatles' status as supporting act was inappropriate. For Epstein, location, in the beginning, was everything. For Barrow, space was the key.

In his column for the *Liverpool Echo* newspaper, he decided to give the boys extra space. After all, they were the breakthrough group from Liverpool.

The headline read: "Big Date for Beatles."

Barrow's review was even more emphatic than the headline, and more powerful. He called the song "an infectious medium-paced ballad with an exceptionally haunting harmonica accompaniment that smacks home the simple tune and gives the whole deck that extra slab of impact and atmosphere so essential to the construction of a Top Twenty smasher."

Was Tony Barrow good? In the words of John Lennon, over and over again in taped interviews on different topics, "You betcha, Larry!"

Tony Barrow's words were smooth as silk. And Bill Harry was doing his thing. In the Liverpool area, "Love Me Do" was ranked number one in *Mersey Beat*, the only publication to give it top ranking.

The most important thing was that the Beatles had a nationwide hit—and number seventeen was not so bad. Young fan Tony Bramwell heard the song for the first time a few months after joining Epstein as a weekend warrior of sorts. After checking out Epstein, Bramwell's mother gave him the green light to work for Epstein and the boys, but only on weekends when school was not in session. Bramwell was impressed with "Love Me Do," even though it was not the element of hard rock he loved so much.

"The kids loved it. The girls swooned over it. My romantic life, if you could call it that at that age, was looking better. 'Love Me Do' was a breakout song for Merseyside."

Lennon House curator Colin Hall, also a budding teenager at the time, remembers the tone and rhythm of the ballad. "Prior to this, I could only think of the Beatles in terms of raw, rough, leather, and wild. This song made the girls and boys dream of love."

One special feature of "Love Me Do" was the soft sound of the mouth organ, with Lennon's lips squeezing out the music. Was it the same harmonica that John Lennon stole from a store on Allan Williams's rocky van journey to Hamburg? Whether the harmonica was purloined or purchased, John's mouth action was a big hit, along with the romantic voice of Paul McCartney.

So, again, a chance walk-in by the unrelenting Brian Epstein ended in a score of untold proportions. George Martin was encountered, quite accidentally. That would be a marriage made in heaven, as they say.

"Love Me Do" would thrill young lovers in Britain and much later in America. Over in Hamburg, the song's first critic was surprised, but pleased.

Forty-nine years later, sipping strong coffee on a cold day in Hamburg, Horst Fascher looks at me with a grin and says, "Although I told Paul it wasn't good, I am happy that I was wrong. I hope he didn't hold it against me."

The breakout song wasn't the Beatles' best, but it was the result of their extraordinary talent being actually recognized. The honest truth? No one gets to their goals alone, which brings us to the story of an unusual ensemble of friends and supporters who changed the boys' lives, and at the same time, changed their own in wonderful ways—in one case with an unhappy ending.

WHEN
THEY
WERE
BOYS

PART SIX:
SECRETS TO SUCCESS

A little help from their friends. Faithful Mal opens up in the Bahamas. Tears. Who's the smart and pretty girl in the office? She's the secret-agent girl. Sister love and the Harrison hug invade America. The boys pick their shoes—Brian gets the best of the rest. Give a hand to Kingsize, and Johnny Hutch, who has the Big Three. Billy Kinsley, Mr. Unselfish, rules the day. Paul the leftie gets up close and personal with Johnny Boy. Raw goes away. Animal magnetism gets a new suit of clothes and the three buddies, Neil, Tony, and Mal, "pave" the way. Hold the lamé, will you, and the lapels: it's time for the makeover. For the boys—it's something borrowed and something new. And all the while, the body shakes and Britain quakes.

CHAPTER TWENTY-THREE

BANDS ON THE RUN

"They were there. Some of them still are. They were extremely talented.
Unlike Billy J. Kramer and Gerry and the Pacemakers, they didn't reach glory,
but in all the cases, the Beatles took a piece of their action. They learned and
watched and learned some more. Especially from Billy Kinsley,
who never got the credit he deserved."
—Spencer Leigh, BBC broadcaster and prolific biographer of Merseyside

"Billy Kinsley was and is the real thing. Of course, if you look at his life
carefully, you'll realize he almost didn't make it. Maybe that's what
drove him to critical success . . . maybe."
—Billy J. Kramer

"They took from each other, not like theft, but a combination of observing,
adapting styles, and just learning by being there."
—Sam Leach, on the relationship between the boys
and the other Merseyside groups

I HAVE NEVER MET KINGSIZE TAYLOR, OF KINGSIZE TAYLOR AND THE
DOMINOES. Teddy Taylor is quite private about the Beatles era, and I
assume, from an e-mail exchange, not a big fan of the boys. Taylor, a former
butcher, is one of three significant music men or groups who left an indelible mark on the Beatles, and almost every young person in the north of
England who grew up on their music. From this perspective, there is no hard
rocker of his generation who can belt out the great songs of the era with such
a definite energy and excitement.

His version of "Long Tall Sally" is a classic. Today he still practices his craft
in Hamburg, where he plays to sold-out audiences.

Did the Beatles pick up Taylor's beat? Possibly. Does any group benefit
from playing on the same bill as other groups? Most likely. But Taylor had a

rhythm that fans of the day described as "pure contagion."

Taylor was promoted by Sam Leach, who understood his appeal: "He got hot, very hot, because he would bring the latest American hits to live audiences. They screamed for him, and he was popular years later because he stayed home, and was devoted to the community."

Many of the fans who watched Taylor at the Cavern or one of the other venues remember that members of the other well-known area groups would watch and take something away.

Paul McCartney was one of those taking notes. He was a quick study, and was never too embarrassed to do so. He loved to learn more, and he learned a lot from Taylor on chords, the latest lyrics, and hard-beat style. Taylor, although not recognized as such back in the day, was a major player in developing the Merseyside sound.

The venerable Bill Harry remembers the impact of Teddy Taylor.

THEY WERE PROBABLY THE BIGGEST BRITISH ROCK 'N' ROLL BAND IN THE EARLY SIXTIES. THEY BLEW LIKE MAD. THEY WERE FANTASTIC. TEDDY WAS A FANTASTIC GUY, BUT A BRILLIANT GROUP LIKE HIS AND OTHERS WERE CRUSHED DOWN BY THE LONDON RECORD GIANTS. THEY TRIED DOING IT TO THE BEATLES, BUT EPSTEIN FOUGHT HARD AND IT DIDN'T WORK. PEOPLE LIKE TEDDY WERE SIMPLY STOPPED BY THE LONDON RECORD PEOPLE. THEY DIDN'T WANT ANYONE FROM THE NORTH TO BECOME BIG. I MEAN, TEDDY HAD THE BEST PURE STAGE BAND IN BRITAIN. THE DIFFERENCE WITH THE BEATLES IS THAT THEY ALSO HAD MUSIC THAT THEY WROTE.

Horst Fascher says that in Hamburg, from a look at pure and raw onstage talent, "there was no band as dynamic as Teddy Taylor and the Dominoes." And this comes from a man who was so in love with the Beatles' music that he tried never to miss a set, even when he was securing the gates of the nightclubs.

Bill Harry also remembers the power of the Big Three. "The Big Three—brilliant, the Cream before the Cream. Brian Epstein wanted Johnny Hutchinson to be the Beatles' drummer instead of Ringo."

Although Harry's comment may be accurate, Spencer Leigh doubts that Hutchinson's hard line and tough, fighting demeanor could ever fit in with the accommodating style of John, Paul, and the gang. Leigh thinks that Johnny Hutch, as he was called, "would certainly have fought with John Lennon."

Bill Harry adds, "He did play with the Beatles on a few occasions, and they were a bit scared of him. But the Big Three were very special."

So special, Leigh adds, "They were the model for . . . Cream. They were the loudest, most intensely raw group in Liverpool. You couldn't miss them."

In addition to Taylor and the Big Three, another group is barely mentioned for their influence on the Beatles, not to mention their influence on almost every group that came after them: Johnny Kidd and the Pirates.

Kidd, who never played an instrument, had such an influence that bands like Led Zeppelin and the Who tried to replicate his band's ultra-dramatic presence. They hit the charts with two classics, "Shakin' All Over" and "Please Don't Touch." They dressed and paraded on stage as swashbuckling buccaneers, testing the limits of outrage and sexual tension. Their physical act was risqué before risqué was routine, before Alice Cooper, Bowie, and others.

"The Pirates," says Leigh, "were the roots of the beginnings of a lot of bands, and no doubt the Beatles were greatly influenced by them."

Denny Somach, American rock historian and Led Zeppelin biographer, says, "They were more successful as an influence on other bands than they were as a group. In fact, Roger Daltrey of the Who shed his guitar because of Kidd's success as a non-playing singer, and Zeppelin routinely covered their songs as they rehearsed."

As with Rory Storm's antics, the Beatles were enthralled by Johnny Kidd and the Pirates. In the real time of the turn of the decade from the fifties to the sixties, it was difficult to measure, but their subsequent music and performance style was clearly affected.

The Beatles were also impressed by other artists during their rise to success, especially the Americans. They said little in public, though, about the local bands, but they showed their respect in different ways. In public—with the exception of Joe Ankrah and the emergence of a younger entertainer named Billy Kinsley—they offered respect, but little praise.

For Billy Kinsley, they had a special respect. Billy Kinsley was a hot property. At fourteen, the youngest entertainer in Merseyside began with his group, the Mavericks. With great audacity, and working through coveted deejay and host Bob Wooler, Kinsley, along with his friend Tony Crane, reached out to *Mersey Beat* publisher Bill Harry to ask if they could borrow the name of the publication for their band. Harry agreed, and the Merseybeats were born.

It is fascinating that Harry and Kinsley both added to the general consensus that the new wave of bands forever would be titled the Merseybeat from Merseyside.

In another era, Kinsley would have been arrested for not being old enough to work, but who knew, and frankly, who cared? What the group did care about was the exposure to all that music, "all that great noise," as Kinsley says today.

There is no question that most of the bands in Merseyside formed somewhat of an educational foundation for their counterparts. They learned from one another. Sam Leach saw all of them in action.

"They took from each other, not like theft, but a combination of observing, adapting styles, and just learning by being there."

And then there were the Beatles.

Tony Crane thought he and Kinsley had made an extraordinary breakthrough—a band with two primary singers. Ambitious, young, and excited about music, Kinsley and Crane were convinced they had developed something new.

Crane recalls the excitement: "We thought we were the first group with more than one lead singer. Then we went to the Cavern. We saw the Beatles, and we realized . . . we were not the first. They were."

Like Crane, Kinsley was in a state of wonderment, first watching, then knowing the boys. Like a wide-eyed kid, which he was, he visually absorbed the style of John and friends, and then systematically watched every step, every movement.

"Frankly, no one had ever heard of two lead singers, and then I saw John and Paul," Kinsley recalls.

No one had ever seen three lead singers, because George always got his turn, and George was really good. They really rubbed

OFF ON US—THE HARMONY, THE SOLOS AND THE DRUMMING. REMEMBER, PETE BEST WAS A DAMN GOOD DRUMMER, AND IS STILL TODAY A GREAT DRUMMER. BUT THE BIGGEST EFFECT ON US WAS WHAT YOU DIDN'T SEE ON STAGE. THEY WERE SO KIND AND SUPPORTIVE, ESPE-CIALLY JOHN AND PAUL, ALTHOUGH GEORGE WAS ALWAYS SO CHARMING AND WARM, BUT A BIT SHY. I THINK SHY WAS PUTTING IT MILDLY—AS YOU KNOW, LARRY, BECAUSE YOU WERE WITH THEM IN THOSE EARLY DAYS BEFORE EVERYTHING BLOSSOMED.

What was also impressive to the young Kinsley was how noticeable the three- or four-year age difference was: "You remember high school, don't you . . . just one grade difference between you and others was a big deal. We looked at these guys like they had a lot of experiences to share, and they did. Stories of stage presence, tuning the instruments, dealing with rowdy crowds, which was a favorite topic, and of course, just the nod of acceptance, of approval, was so important."

It's hard to imagine being so young, so green, and as Kinsley admits, "so scared," but the Beatles helped soothe the young group's anxieties.

Kinsley's life, detailed in one of the best books ever written about Merseyside, Spencer Leigh's *It's Love that Really Counts*, was a difficult one. The Kinsley family faced its tragedies, and one night the future was in serious doubt.

"It is a night I will never forget," Kinsley tells me.

Kinsley was a frequent visitor to a boys' club as he approached the age of thirteen for five-night-a-week workouts. Coming home one night, he was attacked by about fifteen young men, one of whom slashed him with an open razor. The left side of his face would be scarred for life, but the scars of the moment—the bleeding, the helplessness, his family's suffering—would stay with him for a while and then make him even more determined to make it.

"It was horrible," Kinsley recalls, "and what made me more vulnerable was when, as a victim, I had to testify under duress, with at first the police not believing me, even suggesting that I was a member of the gangs, which they learned was not true. It was horrifying."

When things started to settle down, the charismatic youngster, dealt an early life of economic disparity and violence, started his trek to greatness, first as a paper boy and, barely a year later, the cofounder of a skiffle group. As mentioned earlier, age was never an obstacle in his mind.

As the Merseybeats entered their development stage, Crane and Kinsley walked into the Cavern in January 1962, getting their first look at the Beatles. It was love at first sight.

From Billy Kinsley, soon to be a compatriot and colleague of the boys, the view of them in the beginning is emblematic of why teenagers, especially in 1962, were drawn in like flies to light.

"They were just as dirty and scruffy as the Cavern. . . . I was in a trance for days. . . . They were playing rock 'n' roll raw and alive, just as it should be played. . . . The Beatles stood out. . . . Paul jumped into the audience screaming 'Long Tall Sally' and John Lennon lay on the floor and played guitar solos. They were great."

So, there you have it. Billy Kinsley confirms. The Beatles' first attraction, much as it was in Litherland Town Hall, and Hamburg, was animalistic, over-the-top hysteria, partially inspired by Rory Storm, copied with efficiency from the likes of Chuck Berry, bearing a likeness to Teddy Taylor, Elvis, and Little Richard, and with the musical power of the Big Three. But there was a difference, as Kinsley explains:

ALTHOUGH THEY WERE SMOOTHED-OUT AND CLEANED UP BY BRIAN, IN WHAT YOU CALL "THE MAKEOVER," LARRY, THEY TOOK WHAT THEY LEARNED FROM THEIR INFLUENCES, LIKE GEORGE FORMBY AND LONNIE DONEGAN AND THE LIKES, AND THEY MERGED IT INTO A PERFORMANCE LEVEL, NOT JUST ACQUIRED BUT DRAMATICALLY THEIR OWN. THEY WERE THE HOTTEST GROUP EVER SEEN WITH A HARMONY THAT WAS BEYOND ANY OTHER GROUP, AND BEFORE THEIR OWN AMAZING MUSIC, THE STUFF THEY WROTE, WAS WOVEN INTO THEIR ACT, THEY HYPNOTIZED THEIR AUDIENCES WITH A LEVEL OF RAW THAT HAD EXCEEDED ANYTHING BEFORE THEM.

Kinsley and Crane eventually had their own dream come true. In April 1962 they debuted at the Cavern. But it was a rough road. Dave Forshaw, the man who spotted the Beatles at Litherland, got them some gigs and was instrumental in keeping their spirits alive.

Kinsley and Crane were admired by the Beatles, joining them in shows at the Cavern, where the boys were impressed by Kinsley's voice. Paul McCartney was so impressed by the group that he has described their "You Are My Love" as one of his favorite love songs. Kinsley and *his boys* have had a career spanning continents. Never as well known (who is?) as the Beatles, the harmonious Merseybeats had many incarnations—changing their name to Liverpool Express in the seventies—but also had a truly steady career of success.

Aside from Kinsley's work during Apple sessions with George Harrison, many eyewitnesses, including Joe Ankrah of the racial-barrier-shattering Chants, remember the Merseybeats as having a positive influence on the Beatles in 1962. After all, Kinsley and Crane's Merseybeats served a triple role: admiring fans of the Beatles, transitioning to professional musicians, and serving as a motivating group of cheerleaders in the early days when the boys' smashing success was not yet guaranteed.

Billy Kinsley has lived a good life of accomplishment, but in youth, there were moments of uncertainty. One in particular comes to mind, for it might have changed his future—*might have* being the key words here. Although his career would have him recording with the Beatles at Abbey Road and performing for years with them, there was one act he may regret.

In the beginning, when Brian Epstein seemed to be on a signing frenzy, Kinsley and Crane made a choice—they were the third group Epstein signed. The Big Three was also in the stable.

Kinsley remembers being a bit jealous. "We left him because he wouldn't buy us suits. He bought the Beatles suits and we were jealous."

Imagine, Kinsley, Tony Crane, and the boys of Merseybeat *left* Epstein because he wouldn't buy them clothing. They *were* jealous and, as you can imagine, young in years and young in spirit and naive to the ways of business.

Kinsley is, without challenge, the most popular current public figure of the Merseybeat era in Liverpool, and remains an icon for three reasons: he was good, he was caring, and he never left, except to successfully tour, of course.

"The Beatles had a course, a plan: move on and shut the door," recalls broadcaster Leigh. "They never veered from that, rarely recalling, except when pressed, some of the people who put them there."

Although Merseyside groups would always help other groups behind the scenes, they would rarely praise one another in public. Kinsley is as proud of the Beatles and the other groups as he is of his own group.

"Without them, where would we all be?" he reminds me.

Spencer Leigh adds, "Area musicians say bad things about each other. . . . Nobody will have a bad thing to say about Billy Kinsley. Most musicians talk about themselves, but Billy talks about other people and their strengths."

And then there is the truly magical American connection. Kathy McCabe, an admiring Beatles fanatic from Baltimore, a city she describes as being so much like Liverpool with its narrow row homes with steps leading to them, decided as a teenager to find a pen pal. Her choice was fateful.

"I became a pen pal to Robbie Malloy," she recalls. "He was the brother of Sandra Malloy, who became an English teacher and the wife of a young musician named Billy Kinsley. That began a lifelong friendship with a professional connection."

From Baltimore to Liverpool and back many times, McCabe became a close friend of Sandra and Billy Kinsley's, who had developed an extended family in addition to their two girls and a boy. Inspired by the Beatles, and their new friends, they formed a strong emotional bond with McCabe and Freda Kelly ("Freda the Believer"). McCabe, in the spirit of things, married professional musician Mac Walter, in Baltimore. The couples are inseparable, and McCabe actually helped produce the band's Liverpool Express albums.

"I was a Beatles fan, still am, but what I got through my pen pal was a relationship with the most wonderful man in Merseyside, and his most wonderful wife, and through it, I learned that the era, the music, the people have a wonderful side story. Through Billy I learned the other side of the story, that the era was unkind to people who didn't persist. Billy did and created, through ups and down, his own success. He never complains, but he is always aware of what the Beatles did for him."

What the quite insulated surviving Beatles don't know is what Billy Kinsley *did for them.*

Unlike some of the other contemporaries, the unsung leader of the Merseybeats has been a beacon of light, telling the story of what the Beatles were really like. He and his bandmates have never allowed the broad shadow of the Beatles to diminish the flame of their own contribution to music lovers, yet, at the same time, they never forget where they live and who opened the doors for them.

After years of research, I have learned that few people who "were there" will credit others in the region with a knack for credibility or real talent. Billy Kinsley is an exception. Everybody loves him.

Kinsley, hiding the scars of his youth, stands as a tribute not just to the music that he has shared and the lower-profile stardom he has achieved, but as a symbol of the rare artists from that era whose glass is always half full, and whose words and style engender total respect in a tough town where respect has to be earned, year after year.

In that respect, he's one of the few Merseyside success stories who remain viable, and vital, and very much alive fifty years after the Beatles' climb to the top began.

His success, and that of others who mixed their brew of creativity with the boys, is a bit more public than the work behind the scenes of two women who have never been recognized appropriately for their contributions.

CHAPTER TWENTY-FOUR

SECRET-AGENT GIRLS

*"I adored them. And I really adored their parents, especially Richie's mother,
Elsie. She was salt of the earth."*
—Freda Kelly, fan club secretary, assistant to Brian Epstein, teenage fan,
and special friend of the boys

*"You might say I was in a good position, being in America,
and sending decent information every week."*
—Louise Harrison, George Harrison's sister

*Two young women: one transplanted in America, the other a
sometimes-smitten teenager in the heart of Liverpool. The effect they had on the
Beatles' ascension can't be measured in full, because the parts they played
at home and abroad were key in the boys' success story even though,
like secret agents, they had very little visibility.*
—Freda Kelly, Fan and Friend

AND SO I WONDERED: WHAT WOULD SHE LOOK LIKE AFTER ALL THESE
YEARS? I pictured the devoted seventeen-year-old in those old pictures, the
vintage ones. She was just seventeen, and as Paul would say, "you know what
I mean." Imagine being just seventeen and walking into the world of four
sometimes awkward and very sensitive young men, and for more than ten
years being privy to everything that was going on in those raw beginnings.
Imagine seeing them every day, watching them grow from boys into men,
getting as close as millions would want to in the crazy years ahead.

There is no question that unlike the girl in the song, she was not just
"standing there," and there was no romantic connection, but now, in the
new century, she says with a blush, "I had a crush on each one of them,
depending on the week." That's about all you are going to get from Freda
Kelly on her private life, and theirs. Nothing else.

Refreshing, isn't it?

She was crazy about the Beatles. While her parents were so afraid that living in the world of rock 'n' roll would somehow compromise her, in all those years there was never an issue.

"My parents were old-style. They were quite nervous about my job. But there really was nothing for anyone to get nervous about."

The Beatles were always sweet and proper toward Kelly, often giving her car rides home. Not only was this girl with the great work ethic deeply revered—by the four boys and their manager; and by the devoted ones, Tony Barrow, Derek Taylor, and Tony Bramwell; and by the enablers, Sam Leach and Allan Williams; and by all the rest of the Liverpool crowd, some of whom stayed behind—but she was loved, really loved by the families. Kelly had close relationships with a number of the Beatles' relations, including "Uncle" Jim McCartney, Louise and Harry Harrison, Elsie Starkey and Ringo's stepfather Harry Graves, and Aunt Mimi, John's guardian angel, although "angel" would be a stretch.

"Mimi sometimes gets a bad look at," Kelly told me recently. "She was stern. She was strong. And John needed someone strong. Although she might not have expressed it, I believe she had John's best interest at heart."

Kelly was the link between stardom and real life, and her constant calming presence gave solace to the families who found themselves in this bright spotlight. When the girl was around, the parents felt relief and warmth. She was so friendly as a liaison with the family members that they practically became family. Uncle Jim would take her out to lunch. Brian Epstein, stiff, proper, and sometimes a difficult boss, took her to a gilded box at the Empire Theater to watch the boys feted by the Merseyside fans.

She was, *is*, significant—not just some passerby who shook their hands, but whose life was changed, and who made theirs more lively. The revered pressman Tony Barrow says, "She was one of the 'boys' behind the curtain who made it possible for them to rise." He emphasizes the word "boys" with humor and affection.

Is she a character? No. But she *has* character, and as I've learned through some of the people who would rewrite history to suit their own agendas, it is rare to find such a truthful, unaffected human being who was *really there*, and knew them intimately. No, not the way you're thinking, because this woman, funny and natural, has got standards higher than the restaurant she suggests for our meeting.

It is a starry, clear night, as Kelly strolls around the rooftop restaurant and, with her hand, gives me a visual tour of Merseyside—the lights shining brightly over the Liver Building, the river Mersey glowing from the moon. "Across there, across there, that's where I live and work . . . that's the Wirral over there, the Wirral, the peninsula that leads to the Irish Sea. Beautiful, isn't it?"

Secret-Agent Girl is a grandmother now, and the first thing we do, quite naturally, is exchange cell phone pictures of our grandchildren. Odd, isn't it, how life changes. "Freda the Believer," as I call her—the protector, the pride of thousands of fan club members, the girl who stood in the Cavern and watched through the smoke as her guys lit up the crowd—is now a grandmother. And the twenty-one-year-old news guy, who fatefully joined the Beatles on every stop of their North American tours in 1964, 1965, and part of 1966, and kept in touch with them over the years, is now a grandfather.

Our dinner is very relaxed. Then, at a nearby sofa in a glass-coated lounge, Freda Kelly tells me her story.

"I adored them. And I really adored their parents, especially Richie's mother, Elsie. She was salt of the earth."

The beaming woman, Freda Kelly, worked for the Fearsome Foursome in a few different roles from 1962 to 1972, a decade, not interrupted by Epstein's 1967 death.

She still has the same wide grin of the doting teenager who kept company with the four youngsters who would become famous. For years, reporters and inquisitors of every type have asked her for the inside story. She tells it sparingly. In the age of gossip, the era of "anything goes," if you're looking for secrets—sexual scandals, stories of jealousy, sordid tales of life on Mathew Street, what happened behind the curtain of thick cigarette smoke at the Cavern—you won't be getting it from her. It is that enduring loyalty, mixed with a wonderful sense of humor, that made the Believer a powerful force on John's band as it marched to greatness.

While the circumstances of life have changed, Kelly has not. A dedicated grandmother, Kelly remains a loyal and devoted follower of the Beatles, and a devotee of all things Liverpool. What the surviving and missing Beatles never knew was that Kelly would be the unofficial leader of the small but active Beatles community in Liverpool, the enablers, the promoters, the ones who remain with us and were left behind when the four local kids went off into the wild world of stardom and celebrity with all the joy and agony that comes along with it.

Freda Kelly is an organizer. It could be an eightieth birthday party for Allan Williams, or something involving the Best family—Kelly will be there and be involved. She was the go-to girl for the young "boys" and their families, and she remains the center of communication for all the "Beatle people" who make Merseyside their home, from Roag Best, to the surviving Quarrymen, to many, many others you may have found in this book.

Her credentials are amazing. After all, how many people could say that John Lennon saved her job, or that "Eppy" was a tough but sensitive boss? How many people could turn a shade of deep red when they talk about being around the boys?

Tony Barrow met her in 1962 and worked near her in 1963.

"Nobody, I mean nobody was closer to the group in those early days than Freda," Barrow says. "She was young, a teenager like their fans, and was the main conduit to the families. It was always interesting that when Brian moved the NEMS empire to London, Freda never left, not because she wouldn't, but because her parents wouldn't let her go. So she stayed and became our vital link in Merseyside. And what a link she was. She had energy, devotion, and a cheery disposition."

Although there has been minimal contact with the Beatles and the Believer since the seventies, the boys, in their time with her, cherished her. On the Beatles' 1963 Christmas record, George Harrison gives thanks to "Freda Kelly in Liverpool." The three other Beatles shout out in response, "Good ol' Freda!," which now is the name of a first-class film documentary released in 2013 on her life.

Back in the sixties, Kelly was an avid fan of music, the boys, and the Cavern:

I LIVED AND DIED AT THE CAVERN. I WORKED AT A FIRM AROUND THE
CORNER ON STANLEY STREET AND I USED TO GO TO ALL THE LUNCHTIME
SESSIONS. I REALLY LIKED THE BEATLES, THE WAY THEY LOOKED, THEIR
ATTITUDE ON STAGE. IT WASN'T JUST THE MUSIC. IT WAS EVERYTHING
ABOUT THEM AND HOW MUCH FUN IT WAS. WHEN I WENT TO WORK I HAD
A LOT OF CONTACT WITH THEM, DID THEIR LETTERS, WENT TO THE BANK,
AND ALL THAT. THEY ALL LIVED IN THE SOUTH SIDE OF LIVERPOOL AND MY
CRUSHES ON THEM WAS DETERMINED BY WHO GAVE ME A RIDE HOME SINCE
I ALSO LIVED ON THE SOUTH SIDE. THE FIRST CRUSH WAS ON PAUL, AND
THEN I MOVED ON TO RICHIE AND GEORGE. JOHN NEVER GAVE ME A RIDE
HOME BECAUSE HE WAS BLIND AS A BAT AND DIDN'T DRIVE.

She adds, "In 1962 they were just ordinary boys with ordinary dreams. No
stars. Just guys from the area, trying to make some money, and make people
happy with their songs."

She worked in the office of Brian Epstein and was a powerful force of optimism at a time when the boys were celebrating success, but worried almost
all the time what would happen next. More than a secretary and top fan club
organizer, Kelly spent countless hours away from the limelight. She is one of
the few who can tell us, in her soft but clear voice, that the boys were not so
sure that stardom was really their fate, even in the pulsating days of their
most significant year, 1963.

"They were all worried, especially the parents. But Eppy was never in
doubt about the end result, just worried about the present. He knew they
were going to be idolized. Although he was a bit of a dreamer, he was also a
realist, and he thought their music, combined with their personalities, would
take the world. The boys didn't exactly see it that way. They looked cocky,
but, like all young people, they were a bit scared."

Kelly wasn't scared, just a bit in awe, when Eppy offered her the job. She has
a wonderful smile, and she smiles broadly as she explains how she got the job.

"Brian knew I was a follower. [Not the screaming kind, she says.] He had
seen me at Beatles gigs. I knew he was the boss at NEMS Limited, the record
store. He told me about signing a contract with them. It was a Saturday night
at St. Barnabas's Hall in Penny Lane. I was stunned that he even approached
me. I don't know why. I assumed he knew I had secretarial experience."

Over the years, the perky assistant and fan had to hold her emotions in. After all, "I had to be professional," she remembers. And as Beatlemania spread to the human universe, she witnessed the euphoria of her boss and the gradual emotional decline as the grand years of 1963 to 1966 passed into history.

"He had so many goals, and by that year, including a personal challenge. Were the boys growing away from him? I didn't see that, although some say it was going on. His death was such a shock to me, and like others, I don't believe for a minute that he took his own life. He loved his family and he would never do that to them."

One of the most fascinating observations from Kelly is the contrast between the Beatles' fame and the way they were treated on the home front.

"In these parts, they were still just the boys from the neighborhoods, the same guys who played at the Cavern. The nice thing is that, in those days, they were humble in their own community. On the streets, they were still Uncle Jim's kid, or Elsie's boy, or Julia's brother John, or Harry and Louise's George. That's what makes their success even more charming and gratifying."

Kelly was the main liaison between the business and the families, and even after the Beatles, as a group, disintegrated and went their own ways, she kept in close contact with the families.

Her early take on the boys remains an invaluable part of their history, because Kelly more than anyone brings you to the inside of what they were *really* like in the years before I met them, in the days before the world embraced them and changed their lives forever.

"I tell you, they were so innocent. They didn't even know they were naturally funny. They were surprised when people laughed at what they said. And that was part of their appeal as people . . . that young innocence and almost bashful look. To the people they knew, they didn't really change in those days."

Who was the most cheerful?

"Richie. He would bounce into the office, dancing. He always made every day bright, at least for me. Not a day would pass when he didn't ask me how my family was, how *I* was doing."

Who was in charge?

"Well, you know, there were always two people who wanted that position, but it wasn't a battle or anything like that—just two boys who wanted to be running things. Actually, Paul and John played off of each other really well, and Ringo and George would take a backseat, but not when they were alone. George was quite animated when you talked to him one-on-one, and he didn't have the pressure of being the youngest one, a title he left behind as the years moved on and his individual talents started emerging. It was a wonderful experience watching them grow from boyhood to manhood. And then, after Apple came to be, my job was done."

Kelly does not talk about what she did for them. The most important task was keeping them united with their families at a time when the fame was growing, the success was certified, and the parents were thrilled by the success, but concerned about the fame.

"The parents did not sit idle. Mimi was always lecturing John about the future. Elsie still saved, even after Richie became rich. Uncle Jim McCartney and Louise and Harry Harrison answered letters, and devoted their daily lives to their children. One of the untold stories is how much they worked to help their boys. It was impressive."

What Kelly will not tell you is what Tony Barrow will.

"She was the glue that kept so many things together," Barrow says. "She was dedicated to the boys and their families, really committed. Because they loved her, and she returned it tenfold. You know, we wanted to bring her to London. But her parents wouldn't let her go."

So Kelly stayed behind and did the work to develop an amazing fan club, to act as a bridge between John, Paul, George, Pete, Richie, and their families. And here we are in the next century, where she remains in Merseyside, serving as the unofficial but respected truth teller of the past, and leader of all the people who played a role in the Beatles rise, who also stayed behind.

Every successful entity has its own dedicated people who built the blocks to glory. The first secret-agent girl played an unheralded but crucial role in the life of the boys in the early days, the formative years of their remarkable journey.

After all, Brian Epstein, the dreamer, needed a guidepost, a pathfinder to steadfastly pursue the dream. In came Freda Kelly, a Liverpool original and the unsung leader who kept the Fabs fabulous at a time when the disbelievers were crawling out of the woodwork.

Kelly was a believer, and so was the loving big sister to the youngest Beatle.

Louise Harrison—Sister Act

Harry and Louise Harrison had four children. Their daughter Louise was the oldest, and still refers to George as "my kid brother."

To watch the ascension of her kid brother to fast-and-furious fame was uncanny and prideful for a woman in her mid-twenties who had made the trek to the North American continent, first stopping in Canada, then eventually winding up in southern Illinois. These days she lives a modest life in northern Florida and Missouri, where she runs a foundation with a Beatles cover group known as Liverpool Legends.

It was the spring of 1963 when the word came in.

MARCH OF 1963 I MOVED INTO THE UNITED STATES. IT WAS AROUND THAT TIME, RIGHT BEFORE I MOVED TO THE UNITED STATES, THAT MY MOM SENT ME THE FIRST "LOVE ME DO." I WAS STILL LIVING IN CANADA WHEN I FIRST HEARD THAT ONE, AND THEN ONCE I GOT TO THE UNITED STATES I MOVED TO A LITTLE PLACE CALLED BENTON IN ILLINOIS, IN SOUTHERN ILLINOIS, AND SO MOM STARTED SENDING ME THEIR RECORDS. ALL MY LIFE, WHEN I WAS A LITTLE BITTY KID, PEOPLE WERE ALWAYS SAYING TO MY PARENTS, "OH, YOU KNOW, SHE'S JUST LIKE SHIRLEY TEMPLE. . . . SHE SHOULD BE IN THE MOVIES." SO I ALWAYS GREW UP WITH THIS IDEA THAT SHOWBIZ IS MY FORTE. SO WHEN SUDDENLY I HAD THIS BROTHER IN A BAND . . . SO I STARTED GOING TO ALL OF THE RADIO STATIONS AND TRIED TO GET HIS RECORDS PLAYED. I WOULD GO IN AND SAY, "THIS IS MY KID BROTHER'S BAND, AND THEY'RE NUMBER ONE IN ENGLAND, AND YOU SHOULD BE PLAYING THEM."

Louise Harrison was an "advance woman," checking out the territory of North America as a possible new market for the Beatles' music. Brian Epstein was thrilled to have an "agent" on the ground. Louise was aggressive, but along with her hard sell to radio stations, she played an invaluable role: writing to Epstein and the other key players about the real story of America.

I STARTED WRITING TO BRIAN AND TO DICK JAMES, GEORGE MARTIN; I WAS DOING SOME RESEARCH. I GOT A SUBSCRIPTION TO *CASHBOX*, *BILLBOARD*, AND *VARIETY* MAGAZINES . . . BECAUSE I HAD ONLY MOVED INTO THE UNITED STATES IN MARCH OF '63, SO OBVIOUSLY I DIDN'T KNOW MUCH ABOUT THE AMERICAN MUSIC BUSINESS. I KNEW THAT BRIAN DIDN'T, EVEN BY HIS OWN ADMISSION HE DIDN'T REALLY . . . HE WASN'T A SUCCESS AT ANYTHING UNTIL HIS FATHER PUT HIM IN CHARGE OF THE RECORD DEPARTMENT AND HE HAPPENED ON THE BEATLES. . . .

I WOULD HANDWRITE FOURTEEN-PAGE LETTERS TO HIM EVERY WEEK TELLING HIM ALL OF THE STUFF THAT I LEARNED. TELLING HIM ABOUT HOW, GOING TO THE RADIO STATIONS, THEY WOULD TELL ME THAT "THIS STUFF IS NOT COMMERCIAL AND WOULDN'T GO ANYWHERE." ALSO [TELLING HIM] WHAT I WAS LEARNING BEHIND THE SCENES . . . JUST FROM OBSERVATION AND FROM ALL OF THESE MAGAZINES. I WAS LEARNING THAT THERE WAS A WHOLE DIFFERENT ATTITUDE TOWARDS BUSINESS IN THIS COUNTRY THAN WHAT WE WERE ACCUSTOMED TO IN BRITAIN. THERE WAS NO GENTLEMANLY STUFF; IT WAS ALL PUSH HARD, AGGRESSIVE, SALESMEN AND MARKETING. I TOLD HIM THAT WITHOUT A REALLY GOOD, STRONG SOMEBODY BEHIND YOU WITH A LOT OF CLOUT, YOU AREN'T GOING TO GET ANYWHERE. IN BRITAIN, AS YOU KNOW, THERE IS THE BBC; ONCE YOU'RE ON THE BBC YOU'RE OKAY. BUT AT THIS TIME IN THE COUNTRY THERE WERE 6,000 INDEPENDENT RADIO STATIONS. I WAS TRYING TO GET AIRPLAY ON SOME OF THE MAJOR ONES IN CITIES I WOULD GO TO . . . EVANSVILLE, ST. LOUIS, PADUCAH, SPRINGFIELD, ILLINOIS . . . ALL OF THE ONES WITHIN TWO HUNDRED MILES OF MY HOME. I WAS CONSTANTLY BEING PUT DOWN BECAUSE I WAS A WOMAN. WHAT'S A WOMAN DOING POKING HER HEAD AROUND IN MEN'S BUSINESS? THERE WAS ALSO THIS ATTITUDE OF "ARE YOU GOING TO GIVE US A ROLLS ROYCE IF WE PLAY IT?"

Louise was actually engaging radio stations during the height of the payola scandal (pay for play), and she had nothing to give away but her own enthusiasm.

GRADUALLY, OVER SIX MONTHS, I WAS PASSING ALL OF THIS INFORMATION ON TO BRIAN AND I GOT LETTERS BACK FROM HIM SAYING, "I WROTE VERY CAREFULLY EVERYTHING YOU WERE SAYING." I TRIED VERY, VERY

HARD TO TRY AND GET THINGS GOING. I WAS WATCHING THE *ED SULLIVAN SHOW* AND STARTED PUTTING A P.S. AT THE BOTTOM OF MY LETTERS—P.S. GET THEM ON THE *ED SULLIVAN SHOW*. IT WAS KIND OF INTERESTING, BECAUSE TOWARDS THE END OF THE YEAR ED SULLIVAN HAPPENED TO BE IN [THE] LONDON AIRPORT AT THE SAME TIME THAT THEY WERE COMING BACK FROM THEIR LITTLE SWEDISH TOUR, AND HE SAW THIS BIG HULLA-BALOO WITH ALL THESE PEOPLE HERE. SO HE TRACKED DOWN, YOU KNOW, [ASKED] WHAT'S THE BEATLES? HE GOT IN TOUCH WITH BRIAN, AND IT WAS FUNNY BECAUSE BY THAT TIME BRIAN WAS STARTING TO GET A LITTLE BIT BIG-HEADED. HE KIND OF FANCIED HIMSELF THE PROMOTER AND EVERYTHING. HIS EGO WAS TREMENDOUS. EVERY WEEK I SENT HIM ED SULLIVAN, ED SULLIVAN, ED SULLIVAN, SO FORTUNATELY HE TOOK THE PHONE CALL AND OF COURSE WE ALL KNOW WHAT HAPPENED AFTER THAT.

It's hard to say what might have happened without Louise's constant flow of information. Brian Epstein was a smart and intuitive man, but he had limited information on America. If he really knew the American scene, why would he have hired a shaky turboprop for the tours rather than a jet? The distances surprised him. Britain is small compared to the United States. Why didn't he hire scores of security guards, instead leaving the Beatles in the hands of Neil Aspinall and Mal Evans, a devoted army of two? And why would he have invited me, a twenty-one-year-old news journalist from Miami, to travel in their official party on the greatest musical tour of all time, rather than a seasoned music journalist? No complaints here.

On the business side, Louise would prove to be a gem. But yet, after all these years, and all of her support, she credits George's success to her father's uncompromising view of love, laughter, and steadiness.

"He was like a lighthouse . . . calm, steady, on the rocks . . . shining the light to show you . . . to keep you away from the hazards of life." She adds, with tears welling up in her eyes,

MY PARENTS, THEY REALLY STARTED WHAT I CALL MY GLOBAL FAMILY. THERE WAS, OF COURSE, THE HARRISON HUG. ONE OF THE LAST TIMES THAT I SAW GEORGE . . . HE HUGGED ME, HE SAID, "PASS IT ON." AFTER

HE DIED AND PEOPLE WOULD BE TALKING TO ME, PEOPLE WERE GIVING
ME THEIR CONDOLENCES AND I WOULD SAY, "WELL, HERE'S A HUG FROM
GEORGE." THEY WERE ALSO FEELING SAD ABOUT HIM AND I KNEW THEY
NEEDED SOMETHING IN RETURN FOR THEIR CONDOLENCES. I SAID, "THIS
IS A HARRISON HUG, IT'S FROM GEORGE," AND "PASS IT ON." SO, I
STARTED ENCOURAGING PEOPLE, WHEN THEY GET THE HARRISON HUG,
YOU'VE GOT TO PASS IT ON. I'VE BEEN GETTING THINGS . . . I HAD AN E-
MAIL ONCE FROM A LADY IN ARGENTINA, AND SHE SAID, "I GOT A
HARRISON HUG FOR MY BIRTHDAY THIS YEAR; YOU HAD GIVEN IT TO
SOMEBODY IN CLEVELAND IN 2002." AND THEN OTHER PEOPLE E-MAILED
AND TEXTED ME AND SAID, "I'VE NOW GIVEN MY HARRISON HUG TO PEO-
PLE IN SEVENTEEN DIFFERENT COUNTRIES." SO PART OF THIS WHOLE IDEA
OF THE HARRISON HUG IS TO KEEP GEORGE'S LOVE CIRCULATING. THE
HARRISON HUG DID NOT START JUST WITH GEORGE, WE HAD IT ALL OUR
LIVES. NOT ONLY DID WE HAVE IT, BUT MOM AND DAD GAVE THAT HUG
TO EVERY BEATLE FAN THAT CAME INTO CONTACT WITH THEM. THEY FIG-
URATIVELY HUGGED THEM BY ANSWERING THEIR LETTERS.

Louise, startled by the Beatles' ascent, made sure that she would be a factor by serving as an unpaid, totally dedicated volunteer. For her work, she
was invited to various stages of the Beatles' trips to America, including the
two-concert trip in February 1964.

THEY WERE FLYING SO HIGH, I THOUGHT . . . YOU KNOW HOW THEY TALK
ABOUT A NATURAL HIGH? THAT'S THE WAY IT WAS IN THE HOTEL ROOM IN
NEW YORK, WHEN THEY WERE THERE TO DO THE *ED SULLIVAN SHOW*. THEY
WERE IN THE PRESIDENTIAL SUITE AND I HAD JUST ARRIVED A LITTLE
WHILE EARLIER AND THEY WERE RUNNING ROOM TO ROOM BECAUSE
THERE WAS A TV SET IN EACH ROOM AND THEIR ARRIVAL IN NEW YORK
WAS ON EVERY TV SET. THEY WOULD GO, SEE WHAT THEY ARE SAYING
HERE, SEE WHAT THEY ARE SAYING THERE. THEY WERE ALL FLOATING
ABOUT SIX FEET FROM THE GROUND. THERE WAS ALWAYS BRIAN IN THE
CORNER, MAKING SURE THINGS WERE BALANCED.

Keeping George's feet firmly planted to the ground was a priority for the
Harrisons and American-based sister Louise.

"My dad had a similar dynamic . . . because with George being the youngest, Dad had to sign to give permission for him to be in the Beatles. So Brian knew and respected my dad. He knew that he had my dad to deal with, and that George, who I think was more grounded than the others, would be influenced by his solid family ties."

But in time, before their breakout in 1964, young Louise Harrison discovered that even with the sincere, warm optimism of her sweet brother, a certain element of mistrust settled in.

"He started realizing how much they were being manipulated and predatory. Just being ripped off all of the time."

But the group, unlike the split in the later sixties, managed to maintain a level of unity.

"Later on there was all of that legal stuff, but that was the lawyers creating the [tension]. They themselves—and I know from talking to George—they never really had any animosity towards each other. There was animosity brought in from outside and thrust upon them."

Louise Harrison is a spiritual woman. From the beginning, she never imagined their long-range influence, their lasting impression. But as time and age have settled in, she sees a level of divine purpose, as she expressed to me in a 2012 interview.

LK: I have to ask you a very difficult question. 1963. Did you ever have any idea that they would become iconic in the way that they are now?

LH: No. I don't think anybody did. And yet when you do look back, and there's a book on that bookcase there about The Beatles and Philosophy, and I've been invited to many, many sermons that have been given by many ministers across the country, and I've talked to many philosophers and theologians, and the general consensus seems to be that in the past, throughout the known history of our species, there have been people who have come along and have been very, very prominent that have had a teaching role in life. They've come along as teachers. People like Buddha, Muhammad, Christ, and whoever else. All of these various teachers have come along to try to give the species some kind of road map as to how we really ought to be behaving toward each other.

LK: Do you think that the Beatles came around for that reason?

LH: The consensus of opinions of the people that have talked to me have said that it was almost as though the Beatles were the twentieth-century formation of that message, and it had to be done on a different scale to how it had been done in earlier centuries in order for the message to reach all of humanity.

I want to make one thing clear. Louise is not suggesting that the Beatles were bigger and more important than any of the world's religions. She is not echoing John's 1966 comments, taken out of context, that the Beatles were bigger than Christ. But she does offer us the realistic principle that agents of culture can have enormous impact on people's lives.

In that respect, in some ways, the woman with a direct bloodline to George Harrison, the woman who quietly helped so much in the beginning, seems to reflect the philosophies of her eclectic brother, that a belief system can pass the boundaries of established theology.

CHAPTER TWENTY-FIVE

THE BOYS OF THE ROAD

*"All three, in different ways, were invaluable on the road to success
for the people I named the 'Fab Four.'"*
—Tony Barrow

IN THE BEGINNING, THE TRANSPORTATION COULD BE AS WICKED AS THE
WEATHER. Aboard the Lockheed Electra in 1965, in a rare interview, master
roadie Neil Aspinall made a comparison.

"This [plane travel] is much finer than our previous modes of transportation."

That was an understatement. For Aspinall and the boys of the road, those
early, bumpy rides would never escape their memory.

For Tony Bramwell—the youngest traveler, hand-holder, equipment
guardian, and just plain gofer—one episode will always stand out:

WE WERE AT A CONCERT A LONG WAY FROM LIVERPOOL. [IT WAS] WIN-
TER . . . I THINK DECEMBER 1963 . . . THE POLICE GAVE US AN ESCORT TO
OUR VAN AND WHEN WE GOT TO IT, IT WAS COMPLETELY WRECKED—
MIRRORS OUT, WINDOWS GONE, HEATER BROKEN. AND WE HAD TO BE IN
LIVERPOOL, WHICH WAS FOUR HOURS AWAY, FIRST THING IN THE MORN-
ING. WE DIDN'T KNOW WHAT WE WERE GOING TO DO. THE POLICE
ESCORTS SAID THEY WOULD LEAD THE WAY FOR US, AS WE DROVE THE
BROKEN VAN. WE GOT IN THE VAN AND WE MOVED THE EQUIPMENT
BEHIND THE FRONT SEAT AND THE BEATLES SAT ON THE FLOOR BEHIND
THE EQUIPMENT, WRAPPED UP IN THE COATS TO KEEP WARM. THE ONLY
THING THAT WORKED WAS THE STEERING AND THE ENGINE AND BRAKES,
ENOUGH TO GET US THERE IN TIME. WE DROVE THROUGH THE NIGHT.
EVEN NEIL WAS A BIT FRIGHTENED.

YEAH, AND WE DROVE ALL THE WAY TO LIVERPOOL WITH NO WINDOWS—
FOUR HOURS THROUGH THE NIGHT, SITTING ON THE FLOOR BEHIND ALL THIS

EQUIPMENT. . . . THEY WERE STARS, AND THEY DIDN'T ACT LIKE STARS. THIS IS MORE OF A TESTAMENT TO WHO THEY WERE.

It was also a testament to the people they chose to have with them, led by the quiet and determined Aspinall.

Neil Aspinall—Fixer, Father, Kingmaker

The accounting student used his sharp pencil and sharp tongue—the pencil in his salad days as he played the role of helpful boarder to the Bests, unknowing that he and Mona would present a new life to the world. The sharp wordsmith, a bit shy at times, traveled the path from bookkeeper, to protector of the flesh, and finally, guardian of the entire franchise.

And in the beginning, bereft of contacts, he had an important sponsor. His name was Best.

Like so much about his unusual career, history has never adequately credited Pete Best with the lasting gift he bestowed upon the Beatles: an introduction to Neil Aspinall. Of course, Pete never knew they would actually be related one day. Pete also couldn't possibly predict that turning-point moment when he was sacked, and unselfishly urged his good friend to stay on with the band.

Aspinall's connection to the Best family, explained earlier, brought him unknowingly face-to-face with an event that altered the culture of the world, but like so many who were there in the beginning, he had no idea. He was a worker with a zest for excellence, punctuality, and the one most important characteristic in relationships: loyalty.

Aspinall was one of the boys of the road who got the Beatles where they needed to go—except for the time he got lost while driving the boys to London for their infamous Decca audition. But it would take more than bad weather to stop Neil Aspinall.

I viewed him as the ultimate roadie, with a twist. Aspinall was first and foremost interested in the boys' safety and protection—safety being the art of securing them through secret passageways and narrow corridors away from screaming hordes of teenagers; protection being the assurance that their trysts with women were conducted under layers of secrecy and security that resembled that afforded to heads of state.

In both regards, safety and "social" security, Aspinall had no equal.

He was cunning and cool. He did have some drawbacks: for one, he hated the press, and in the early days never understood their pivotal role in branding the Beatles to success. Eventually, after I traveled for weeks with him, he learned to trust me, but reluctantly. He was one of the group, including Brian Epstein and 1964 Beatles press chief Derek Taylor, that roused me in the middle of the night to help convince a mother that her two young daughters, who found their way to John's room in Las Vegas, were treated to nothing more than some candy and company. The episode, as you will learn, was much ado about nothing.

Even after my help there, he treated me and the print journalists with indifference, sometimes trying to deny us access, even when the boys insisted we come into a bedroom or dressing room.

Despite his attitude, I had a deep respect for Aspinall. He was so devoted to the boys in their playing years, and after that, he was a devotee and keeper of the flame as he protected the Beatles' empire as a shrewd business leader for four decades. He ran Apple, the Beatles' company, as smoothly as he maneuvered their tricky travels in the beginning.

He was also a proud and active father to his first child, Roag, whom he produced with Mona Best.

"He was a devoted dad, always there for me," Roag remembers. "He had a later family, but never was far from my interests. And he taught me a lot."

In truth, many of the traits that Aspinall passed on to Roag have made the youngest of the Best sons the most protective of his brother Pete, much in the same style as Aspinall.

In the beginning, Aspinall was the king of transit. His mode was a van, a secondhand Bedford, hardly the stuff of luxury. And in that van Aspinall had his trusty assistant, Tony Bramwell, who had a front-row seat to some of the best songwriting in history.

Tony Bramwell—Friend Forever

The boy who used to play with Paul and George in and around the once-bombed air base in Liverpool, as we now know, is the same boy who had that later chance meeting on the bus with George en route to what would become the thrilling concert at Litherland.

As a teenager, given a chance by Brian Epstein, he was a helper to Aspinall on many of those bumpy van trips. Like Aspinall, Tony Bramwell heard many of the songs before we did, worked out by John and Paul in the creaky seats of Aspinall's Bedford.

"We didn't have a lot of room," Bramwell remembers. "Neil would drive and John would often sit up front, smoke, and chat it up. In the back, the rest of us found little room around the equipment. Sometimes we would try to sleep on our coats, or lean against an amplifier. I'll tell you . . . the most interesting times were when Paul went up front with John. They would sing some things, then one of them would doze off. A little later, they would continue, their notebooks scattered with lyrics, or proposed lyrics. We would pay some attention, but the words and tunes would come back months or years later, when I heard them on stage or on records. It's always kind of amazing that we heard them in the beginning, and had no idea that years later, curious minds everywhere would be trying to figure out what the words meant."

Trying to figure out Tony Bramwell is not hard. He is a genuine character, whose own personality is as unique as the story he lived through.

Bramwell skips along the ancient streets of his adopted town, Totnes, soaking in the sun and enjoying every moment as he points out the landmarks, the river, and the shops, and snakes through the alleyways to lead me to a pub with a beautiful river view. Bramwell has worked for so many rock groups over the years, witnessed so many substance breakdowns, and traveled so far and wide, that it's amazing that he is as healthy as he is, at his age. The man has a reputation for hard drinking, and in the twilight of his youth, for "shagging," the unique British word for the root of all civilization.

"He shagged [her]," he would say, "and they shagged them, and I shagged them, too." To say he's just a "character" is a gross understatement—the man is also a writer and a star promoter who wrote one of the most underappreciated titles, *Magical Mystery Tours: My Life with the Beatles*, in the vast history of Beatles books.

Totnes is in Devon, a county in southwest England that features some of the most breathtaking views in the United Kingdom. The air is clear and the town is ideal for walking, shopping on beautiful High Street, searching for the New Age life, and reveling in the vivid memories of a not-so-ancient past when talent, fate, and numerous acts of God created the immortals of Tony Bramwell's life. Artists, painters, and musicians live among the 7,500 permanent residents of Totnes, named by *Time* magazine in 2007 as the "Capital of New Age Chic." It has been subsequently labeled one of the top ten "Funky Towns" in the world, a perfect fit for Bramwell, who grew up in Liverpool not a quarter of a mile from a skinny, bike-riding kid named George Harrison.

Bramwell, whose career in publicity and music promotion is legendary, appears weathered by the years of drinking and smoking and traveling, but his mind is as clear as the blue Totnes sky as he sips his Guinness slowly on a tavern terrace overlooking the scenic river Dart. Tony Bramwell is a modern Zelig. He rolls his own cigarette in brown paper and inhales deeply, washing the smoke away with the froth of the beer.

Promoter, marketer, writer, and pop music bon vivant, Bramwell became the first independent record promoter in Britain in the sixties, and remains involved in the music industry today, especially in the movies. Bramwell has known George, Paul, and John ever since they grew up together in Liverpool. And after the Beatles split, he became an independent record promoter representing superstar artists including the likes of Bruce Springsteen, and coordinating and promoting the music for films including Harry Saltzmann's James Bond movie *Live and Let Die* (with Paul McCartney's eponymous theme song), *Chariots of Fire*, *Dirty Dancing*, and *Ghost*. Through it all, he has never strayed far from the interests and work of his childhood buddies. When Macca is entertaining these days, Bramwell is often backstage sharing a laugh and the support of a longtime friend, someone who remembers the way it was.

Interviewing Bramwell is risky business. In our scenic afternoon in Totnes, in January 2011, he wears a black T-shirt with white letters that read, "Still Pissed at Yoko." He despises Yoko Ono. Calling her "the Princess of Darkness," and claiming her responsible for a much different John Lennon than the one he knew, Bramwell has not only burned bridges, but torched the countryside with his exorbitant candor. When I wrote the foreword to his incredible memoir of life with the Beatles, *Magical Mystery Tours*, I was confident that Yoko and her supporters might consider me a dead-on-arrival reporter thereafter. But if there's one thing I've learned in memory land of the boys, it is that personal feuds are often abandoned when people are interested in telling *their* story. And Bramwell's account of the beginning, as you will learn throughout this story, is believable.

Paul McCartney, who searched the fields surrounding Liverpool Air Base for unexploded bombs with friends George Harrison and a raggedy young Tony Bramwell, attests to Bramwell's photographically creative memory, saying, "If you want to know anything about the Beatles, ask Tony Bramwell. He remembers more than I do." Bramwell's memory also includes the chronicle of, as he puts, "the shagathon," the wondrous sexual adventures that liberated him from the streets of Liverpool to the capitals of the world. His knowledge is so vast on that subject that he arguably could have expanded his career beyond expert record promoter to an on-the-job author of studies on the male sexual endurance.

Bramwell is a rare witness, five years younger than the boys, who was in towns, places, and situations that few have been. But he has a long-term memory that shines the spotlight on the real boys, not the cartoon-character "Fabs" who were characterized in the early years by some of the older journalists with an envy for and vengeance against anything to do with young people.

"George and I lived about a quarter of a mile from each other. He was wiry. He was always wiry, and he had wonderful parents, especially his father, Harry, who let us ride free on his bus. Harry was a wonderful man. I was six, George was nine. We used to build dens, hide in haystacks, play Robin Hood. Paul lived a few miles away. The three of us did some boy things, like look for unexploded bombs at the air base. George was kind and considerate, and warm."

While Bramwell remembers the long summer days of boyhood fancy, his skin turns flush when he talks about the kindness of George, and the exuding confidence of a twelve-year-old Paul.

"He was a charmer," Bramwell says. "And very Paulie, if you know what I mean."

What *does* he mean?

"Everyone just, you know, liked him. He was always confident. He's always been the most Beatley Beatle, but when he was a kid, he was just that—he's always been that."

As Bramwell puts two thumbs up in a "Paulie salute," he continues, with much pride.

"He was never embarrassed about anything he had to do. He was up for it, as he would say, 'I'm Paul McCartney and I am what I am.' He was then, and today, always very confident."

Bramwell, who believes that Paul's mother delivered *him* from the womb, has always felt a comfortable intimacy around McCartney, but didn't meet up with young John Lennon until John was twelve.

"He was rough, kind of a Teddy Boy. There was always that special, beguiling smile. I met him a few times, and then, on a beautiful July day, I walked over to a church in Woolton, and saw John from a distance. He was playing with a band. It was a skiffle group called the Quarrymen. Did you ever hear of them?" he quizzes with a wry smile.

That chance second meeting with George on the bus would change Bramwell's life, and the lives of playmates Paulie and George, and in many respects, through six and a half years of motion, madness, and an extraordinary leap of faith and talent, the life and times of a city, a nation, and amazingly, the planet Earth.

Back in Totnes, Bramwell skips again through the town, helping me to make the 5:30 train back to London. His sneakers are pounding the earth in joy; his legs seem to be on fire. Maybe the Guinness is taking hold. Both of us are out of breath when we see the train in the station. Daringly, he walks across the track and holds his hand up in a gesture to stop the train. I board the train at the same moment that the train starts moving. Bramwell is now on the platform, waving and waving like a little boy, and as the train moves through the seascapes of Devon, I think about the boy and his mates and the fickle fates of chance, hope, and destiny.

Malcolm Evans—Gentle Giant

The pages of history are strewn with asterisked names, brief references to people who were along for the ride. When the dead are not around to explain their influence, the living quite often have a diluted memory when they write the credits for their own successes. And individuals who may have helped craft a larger success story are often forgotten.

Therein lay the bittersweet saga of the Beatles' roadie and touring friend whom I admired the most—a man with a hell of a story.

When memorial services were held for Malcolm Evans on January 7, 1976, none of the boys were present—surprising, considering the enormous contribution he made as a pal, an employee, and an affectionate protector of their bodies and their privacy, especially during their infancy. It was not the first time the boys, usually so sensitive to others, ignored the rites of passage. Stuart Sutcliffe, so instrumental to the crafting of their style, and even their name, their birthright, was not honored appropriately either when he died in Hamburg after his painful ordeal.

Fittingly, it was the quietly "compassionate Beatle," George Harrison, who sent Mal's family, at the end, a check for over 5,000 British pounds. Also, in 1997, George was the only Beatle who attended the funeral of pressman and promoter extraordinaire Derek Taylor, whose contributions resonate through these pages.

Mal Evans was hardly a Beatles fan in the beginning when he first watched them at the Cavern Club. In fact, he was "crazy" about Elvis, whom he met along with the boys in Los Angeles in the summer of 1965. At six-foot-six, described as a "gentle giant" by many, Mal was not easy to miss. He befriended George, and within weeks in early 1962 became a part-time bouncer at the Cavern. His role in the formative years, as a friend, protector, and musical muse to the boys, is probably one of the greatest untold stories of their lives.

In fact, of all the people in the inner circle of the young artists, no one felt more intimate on an emotional level with the Beatles, with the exception of Brian Epstein and Neil Aspinall.

Mal carried their bags, listened attentively to their high and low moments and moods, and in every moment, big or small, helped them cling to their hopes and heartaches. He occasionally shared the benefits of touring life with them, including access to women and drugs in the later years, but never allowed them to put themselves in a dangerous position. Malcolm Frederick Evans was a man clearly with only one agenda: friendship with the boys. And I can tell you that, for much of his life, they loved him back. After all, it was Mal who put his body between surging crowds and the boys.

In Detroit in 1964, after the police had mistakenly left us, I ran alongside Mal and Neil and a few other reporters to create a makeshift wedge as the maniacal crowd, penetrating the defenseless parking garage, circled in on the Beatles. Mal pushed and shoved through the crowd with his massive arms, elbows protruding just at the right moments. It was a sweaty and scary confrontation. There is no question, in my mind, that Mal, if necessary, would have killed for them. He often boasted of coldcocking a desperate photographer in Paris. I wasn't there. But the legend of the fight, at least among the boys, remained solid.

Aspinall, too, offered total dedication, but his edges were harder. Quite often, early on in the boys' touring career in Britain, Aspinall enjoyed pushing and shoving away legitimate reporters. He was extremely jealous of anyone getting close to the boys. He was rude to me on several occasions, but Mal and Epstein intervened and made things right. While Aspinall never understood the role of media, so critical in the rise of the Beatles, Mal, with no prior experience, seemed to get it. Even later, when Aspinall assumed control of the Apple empire of the original Beatles, he tended to manage with an exclusionary style. Despite that, his knowledge of security, dedication to the Beatles, and maturing business prowess made him invaluable.

But Mal was the popular one, with the body of a lion and the heart of a pussycat. Eleven years before his ugly end, the tall and broad former technician for the postal service traveled to Nassau, the Bahamas, to be with the boys. It was February 1965, almost six months after the end of the first great summer tour of North America. It was there that I reunited with my traveling companion.

"Larry, Larry. It's you, you fucking bastard. I love ya, Larry."

He hugged me hard when I walked through the doors of the boys' rented cottage on the Nassau beachfront, so hard that the differential between our height caused him to grab my neck and press me to him, causing a troubling nosebleed. The gentle giant had inadvertently injured me. He got some ice and some napkins, and I laughed so hard I couldn't stop the bleeding.

The Beatles were in Nassau to film the movie *Help!* Mal, as always, was with them, helping to guard the beach in front of them and the winding road behind them. George and John were relaxing in the unkempt living room, with the smell of marijuana smoke hard to miss. Paul arrived from the beach with a pair of swimming fins in his hand, accompanied by Neil Aspinall. Ringo was out of sight. I laid out my tape recorder and did a few interviews. Mal seemed more interested in the content of the interviews. In fact, both he and Aspinall asked me to avoid reporting on what the guys were smoking. I agreed.

Shortly after I turned my recorder off, Mal motioned me over. He asked me where I was staying. My hotel was a modest two-story house just off of the old docks on Bay Street, the main commercial street in Nassau. There were two beds in the room.

"Could I come along tonight, mate?" he whispered to me.

"Sure," I said, "but why?"

"Want to spend a night away," he replied.

I got it. Aspinall was in the house. The security was set. It was a pleasantly cool February night in the Bahamas. The shooting schedule for the movie was tight. He wanted a night on the town.

We took a cab into the downtown of Nassau. He left his little overnight bag in the room. A few minutes later, we went to the waterfront.

"Could I take notes of our conversation?"

"Of course, man, but no recordings. Just stuff on paper."

I knew I had to work fast. He would be seriously drunk within two hours, but his insight into the boys would be valuable, someday, if not in the heady days of 1965. I was curious, because the story of Mal Evans was often elusive.

We walked to a restaurant and bar on the bay front, and I asked a few questions over dinner and drinks.

So, how did it all begin?

"I'm working for the phone company. I often took walks at lunch. Dropped in to this Cavern nightclub, took a smoke, and watched this band. It was 1962, just three years ago."

What was it like?

"Well, the place was smoky and these guys, Pete, Paul, John, and George, were doing a very good set of rock . . . a little bit like Elvis music. A lot of businessmen there, and some kids. The music was really good. Got my Elvis groove going. You know I was a member of the Elvis fan club, did ya? Loved their music. They were very high-pitched and there was harmony . . . walked away with an impression."

What happened next?

"I kept my job, but found part-time work at the Cavern. I was a security man."

A bouncer?

"Yes. I bounced them round and round, but no problems really. I got to know the guys really well. Really nice guys, who were getting crowded, you know what I mean. Each month from the fall of '62 to the winter of '63, more and more of the kids showed. After Brian got working with them, I got to know him, and Barrow [press officer Tony Barrow] and everyone. Then my life changed when Brian asked me, in the spring, I think, of 1962, to become their assistant road manager. Me wife Lil didn't want me to go. We have a son, you know. But I went. Larry, I fell in love. No, not what you're thinking, man. I fell in love with all of them, the music, the fame. I feel like a brother."

Who's your favorite?

"Wanna get me sacked? As it is, I didn't know what the hell I was doing when I first set up the stages. I think I was fired a couple of times, but I think they view me as a friend . . . almost a family member. Do love George, you know . . . there is a soul inside that skinny face. . . . Paul is a sweetheart. Yeah . . . I'm an errand boy . . . fixer . . . handy mate, ya know . . . but I would do anything for them. Paul is easier to like than John, but John's a mad genius . . . and Ringo . . . just a sweet man."

The conversation gave way to dinner and drinks and a night in a club deep in the heart of a Nassau neighborhood. The next morning I awakened

Mal at seven to make sure he got to the film shoot. After all, he was in one of the scenes.

I saw him later that year on the 1965 summer tour, his highlight being the Beatles' meeting with Elvis in Hollywood. We saw each other again in 1966 on tour, in 1968 in London, and in 1969 in Philadelphia. Sometime in the early 1970s, Malcolm moved in other directions. Almost as much as Ringo, he felt like a man without a family when the group split. George, Paul, and Ringo quickly demanded that Mal be hired back, but much to their chagrin, Apple Corps President Alan Klein could not find a job for Mal.

After all, he had mended their socks, picked up clothing and people for them, accompanied them to India, traveled the world at their beck and call, but most of all, during the critical year of 1963, shepherded them with friendship, love, and solace when necessary, and later, sound and creative advice for their music from 1966 to 1970. Some eyewitnesses from the boys' early days state that Mal helped Paul come up with the name "Sgt. Pepper" on the album that many consider the band's most important—*Sgt. Pepper's Lonely Hearts Club Band.* While that may be questionable, one thing is certain: he contributed to many of the album's songs, helping them with their lyrics and songwriting.

Although he was never properly compensated for his creative work, love and respect poured out from the boys. Evans was a witness at the March 12, 1969, marriage of Paul McCartney and Linda Eastman. He was the only member of the Apple Corps staff who was invited to the London ceremony.

Mal accompanied John in Los Angeles, where he had traveled with his girl-friend, May Pang, on the legendary "Lost Weekend." He discovered and guided the successful Apple Corps group Badfinger. His credits for input and support could fill a chapter in this book. But one accomplishment goes deep beyond the real glory and fame of the Beatles.

Mal played a pivotal role, along with Neil Aspinall, in the most important year of the evolution of the boys: 1963. He shepherded them with protection, love, solace, kindness, and sensitive advice when they, as you will soon read, were close to jumping across the line between right and wrong in their private lives.

Unfortunately, by the winter of 1975, nearly divorced, almost broke, and dependent on drugs, Malcolm Evans, who gave so much input and effort to *Sgt. Pepper's*, became a lonely heart.

In an interview before his death, he was asked about his lack of financial return, and answered, "Hey, loving them as I do, nothing is too much trouble, because I want to serve them."

The man who idolized them from the beginning remained committed to them at the end.

On January 5, 1976, fourteen years after meeting the boys, Malcolm Evans, living with a girlfriend, Fran Hughes, in Los Angeles, was despondent. His girlfriend called John Hoernie, his cohort on his book, *Living the Beatles Legend*. Hoernie arrived at their rented motel apartment to see Mal looking groggy and incoherent. At one point, Mal picked up an air rifle. Hoernie expected the worst. Hughes summoned the police. And thus the tragedy unfolds. Despite repeated warnings from the police to drop the weapon, the police say Mal pointed the rifle at them. He was shot four times, and died immediately.

Malcolm Evans, who had lived the legend, took his memories to the grave. When the story of his death came over the United Press International (UPI) wire machine in the newsroom in Philadelphia where I then worked, I stood there in a state of shock and wondered, "How could such a gentle and kind man suffer such a violent death?" Yoko Ono tells me that John cried uncontrollably when he heard the news. Longtime Beatle buddy Tony Bramwell talks of Paul's shock and grief.

In a brief story following his death, the *Los Angeles Times* described Mal Evans as "a jobless former road manager for the Beatles."

He was more than that. Much more.

Billy Kinsley, founder of the Merseybeats, describes Mal as a "constant companion, defender, and a sweet guy who would never harm a soul, unless they were running in the direction of the boys."

Kinsley, with bittersweet memories, adds, "As they say, he was a gentle giant who had this enormous sense of satisfaction, and was there in good times and bad, always ready with a smile and a wonderful body block."

CHAPTER TWENTY-SIX

THE MAKEOVER

*"They were ahead of their time, but what Brian did for them,
shaping the imagery, brought them a futuristic look
that was so influential in their success."*
—Derek Taylor, talking to me somewhere over America in August 1964

MONA BEST, THE OFTEN-FORGOTTEN FORCE BEHIND THE FLEDGLING BEATLES' EARLY PERFORMANCES IN HER CASBAH NIGHTCLUB, did much more than get the boys gigs. In fact, one of her influences may be more important than all the others: her recommendation to Brian Epstein that he "polish up" his unpolished band. She suggested he change their look, which was similar to many other bands at the time, and give them a look that was new and fresh. It was advice he took to heart.

The music was dynamic. The bookings were improving. Although Brian Epstein was struggling to get them a genuine recording contract, he knew that there was another more urgent mission in the late winter of 1962. And so he proceeded to engineer "the makeover."

The world was indeed changing. The rock groups of the fifties, although fairly well dressed, began to symbolize a move toward the outer limits of what Americans would label as a growing problem: "juvenile delinquents." Every generation has had its form of juvenile delinquents, but in the late fifties, the groups were famous for Elvis-style longer black hair, leather jackets, and an outward irreverence to anyone over twenty-one. Sound familiar?

Irreverence for adults was one thing, but Brian Epstein knew very well the secret to the long-term success of the Beatles: *acceptance.* He knew that the quality of their music, the factor that was bringing them early success, could be trampled by the rough-tough imagery that came right out of the Teddy Boy handbook. So he moved, and he moved fast.

Soon after his first glimpse at the group, Brian Epstein was determined to make the group more palatable to all audiences. But there was a challenge.

As Derek Taylor remarked to me much later on, "How in hell do you take away that raw radiance without destroying the act?"

The answer to that question might have determined the boys' fate, and Epstein knew that from the beginning. In fact, Taylor's early notes of Epstein's remembrances for the ghostwritten autobiography, *Cellarful of Noise*, confirms Epstein's early concerns.

He wrote, "The Beatles were scruffy and rather dirty. They were all shaved and they were neither as untidy or dirty as anyone else. . . . They smoked and ate on stage. The response was falling off, but they *were* very funny on stage."

In the beginning, Epstein felt that the only reason the Beatles were interested in doing a deal with him was that he had some money, a car, and a good job. He was accepting of them when they set a meeting to talk about a management contract, but he was none too happy that Paul was an hour late for the first real discussions.

It was during these talks that Brian realized he would have to clean up their act without really cleaning up their act. From the beginning, he wanted trust. So the makeover would have to be executed in time. They couldn't feel hammered immediately upon signing. Like all young people of a certain age, they relished their style, and conformity is such a fashion statement in its own right for teenagers and young adults of every generation.

"In truth," he would say later, "in truth they had already made themselves over with their boots and the acceptance of the Franco-German mod hair style. All I did was get them the clothes, and tell them to bow."

In truth, as Epstein would say, he did a lot more.

Joe Flannery explains that "the boys were independent. . . . They liked the way they dressed. After all, the leather jackets and wilder hair gave them a real reputation when they came back from Hamburg. What Brian brought to them was not really a clean-cut look, but a dramatically futuristic fashion look. It was advanced for the time, sort of futuristic with elegance. And the only reason they accepted it was John's reluctant acceptance of Brian as an authority, a father figure."

In reality, the makeover was a real struggle. Even though John Lennon could be satirical and offensive in his remarks chiding Epstein, sometimes driving him to cry when the boys were not around, he deeply respected the man when it came to business. But he was reluctant to change their "raw" look—jeans, T-shirts, leather jackets, and "creeper" shoes. Paul and George also liked the raw look, but in the end, it had to go.

The new look was a combination of the sleek look of the John F. Kennedy Camelot era and the growing ascension of the space race in America. In addition to the polite bow, the made-over Beatles had a complete look from head to toe. The hair came from their friend in Paris, Jürgen Vollmer, and Astrid Kirchherr in Hamburg. The suits were from suburban Liverpool, the shirts and ties an inspiration offered by the elegant Epstein. And the shoes? The change in footwear was a direct result of the daring of John and Paul, who first noticed the Chelsea boot in a high-end store in London's Chelsea neighborhood. The boots were born in the Italian culture of the late fifties and early sixties, although the boys adapted them to have Cuban heels. The boys provided the boots. They saw them, they wore them, but they were still convinced that for the rest of the body, the Hamburg style, inspired by Astrid Kirchherr, was very good for them—leathered up in black with tight trousers. It was Epstein who at first pressured them, and then mandated, a more streamlined look—out with the leather, and in with what he thought was a more modern look.

To me, who observed their new look close up—in the airplane, on stage, and in all the Beatles' public moments—it was pure genius. Of course, at that time I didn't know the real history, but I was impressed. The boots as well as the rest of the collection set a fashion trend, only, of course, to be replaced by colorful uniforms and psychedelic outfits during the Beatles' so-called acid era in the late sixties. It's also interesting to note that the dress code, in strict conformity to Brian Epstein's wishes, vanished after his death.

But in 1962, there was a reason for the makeover. Epstein was able to alleviate—even diminish, quite methodically—what would turn out to be a major concern about the boys.

One has to think what the domestic reaction in America would have been in 1964, if the Beatles had arrived in those tight leather pants and the gang-style jackets. By 1964, the aura of the movie *Blackboard Jungle*, with

Bill Haley's melodic tune "Rock Around the Clock," was done and over with. The gang mentality of the "JDs" (juvenile delinquents) in America had given way to the dreamy songs of the Philly sound—the clean-cut performances of Bobby Rydell, Frankie Avalon, and James Darren.

And think about this: all the fuss about the Beatles' hair was neutralized by the neatness of their look. They were always in modern, sleek-fitting trousers and jackets, some of those jackets with no lapels. Their ties were always tied neatly. Their high-heeled boots looked sharp and appeared to be uncomfortable, but they were not. It was rare to see them in public without the proper attire. Once inside the touring aircraft, they would loosen up considerably, happy to be more informal, but rarely did they allow themselves to be photographed like that, with the exception being a vacation at the beach, or that quick trip they took near the end of 1964 to ride horses and relax in the Ozark Mountains.

Ultimately there was a plan, and the plan was always etched in stone at the hands of Brian Epstein, who was a regal dresser himself. He never hoped they would emulate his English businessman style; all he was looking for in the makeover was to make them look legitimate with a touch of style. Little did he know that the touch changed the way men around the world tried to look.

When I returned to Miami after the first summer tour, in 1964, so many people would ask me the question, "Are they as clean-cut as they look?" The answer was yes. The so-called mop tops were easily recognized for their music as well as their appearance, which to adults and children in 1964 was viewed as shocking and provocative. But the makeover allowed them to be viewed as serious and refreshing artists, as well. It offered a level of credibility. Just as the Boston Pops' recording of their music legitimized the Beatles in the eyes of most Americans over the age of eighteen, their fashion change made them look distinguished and important. An important note: the boys were always sharply shaved; I never saw anyone in the group unshaven at any point.

Tony Bramwell remembers the contrast from the early look to the iconic new look:

MOST OF THE LIVERPOOL GROUPS, RORY STORM FOR EXAMPLE, WORE GOLD LAMÉ, DAYGLO PINK, OR WHITE TUXEDOES, THE TUXEDOES BEING

COSTLY TO CLEAN. QUITE OFTEN, THEY WERE NEVER CLEANED. THAT WAS BAD. . . . THE EARLY BEATLES WORE BLACK-AND-WHITE TWO-TONE LOAFERS . . . THEY GOT SMITTEN WITH THAT HIGH-HEELED BOOT LOOK, INFLUENCED BY CUBAN AND SPANISH DESIGNS. BUT WHEN BRIAN SAW THEM AT FIRST, AT THE CAVERN, HE WAS IMPRESSED BY THE SKIN-TIGHT LEATHER TROUSERS AND THEIR ZIPPED-UP BOMBER JACKETS. HE REALLY LOVED IT, BUT AS THEIR MUSIC WAS MORE ACCEPTED, HE HAD TO MAKE THEM MORE ACCEPTABLE TO AS MANY PEOPLE AS POSSIBLE.

Even early promoter Sam Leach admits there was genius in Epstein's moves, but he still savors the early days.

HE TOOK THE RAW OUT OF THEM. WHEN THEY CAME BACK FROM HAMBURG, THEY WERE GREAT. BEFORE THEY WENT TO HAMBURG THEY WERE PRETTY POOR. WHEN I FIRST SAW THEM, I WAS CONVINCED THEY WOULD BE AS BIG AS ELVIS. THEY HAD THIS CHARISMA. WHEN YOU SAW THEM ON STAGE IN THEIR LEATHER JACKETS, BACK IN THE EARLY DAYS BEFORE THEY WERE MANAGED BY EPSTEIN, THEY WERE THE BEST ROCK 'N' ROLL ON THE PLANET, I THOUGHT, AND WAS CONVINCED THEY WOULD BE REAL BIG. UNFORTUNATELY, BRIAN TOOK AWAY THE HARD, RAW WILDNESS OF THEM AND HE MADE THEM MORE PRESENTABLE, YES, BUT THAT THING THEY HAD WAS UNBELIEVABLE. PAUL USED TO GYRATE ROUND THE STAGE LIKE A LUNATIC. BRIAN GROOMED IT OUT OF THEM AND MADE THEM MORE PRESENTABLE, BUT IN '61, I THINK, THAT WAS THEIR BEST YEAR. THEN IT WAS ON WITH THE SUITS. ON TO MOM AND DAD.

Although Leach longs for the early memories, loving the magic after Hamburg, he admits the change was fundamental to the group's worldwide success.

"Brian did the right thing, but in the climate of those days, although I liked the early feel, it was quite important for them to be presentable."

The makeover began with Epstein's campaign to get the boys to trash their Hamburg suits. The leather disappeared. Their first big change was in a concert on March 24, 1962, at the Barnston Women's Institute. After shopping at Burton's chain outlet in Liverpool, the difference was dramatic—very thin lapels on lounge suits, and collars in velvet. Within months, they would at times wear collarless jackets as well.

In a later appearance at the Manchester Playhouse, they wore mohair suits tailored by Beno Dorn, of suburban Liverpool. The shirts were buttoned down, the tie quite thin but neat and kempt. As time moved on, the outfits became more sophisticated.

The Beatles' look changed fashion worldwide. It became the standard for menswear for much of the sixties. Did they know that would happen? John was so concerned about the exit from leather, but was convinced that there was reasoning in Epstein's makeover. According to Joe Flannery, John said, "If it takes a suit to give us all more money, let's do it."

They did. The makeover was in progress by the time of the Parlophone success in the summer of 1962.

Historian Denny Somach believes that Epstein's basic instincts made such a difference:

BASICALLY WHAT BRIAN DID, LOOKED AROUND AT ALL THE OTHER GROUPS, AND HE DIDN'T LIKE THE TOUGHNESS. HE ALSO BASICALLY LEG-ISLATED THAT THEY WOULD ALL WEAR MATCHING SUITS. THE CONCEPT OF MATCHING SUITS WAS NEW, ESPECIALLY SINCE MANY BANDLEADERS WORE A DIFFERENT JACKET THAN THE REST. BUT WHAT IS INTERESTING, THAT BY WEARING THE SAME OUTFITS, THERE WAS NO PERCEIVED LEADER, EVEN THOUGH JOHN AND PAUL HAD A SPECIAL PLACE. THE UNIFORMITY MAY HAVE DISCOURAGED INDIVIDUAL STYLE, BUT IT CERTAINLY MESHED WITH THE MUSICAL HARMONY.

By the end of 1962, Johnny's boys had gone from grunge to sleek and futuristic fashion, and the timing was, excuse the cliché, "picture perfect."

The imagery was set, although the biggest tests were yet to come. Would the small Beatles bubble burst, and would the genuine movement fly in Europe and the States? Thanks to ingenuity by two powerful journalists-turned-promoters, and an amazing nonstop schedule, the year of 1963 turned into 365 days of imagery and success that began with an unusual cascade: the Beatles versus the Beatles.

WHEN
THEY
WERE
BOYS

Part Seven:
1963—New Year's Day

"People forget the time frame. When you think about it, Larry,
it was just over seven hundred days since they thought it was all over.
Seven hundred days . . . "
—Tony Barrow

"My friends were in lights. My bus buddy George was now
riding in cars driven by strange people."
—Tony Bramwell

"Of all the craziness of 1963, the queen's event, even without the queen,
was the highlight, even if I may have pissed her off
by returning her medal years later."
—John Lennon, in 1975

The time frame of this story is astonishing. New Year's Day 1963 came a little over two years after the first Hamburg visit ended with a nightclub fire, Paul and Pete's quick exit, and George's embarrassing underage deportation dilemma.

It was two years after the terribly despondent boys looked inward and saw nothing worth continuing, with John Lennon beyond despair.

It was two years and three days after the Litherland concert provided a brief tonic for the boys' loneliness; exactly one year after the Decca crisis; and almost a year after Bill Harry declared the Beatles number one in *Mersey Beat*. A new year dawned, and it would be no ordinary year at that.

On January 1, 1963, Astrid Kirchherr was alone in her solace, the Sutcliffe family longed for Stuart, and fans in Hamburg recollected the sweet and sometimes high-pitched tones of the boy singing "Love Me Tender," the boy whose face could light up the night.

Sam Leach was still promoting, but the boys had passed him by. His toothy smile and that wonderful, melodic accent illuminated even the most boring of conversations. Would his place in history be bookmarked for future generations?

Julia Baird, sister of the child Mimi was "waiting for," watching from a bit of a distance, was shell-shocked by the rise of John and the boys. Sister Jackie was startled; Baird remembers: "It was amazing. The radio, the TV, the papers. It was totally unreal, but from that Woolton church fair that we witnessed back in 1957, and now to this . . . and to think, this was my mother's little boy . . . my brother."

Tony Bramwell, wide-eyed and still by their side whenever he could be, remembers:

"It was hard to imagine, but Eppy was roaring on all engines. We still had to take long road trips, although I had to stay in Merseyside, but the outlook was brighter. He always seemed to be worrying a lot, but his worrying was a lot less. He would have periods of being down, but I noticed he seemed a bit more self-assured. The boys knew they were going places . . . now their eyes were on America. That was the big unknown."

Many of the other players were watching and listening. Colin Hanton was training for work as an upholsterer, Rod Davis was at Cambridge—the heady and classy banjo man of the Quarrymen says he was "watching the boys closely" as 1963 arrived. Pete Shotton, he of the washboard for the Quarrymen, stayed close to John, still with the memories of John striking his head with a washboard after he quit or was fired from the Quarrymen, depending on whose version you get. Shotton, who would become a fast-food millionaire, never knew in early 1963 that John and George would later help him buy a grocery store, setting him on his way.

For Freda Kelly, the fan club secretary and intimate to the Beatles' families, life was but a dream, but did she know what would happen in 1963? "Not quite," she says today.

"I always believed in them," Kelly says, "but soon what was word-of-mouth through neighborhoods was spreading through the country. But the parents were still worried. Mimi, the Harrisons, Mrs. Starkey, and Uncle Jim [McCartney] were praying that it would last. As for me, I felt I was living a dream, but the dream was far from over. I would stay with them for years."

Kelly, seen in pictures with the boys near a farm field, was electrically attractive, and she had the chance of a lifetime to work with them, to see them up close, to bond with their families, to understand their roots, to cheer for them, and to be, mostly while they were in Liverpool, living every girl's dream.

"In many ways, I was like them," Kelly says. "Humble beginnings, and just hoping for a break. My break was working for Brian, meeting them, and getting butterflies in my stomach every time I heard of another success, another concert. Now they had Britain. I knew the world would follow."

"How did you know?" I ask.

"They were just too good to be missed," she replies.

Bill and Virginia Harry were not married yet, but they had spent so much time together that the union was inevitable, or so John Lennon thought. And so he was right. With a wink and a smile, Harry stares ahead and remembers wistfully: "She loaned me the fifty pounds to start *Mersey Beat*. I was indebted to her, you might say, but we were in love."

On March 16, 1963, the duo would make it official. They would take their vows. As of this writing, like the Beatles, they've reached the golden fifty-year anniversary—theirs is the longest-playing love song in the Beatles family.

With love, anticipation, and a lot of support, the boys looked ahead to a year of emotional highs and lows, physical exhaustion, and hope that their own music would continue to sell.

CHAPTER TWENTY-SEVEN
MUSIC STAMPEDE—
A STORY OF TWO COUNTRIES

"The failure by Vee-Jay Records to cash in on the Beatles . . . may be one of the greatest misses in recording history, while the sheer guts of Alan Livingston put the Beatles and his own company over the top."
—Bruce Spizer, prolific author and the world's expert on
the business practices of the Beatles

"It was amazing how clueless we were in America. All this incredible music was piling up in Britain, and we had no idea how big it was."
—Chris Carter, host of Breakfast with the Beatles on XM Sirius and
KLOS radio, Los Angeles

"It was happening so fast. The press was eating it up. The hits were coming, and we never knew what speed of success was, until this."
—Derek Taylor

THERE IS ALWAYS A SONG THAT YOU REMEMBER IN YOUR LIFETIME, a memory grabber that takes you back. For most early Beatles fans, those who loved them before the iconic years, there's one song that will always be most vivid: "She Loves You."

Most people thought the title was "She Loves You, Yeah Yeah Yeah." The "yeah yeah yeah" was so much a part of the early imagery of the boys, along with the much-maligned "mop tops" haircut. Essentially the boys' performance of "She Loves You" embodied the whole early Beatles package.

"It was everything in one song. The 'yeahs,' the boys shaking it up, the grand harmony, the scene of Paul and George face to face at the microphone," says Chris Carter, host of *Breakfast with the Beatles* on Sirius Satellite Radio and KLOS Los Angeles, and one of the world's real masters of the boys' music.

It was the Beatles' all-time number-one single in England. But there was a much more significant meaning to that song. The Beatles were originally appealing to kids, but "She Loves You," beginning in 1963 in Britain and continuing in America awhile later, signaled the changing of the fan base. The song solidified their growing appeal to all age groups, from teens, to young adults, to the mothers and fathers in their thirties and forties. And there was one other thing. Although they had written plenty of earlier songs, "She Loves You" sealed the deal for John and Paul as songwriters.

As an eyewitness to so many concerts, in addition to the hard-rock songs like "Long Tall Sally," I can attest that "She Loves You" always brought the house down like no other tune.

"From an historical perspective, it certainly was the grabber that left its mark," remembers promoter, roadie, driver, friend, and sometime gatekeeper Tony Bramwell. "I remember that it was the song that everybody played in their minds."

For a while in 1963, it was the Beatles versus the Beatles. There was a music stampede as their songs jockeyed for position on the charts, and with very few other artists in between. There was one glaring reason for this phenomenon. John, Paul, and George had been writing songs for so long that their sudden rise in late 1962 and most of 1963 provided a real traffic jam of sorts on the charts.

Their eventual song that startled America, "I Want to Hold Your Hand," was recorded in October 1963. It was not only the first mega-hit in America after its late-December release, it was also George Martin's first attempt to use four-track technology. The multitrack system would enhance the recording experience, and would enable Martin to mix the different tracks in a single song.

So, why was "I Want to Hold Your Hand" not an instant number-one hit in the UK? Blame the Beatles on that score.

The song was released on November 29 in England. There were one million preorders in Britain. It would have been an instant number one if the Beatles had not collided with the Beatles. "She Loves You," the first million-seller, was at the top of the charts. So, "I Want to Hold Your Hand" had to wait a couple weeks to claim the number-one spot.

The history of Beatles albums in Britain is extraordinary. The LP *Please Please Me* was released on March 22, 1963. It remained number one for thirty weeks. Their second album, *With the Beatles*, released on November 22, 1963, the day President John F. Kennedy was assassinated. That album stayed in the number-one slot in Britain for twenty-three weeks.

The Beatles' music stampede was unprecedented. Remember, it was two years earlier that Paul played "Love Me Do" for Horst Fascher, their protector in Hamburg, who loved the group but didn't like the song.

Many of the Beatles' releases in 1963 were recorded in a most unusual session, under the direction of George Martin at Abbey Road Studios, on February 11. Ten songs were recorded in thirteen hours. The boys' schedule for 1963 was almost overbooked, and Martin insisted on getting them to record as much as possible and in whatever time was available.

There was a fascinating theme during the golden days of 1963, one that has been mostly overlooked. Even with their escalating fame and success, they treated their jobs as though it was 1962 all over again. Still hungry for success, the boys never took anything for granted.

Billy J. Kramer, already a hit in his own right, remembers how methodical they were, even with hit records topping the charts one after another.

"Everywhere I played with them, they played their hearts out," Kramer recalls. "They were the same in 1963 as they were in 1961. They might have had better clothing and extreme fame, but they weren't sure of it, in their own minds."

Freda Kelly, staying in touch with the families, watched the fan club grow and had a hard time coping with the gifts, the perfumed letters, and all the excitement. The boys came back to the Liverpool office, but not as frequently, and yet, she remembers, they came back as the same people she remembered first meeting.

"To us, they were just the boys," Kelly recalls. "Pete was no longer there but we stayed in touch. The egos were the same as the egos earlier. If they were changing or full of themselves, I didn't see it."

Kelly was, as always, a believer, and what she may not have noticed was Paul's growing influence on John's band. Although he always deferred to

John in public, Paul was spending more time with Brian Epstein. As usual, he avoided controversy. Paul was now twenty-one and exerting a stronger influence on the group. There was no feuding. That would come later— seven years later. In 1963, for Paulie and his three buddies, the work ethic remained priority number one.

Tony Bramwell, Mal Evans, and master roadie Neil Aspinall never saw anyone let up in the work ethic.

"They always worked so hard . . . never let up . . . never said 'we are on top,'" Mal Evans remembered during an interview in 1966. " . . . I would be so taken by their work habits, especially in the late 1963 time when they could have been out of control."

While the music stampede in Britain was overwhelming, the initial impact in the United States was not encouraging.

The new *fever*, 1963 style, was punctuated by a strange cycle of events as the boys' recordings slowly made their way to the United States. In the background were wise men and women, ineffective leaders, and a scoundrel of sorts.

When Paul and John wrote "Can't Buy Me Love," it wasn't intended to be autobiographical, yet it was symbolic of the legal scrapes going on in the United States. For a while, the boys couldn't get attention in America. The frustrating failure of American record companies to see the boys' potential was painful, especially to Brian Epstein. The mess over music rights in 1963 could never have been told in a three-minute song, but maybe in a full-length feature movie. It might have been titled *A Hard Year's Fights*.

Once again, the slope was slippery, and the Beatles efforts, with Epstein's intense push, almost collapsed over the edge into ruin.

In the early part of the year, Capitol Records, a division of EMI, had very little interest in the first song that Epstein dispatched to America—"From Me to You"—which ended up being distributed by Vee-Jay Records, a company that produced only black artists before signing the Four Seasons in 1962.

Through a series of legal machinations, and Capitol's indifference, Vee-Jay Records got the right of first refusal to the Beatles records, and conversely, Capitol executive Dave Dexter, the man in charge of approving new releases, did not view the Beatles favorably. Perhaps he agreed with the Decca chief who advised Epstein 1962 that guitar bands were history.

Capitol's failure to act, and its lack of awareness of the Beatles' rise in the UK, placed Vee-Jay in a great position. As early as February 1963, Vee-Jay released "Please Please Me" in America. It never made the early Billboard charts, but in Britain it began a thirty-week run as number one on March 22. Was that a testament to the payola-and-plugola days of American music? After all, pay-for-play was under federal scrutiny. Vee-Jay's promotional budget was moderate, but the fact is that the Beatles' music was quite available in the United States in 1963. But they didn't click. Or was it all about the fever not yet reaching America? The latter is the key question. Vee-Jay also released "From Me to You" in the United States and it managed to reach number 115 on the charts. The company did recoup its investment with the singles it still owned in 1964, including "Please Please Me"/"From Me to You"; "Do You Want to Know a Secret?"/"Thank You Girl"; "Love Me Do"/"P.S. I Love You"; and "Twist and Shout"/"There's a Place."

In all, over 2.5 million Beatles singles were sold on the Vee-Jay label. The company was flying high and had been aggressive in signing new acts during the early rock 'n' roll years of the fifties. After all, Vee-Jay had even signed a deal with Little Richard.

Then the sky fell.

Vee-Jay's president, Ewart Abner, was in trouble. Abner was hugely successful as an executive, but he had a fault line, a gambling problem, and was accused of embezzlement. The company's funds were depleted. The sixties version of Vee-Jay was over.

Into the breach came a successful label—a rare mix of the Philadelphia-born dance-craze super hits and the boys from Liverpool. Cameo-Parkway Records, the Philly hit maker, famous for "The Twist" and "The Bristol Stomp" and many early-sixties dance themes, and partially owned by Dick Clark, got into the mix.

And here lies a story of "no guts, no glory." It is the story of two Bernies. Bernie Lowe was the chief of Cameo. Bernie Binnick, who ran Swan Records, shared nearby office space with copartner Tony Mammarella.

Jerry Blavat, an original dancer on *American Bandstand* and a music legend in Philadelphia and across the country as a deejay, writer, and friend to all the major rock entertainers of the past sixty years, remembers how the "Bernies" reacted to the Beatles:

BERNIE LOWE AT CAMEO-PARKWAY WAS NOT INTERESTED IN THE BEATLES, BUT BERNIE BINNICK, HE WAS A FORMER SHOE SALESMAN IN PHILADELPHIA, WAS *VERY* INTERESTED, AND RELEASED "SHE LOVES YOU" ON HIS SWAN RECORDS LABEL SEPTEMBER 6, 1963. IT WAS FAIRLY INVISIBLE ON THE RADIO, BUT BY THE TIME OF THE DECEMBER CAPITOL LAUNCH, THE COMPANY'S RELEASE FINALLY PAID OFF. "SHE LOVES YOU" FLEW INTO ORBIT IN 1964. . . . DICK CLARK DIVESTED HIMSELF OF INTEREST IN CAMEO-PARKWAY AND SWAN RECORDS. IT WAS A GOOD CHOICE.

Clark, who graciously wrote the foreword for my first Beatles book, *Ticket to Ride*, wanted to avoid any conflicts of interest as the pay-for-play investigations began in Washington.

Bruce Spizer notes that Swan had an option on the next Beatles record but didn't exercise it.

"It's kind of interesting that Bernie Binnick liked what he heard, but obviously he wasn't sure about what would come next," Spizer says. "He did, though, cash in when the Beatles hit the airwaves in late December."

But that mass eruption of the Beatles on American radio stations almost never happened.

The Swan gambit paid off, but it took tremendous patience. Remember, 1963 was a boom year in Great Britain and Europe for the Beatles, but it was a bust year in the States. For eleven months of 1963, the Beatles were unknown in America. All those months earlier, the boys' songs were on sale, but outside of the overly ambitious deejay Dick Biondi in Chicago, few people actually heard them.

And then Capitol Records and Dave Dexter got a second chance when "I Want to Hold Your Hand" was offered to Capitol. Once again, Dexter showed his hand. He said no.

Incredibly, there would be a *third* chance for Capitol to get it right. Bruce Spizer recalls,

Dexter turned down "I Want to Hold Your Hand." Brian Epstein had enough. He went over David Dexter's head to Alan Livingston, the president of Capitol Records. Livingston listened and listened again, and by late December and early January, "I Want to Hold Your Hand" was on its way to becoming champion of American radio. Dave Dexter had also turned down "She Loves You," which Swan cashed in on. Epstein's leap over this executive's head, directly to Livingston, guaranteed the eruption of emotion that would go out of control among American teenagers. Without Alan Livingston, and a largely unknown deejay, there might not have been the great timing of the December 26th launch of "I Want to Hold Your Hand," and along with it, also one of the great relationships, to that point, in musical history.

I met Alan Livingston once. During the 1964 tour, he hosted a VIP party in Brentwood, California—a charity fund-raiser featuring the four Beatles, standing under a tree, taking pictures and signing autographs. Lloyd Bridges and teenage sons Beau and Jeff were there. As the stars marched in, one by one, I was duly impressed.

But the boys were not happy.

The next day, John said to me, "It's rubbish that only the big spenders get to meet us. But then again, Larry . . . "

"Yes?"

"Then again, the charming Mr. Livingston helped us so much, that . . . could we really say no?"

Paul McCartney, gracious and charismatic toward more than seventy of Hollywood's finest, would later sympathize with John.

"To think that police in America don't even allow us to wave at the fans. It doesn't seem fair, does it?"

But Livingston certainly deserved respect and payback. Without him, the flame for the Beatles in America may never have been lit.

It's ironic that a forty-six-year-old executive, far from the madding crowds of teenagers, got what the Beatles were all about.

For Bruce Spizer, the Capitol acquisition of "I Want to Hold Your Hand" is a classic case of good business/bad business:

THE FAILURE BY VEE-JAY RECORDS TO CASH IN ON THE BEATLES BECAUSE OF THE BOSS'S GAMBLING PROBLEM MAY BE ONE OF THE GREATEST MISSES IN RECORDING HISTORY, WHILE THE SHEER GUTS OF ALAN LIVINGSTON PUT THE BEATLES AND HIS OWN COMPANY OVER THE TOP. THE FACT IS . . . LIVINGSTON'S ABILITY TO READ THE PUBLIC, AND THE YOUTH, WAS EXCEPTIONAL. HE SENT HIS COMPANY INTO OVERDRIVE BY SECOND-GUESSING A WELL-LIKED EXECUTIVE WHO HAD REJECTED THE BEATLES AT EVERY TURN. I OFTEN WONDER WHETHER DAVE DEXTER HAD BEEN READING ANY NEWS REPORTS FROM GREAT BRITAIN.

Livingston's intuition would become even more legendary. Throughout the rest of his career, he produced and wrote many TV series, sponsored artists like Don McLean ("American Pie"), and was influential in his years at NBC-TV for a number of major hits, including *Bonanza*. He was a renaissance man who constantly offered new vistas in music, TV, movies, and the arts.

The Capitol boss became a Hollywood icon, and maintained a close business relationship with Brian Epstein.

Joe Flannery offers more about Brian's decision to go directly to Livingston: "He had made a clear choice. 'I Want to Hold Your Hand' had to be released with drama and promotion, and on the signature of a big label. He knew it might be risky to go over people's heads. But he had come too far and he decided to take the risk."

Two years later, during the 1965 tour, in a conversation in his cottage room at the Beverly Hills Hotel, Epstein told me, "Larry, I think he must have thought I was out of my mind when I told him, 'They will be bigger than Elvis.' But it worked, and here we are. Without his intervention, who knows what might have happened."

The "bigger than Elvis" theme was familiar. Sam Leach had uttered those words three years before, directly to the startled Beatles.

Allan Williams thought Leach was crazy. "Bigger than Elvis?" he said to me doubtfully. "Did I believe that back in the post-Jacaranda days? No."

Williams never looked at the boys' future that way, but Leach did, and one year after he negotiated their first legitimate recording contract, Brian Epstein would bet the future on his forecast. It was a bold move by Epstein, forecasting a meteoric rise for the group, telling an American music mogul that they would overtake Elvis. "I Want to Hold Your Hand," the block-buster that paved the way for the Beatles' American domination, was the biggest-selling Beatles single of all time. It sold 11 million copies decades before MP3s and the electronic revolution. Livingston got his payoff.

But there were other players.

One pioneer is almost forgotten in the rise of "I Want to Hold Your Hand." Carroll James of WWDC radio in Silver Springs, Maryland, serving the Washington area, played the song for the first time in America. Deejay James received a request from a young fan, Marsha Albert, who had seen a clip of the Beatles on the December 10, 1963, broadcast of the *CBS Evening News with Walter Cronkite*. James arranged for an airline flight attendant to bring the record over. He played it on December 17.

James got the first play of "I Want to Hold Your Hand," but a small-market station in New England beat him to the punch with two other even-tual hits. It was WORC in Worcester, Massachusetts, that set the real early pace, and made some news.

On December 6, 1963, WORC started playing "I'll Get You," followed by "She Loves You." WORC made history. Based on listener requests, the station proclaimed "I'll Get You" as number one, and "She Loves You" as number nine. Word of the Beatles' success on WORC started spreading around the country.

Between Carroll James in Washington and the aggressive play of WORC radio, Capitol Records was forced to move quickly. Capitol had wanted to wait till the Beatles' arrival in February to release their music in the States. But Carroll James's sneak preview changed all of that. By December 26, the song was being played in almost every market in America. Capitol ended up contracting RCA and Columbia Records to press extra copies of the single to meet demand.

Soon the song would become number one in America, John and the boys remembering that they got the news during their marathon Paris run in January.

Once again, I vividly remember the conversation years later.

"What was the most exciting moment in those early days?" I asked John during a film interview with Paul at the St. Regis Hotel in New York.

"Larry, it was Paris when we got the word that the song was number one, and we celebrated . . . milk, you know?"

Again, John loved being vague and eclectic.

"Milk?" I asked.

"Milk, Larry," John replied.

The news they received in Paris prompted a sense of victory for the boys, getting ready for their first trip to the States. All of them were extremely, and sometimes painfully, nervous about the kind of reception they would face on their February visit to the United States.

The nerves didn't last long. Before they arrived in America, "I Want to Hold Your Hand" had become the group's first American number-one song, entering the Billboard Hot 100 chart on January 18, 1964, at number forty-five and reaching number one by February 1. It held the top spot for several weeks before being replaced by "She Loves You." It was again Beatles versus Beatles, an avalanche of old songs and new that collided on the way to Hit Land, a reverse scenario of what had occurred in Britain. And in retrospect, the Beatles' explosion on the US scene in the first months of 1963 previewed the British Invasion of the American music industry that would soon follow.

Once again, record executives who passed on the boys were left to despair, and those who saw the light became heroes forever, which, in the life of the Beatles, is a very long time.

And as we see repeated in this story over and over again, it was persistence by Brian Epstein, and the courage of one man, in this case Alan Livingston, that changed everything.

There were other components in the Beatles' success in America, which was speedier than their rise in Britain. Two men with diverse talents carefully crafted the words and images that paved the way.

CHAPTER TWENTY-EIGHT

BARROW ON THE BEAT

*"With all the royalty in attendance, John had the cheeky request that
the rich people in the audience should rattle their jewelry."*
—Tony Barrow

*"Yes, it's true. I did use the term 'Fab Four' in an early press release,
but I never knew what I was unleashing at the time, did I?"*
—Tony Barrow, talking to me on the Beatles' chartered plane
in August 1965

WORDS. CAN'T LIVE WITHOUT THEM, especially when they help create imagery, and for the Beatles, that imagery was created before they really made it. Along with the lyrics of so many songs, the fanaticism, and the pure songwriting talent, words helped put the boys in play, even though at the time they were really too busy and all-consumed to realize where the written words had placed them.

Bill Harry in print, and Bob Wooler via voice, had started it. And Derek Taylor and Tony Barrow had finished it—both extraordinary wordsmiths who could put feelings into type, not to mention having an ability to dramatically speak to groups, large and small, with elegance and clarity.

While, as you will soon learn, Taylor seemed to channel the life of a Beatle—cool, very funny, Beatle-like, and at the same time, protective—Barrow was demure and avuncular, a model of the press officer, dressed for the world of finance but hip enough to deal with the vagaries of rock 'n' roll. Both shared an amazing talent—grace under fire—in one case, literally.

When our chartered aircraft, stricken by a small engine fire, made a cautionary landing at Portland, Oregon, in the summer of 1965, the well-traveled Mr. Barrow walked up and down the aisles making sure everyone's seat belt was fastened, way before he fastened his own. The landing was soft, but with all the pressure of the moment, Barrow held his own while remaining calm, proper, and dressed to the hilt. If war broke out, you knew that you would want Tony Barrow in the foxhole with you, no doubt about it. While he may not have had Taylor's dramatic and sometimes overextended flair, Barrow, on the beat, on tour, or simply one-on-one, was an image-maker supreme. His eyes would wander during the press conferences, looking at the reporters, sizing them up, knowing by body language and facial expressions what was coming next.

His road to joining the boys' inner circle began with presenting local pop groups in his hometown of Crosby, in north Merseyside. His hosting duties led to a weekly column, at the age of seventeen, on pop and entertainment for the *Liverpool Echo* newspaper.

Barrow had a unique job when he arrived at Decca Records' London offices, writing liner notes on the back of albums. He managed to continue his *Echo* column at the same time.

Brian Epstein noticed. In late 1962, Barrow survived a real conflict of interest: signing on with Epstein as a freelancer to promote the Beatles' first single in Britain, "Love Me Do." The song was released on the Parlophone label of EMI, and Barrow put together press materials while he was working at Decca, a major competitor to Parlophone. After joining Epstein and company in May 1963, Barrow became a progressive innovator—creating a disc that would be sent to every member of the fast-growing international Beatles Fan Club at Christmastime. The unique holiday greeting was so successful that it was then produced annually, an innovative electronic well-wishing that was created decades before the age of iTunes and social media networks.

But his most startling contribution was his talent as a promoter through words and creative advertising. Although like Derek Taylor he would clash at times with Epstein, the intuitive manager was amazed at Barrow's cunning and capacity to think differently.

"I shall always appreciate the role that the press officers played for us," Epstein graciously said to me in 1966. "Tony is one of the best in the business. Derek was so formidable."

"I guess you like writers?" I asked.

"Not all, but I hired away two of the best, and you see what they did."

For all of Epstein's early naïveté about contracts and such, he was unbelievable in understanding the power of words, and the imagery that was created in people's minds. He was adamant about banning film crews from many of the early concerts, and that was probably a bad move, considering the power of film. But he viewed the written word, in the early days, as more important than film. Then Tony Barrow arrived.

In the final six months of 1963, Barrow pulled off one of the greatest public relations and marketing campaigns in history. At selected engagements, at small and cozy movie theaters, Barrow cleared the way for film crews to shoot small portions of the performances. Most of the 1963 concerts were bigger than the previous year's performances, but still intimate enough to allow a roving camera crew. In a masterpiece of planning, Barrow picked locations where he knew the crowds would be mostly girls who were sure to rise into a wild, screaming frenzy.

What Barrow did was exceptional marketing. The film cameramen would get just enough of each concert so they could show that fraction of a song on the evening news, but Barrow made sure that they got all the film they wanted of the screaming audiences. The result was an image of mass hysteria, even though the theaters were small and compact. This technique is mentioned at several junctures of this story, because it was so important every time it was employed. It also set a standard that is practiced today in the highly proprietary world of popular music. At mega-concerts far and wide, TV cameramen are allowed to take only a portion of video of one song at a concert, just enough to get it on the evening news, but not enough to make it commercially saleable, or material for exploitation. Epstein and company were so wary that one time Epstein followed a radio colleague of mine up a giant tower in the Rocky Mountains to make sure he wasn't secretly making an audiotape of a concert.

Epstein, always looking ahead, feared that too much film could compromise the business later on. But Barrow and his work buddy Derek Taylor understood the technique of showing the film that counted the most, the wrenching and sometimes hysterical screaming, the girls flailing their arms, looking passionate and a bit delirious. It was this kind of footage that first appeared on the *CBS Evening News with Walter Cronkite.*

This strategy helped the Beatles' explosion in forthcoming locations—Sweden and Paris—and of course, sparked the interest and anticipation in the biggest prize, America. It was controlled marketing at its best. Today our business would call it "staging." But whatever they called it in 1963, it worked.

As summer moved into autumn in 1963, Tony Barrow and Derek Taylor guaranteed that the words and images reflected an avalanche that was out of control. Taylor was still writing, and Barrow was already on the job for Eppy.

It was around that time that Barrow also coined the term "Fab Four."

He recalls, "Yes, it's true. I did use the term 'Fab Four' in an early press release, but I never knew what I was unleashing at the time, did I?"

For a while, Barrow was a not-so-quiet moonlighter. He was writing for the *Liverpool Echo* happily promoting the Beatles while his bosses at Decca Records were rejecting them. He also wrote columns *after* joining Epstein's NEMS organization.

To describe Tony Barrow is to envision an English gentleman with the poise and class of royalty. Always dressed well, most of the time wearing a jacket and tie, Barrow was "in command" at all the press conferences on the international tours, especially in America in 1965, when the Beatles conquered Shea Stadium. In Hollywood, he delicately arranged the Beatles' historic meeting with Elvis Presley. A few nights before that, when the engine dimmed on our turboprop as we headed into Portland, Barrow was the calm force surrounding a minor panic from John and George as we approached an emergency landing. Barrow came down the aisle and calmly assured everyone that "everything is on schedule . . . all just routine, you know."

In many respects, from the beginning of his official tenure as an employee of Epstein and the band's, Tony Barrow was a powerful presence in the Beatles camp during their most critical months. With the media, he was a cheerful offset to the intense and security-conscious Neil Aspinall, whose job was to keep away the unruly and the unfriendly. As with Derek Taylor, there was always a smile, a drink, a joke to clear the tension of traveling and crowds.

Great adventures are produced by exceptional people with unlimited energy, but for many of those who worked in the background to ensure the Beatles' success, there was a price to be paid.

One of the untold stories of the Beatles' early life was the price an individual endured amid the concern and chaos of the crowds, the would-be hangers-on, the lack of sleep, and this new, brave, unchartered world of an always-hungry public, if not berserk fandom. All of a sudden, the normalcy of the human spirit was shattered by the fear of the unknown, the fright of watching near-violent crowds around you, and the changes it brought about in your own behavior.

Today Tony Barrow savors the memories, but also knows very well that for all the joy, there was a good dose of suffering, especially in 1963.

MY LIFE WAS TURNED UPSIDE DOWN BY THE COMPLETE CHANGE OF DAILY WORKING SCHEDULE. AS A WRITER AT DECCA I HAD WORKED FROM TEN UNTIL SIX, MONDAY TO FRIDAY, PERIOD. ONCE THE BEATLES BECAME INTERNATIONALLY POPULAR, AS SOON AS THE PHONE STOPPED RINGING IN THE OFFICE I'D START GETTING CALLS ON MY HOME LINE FROM JOURNALISTS AND OTHER MEDIA PEOPLE ALL ROUND THE WORLD. I WAS NEVER OFF DUTY, 24/7. AS I TRAVELED MORE AND MORE, I SAW LESS AND LESS OF MY WIFE AND OUR FAMILIES. ON REFLECTION THIS BECAME PARTICULARLY UNFORTUNATE AFTER THE FIRST OF OUR TWO SONS WAS BORN IN 1967. I CHERISH ALMOST ALL THE EXPERIENCES I HAD WITH THE BEATLES, THE LOWS AS WELL AS THE HIGHS, BUT I FEEL SAD NOW THAT I MISSED OUT OF WATCHING MY BOYS GROW THROUGH THEIR EARLY CHILDHOODS SIMPLY BECAUSE MY JOB DEMANDED SUCH NONSTOP ATTENTION.

That nonstop attention could wander into the middle of the night, which leads to the question: Would the Beatles have made it if a real scandal erupted? The answer is no, especially in the early days.

And on that subject, my mind wanders back to Las Vegas in 1964, when John was asleep in his hotel room, with two very young sisters on the bed watching black-and-white TV. It was about 4 a.m. Team Beatles—including Brian Epstein, Derek Taylor, and Neil Aspinall—rushed to my room and pleaded for help. Nothing happened in John's room. I checked that out thoroughly. John was his usual self. The girls, about eleven or twelve years old, had broken through security. John invited them in and that was that. He loved talking to the kids, and yet there was an air of impropriety. But since

I was a so-called reputable member of the media, Taylor urged me to go down to the lobby and convince their mother, who had been gambling all night, that it was all innocent, since it was. The mother was skeptical but may have later reached a court settlement with Epstein. For that moment in time, there was no scandal, and the Beatles marched on.

In those days, an alleged scandal would have destroyed the boys, especially in the puritanical 1960s of America.

What would have happened in this unfortunate and erroneous close call if the minds had not moved quickly, if headlines had overwhelmed the group, if a phony report of "trouble" backfired?

It is in those moments, when the forces of human nature can overwhelm the big picture, that you have to vividly appreciate the Beatles' handlers, led by Brian Epstein.

Over the years, I have argued and laughed with dozens of press secretaries to mayors, governors, and even presidents. In truth, I have never met anyone quite as classy, direct, and protective of his clients than Tony Barrow. He set a standard that few have gotten even close to.

When it came to expertise with press and messaging, the boys were so fortunate to have not one, but two masters of the art, both as different as night and day. The second man was more suave and Beatle-like than Barrow. He had a different style, but they both shared one common gift: total loyalty. Together, their impact on the Beatles' success was impressive.

CHAPTER TWENTY-NINE

PEN PAL #2–DEREK TAYLOR

"I tell you, Larry, that this is the greatest band ever. In the past, now and forever, as Brian says, people will still be listening to them in the next century."
—Derek Taylor, speaking to me on the Beatles' chartered
American Flyers airplane, August 1964

"I've always had a connection with Derek. In a way, Larry, he was encouraging to me. . . . I think he understands where I came from . . . if you know what I mean. He is really a friend."
—George Harrison, to me during the 1965 tour of America,
where Taylor was replaced by his colleague, Tony Barrow

HE LIVED A LIFE OF EXCITEMENT AND DRAMA, but it was what Derek Taylor did in the early 1960s that made his mark—proof of how what some key members of the press witnessed and wrote created the imagery that allowed the Beatles to prosper at such an accelerated pace. The fact that two journalistic giants later traded in their typewriters for flak jackets to protect and serve the Beatles became even more meaningful. Tony Barrow was first to join Epstein's team, followed by Derek Taylor. The latter was press officer in America in 1964, while Barrow covered the home front and the rest of the world. In a strange turnabout, Barrow covered the 1965 tour and Taylor moved to America and became an independent press agent.

In 1966, in a lounge at the Deauville Hotel in Miami, Derek Taylor and I reunited over a few drinks, and lots of talk. Taylor was probably the smoothest and most *entertaining* reporter, news professional, and communications executive I had ever met. While Tony Barrow fought for and protected the Beatles forcefully and without fingerprints, Derek Taylor was effusive and blunt. Sometimes, to some of the Beatles, he was a little too blunt. But while he could be a bit on the wild side, he was fantastically entertaining—though "entertaining" is a pure understatement. While Tony

Barrow was intense and absolutely serious back at the home office in London, or on the 1965 and 1966 tours, Taylor was a show within the show. And the show continued on that spring evening in '66.

"Larry, I tell you, the Byrds may be bigger than the Beatles."

"That's crazy," I said. "Really? How could that be?"

"Just listen to the music, and watch them."

"I doubt it, Derek."

"I know. But just watch."

One wonderful talent that Derek Taylor possessed was his skill as an illustrative writer. And his writing abilities and mastery of the language made him a dynamic promoter throughout his career. In the next year after our meeting in Miami Beach, he managed to create the imagery that the Byrds were indeed a decent challenger to the Beatles' early legacy, even though they really were not. He subsequently helped create the image of Brian Wilson of the Beach Boys as a developing musical icon, and practically *made* the early career of the eccentric musical artist Harry Nilsson. The rest of Taylor's remarkable career had him joined with such high-level groups as the Rolling Stones. Such were the talents of the smooth, extremely well-dressed, and strikingly handsome Derek Taylor, a man whose words, along with those of the distinguished Mr. Barrow and the demonstrative and prolific king of the home front, Bill Harry, created the early spark for the boys. There is no question in my mind that the words of Derek Taylor, Bill Harry, and Tony Barrow catapulted the Beatles. Taylor may have had a fleeting public relations affair with the Byrds, but in his life, it always came back to the Beatles.

He was a most interesting man.

If Derek Taylor could sing, his looks alone might have made him a pop icon. Of course, he was in room 1742 at the Queen Elizabeth Hotel in Montreal, a room packed with musical and other celebrities, when John Lennon put to music the song "Give Peace a Chance," a song that was played over and over again by antiwar activists in the early seventies. It appears that Taylor was singing, but it doesn't really matter. He used his expertise, now back in the Beatles sphere, to publicize and uniquely promote one of the most familiar peace songs of all time. The date was June 1, 1969, and Taylor was now with the Beatles' new Apple Corps. He told me then that the Beatles were "on their way to being the all-time standard for music," his beloved Byrds notwithstanding.

When Apple became embroiled in legal warfare in the seventies, Taylor moved on to even more groups. Once again, he came back to the nest, resuming work for Apple Corps in the 1990s until his death in 1997. In between those assignments, he did everything you could possibly imagine in the music business, including, much to my surprise, a short stint as a radio reporter in the Bahamas, visiting the Beatles as they filmed the movie *Help!* in February 1965. I was also there, doing the same job for my station in Miami. Sadly, Taylor, who had ghostwritten Brian Epstein's biography, helped George with his own national newspaper column, and supported the boys through thick and thin—a lot more thick than thin—got a rude welcome. He told me about it, and along with Beatles roadie and friend Malcolm Evans, we commiserated in a bar on Bay Street in Nassau, the first time I had seen him since he resigned as Beatles press officer at the end of the 1964 tour.

"Paul was a shit, pure fucking shit to me," he said.

"Why?" I asked.

"It's a long story, so piss off, Larry, and get your *own* interviews."

"I will."

"Fuck off. But on the other hand, can I use some of *your* interviews?" Taylor was now a "reporter," and Paul didn't like it.

"Of course!" I answered. "You can *borrow* any of my interviews."

When I emphasized "borrow," he laughed and hoisted another drink.

I laughed very hard, and so did Mal Evans.

Paul was irritated because Taylor was using his knowledge of the boys to acquire interviews and dig up stories. There is an irony to that point of view.

In one of his wonderful books, *As Time Goes By*, Derek, still hurt after all these years, wrote about his encounter with the Beatles during an assignment for KRLA radio in Los Angeles to raise money for his hoped-for public relations and marketing company.

"Paul was very mean in the Bahamas. I mean, mean," Taylor recalled.

Who is to blame him for feeling that way? Taylor remembered Paul saying, "Bloody hell, Derek. You with a tape recorder asking us questions?"

And what about John's reaction?

"I took John first . . . 'caustic' John, who was really nothing of the sort. He pulled a couple of desultory put-downs and then gave me as good a tape as you'll get if you're asking questions like, 'Whereja buy your boots?'"

George gave him a warm interview, talking about a wedding he attended; Ringo talked about marriage, and Paul. As he always did, Paul came around, giving Taylor an interview on songwriting. As Taylor remembered, "Paul decided not to be mean any longer, guessing correctly that life was bad enough without rubbing my nose in it. . . . "

But Taylor felt uncomfortable about his assignment for KRLA. For all the swagger and charm that I had witnessed Taylor display while traveling with him, he was emotionally devoted to the boys, a devotion that lasted until he died.

It was, after all, Derek Taylor who defied conventional wisdom and wrote a column in the *Manchester Daily Express* about the Beatles' performance at the Odeon Theater. As an "older man," in his thirties, Taylor shocked his bosses with his writing of the young group. If he liked them, would other adults fall in line? The piece was a big catalyst in their success. It was Taylor whose pen was mightier than the power of all those early promoters. He didn't help the Beatles get a recording contract, like Tony Barrow did, but, in love with their music and style, the extremely honest pressman chronicled and fanned the flames of their dramatic rise. He eventually made his peace with Paul McCartney, and with the help of Neil Aspinall, worked for Apple until his death.

But back in Nassau, with him as a journalist again, we all understood what was happening. In that location, John and George were especially helpful. George had admired Taylor as a passionate friend from the beginning, and in Nassau made sure he got all the interviews he needed.

One of the reasons Taylor had resigned as their press officer after the famous 1964 summer tour was that he had a falling-out with Brian Epstein, who felt that Taylor had become too close to the boys, and had a bit too much power. Taylor also realized that becoming "one of them," as he had, brought a familiarity that could also breed contempt. And although he was the happiest human being in public, Paul McCartney was the self-appointed emotionless conscience of the group when it came to complaining about friends trying to exploit their success. Never mind that Derek Taylor practically put them on the map with his detailed, super-descriptive journalism for the *Manchester Daily Express*.

And the man had ups and downs—with the most notable down being the falling-out with Epstein, who hired him to join his organization in 1964, and selected him to ghostwrite Epstein's own autobiography, *A Cellarful of Noise*. There was a friction-filled relationship with Paul McCartney, whom he really admired. John was always respectful. George was really his friend, to the end. And toward the end, Taylor understood that the biggest part of his nonfamily life was the boys. It's an irony, though, that they rode to triumph partly on his words. And the words of Derek Taylor, *the reporter*, will tell you all you need to know.

In his collector's-item book of 1984, *Fifty Years Adrift*, with George Harrison as editor, I found, along with some mentions of me (a gratifying ego boost), some extraordinary gems, including a nod to his wife, Joan, from the spring of 1963.

"Joan's recall of the events leading up to the 'Night Our Brains Caught Fire' [i.e., the first time they saw the Beatles] is more exact than mine. She first heard of the Beatles in late 1962 from her teenage sister Diane who still lived in Merseyside. Of all of the groups, Diane said, it was the Beatles who stood out. Indeed I heard her say that many times before they became famous. Then Joan saw them for herself on Granada TV. . . . 'They were astounding,' [she said, adding that] they seemed so confident and appealing."

Taylor added:

"There was nothing about them in the national press. . . . Time passed. The Beatles' second single, 'Please Please Me,' went to number one. The event was not front-page news, nor were the Beatles. . . . To the west . . . *Mersey Beat*, a newspaper edited by the estimable Bill Harry, had everything covered; but we in Manchester were not going to be left out of this for much longer."

In several months, Derek Taylor would see it for himself.

The Beatles had made an earlier appearance at the Manchester Playhouse in 1962, the night Pete Best was attacked with the scissors, the night Paul McCartney's usually warm and generous dad Jim scolded Pete for taking attention away from the boys, presumably because he became a victim of attack.

But their biggest date in Manchester was yet to come—May 30, 1963—as part of a national tour with American star Roy Orbison and Liverpool's Gerry and the Pacemakers. The setting was the venerable Odeon Theater, and Derek and members of his family were there. Writing for the *Daily Express*, Taylor shocked his readers and his bosses with his review. The editors thought that, at the age of thirty-one, real adulthood, Taylor would be unfazed by the Liverpool music craze. The editors were wrong.

In his book, Taylor recalls the night:

"This beguiling and beguiled postwar generation of teenagers was about to see the greatest group of entertainers the world had ever seen. . . . Two hours later, it was over bar the screaming. Joan and I knew that something of extraordinary power had been acted out before our eyes. Went to the telephone and in a rush of blood and words to the head, I dictated the review without a note, just as it came, and they printed all but one paragraph of it."

The actual review, headlined "Derek Taylor Gaily Crashes Through the Liverpool Sound Barrier," became a dynamic moment in the boys' career. It was read throughout the nation on May 31 and after. It was written with the same "bite" and "edge" that Taylor displayed a year later as press chief for the boys and traveling companion to me and a lucky few on that insane 1964 North American tour. But who knew at the time that Derek's words, vision, and expertise would lead to something else. The review was at once skeptical but prophetic. It read, in part:

BECAUSE OF THE CITY OF LIVERPOOL, POPULAR MUSIC, AFTER YEARS OF TURMOIL AND UNSPEAKABLE RUBBISH, HAS BECOME HEALTHY AND GAY AND GOOD AGAIN. THE LIVERPOOL SOUND CAME TO MANCHESTER LAST NIGHT AND I THOUGHT IT WAS MAGNIFICENT . . . INDECIPHERABLE, MEANINGLESS NONSENSE. . . .

THE SPECTACLE OF THESE FRESH, CHEEKY, SHARP YOUNG ENTER-
TAINERS TO THE SHINY-EYED TEENAGE IDOLATERS IS AS GOOD AS A REJU-
VENATED DRUG FOR THE JADED ADULT. . . . THE BEATLES AND GERRY AND
THE PACEMAKERS WERE A FAIR-SIZED SENSATION. . . . THEY HAVE IN
ABUNDANCE THE FUNDAMENTAL GOOD HUMOUR OF THEIR NATIVE
CITY. . . . IT WAS REALLY THE BEATLES WE HAD GONE TO SEE. . . . WHEN
THE NO-LAPELLED, SHINY BLACK SUITS AND THESE BLACK ROMAN HAIR-
CUTS APPEARED TO A CASCADE OF OUTRAGEOUS PRAISE FROM THE
COMPERE [EMCEE], THE CINEMA WENT WILD. NOBODY COULD HEAR
THEMSELVES TRYING TO THINK. THE ACT WAS LARGELY DROWNED, BUT
IT DIDN'T MATTER AT ALL. IT WAS MARVELOUS, MEANINGLESS, IMPERTI-
NENT, EXHILARATING STUFF.

Taylor knew the music world would never be the same. He began covering the Beatles on a regular basis, and the column he wrote on Brian Epstein
was another headliner. Epstein was formal to Taylor's casual; careful to
Taylor's candid; and somewhat shy to Taylor's brash command of the language. But Taylor was fascinated by Epstein's intuition, and almost overnight
turned the former retailer into a management sensation.

On June 20, 1963, Taylor wrote in the *Express*, "Epstein, the brain behind
the Beatles . . . Epstein knows a hit when he hears one, and twenty months
earlier he heard such a hit [from the Beatles]."

Taylor profiled the unlikely pop master, who at that point had signed the
Beatles, Gerry and the Pacemakers, and Billy J. Kramer and the Dakotas.

Taylor wrote many stories about the boys, but perhaps his most significant
piece, now read *around the world*, published on January 15, 1964. Dateline:
Versailles: "As midnight struck in Versailles . . . the Beatles conquered the
town, and by implication, France."

Next was the world. And after France, the United States was waiting.

By the spring of 1964, Derek Taylor was a personal assistant to Brian
Epstein, and in the summer he joined the Beatles on tour. The reporter
suddenly became the man who protected the boys from other reporters. His
relationship with them lasted thirty-four years in all.

His most significant impact, though, was in the words he wrote—how he phrased them—and his wry but illustrative description of the boys and their music.

When I think of Taylor, I think of what George shared with me one night: "Derek is the most honest person. We've always been close, always will be. . . . He taught me so much, some of it surprising, about life . . . things like the royal family's original softness toward Hitler. . . . He taught me to just be myself . . . which I always tried to be."

Derek Taylor was a master ghostwriter, especially for George. And during his early friendship with George, he learned quickly that George was more than just a musician. While John and Paul may have discounted George's input, Taylor discovered early on that George was a heavy-duty thinker.

During one of our soul-searching conversations on the meaning of life, and the meaning of the Beatles, Taylor made a memorable point.

"Just remember," he said, "[George] has enormous intellectual curiosity; he wants to know everything. I won't go into detail, except to say that he has critiqued some of my writing attributed to him. That's always a risk, but it's worth it when you can have a candid talk and understand exactly what that person means. George may be the youngest Beatle and all that, but he is beyond his years in his values, and his pursuit of the truth, and I might add quite candidly, his ability to [be] direct and sometimes painfully honest."

George always had fond memories of Taylor, whom he helped profile in their joint book, *Fifty Years Adrift*. Taylor is an easy man to remember, a distinct personality, a man with a wonderful sense of the language and a pure instinct for when to intervene, as I remember from one of my first experiences with the boys.

When I think of Taylor, I recall the time I met John for the first time. John, looking me up and down, asked me if I was a "nerd" from the fifties. I called him a "slob." As I left the room, dejected about my first encounter with the boys' founder, Taylor said, "Well, that was a fucking piss!" I laughed hard, then realized that I had erred. Moments later, John ran out into the corridor, hugged me, and apologized—very un-John-like.

I will forever believe that it was Taylor who sent him out to make things right.

Derek Taylor had another rare and important talent: he could calm down both the boys, and an audience of thousands, at the same time. His only unsuccessful attempt at this enterprise was his attempt to stop 7,000 fans from storming the stage in Vancouver, British Columbia, in August 1964. But a month later, in Cleveland, he was successful in addressing the audience. Frightened Cleveland police officials, with no real reason, surrendered to the hysteria of the crowd and shut down the concert. The Beatles were angry in the dressing room; the crowd was ready to explode. Taylor talked both City Hall and the boys into resuming the show. Then, in his smooth and charismatic way, he walked up to the microphone, addressed the crowd, and soothed them with a soft warning that they had to calm down so the Beatles could come back on stage.

It worked.

At their Seattle hotel in 1964, the boys pissed on the rug of their suite after hearing that the staff wanted to cut it up and sell it to fans.

When reporters asked Taylor about this, he replied, "In the case of the alleged moisture on the floor covering, I can neither confirm nor deny. The truth is that . . . well . . . well . . . I think *I have to go now!*" Taylor was a wonderful teaser.

Both Derek Taylor and the amazing Tony Barrow had a finite understanding of how to promote the aura of the Beatles. Taylor was especially interested in visuals. And both men continued employing a technique mentioned earlier. In most of the movie-theater concerts, they would allow limited film by the newsreel photographers of the day. The photojournalists were encouraged to show the delirious crowds, and in some cases, the fans chasing cars down the street. By the time the boys got to America in 1964, American fans were quite ready to emulate the UK hysteria—and they did, with gusto. There is no doubt that the two press giants were able to stage the filming of the wildness and love of the crowds. Was it a distorted look? Quite the contrary. The original newsreel footage in the UK, mostly of smaller crowds and smaller venues than the Beatles would face in America, did show a realistic sense of the rampages and uncontrolled crowds that followed the boys and their music. The images gave a picture of emotion, regardless of the size of the crowd. Imagine the work of two great and former writers and promotion men carefully serving as gatekeepers to the British press. The Beatles were already the stuff of legend, but the pictures reinforced their imagery.

There is no question that Taylor channeled the Beatles in his appearance and style. For that, he would always get heat. Epstein was especially wary of his style. But as a pen pal, a buddy of sorts, and a real crowd-pleaser, Taylor did the job both on stage and off.

CHAPTER THIRTY

MOMENTUM WITH A ROYAL AND FOREIGN TOUCH

*"Suddenly, they were a real happening. Even the adults were digging them.
As I said, 'It was big.'. . . They were about seven to eight years older than me,
but the shoes, the hair, the dynamic style . . . all of that became a standard
for the times. I just thought, 'If only I could play with them . . . '"*
—Alan White, drummer for the band Yes and for the Plastic Ono Band

THERE WERE TRIUMPHS AND DANGER LURKING BEHIND THE SCENES IN THE FALL OF 1963.

Many dates have been described as the beginning of Beatlemania, but only one really qualifies, and that is October 13, 1963, when the Beatles appeared on the TV show *Live at the London Palladium*. The national showcase was a blockbuster, and the British press covered the event in the Monday papers as a major cultural event.

Part of the success was due to the mother of all photo ops. "Looking back," Tony Barrow says, "I would like to have taken credit for staging this event, and some press agents would have said they did stage it, but I had nothing to do with it."

"It" was a spontaneous near-riot near the Palladium's entrances, with teenage girls and boys straining the patience of usually reserved London police officers, resembling a modern-day flash mob, moving back and forth in waves and hoping that strength in numbers would help them get to the boys.

The press responded in kind with Monday headlines like "Beatles Fever," and yes, the first occasion of the printed word in the national media— "Beatlemania." The photos and the story of this new phase of fever were noticed by the nation.

Alan White, future drummer of the progressive rock group Yes and John Lennon's drummer on the immortal track "Imagine," was fourteen when he saw the show, and read the papers. He chose his career path early, first as a guitarist, then as a drummer. In 1963, he was looking for inspiration at all levels, and the ascent of the Beatles got him excited and inspired him to make a career of it.

"I was so thrilled. Four northern boys [Alan was from northern England] suddenly the rage of the nation. Like all young musicians, I thought that could be me out there. And they were so good. Watching them on TV, listening to the records."

During a chat with me before a Yes gig in Atlantic City, New Jersey, in 2010, White remembered the impact of that appearance.

"Suddenly, they were a real happening. Even the adults were digging them. As I said, 'It was big.' . . . They were about seven to eight years older than me, but the shoes, the hair, the dynamic style . . . all of that became a standard for the times. I just thought, 'If only I could play with them . . .'"

White got his wish when he received a call from John six years later, inviting him to Toronto for the "Live Peace" effort, along with Eric Clapton and, back again with John, old friend from Hamburg Klaus Voorman. Two years later, White would play the drums on "Imagine."

"I lived the dream of every young musician. When I got that call from John, who had seen me in some clubs in London, I thought it was a prank. I said, 'No way it is John Lennon on the phone.' But it was."

So, really, along with the music, the Palladium appearance was an emotional moment for White, and for the nation. People in Liverpool watched with awe. After all, Tony Bramwell remembers, "It was those same boys at Litherland Town Hall in December of 1960, the friend [George Harrison on the number 61 bus], but now they were on the national TV."

Ten days after the Palladium, there was a journey that proved beyond doubt that John, Paul, George, and Ringo had gone international—arriving for their first real foreign tour, in Sweden. If you don't count Hamburg, which the Beatles first visited as an unknown band, Sweden was their first journey overseas as a hit group.

Behind the scenes, though, the boys' obsession with sex almost got out of control.

Mal Evans remembered the "selection process": "There were many beautiful girls in Stockholm, but I was getting a bit upset because the guys were taking too many chances, going where they shouldn't have been going."

"Where is that?" I asked.

"Not going to say," Mal replied, "not even to you, Larry."

Turns out that Brian Epstein was also concerned, for fear that winding up with more teenagers would be a scandal. But Neil Aspinall, always loyal, and John, always looking, convinced Epstein that "all was in order." That was Epstein's version of things.

The "selection process," as Mal described it to me, was fairly organized: find the young women, screen them to determine their safety and maturity, and make sure their ages were appropriate. How Mal and others could make those judgments always fascinated me. As it turns out, the episode in Las Vegas with the young girls was the closest to a full-blown scandal, even though nothing happened. But it is very obvious that in the contemporary environment, the Beatles and their buddies would never have survived the tabloid press. That they did survive the press in 1963, and later when I toured with them over three summers, is a testament to the protectionism of Neil Aspinall and the guile of Mal Evans, and their intense loyalty to the boys. There were "tell-all" books published that presumed to know how the boys "operated," but none came from the immediate traveling circle. Tony Barrow, Derek Taylor, and Tony Bramwell all wrote memoirs, but none included any play-by-play of the boys' sex lives. In the modern day, that would be expected, but not so in the sixties.

Bramwell, one of the most fascinating people I've ever met in the entertainment world, does admit that sometimes the fruits of celebrity were shared, especially in the early rush of fame in 1963. "We all shagged the same people, at times. And the boys had a great time in Sweden."

Outside of what might have been unnecessary risk-taking, the Beatles were a big hit in Sweden, an omen that the American tours might also be a hit. The biggest problem, according to Aspinall, was that "local authorities were not ready for the security measures that were necessary," though some of the concert halls were not sold out. One newspaper reported that even though there were some empty seats, the people who *were* there were "in a state of craziness."

The Sweden tour—nine concerts in five days—was covered as a huge international success. In their lives, news coverage played a big part in the "avalanche" of success. When the Beatles returned to London on October 31, 1963, 20,000 fans were waiting at the airport. Epstein remembered, "The boys thought the crowd was waiting for the queen. They couldn't believe they were there for them."

Though the queen was not there, the Beatles would soon be breathing the same air as royalty.

Back home, safely on British soil, the Beatles got ready for the biggest show of all, one that cemented their early success and accelerated the tremendous wave of national pride that was already rolling through Britain. The Beatles had received an invitation from Buckingham Palace to entertain at the Royal Command Performance at the Prince of Wales Theater in London's West End. The charity gala was a tradition going back to the Victorian era. The queen would be there, along with other royalty and members of high society.

It was not a solo engagement—there were nineteen acts on the bill—but it may have been the boys' most important gig yet. Also on the bill was American entertainer Sophie Tucker, movie icon Marlene Dietrich, and others. Would the boys win over England's society crowd, and how would the royal family accept the phenoms of the North?

Despite urgings from Epstein to tone it down, the boys stuck true to form, ending a four-song set with the always raucous "Twist and Shout."

Mal Evans was more nervous than he would be the night he met Elvis in the summer of 1965 when, he later told me, "Met me idol. I was a fan all the way."

In the fancy dressing room, Mal remembered, "I was nearly paralyzed—all those royals out there. Even [usually unflappable] Neil was very, very nervous."

While Mal and Aspinall and George and Ringo were "terrified," according to Mal, Epstein was nearly a "wreck."

He was nervous that John would say something. And he was right; there turned out to be a "something." Looking upbeat and totally animated, the former milkman of Menlove Avenue addressed the well-heeled audience on his own terms.

"Will people in the cheaper seats clap your hands? All the rest of you, if you'll just rattle your jewelry . . . "

Laughter filled the house. The crowd, roused by young people in the audience, saved their most strident applause for the Beatles.

The *Daily Mail* proclaimed in its headline, "The Royal Box Was Stomping." And the *Daily Express* noted, "Night of Triumph for Four Young Men."

The *Daily Mirror* was the one Fleet Street tabloid that from the beginning tried to "own" the Beatles. The newspaper had 6 million readers, and they were treated to a magnanimous review, with the use of the word "Beatlemania" and several image-making lines:

"It's plain to see why these four cheeky energetic lads from Liverpool go down so big."

"They're young, new. They're high spirited. . . . They don't have to rely on off-colour jokes about homos for their fun."

Incredible words from today's perspective, and even more incredible considering their authors were unaware of Epstein's sexual preference and John's incessant obsession with satirizing homosexuals, who were not referred to as "gay," but as something more offensive.

Obviously, neither Tony Barrow nor Derek Taylor wrote the story. Barrow, though, knew the impact that the concert would provide. Though Queen Elizabeth II was pregnant and could not attend, her mother, also known as Queen Elizabeth the Queen Mother, was there, along with her daughter, the popular Princess Margaret, and her husband, the photographer Lord Snowden.

Once again, writer and press chief Tony Barrow was overwhelmed.

"The combination of the Palladium, TV, the first full foreign tour to Sweden, and the Royal Performance on November 4th, had already built up bits and pieces of major publicity in America. It was all an unstoppable barrage, and since we were planning a brief visit to the US in February, this was more than we could ask for."

Add to all of this Epstein's master plan for nonstop concerts in December at cinemas all across Britain, and the charge of the Beatles was in manic mode.

The year 1963—early, mid, and as you will learn, much later—was the biggest year for the boys and Brian. For Tony Barrow, there were seminal moments when everything came together.

THE FAVORITE MOMENTS WERE WHEN THE SINGLES "PLEASE PLEASE ME," AND THEN "FROM ME TO YOU," BECAME NUMBER-ONE HITS IN THE UK. LATER WE BECAME WELL USED TO THE GROUP TAKING EACH RELEASE ALMOST AUTOMATICALLY TO THE TOP, AND THERE WAS NEVER THE SAME THRILL FOR US; IT BECAME AN EXPECTATION. I HAVE ALWAYS DATED THE BIRTH OF BEATLEMANIA TO THE AUTUMN OF THAT YEAR WHEN WE GOT A HUGE AMOUNT OF MEDIA PUBLICITY IN THE WAKE OF THE BEATLES' APPEARANCE ON UK TELEVISION'S SUNDAY NIGHT AT THE LONDON PALLADIUM—WHEN PRESS PHOTOGRAPHERS CAPTURED THE ENORMOUSLY EXCITING ATMOSPHERE OF THE FANS GATHERING OUTSIDE THE THEATER IN LONDON'S ARGYLL STREET—FOLLOWED ONLY A FEW WEEKS LATER BY THE SECOND BURST OF PUBLICITY THAT SURROUNDED THE GROUP'S APPEARANCE IN THE 1963 ROYAL VARIETY PERFORMANCE, WHICH INCLUDED JOHN'S CHEEKY REQUEST FOR PEOPLE TO "RATTLE THEIR JEWELRY."

What about the boys?

"It was so nonstop, we were so tired," Barrow said.

"So much to do and so little time to do it," John Lennon remarked months later.

"The Palladium was exciting," Paul McCartney recalled. "The queen's concert . . . well, that was highbrow, and we were nervous. It was a case of 'touch me, is this really happening?'"

Back home, Allan Williams was incredulous. Could this be happening? In a recent late-morning conversation at the Hard Day's Night Hotel, Williams's cheery cheeks turn flush, as he remembers:

"We used to have a very important national television program every

Sunday. *Live at the Sunday Palladium* or something like that, and I was watching that show [when] the Beatles came on, and they were sensational, and I thought, 'Fuckin' hell, that's my group!' As they progressed, I was quite pleased, because even though I was only a small item in life, at least I was a cog in the wheel of . . . what was to become one of the most famous pop groups in the world."

The pioneers in Liverpool—Sam Leach, Allan Williams, Bob Wooler, Brian Kelly, the somewhat angry Mona Best, the family members—were in a state of shock, disbelief, and in some cases, joy. And John's sibling states the simple fact:

"That was my brother."

The very intense Julia Baird (Lennon) sips her soda, her eyes wandering around the back room of the new Cavern, remembering the excitement in 1963.

"This was the same boy who danced with our mother, lived under the tyranny of Mimi, skipped school—the irreverent but passionate older sibling. He was leading the group that started as a ragtag skiffle gang. He was *famous*. All of England was into him. It was disbelief. But it was so much fun. I wished Mother would have been around to see this, to see where that first guitar had taken him."

Mal Evans, the unfortunate Mal, recalled the fall of '63 as we reminisced in 1966.

"For Neil and me and Brian, it was, you know, the most amazing time. We went from helping them, to driving them, to protecting them. I tried to be a gentle lad, but now I had to use my size to keep people away. And now we thought, 'What would happen in America?'"

The seeds for that journey were planted.

That October and November were indeed sensational, but in the offices of some Hollywood executives, the stage had been set for a dramatic sequence of events in a December to remember. And it all happened before the boys' feet touched American soil.

CHAPTER THIRTY-ONE

A DECEMBER TO REMEMBER—
THE END OR THE BEGINNING?

*"Could I have imagined a future like that? Who could? But, looking back,
I knew they had something special, and a level of compassion
that was truly unusual for a band on the move."*
—Joe Ankrah, Beatles friend whose band was pushed
through racial barriers by the boys

*"I knew they were now beyond Merseyside, but I never knew
they would go that far."*
—Billy J. Kramer, on his feelings about the group in late 1963

DECEMBER 1963 HAD ONLY ONE SIMILARITY TO THAT BLEAK, DEPRESSING, and uncertain December 1960 in the aftermath of Hamburg—the weather was damp and cold.

Three years earlier, a chance appearance at Litherland Town Hall revived the sagging Beatles, with the screams of the fans, the sudden chemistry, and the animal instincts flowing from the stage reigniting that one element of life that you can't put a price on: hope. After all, December 1960 was the month the boys almost called it quits.

Now, three years later, Brian Epstein's Beatles were on the verge of the unthinkable—world domination—although again, even in late 1963, there were doubts.

"If we couldn't make it in America, it would be another setback. America would be the key," John Lennon shared with me almost exactly a year after December 1963.

If there was any problem facing the boys, it was the schedule—at least 223 concerts in 1963, and twenty in December alone, from De Montfort Hall in Leicester on December 1 to New Year's Eve at the Astoria Cinema in London, where they continued their Christmas show for the first eleven days of 1964. That's thirty-one concerts in forty-two days. And one day later, January 12, they finished with a concert at the London Palladium, the scene of an earlier nationwide TV spectacle. They had just three days left before heading to Europe. There were few breaks in their schedule, rare time off, and the suffocating, almost paralyzing life of arrival, hotel, concert venue, hotel, and departure, complicated by the reality that the boys were known to stay up late, discover sunrise at 11 a.m., and eat poorly. All that, combined with heavy smoking and bouts of heavy drinking, made for an unhealthy environment.

Buddy Tony Bramwell remembers the total exasperation and sense of frustration on the part of the boys, anxiety mixed with excitement. He recalls, when he joined them in their wild finish to 1963, that they were haggard, drunked-out, flush with cigarette smoke, and at the same time sleepless, "yawning with joy, wondering if the ride would continue as it was, getting bigger and bigger."

Compared to today's helter-skelter tours, the boys' schedule was breathless. The best band in the world was the busiest, and at times, the most tired. But while they were playing, things were stirring, not only across the English Channel in Europe, but to the west, across the ocean.

Press reports began emerging in America. They were spotty, but pen pals Bill Harry, Tony Barrow, and the ever-smooth Derek Taylor made sure the best pictures of the boys and screaming fans made their way into the newspapers. After all, especially late in the year, Americans themselves were in a state of high anxiety, still in shock after the November 22 murder of President Kennedy. A little diversion from national mourning was well received by the press and the people.

There was little film available, although the *CBS Evening News with Walter Cronkite* aired a short clip of the Beatles and their surrounding fanatics on the December 10, 1963, broadcast, leading Cronkite to claim later that he had the Beatles first. He did, in America at least.

The man who had so much impact on the Vietnam War, the man who conquered the space race on TV, claimed the Beatles as his own.

In late 1989, I hosted Cronkite at a community luncheon in Philadelphia.

The news legend said, "Larry, heard you traveled with the Beatles."

I responded, "Well, yes."

"You know," he said, "I had the first film of them."

"Really," I replied.

What Walter didn't know was that Tony Barrow and Derek Taylor were unleashing that campaign of specified distribution of Beatles information that may have been one of the most coordinated media campaigns in history, with bits and pieces of film, information, and pictures of hysteria combining to create an imagery of combustible emotion. Crowds in small theaters and ballrooms looked like thousands, when really they were mostly in the hundreds. News reports of a coming "British Invasion" were rampant, with most of the attention paid to the boys' hair, which at that time in history had an effect of shock on adults in America. The buildup was working. And then Christmas came, with a day-after surprise.

The day after Christmas was important. Although a few stations had claimed earlier broadcast, most American Top 40 radio stations began playing "I Want to Hold Your Hand" on December 26. Its flip side, "I Saw Her Standing There," was also instantly popular. The 45-rpm record sold over 250,000 copies in the first few days.

In Liverpool, Freda Kelly did her usual due diligence, treating the boys' families like her own, keeping lines of communication open to the growing fan-club base. Barrow and Taylor, on tour and in the offices in London and Liverpool, plotted. The American invasion was not far away. Kelly was still trying to convince Elsie Starkey that while her piggy bank was smart thinking, it was time to stop worrying about filling it, that Richie would be fine.

The tired Fab Four, a term coined by the talented Tony Barrow, was trying to cope with their December schedule, while thinking about what January would bring.

First, there would be a long stint in Paris. It was in Paris that Epstein and the jubilant boys, still in the discovery phase of huge celebrity, would learn that "I Want to Hold Your Hand" had reached number one in America. John would later say to me, "We celebrated with milk." And he said it with a straight face.

As 1963 drew to a close, Pete Best chatted, when he could find him, with his friend Neil Aspinall. Pete, depressed but unselfish, congratulated Aspinall on the good fortune of the group that had left him behind. The Prince of Mathew Street, Sam Leach, watched with curiosity as the local boys began screaming into Earth's orbit. Allan Williams, the man who let them get away, and who told Brian Epstein, "Don't touch them with a fucking bargepole; they will let you down," was fascinated by their ascent. Deejay and writer Bob Wooler was bittersweet—proud but sad that his boys, even errant John Lennon, who had beaten him up, were headed for America. Tony Bramwell, their helper for so many horrible road trips on so many rugged roads, was humbled, and ready for new worldwide adventures with the boys and many who came after them.

As the clock struck midnight ringing in 1964, Mona Best remembered the warmth and charm of a Beatles performance at the Casbah on New Year's Eve 1960. She was melancholy about those days and worried about Pete, who took an immense interest in his much younger brother Vincent Roag, who was about to turn eighteen months old. Roag, as he was called, the product of Mona's affair with Neil Aspinall, brought brightness and joy to the Best household. Aspinall, who had emerged early as one of the most savvy "protection" people in the business, was mentally preparing himself for France and, of course, America. In another life, Aspinall surely would have been an advance security chief for the White House or 10 Downing Street. He was that good.

Cynthia Lennon was in love and caring for her and John's almost nine-month-old son, Julian. The coming year of 1964 would see a changing relationship with Johnny Boy, although in late 1963 Cynthia was described by friends as "blissful."

In December 1963, Yoko Ono's first child, Kyoko, was four and a half months old, the child of her relationship and marriage to entertainer and producer Anthony Cox. It would be a little less than three years later when she met John at an art gallery in London.

The Quarrymen were scattered around Europe: Colin Hanton, the last of the Quarry boys to leave the band, was developing his skills as an upholsterer.

Rod Davis continued his brilliant march through higher education, graduating in 1963 from Cambridge and looking for a teaching job at home in Liverpool. Len Garry, somewhat of a teen idol, in his mind rivaling Paul McCartney in the very early days, was aiming to become an architect.

Horst Fascher could only watch with wonder. Just a year earlier, he claimed to me, he had "slipped thirty dollars under the table in 1962 to persuade Brian Epstein to allow the Beatles to perform one last time in Hamburg."

Members of Kingsize Taylor and the Dominoes could only watch in disgust as the Beatles were about to extend their stardom across the sea. Teddy Taylor, the leader of the group, was especially bitter. He is still a popular performer in Hamburg, where he lives. Many friends, family, and survivors of that era believe that Kingsize could have been as big. Others remain friends with him but say his songwriting abilities were lacking. Like that of Pete Best, the name Teddy Taylor still, to this day, evokes words of respect in Liverpool.

The sweetest man in the Beatles' inner circle, Malcolm Evans, received the okay in late December to bring his wife and son on the Beatles' January invasion of Paris. Malcolm, who loved the boys almost as much his own family, became legendary for fighting with a journalist in Paris, an incident, he told me later, that "I would be proud of for the rest of my life." From my perspective, Malcolm would have gone to any extreme to protect the Beatles, but especially John and George.

And then, of course, there was the continuing "campaign."

In mid-December an internal memo from Paul Russell, national album merchandising manager for Capitol Records, outlined a series of actions under way in advance of the arrival of Beatles music in America. Russell wrote: "A film clip of the Beatles in writhing action will be shown on the Jack Paar show January 3 [Paar was the host of *The Tonight Show*]. . . . The Beatles are scheduled to make two live appearances on the *Ed Sullivan Show*." A third would actually be taped for broadcast.

"United Artists, which will be distributing the Beatles' first film [*A Hard Day's Night*] this summer . . . is already . . . 'booming' the Beatles."

Russell's memo, to all key Capitol executives, had a lot more, but the final paragraph said it all:

"The message is certainly clear. There are a lot of people who are putting up big money to ensure that the Beatles are the biggest thing yet in America. We should be fully prepared to take every possible advantage of the 'Beatles Snowball.'"

The "snowball" was rolling on and on. On December 27, 1963, I was driving south from St. Louis to take a job as news director of WFUN radio in Miami, when I entered the city limits of Paducah, Kentucky, a community based at the confluence of the Ohio and Tennessee Rivers. I remember the city for two reasons. First was the dramatic site of the two rivers churning into each other; I had never seen the beauty of nature that way, actual white-caps on a river. As I passed through Paducah, after traveling through southern Illinois and then into Kentucky, the second memorable moment hit me—the realization that the "boys" were everywhere. Every time I switched the dial to a new radio station, it was the same song, "I Want to Hold Your Hand." It was catchy and it was catching on. Once in a while, something else would play—"It's My Party" by Lesley Gore, "Walk Like a Man" by the Four Seasons, "Surfin' USA" by the Beach Boys, who were themselves growing in popularity, and some others. The station in Paducah also had a surprise for me—the playing of "She Loves You," already number two on the charts in England and a close second to "I Want to Hold Your Hand" in America. "She Loves You" was actually sneak-released by some stations in the summer of 1963, but no one paid attention. Now it was dug out of the files, and there it was. "Another catchy song," I thought.

At the time, the Beatles were just a curiosity for me, as they were for most. I was used to fads and one-hit wonders. Having heard a few reports about these shaggy-haired kids from northern England, I had serious doubts until I heard their songs for the first time. By the time I reached Miami, I had heard two other new Beatles songs, "Love Me Do" and "I Saw Her Standing There."

Now *that*, as I consider Paul Russell's memo, was really a snowball.

But, being a reporter, I was fascinated but hardly convinced. It was that skepticism, and more challenging questions than they were used to, that I truly believe brought me closer to the boys when fate and a little bit of luck took me into their world eight months later.

In a way, my story of the Beatles was told in reverse. I first met them in Miami on their first trip to America in February 1964, was the only reporter to travel with them on their complete 1964 and 1965 North American tours (plus most of the 1966 tour), and thirty-nine years later, wrote about the adventures in my book *Ticket to Ride* (Running Press, September 2003). Two years after that, I chronicled the adult life of Johnny Boy himself in *Lennon Revealed* (Running Press, September 2005). But even then, I never knew the story of how it really was in the beginning, before I knew them.

That story is, to me, as fascinating as their success, which endures. The other story, of the people who helped make them enduring, was elusive at the time.

The truth is that in the waning days of 1963, people like Bob Wooler, Sam Leach, Freda Kelly, Allan Williams, and many, many others knew that their part of the drama was beginning to end, although Tony Barrow, Derek Taylor, Tony Bramwell, and their friends would stay on for decades. For Mal Evans and the multitalented Neil Aspinall, there would be plenty of drama in the years ahead. Other entertainers knew already that the Beatles were moving to a new level.

But did they know just how big the band would become?

Billy Kinsley: "Did I know in '63 that they would be the greatest of all time? No one did, but we did know that Liverpool would soon be but a memory."

Billy J. Kramer: "There was no sense of competing. I felt that I was good, and I knew they were climbing. I appreciated everything they gave me, and taught me. I knew they were now beyond Merseyside, but I never knew they would go that far."

Joe Ankrah: "Could I have imagined a future like that? Who could? But looking back, I knew they had something special, and a level of compassion that was truly unusual for a band on the move."

As best buddy Bob Wooler closed out the year of 1963, he told friends that there was a feeling, bittersweet, of happiness and regret. "They [will] soon leave us," he said to some fans at the Cavern.

The truth, and a sobering truth it is, is that talent does not necessarily succeed. I wonder how many great songs are mothballed in someone's attic, never to be recorded, and how many truly great novels sit unpublished, never to be read. And with thoughts like that, life invariably brings you to consider all the "ifs" and all the "what-ifs."

What if all the "players" had not been in place? What if the "pen pals" had not been so smart, talented, and loyal? What if the families had not been so driving and supportive? What if the media manipulation had not been so beautifully orchestrated? What if so many different people had not been as dedicated as they were? What if . . .

So the story is really more than just the "boys," but also about all the "ifs" that materialized and the talent that emerged with a lot of help from their friends. There was the strong belief and dedication from a young and forceful businessman, shining through the fog of indifference. There were setbacks and internal struggles juxtaposed against extraordinary luck and good timing.

When they were boys, it was John, Paul, George, Pete and Ringo, and Stu. But whether it was the Casbah, the Cavern, the hundreds of church and community halls, and whether it was fifty or five thousand people, the boys' early moments of success and their eventual musical immortality was a mutual affair—small or large, the crowds feasted on the Beatles and the boys were driven by them. Perhaps the greatest tribute to each of them is the amazing discovery of this group by millions of people over the past fifty years, after they became men.

So, the story of the early days, "when they were boys," is in fact the story of four lives, and the people who molded them, for better and for worse. It remains the ultimate rags-to-riches story, the kind that we revel in. But it is also a story of amazing good luck, discovered and nurtured talent, and a band of buddies, confidantes, and savvy operators who helped them "snowball" their way to success. It is also the story of those left behind who made invaluable contributions, but who were not, in some cases, acknowledged by the stars they helped make. It's a story about millions of people around the globe who savored their music. Once they got there, the elements of human emotion took over, and like the early days, division and rancor ruled at times, along with drug use and a search for happiness.

The history is filled with many crevasses, deep moral failures. They made their way to the top with great skill, but in the beginning, when they were just boys, when their music was rejected, they leaned on the embrace and support of many people who, in turn, were never beneficiaries of the gigantic largesse, whether with fame or fortune. Many of them have the real knowledge that they were blessed to lend a helping hand. Some of them were rarely acknowledged, and yet others were completely forgotten. When Hunter Davies wrote the Beatles' authorized biography in the late 1960s, it was really their version of events, much like *The Beatles Anthology*, released in 2000, which was again produced and distributed by the Beatles empire. Davies's book *The Quarrymen* was an outstanding look at the first band. But yet, over time, the lives of Freda Kelly, Sam Leach, Billy Kinsley, Bob Wooler, Pete Best, Mal Evans, and so many others have been mere footnotes in the boys' own history. You could probably say the same about many successful people, but in this case, the people left behind made a major contribution.

On October 9, 2010, a John Lennon tribute in Liverpool marked what would have been his seventieth birthday. Bill and Virginia Harry were invited, but Virginia was ill, so Bill trekked solo to the north to check it out. When he got to the event, he was surprised that he had just a ticket, like anyone else, to get in—no special pass or any recognition of his role.

When I last interviewed Yoko Ono at the Dakota, and shared some of the accounts of my research for this book, she seemed fascinated by some of the background stories and actually took some notes. She was sorry that Bill Harry, the man who did so much to create the early legend, was omitted from the VIP list at that Merseyside celebration of John Lennon's birthday in 2010. She said she was truly sorry, and I believe her.

When I saw Paul briefly at the White House celebration in 2010, I mentioned that I was trying to get some time with him to chat about the people who helped put him and his buddies on top. Although he was warm and gracious to me at the White House event, he never responded. Both he and Ringo clearly are not interested in the past. To counter some of the controversy in this book, I asked for their cooperation on many occasions. It was declined, politely, of course.

About one aspect of the boys' lives there is no dispute. They wrote the songs, or most of them, but their style was accrued from watching the likes of Rory Storm, Billy J. Kramer, Kingsize (Teddy) Taylor and the Dominoes, Billy Kinsley, the Big Three, Gerry Marsden (and the Pacemakers), Johnny Kidd and the Pirates, and the a cappella sounds of Joe Ankrah and the Chants. Don't we all gather our knowledge and ability from the people we meet, and the experiences we have?

When you download the songs of Kingsize Taylor and his group, you hear the carefully manicured harmony of the young Beatles. There are other similarities, not the least of which is Rory Storm's stage drama, the gyrations, the vivacity of it all. Much was learned, and then, the boys turned around and changed the world of music with their own unique touches.

Where the boys separated themselves from their Liverpool and Hamburg contemporaries was in their own original writing, the extraordinary range of John Lennon and Paul McCartney, and the hidden (until much later) songwriting ability of George Harrison. Even Ringo held his own, recording several number-one hits in the seventies.

So, here in the century that Brian Epstein forecast young people would still be listening to the Beatles with the same awe of the delirious fans of the sixties, we continue to feast on what happened in just eight years of music-making, before they went their separate ways. But those eight years turned out to be enough to make them relevant forever.

What is "forever"? Is it the span of a single lifetime, or even the next century and beyond?

For a while, "forever" was the sum of eight years, 1961 to 1969, when most of the music was created. What we forget is that before the eight years, there was a period of time when dreams were brought to reality by hard work, luck, some really fine people, and the fortunes of fate, with some betrayal thrown in. We also often fail to recognize that much of that music began in scenes of squalor, even depravity, when frankly few noticed or cared, except the hometown believers, the silent champions of the boys. And even among them, who knew it would last this long, except for Brian Epstein, Freda Kelly, and a few others?

In our lives, with the instant fads and fading celebrity, with the one-hit-wonder musicians, and with many pretenders to the throne, fifty years is truly as close to forever as anyone could imagine.

BIBLIOGRAPHY

Baird, Julia. *Imagine This: Growing Up with My Brother John Lennon*. London: Hodder and Stoughton, 2008.

Barrow, Tony. *John, Paul, George, Ringo, and Me*. New York: Da Capo, 2006.

Bedford, David. *Liddypool: Birthplace of the Beatles*. London: Dalton Watson Fine Books, 2011.

Best, Pete, and Bill Harry. *The Best Years of the Beatles*. London: Headline, 2006.

Best, Roag, Pete Best, and Rory Best. *The Beatles: The True Beginnings*. New York: Thomas Dunne, St. Martin's Press, 2007.

Bramwell, Tony, and Rosemary Kingsland. *Magical Mystery Tours—My Life with the Beatles*. New York: St. Martin's Press, 2009.

Brocken, Michael. *Other Voices: The Hidden Histories of Liverpool's Music Scenes 1930s–1970s*. Farnham, UK: Ashgate, 2010.

Brocken, Michael, and Melissa Davis. *The Beatles Bibliography*. Manitou Springs, CO: Beatle Works Ltd., 2012.

Coleman, Ray. *Lennon, the Definitive Biography*. New York: Harper Perennial, 1992.

Davies, Hunter. *The Beatles: The Authorized Biography*. New York: McGraw-Hill, 1968; Dell, 1978.

———. *The Quarrymen*. London: Omnibus, 2001.

Dogget, Peter. *You Never Give Me Your Money: The Battle for the Soul of the Beatles*. Oxford: Bodley Head, 2009.

Ellis, Ron. *Ears of the City*. London: Headline, 1999; Southport, UK: Nirvana, 2005.

Epstein, Brian. *A Cellarful of Noise*. New York: Doubleday, 1964.

Fascher, Horst. *Let the Good Times Roll! Der Starclub–Grunder Erzahit.* Munich: Eichborn Verlag, 2006.

Gannon, John, and Kevin Roach. *The Beatles: Living in the Eye of the Hurricane.* Liverpool: Liverpool Authors, 2011.

Geller, Debbie. *The Brian Epstein Story.* Ed. John Savage. London: Faber and Faber, 2000.

Gruen, Bob. *Sometime in New York City.* Guildford, UK: Genesis, 1995.

Harrison, George. *I, Me, Mine.* London: W. H. Allen, 1981.

Harrison, George, with Derek Taylor. *Fifty Years Adrift.* Guildford, UK: Genesis Publications, 1983.

Harry, Bill. *The Beatles Encyclopedia.* London: Virgin, 2001.

———. *The George Harrison Encyclopedia.* London: Virgin, 2004.

———. *The John Lennon Encyclopedia.* London: Virgin, 2001.

———. *Lennon's Liverpool: In My Life, a Magical History Tour.* Liverpool: Trinity Mirror Media, 2010.

———. *Liverpool: Bigger than the Beatles.* Liverpool: Trinity Mirror Media.

———. *Mersey Beat.* London: Omnibus, 1977.

———. *The Paul McCartney Encyclopedia.* London: Virgin, 2003.

———. *The Ringo Starr Encyclopedia.* London: Virgin, 2004.

Kane, Larry. *Ticket to Ride: Inside the Beatles' 1964 Tour that Changed the World.* Philadelphia: Running Press, 2003; New York: Viking Penguin, 2004.

———. *Lennon Revealed.* Philadelphia: Running Press, 2005.

Kessler, Jude Sutherland. *Shoulda Been There.* Dothan, AL: On the Rock Books, 2008.

Kirchherr, Astrid, Matthew Clough, and Colin Fallow. *Astrid Kirchherr, a Retrospective*. Liverpool: University Press, 2010.

Leach, Sam. *The Rocking City: The Explosive Birth of the Beatles*. Gwynedd, UK: Pharaoh Press, 1999.

Leigh, Spencer. *The Beatles in Hamburg: The Stories, the Scene, and How It All Began*. London: Omnibus, 2011.

———. *It's Love That Really Counts: The Billy Kinsley Story*. Liverpool: Cavern City Tours, 2010.

———. *Let's Go Down the Cavern, the Story of Liverpool's Mersey Beat*. London: Vermilion, 1984.

Lennon, Cynthia. *John*. New York: Crown, 2006.

Lennon, John. *In His Own Write*. London: Jonathan Cape, 1964.

Lewisohn, Mark. *The Beatles Day by Day*. New York: Crown, 1990.

———. *The Beatles Recording Sessions: The Official Abbey Road Studio Session Notes, 1962–1970*. London: Hamlyn, Random House, 1998.

Martin, George. *All You Need Is Ears*. London: Macmillan, 1979.

Miles, Barry. *Paul McCartney: Many Years from Now*. London: Secker and Warburg, 1997.

Norman, Philip. *Shout: The Beatles in Their Generation*. New York: Simon & Schuster, 1981.

Ono, Yoko. *Memories of John Lennon*. London: HarperCollins, 2005.

Pawlowski, Gareth L. *How They Became the Beatles 1960–1964: A Definitive History of the Early Years*. New York: E. P. Dutton, 1989.

Porter, Alan J. *Before They Were Beatles: The Early Years 1956–1960*. Bloomington, IN: Xlibris, 2003.

Riley, Tim. *Lennon: The Man, the Myth, the Music—The Definitive Life*. New York: Hyperion, 2011.

Somach, Denny, Kathleen Somach, and Kevin Gunn. *Ticket to Ride: A Celebration of the Beatles.* New York: William Morrow, 1989.

Somach, Denny, Kathleen Somach, and Scott Muni, with Kevin Gunn. *Ticket to Ride: A Tribute to the Group that Symbolized the Sixties Era.* New York: William Morrow, 1991.

Spizer, Bruce. *The Beatles Are Coming! The Birth of Beatlemania in America.* New Orleans, LA: 498 Productions, 2003.

———. *The Beatles Records on Vee-Jay.* New Orleans, LA: 489 Productions, 1998.

———. *The Beatles for Sale on Parlophone Records.* New Orleans, LA: LLC Productions, 2011.

———. *The Beatles Story on Capitol Records, Part One: Beatlemania and the Singles.*
New Orleans, LA: 498 Productions, 2000.

———. *The Beatles Swan Song: "She Loves You" and Other Records.* New Orleans, LA: Midpoint Trade Books, 2007.

Sutcliffe, Pauline, and Douglas Thompson. *The Beatles Shadow: Stuart Sutcliffe His Lonely Hearts Club.* London: Sidgwick and Jackson, Pan Macmillan, 2001.

Taylor, Derek. *As Time Goes By.* New York: Quick Fox, 1974.

———. *It Was Twenty Years Ago Today.* Guildford, UK: Genesis, 1987.

Williams, Allan, and William Marshall. *The Man Who Gave the Beatles Away.* London: Elm Tree, 1975.

INDEX

PHOTOGRAPHY CREDITS